Dealing with Individual Differences in the Early Childhood Classroom

P. 15
p. 24

Bernard Spodek
University of Illinois

Olivia N. Saracho
University of Maryland

Longman

New York & London

**DEALING WITH INDIVIDUAL DIFFERENCES IN THE EARLY
CHILDHOOD CLASSROOM**

Longman, 10 Bank Street, White Plains, N.Y. 10606

Associated companies:
Longman Group Ltd., London
Longman Cheshire Pty., Melbourne
Longman Paul Pty., Auckland
Copp Clark Pitman, Toronto

Acquisitions editor: Stuart B. Miller
Sponsoring editor: Naomi Silverman
Production editor: Linda Moser
Cover design: Robin Hessl-Hoffman
Production supervisor: Anne Armeny

Library of Congress Cataloging-in-Publication Data

Spodek, Bernard.
    Dealing with individual differences in the early childhood
classroom / Bernard Spodek, Olivia N. Saracho.
        p.   cm.
    Includes bibliographical references.
    ISBN 0-8013-0451-2
    1. Early childhood education—United States.   2. Individualized
instruction—United States.   3. Mainstreaming in education—United
States.   4. Special education—United States.   I. Saracho, Olivia
N.   II. Title.
  LB1139.25.S65   1994
  372.21'0973—dc20   92-35209
                                                       CIP

1 2 3 4 5 6 7 8 9 10-MA-9796959493

Contents

CHAPTER 14   DEVELOPING PROFESSIONAL GROWTH   369

Preface

In the last several decades American schools have expanded their mandate to provide an appropriate education for all children. During this period, the schools have also been required to serve an increasingly diverse population of children. From the 1960s onward, schools have moved from excluding children with disabilities, to educating them in separate—often segregated—classrooms, to including them in increasing numbers in regular classrooms. Schools have also been concerned with providing an appropriate education for children who are at risk of future educational failure, especially as a result of environmental conditions, such as poverty. In addition, during this era the schools have shown a growing concern with providing an appropriate education for children who are gifted and talented.

During this time, the fields of early childhood education and early childhood special education developed separately and became isolated from one another. Not only were children with disabilities separated into different classes from children without disabilities, but the methods used to educate each of these groups became increasingly different from one another. The organizations in the field of early childhood education and early childhood special education, such as the National Association for the Education of Young Children and the Division of Early Childhood of the Council of Exceptional Children had little to do with one another.

The trend has been reversed in recent years. These organizations are working together more often than ever before. Children with disabilities, children who are considered to be at risk of future educational failure, and children who are gifted are increasingly being provided with appropriate educational programs in regular classrooms.

The process of including children with diverse educational abilities in regular classes, however, has placed a heavy burden on classroom teachers. Teacher training too often has not adequately prepared regular classroom teachers for the task.

Teachers do not need to become experts in the education of children with each kind of educational need. Rather, they need to be helped to modify their classrooms and their educational practices to serve the increasingly diverse population of children attending their classes. They must also be provided with necessary resources—both physical and human—with which to serve all children's needs.

This book is an extension of the move to serve diverse populations of young children in regular early childhood classes. It is designed to provide regular classroom teachers with the information they need to know about children with diverse educational needs: children with disabilities, children who are gifted, and children who are at risk of future educational failure. It should help teachers modify their programs to respond to the extended range of individual differences that are currently being included in their classes.

The book is divided into three parts. The first part presents background information, including an historical perspective and a description of characteristics of children with disabilities, children who are at-risk, and children who are gifted. The second part deals with the concerns of teachers other than actually teaching children, including identifying children, evaluating children, planning and modifying the classroom for teaching, creating a positive social environment, and working with parents. The third section deals with modifying teaching to deal with diverse populations. Each content area is addressed separately in this section. The final chapter deals with strategies for continued professional development.

The basic values of early childhood education—respect for each individual child and his or her particular pattern of development; concern for comprehensive education related to all areas of development and grounded in personal expression and creativity; concern for the autonomy and freedom of the individual; a belief that education should be relevant to the current lives of young children as well as preparation for their future; and a view that children's educational experiences be joyful ones—are reflected throughout this book.

In addition we view the classroom teacher as the focal element in the education of young children. Thus, we are addressing the individual teacher in the early childhood classroom and those preparing to be teachers. The book brings together a wealth of information about the education of young children culled from the experience of practitioners as well as the studies of scholars and researchers. It provides examples of ways to modify the classroom in response to the educational needs to individual children as well as the theory and research underlying those modifications.

Parts of this book have been taken from a previously published text, *Mainstreaming Young Children*. Richard C. Lee was a co-author with us of that book. Although he did not participate in the preparation of this volume, we are grateful for his contribution and wish to acknowledge it. We also wish to acknowledge the many other individuals who have helped us in the preparation for this volume. Mary Ellen O'Farrell and Eunah Huang helped with the gathering of reference materials. We especially wish to acknowledge the following reviewers for their helpful comments:

Joann Ericson, Towson State University

Jan Ewing, University of Alabama at Birmingham

Susan Fowler, University of Illinois

Jeanette Hartman, Indiana University of Pennsylvania

Stevie Hoffman, University of Missouri at Columbia

Esther Hovey, California State University at Long Beach

Susan Hupp, University of Minnesota

James Johnson, The Pennsylvania State University

Jennifer Kilgo, Virginia Commonwealth University

Margaret Lay-Dopyera, Syracuse University

Philip Safford, Kent State University

Rosemarie Slavenas, Northern Illinois University

Susan Trostle, University of Rhode Island

In addition we wish to acknowledge the help, encouragement, and support of our families during the preparation of this book: Francisca and Pablo J. Villareal, Saul M. Villareal and Lydia Gonzales, and Prudence Spodek.

PART ONE

Foundations for Including Children with Diverse Abilities in a Regular Classroom

CHAPTER 1

Introduction

CHAPTER OVERVIEW

This chapter presents:

1. An overview of the book.
2. The rationale for creating an integrated classroom.
3. The concept of least restrictive educational setting.
4. Ideas about teaching in an integrated classroom.

Early childhood teachers are being asked to educate an increasingly diverse group of children. This requires that they become more sensitive to individual differences among these children and more competent in providing an appropriate education for each child. Children who were withheld from school before or who were provided with a segregated education increasingly are being included in regular classes among a wide variety of children. Integration provides a degree of educational equity not previously available to some populations of young children. In addition, education of children from diverse backgrounds and with diverse abilities is more effective for all children involved (Zimiles, 1991).

This book is designed to help teachers of young children—in preschools, kindergartens, and grades 1 through 3—adapt their classroom practices to respond to the developmental needs of a range of children, including those who are at risk of future educational failure, those who have disabilities, and those who are gifted. These children are being integrated to a greater extent than ever before, although programs for preschool children with disabilities and those who are considered to be at risk remain more segregated than programs at other levels of education. However, teachers who have not been prepared as special education teachers are now meeting the challenge of dealing with a broad array of individual differences in their classrooms.

In order to accommodate to the range of differences, teachers need to adapt classroom practices. They need not become special educators, or specialists in a particular disability, but they must become more aware of the needs of diverse children. Children need to acquire techniques to meet their particular educational needs. They must work with a range of specialists, each of whom brings a particular set of expertise, so that together each child can be provided with a program that is developmentally and educationally appropriate.

This book is addressed to general early childhood teachers—in preschool, kindergarten, and the primary grades. These teachers are finding children enrolled in their classes who differ from the norm either developmentally, physically, or psychologically, and therefore it is inappropriate to offer them a regular educational program without some modification. These differences include disabilities such as behavioral disabilities, learning disabilities, mental retardation, visual impairment, hearing impairment, communications disorders, and physical and health impairments. Also included are children who are considered to be at risk of future educational failure and gifted children. The characteristics of these children are discussed in chapter 2.

The increased integration of a wide range of children in early childhood programs seems to be the result of new educational and legal initiatives. However, this is not a new phenomenon. It has its roots in the long history of early childhood education. It is the convergence of concern for social equity that has been voiced in legislation, an increased awareness of the needs of young children, and the availability of theory and technique that support integrated education that is new.

A BIT OF HISTORY

Not too many years ago, children who were regarded as "special" were not educated in public schools. In many schools before the 1960s, for example, a child who was not considered "ready" for kindergarten was sent home and allowed to wait another year to mature. Unfortunately, this practice still exists in some schools today, despite the fact that research in early childhood education has overwhelmingly shown that such children benefit from early childhood education. Children who were unable to navigate the school's stairways and corridors because of an orthopedic problem were educated in a separate school, or at home, and were therefore denied contact with any children who did not have disabilities. There were few resources available in public schools to help children who had vision or hearing problems or behavior problems.

Pioneer Programs in Early Childhood Education

Many early childhood programs were initiated for children who today would be considered at risk or in need of special education. The original Infant School, one of the pioneer early childhood programs, was begun in New Lanark, Scotland, by Robert Owen in 1816 (Spodek, 1973). Owen's school was designed to provide an education for children who might otherwise be working in mills starting at an early age and who would have been denied any education. When the idea of infant education came to the United States in the 1820s, some of these schools were developed for children of the poor—children we would now consider to be at risk. These schools allowed the children to be educated and often allowed their mothers to seek employment outside the home (Harrison, 1968).

Similarly, the nursery school began as a preschool program for children who today would be considered at risk. Rachel and Margaret Macmillan opened their nursery school in the slums of London. These children of poor families were bathed, fed, given medical and dental examinations, and provided with a well-rounded education. The children were taught self-caring skills. Music, art, language activities, and especially play activities were provided to help these children gain those benefits in the nursery school that wealthier children might be given by professional nursery nurses in their affluent homes (Steedman, 1990).

Montessori education had its origin at about the same time as the nursery school. It provided education for children with special needs as well. The method originally was designed for children with disabilities. Maria Montessori originally was employed as a physician in an institution for these children. She adapted approaches to education that were developed by Freidrich Froebel, the father of the kindergarten, and by Edouard Sequin, a French educator of children with disabilities who migrated to the United States. Sequin had been a student of Jean Marc Gaspard Itard, who had worked with the famous "Wild Boy of Aveyron" (Lane, 1976). He adapted Itard's work to address more broadly the needs of children who were mentally disabled. Montessori, using the idea of sensory education and education for practical life needs, combined with academic education, created a method that worked with children with disabilities. She then adapted her method to apply to children from the slums of Rome—children we would consider today to be at risk (Kramer, 1988). Unfortunately, when they came to the United States these approaches to early childhood education—the nursery school and the Montessori school—became forms of education for middle-class young children without disabilities. Only recently have we begun to see the convergence of early childhood education with early childhood special education.

Concerns for Educating Diverse Children

Although there was research on the education of young children with special needs in the 1930s, the biggest impetus came in the 1960s. Early in that decade there seemed to be a convergence of social concerns for children growing up in poverty, with newer conceptions of human development. The prime approach to human development in America until that time was the maturational conceptions of Arnold Gesell and his followers (1952). Given that view, human development was seen as a function of heredity: What a person could become was determined genetically at birth. The educator's role was to match the experience provided for children with their capability. The works of J. McVicker Hunt (1961) and Benjamin Bloom (1964), however, suggested that this maturational approach was not necessarily valid. They reviewed a great deal of existing research and came up with conceptions of development that suggested that human capability is a function of experience as much as it is of heredity. In addition, the early childhood period is critical to human development. It is the period when individuals are most malleable. This concept suggested that early childhood programs for children who were considered disadvantaged (we would now consider them at risk) had great potential for helping these children, who might otherwise be failures in the school system, to increase the probability of their success.

The research programs of the 1960s led to a number of different program models (Spodek, 1973). By 1965 they led to the creation of the Head Start program, which was the first large federally funded program in early childhood education. In 1968 the federal government extended its concern in early childhood education to include children with disabilities. Legislation was established in 1968 to establish the Handicapped Children's Early Education Program. Projects under this program developed different models of early intervention. Each program included parent-involvement activities and training programs for teachers. Each program was also responsible for disseminating its model (Karnes & Zehrbach, 1977).

RATIONALE FOR AN INTEGRATED CLASSROOM

The integration of persons with and without disabilities of all ages in educational settings is a sound and ethical policy. Bricker (1978) has identified social-ethical, legal-legislative, and psychological-educational arguments on behalf of the educational integration of preschool children that hold for older children as well. These arguments relate to the possibility of altering societal attitudes toward people with disabilities, to the negative effect on children with disabilities of educational segregation, and to the increased efficiency of allocating resources to all children through integrated programs.

In the last two decades, there was also an effort to integrate children with disabilities into regular programs. A number of legal decisions supported that integration, providing (1) the right of all children with disabilities to a free public education, (2) the right of children with disabilities to be educated in the least restrictive educational setting, and (3) the right of parents to review and approve of educational decisions relevant to their children with disabilities.

In earlier times, programs for children with disabilities generally were designed for children who had reached the age of compulsory school attendance, usually 6 or 7 years. Research has suggested, however, that for some children there is a greater possibility of overcoming educational deficits if these are addressed before kindergarten or the primary grades. Early intervention has been found, for example, to have pervasive and long-lasting effects on children who are environmentally disadvantaged. Their success in school increased and their need for later special educational services decreased (Lazar, Darlington, Murray, Royce, & Snipper, 1982). Indeed, such research has been the basis for the creation of Head Start, one of the longest lasting and most successful programs serving large numbers of children who are considered to be educationally at risk. Early education experiences have also been found to be effective with children who are mentally retarded. In addition, early experiences help children make the best use of their personal resources and capabilities even when there can be no developmental reversal of a disability.

There have been studies of at-risk children who have been withheld from school for a year as well as studies of such children who have been tracked into a separate kindergarten, sometimes called a "developmental" kindergarten. These children may be given remedial work or may be drilled on isolated skills defined as the basis for academic readiness. There is no evidence that children educated this way improve their learning of academic subjects (Shepard & Graue, 1993). In contrast, there is evidence that when such children are educated in a regular kindergarten class, there seems to be no apparent difference between them and their classmates by the time they reach third grade (Shepard & Smith, 1989).

Although some children with disabilities must be educated in isolation, educating children in segregated settings has a number of shortcomings. By its very nature it is an unequal form of education. This principle has been articulated for children from cultural minorities, but it is equally valid for children with disabilities. It deprives them of many informal incidental learning opportunities that result from interacting with other people within a normal setting. Knowledge and skills gained in segregated settings often are less transferable than those gained in integrated settings. In addition, serious questions have been raised about the effectiveness of segregated special education programs for such children. A number of these studies have shown that in certain areas of education, children with disabilities educated in normal settings do as well as, if not better than, those educated in special classes. Thus the call for *mainstreaming*—the inclusion of children with disabilities in integrated educational settings with their normally developing peers—has been mounted, and all children with disabilities are required by law to be educated in the least restrictive educational setting.

Educational research findings support the move toward providing socially integrated educational programs. The reviews of research by Cegelka and Tyler (1970) and Semmel, Gottlieb, and Robinson (1979), for example, found no advantage of segregated placement for children who were mentally retarded. Studies by Goodman, Gottlieb, and Harrison (1972) and Gambel, Gottlieb, and Harrison (1974) show that the social behavior of children with mental retardation in integrated classes tends to resemble that of their normal peers and has increasingly less in common with their peers who were educated in segregated classrooms.

Growing out of the thrust of legal decisions and research knowledge has come the move to educate children with disabilities within regular classrooms with their normally developing peers. This policy is in effect for children in public schools and has impacted on preschools as well. In Head Start, the policy since 1972 has been that at least 10 percent of the enrollees in each center be children with disabilities. Despite this movement, programs for preschool children with disabilities, especially those in the public schools, have been the most segregated. This has been the case because in most instances, although children with disabilities below the standard entry age have been enrolled in programs, other children of the same age have not. However, this situation is slowly changing.

Two court cases were particularly important in establishing the rights of children with disabilities to an appropriate education. In the 1971 case of *Pennsylvania Association for Retarded Persons* v. *Commonwealth of Pennsylvania*, the right of a previously excluded group of retarded children to a free public education was ensured. The state also acknowledged the right of children with disabilities to education in the least restrictive setting possible, separated from their peers only to the degree that is necessary for educational purposes. Although this was a landmark case, it covered only the rights of children with mental retardation. In a similar ruling handed down in 1972, *Mills* v. *Board of Education of the District of Columbia*, these rights were extended to all children with disabilities. In addition, the lack of school funds was declared to be an unacceptable reason for excluding children with disabilities from public schools.

Legislative Initiatives

At about the same time, a number of states were enacting legislation intended to promote the education of school-age children with disabilities in the most appropriate educational setting. Most of that legislation reflected the basic rights of children with disabilities and guaranteed due process procedures for their parents.

These rights were extended to all school-age children with disabilities in the United States when Congress enacted the Education for All Handicapped Children Act (Public Law 94-142). This was the first of a series of federal laws that have significantly changed the service provided to young children with disabilities. It has also significantly influenced the relationship between early childhood education and early childhood special education. The result of these mandates has been the integration of children with and without disabilities into the same educational programs. Public Law 94-142 provided for the education of all children with disabilities between the ages of 3 and 21. However, it relieved the states from that requirement for children with disabilities from age 3 to 5 and 18 to 21 if normal children in these age ranges are not served by a state's public school.

The requirements for the education of all children with disabilities in schools was extended downward to the preschool level in the amendments to the Education of the Handicapped Act (Public Law 99-457). Part B (the Preschool Grant Program) and Part H (the Handicapped Infants and Toddlers Program) of this act provided financial incentives to states to establish early-intervention programs for children with disabilities from birth through age 5. Each of these laws was extended through the Education of the Handicapped Act amendments of 1990 (Public Law 101-476), which changed the name of Public Law 99-457 to the Individuals with Disabilities Education Act and its 1992 amendments (P.L. 102-119) and extended P.L. 99-457. Placing children with disabilities in community programs for the nondisabled is encouraged as one way of enrolling these children in more integrated settings. Another possible way is "reverse mainstreaming," where limited numbers of children without disabilities are enrolled in programs primarily designed for children with disabilities.

Part B of P.L. 99-457 and P.L. 102-119 require significantly different types of services for infants and toddlers (children from birth through age 2) and preschoolers (children between the ages of 3 and 5). Infants and toddlers are not involved in integrated educational programs, nor are they served by classroom teachers in schools. Special services, often delivered in the context of the family, are required and special educational personnel are needed to supply those services. Thus, it is Part B of these acts, related to preschool education of children with disabilities, that is addressed in this book. However, the services provided to preschool children may be identified in an Individualized Family Service Plan (IFSP), as with infants and toddlers, rather than an Individualized Educational Program (IEP), as long as the IEP requirements are met. For an excellent review of the legal basis for early childhood special education programs, see McCollum and Maude (1993).

Another federal law that impacts early childhood education is the Americans with Disabilities Act of 1990 (ADA). The ADA has four titles related to (I) equal employment opportunities, (II) discrimination in services provided by public entities such as public transportation, (III) discrimination in public accommodations and a range of businesses, and (IV) aids to persons who are disabled in the area of telecommunications. Most visible of the consequences of the ADA are the increased access provided to individuals who are physically disabled in public buildings (including public school buildings) and public accommodations and transportation.

The key areas of early childhood education that are impacted by the ADA include child-care centers and family day-care homes, which are included in the definition of public accommodation of the act. Such facilities are required to provide readily achievable actions to prevent discrimination on the basis of disability. These actions, however, should not create an undue burden. Thus, the physical facilities of such programs would need to remove barriers that would impede access to them, as long as such actions do not create a major budgetary impact. Programs may not refuse to enroll a child with a disability because such enrollment would change the cost of insurance. Transportation that is provided would have to accommodate children with disabilities, and facilities that have 25 or more employees would have to avoid job-related discrimination (Surr, 1992).

Although integrating children with different competencies and backgrounds is considered desirable, especially to enhance social competence, it should be noted that simply placing children in integrated settings will not achieve the desired results. Social interactions will not occur and social skills will not be learned without careful planning and implementation of strategies to achieve these goals (see, Guralnick, 1990; Strain & Kerr, 1981).

LEAST RESTRICTIVE SETTINGS

Not all children with disabilities can be integrated into regular classes, although the overwhelming majority of these children can when appropriate support is provided. The greatest degree of integration is done with children with mild and moderate disabilities. Even with these children, special resources and additional services need to be provided along with special adaptations of regular class programs. For some children, however, the most appropriate educational placement is outside the regular classroom. A determination should be made as to the needs of a particular child and the educational setting best suited to providing for those needs. Evelyn Deno (1970) identified a continuum of placements for children with disabilities:

1. Regular classroom assignment, possibly with classroom modification and supportive services provided.

2. Regular classroom assignment plus supplementary instructional services. (A resource room or itinerant teacher may offer this.)
3. Part-time special classes with the balance of the day spent in a regular class or resource room.
4. Full-time special class with the child segregated into a special class in a conventional school.
5. Special day school.
6. Homebound instruction.
7. Institutional or residential assignment.

Each succeeding placement on the continuum provides a more segregated and therefore a less normal educational environment for the child with disabilities. Only the first three of these levels can be considered to have some degree of integration. However, relatively few children are found in the lower categories.

TEACHING IN AN INTEGRATED CLASSROOM

Enrolling children with disabilities in a classroom does not require that the teacher become a special educator. The purpose of such placements is to allow the children to experience as normal and regular an educational program as is possible. On the other hand, the classroom teacher cannot take a business-as-usual stance, either. Classroom teachers know a great deal about children and about teaching that is as relevant to educating children with disabilities as to educating normal children. In fact, there is much that special educators can learn from regular classroom teachers and teaching (Spodek, 1982). However, classroom organization and practices must be adapted to accommodate the extended range of individual differences in the integrated classroom. Teachers in integrated classrooms also need to work with a wider range of educational personnel (including resource teachers and evaluation specialists) and may have to coordinate a range of services that are offered both within the school and by outside agencies.

Teachers in integrated classrooms also have to develop different relationships with parents. Some contacts with parents are mandated by due process procedures. Others are determined by the particular needs of the children and their parents. Engaging parents in a partnership with the schools is important for all early childhood programs. It is doubly important in programs where children with disabilities or those who are at risk are involved. Indeed, the research is clear that parent participation is one of the key elements in successful programs for such children.

Teachers will also have to plan differently, use different assessment techniques, and review their regular teaching strategies to determine if they are equally effective with all children in their classes. They will also have to learn more about normal and exceptional patterns of development, about different ways of learning that are effective for different children, and about the different ways of teaching that support each form of learning.

Classroom teachers must assume some responsibility for identifying children with disabilities in the school and in the community, although the total responsibility will not fall on them. Some children are identified as having disabilities only after they enroll in regular classes and are observed by a teacher in relation to other children of similar age. In such cases, it is the teacher's responsibility to set into motion the process of assessing the nature and extent of the child's disability and of determining the appropriate method of working with that child. In other instances, teachers will work with other school personnel to identify children with disabilities in the community before they enter school. Even when minimally involved in the process of identification and assessment, the classroom teacher must be aware of the work of the multidisciplinary team as well as the actions taken in relation to specific children.

Once a child is identified as having a disability, the nature and extent of the problem must be assessed. A range of specialists, including psychologists, social workers, and speech and language specialists, help determine the child's needs and plan appropriate educational treatment. In this process, too, the classroom teacher should play a significant role. Often only the classroom teacher has observed the child in the context of interpersonal relations and in the process of coping with the demands of everyday life. This knowledge is important in determining the appropriate form of education the child should receive.

The program that develops as a result of an assessment must be recorded in a formal document called an *individualized educational program* (IEP). Parents must approve of the program to be established for their child and, if possible, should be involved in its development. Often the teacher has the best relationship with the parents and is in the best position to interpret the IEP to them, although social workers and parent liaison workers may assume responsibility for this. If parents disagree as to the appropriateness of the program, reviews must be made available to them, including due process appeals, and the teacher must inform the parents of their options.

Much of the IEPs designed for most children with disabilities will be implemented by the teacher in the regular classroom. Many times children are removed from the regular classroom to a separate room within the school where they are provided with special services or instruction. This separation of the child for special instruction has been characterized as a *pull-out program*. Although the pull-out strategy is often used, we know little about its educational effectiveness for children with disabilities. An interesting meta-analysis (or an analysis of analyses) has been made of pull-out programs supported by Chapter 1 of the Elementary and Secondary Education Act. These children might be considered to be in the at-risk category. After reviewing and re-analyzing studies of such programs, Glass and Smith (1977) concluded that the pull-out procedure per se has no clear academic or social benefits and, in fact, may be detrimental to students' academic progress and social adjustment to school.

These conclusions strongly suggest a need for studies of pull-out programs used for children with disabilities who have been placed in integrated settings. Such sessions may not be the best way to provide for children's special needs. Too often they do not take into consideration the learning that might have taken place for that child in the classroom. As an alternative, the special education resource-consultant teacher might work directly with the child in the regular classroom. In this way, the special education teacher can become more aware of what is happening in the classroom and be better able to integrate special activities with the ongoing classroom program. Resource teachers can also serve as consultants to the regular classroom teacher, providing additional resources and materials and suggesting activities that might be effective with the disabled child. The appropriateness of the option depends on the characteristics of the child, on the ability of the classroom teacher to cope with the responsibilities of the entire class as well as the needs of the child with a disability, and on the nature of the relationship that develops between the regular teacher and the specialists in the school.

In any case, it is likely that modifications will be made in the way an integrated class functions when a child with a disability is included. Such a class always requires additional work for the teacher. The necessary schedule changes, the additional conferences with resource people, the formal evaluation and record keeping, the selection and use of special supplies and equipment, and the need to work more intensely with parents place additional demands on the classroom teacher. Many schools recognize this burden and compensate by providing smaller classes or a teacher's aide. Other schools assign as much responsibility as possible to the special education resource teacher or to a special education coordinator. No matter how the responsibility is shared, however, knowledge of children and of educational practice must be brought to bear to respond to the range of individual differences found among children in the class and to provide the best possible educational program, both for the children with disabilities and for the normal children in the integrated class.

The requirements for dealing with children who are developmentally or educationally at-risk children and with children who are gifted in the integrated class are not as formal as those for children with disabilities. The need to respond to individual differences, however, is just as significant. Although no IEP may need to be filed for these children, the teacher must still respond to the child's individual needs and plan specifically for them. Classroom procedures, schedules, and activities may need to be modified and special supplies and materials may need to be provided. There may still be the need to work with others as part of a team, with Chapter 1 teachers or special personnel for gifted children provided by the school. Parent programs might be provided for these children as well. In any event, the teacher is still the key in the educational process and must coordinate the programs provided, ensuring that these children are well integrated into the classroom.

This book is addressed to early childhood teachers or those preparing to be teachers who will have to respond to the range of individual differences in the integrated preschool, kindergarten, or primary classroom. Part One provides background information for the teacher. In addition to this chapter, which gives a historical and theoretical perspective to practice, chapter 2 provides descriptions of characteristics of children with disabilities, as well as characteristics of children who are gifted or at risk. These descriptions are generalized ones. Children with these conditions will be somewhat different from the descriptions and from each other. In addition, a child may have a number of disabilities at the same time. The information is presented to provide teachers a background for understanding the range of children who might be integrated in their classroom and to serve as a beginning point for individual identification and assessment.

Part Two presents the many professional activities in which teachers must engage before, after, and while teaching a diverse population of children in the regular classroom. Identifying children with disabilities, assessing children's needs and educational outcomes, planning for their diverse educational needs, modifying classroom organization, preparing the social environment, and working with parents are all necessary parts of the educational process. Because children with disabilities may have specific difficulties in dealing with a learning environment and because particular laws and regulations apply to them, these processes, so important to the education of all children, must be dealt with more explicitly.

Part Three presents background information and suggestions for helping the teacher modify the content and procedures of the early childhood education program. Each subject area is analyzed in relation to helping all children achieve the goals that are appropriate to them. Particular attention is given to the expressive arts and to the area of play, both of which are critical to a sound education in the early childhood years. The chapters do not provide suggestions for dealing with all forms of difference. The book has not been designed to be encyclopedic. However, enough suggestions are provided within the entire section to allow teachers to become aware of the program modifications that are needed and to create these modifications for each individual child in the class.

The final chapter deals with the professional development of teachers and identifies resources that teachers can use to serve their own educational needs. We believe this is a useful resource for teachers who are working at creating integrated classrooms where the educational needs of all children can be met within the context of a sound educational program within regular classrooms.

SUMMARY

Early childhood teachers today are dealing with a broader range of individual differences than has been the case in the past. This is due to the broader range of young children enrolling in schools as well as to recent legislation that requires schools to offer programs to younger children and to do this in the least restrictive educational setting. The chapters that follow will deal with ways to modify current early childhood programs to serve the needs of a broad range of individual differences among young children.

REFERENCES

Bloom, B. S. (1964). *Stability and change in human characteristics.* New York: Wiley.

Bricker, D. D. (1978). A rationale for the integration of handicapped and nonhandicapped preschool children. In M. Guralnick (Ed.), *Early intervention and the integration of handicapped and nonhandicapped children* (pp. 3–26). Baltimore, MD: University Park Press.

Cegelka, J. J., & Tyler, J. L. (1970). The efficacy of special class placement of the mentally retarded in proper perspective. *Training School Bulletin, 67,* 33–68.

Deno, E. (1970). Special education as developmental capital. *Exceptional Children, 37,* 229–237.

Gambel, D. H., Gottlieb, J., & Harrison, R. H. (1974). Comparison of behavior of special-class EMR, integrated EMR, low IQ, and nonretarded children. *American Journal of Mental Deficiency, 79,* 16–21.

Gesell, A. (1952). *Infant development: The embryology of early human behavior.* New York: Harper & Row.

Glass, G. V., & Smith, M. L. (1977). *"Pull-out" in compensatory education.* Paper prepared for the Office of the Commissioner, U.S. Office of Education.

Goodman, H., Gottlieb, J., & Harrison, R. H. (1972). Social acceptance of EMRs integrated into a nongraded elementary school. *American Journal of Mental Deficiency, 76,* 412–417.

Guralnick, M. J. (1990). Social competence and early intervention. *Journal of Early Intervention, 14*(1), 3–14.

Harrison, J. F. C. (1968). *Utopianism and education: Robert Owen and the Owenites.* New York: Teachers College Press.

Hunt, J. McV. (1961). *Intelligence and experience.* New York: Ronald Press.

Karnes, M. B., & Zehrbach, R. (1977). Alternative models for delivering services to young handicapped children. In B. J. Jordan, A. H. Hayden, M. B. Karnes, & M. M. Wood (Eds.), *Early childhood education for exceptional children.* Reston, VA: Council for Exceptional Children.

Kramer, R. (1988). *Maria Montessori: A biography.* Reading, MA: Addison-Wesley.

Lane, H. (1976). *The wild boy of Aveyron.* Cambridge, MA: Harvard University Press.

Lazar, I., Darlington, R. B., Murray, H., Royce, J., & Snipper, A. (1982). Lasting effects of early education: A report from the Consortium for Longitudinal Studies. *Monograph of the Society for Research in Child Development, 47* (2–3, Serial No. 195).

McCollum, J. A., & Maude, S. P. (1993). Portrait of a changing field: Policy and practice in early childhood special education. In B. Spodek (Ed.), *Handbook of research on the education of young children* (pp. 352–371). New York: Macmillan.

Semmel, M. I., Gottlieb, J., & Robinson, N. R. (1979). Mainstreaming: Perspectives on educating handicapped children in the public school. In D. C. Berliner (Ed.), *Review of research in education, Vol. 7.* Itasca, IL: F. E. Peacock.

Shepard, L. A., & Graue, M. E. (1993). The morass of school readiness screening: Research on test use and validity. In B. Spodek (Ed.), *Handbook of research on the education of young children* (pp. 293–305). New York: Macmillan.

Shepard, L. A., & Smith, M. L. (1989). *Flunking grades: Research and policies on retention.* New York: Falmer Press.

Spodek, B. (1973). *Early childhood education.* Englewood Cliffs, NJ: Prentice-Hall.

Spodek, B. (1982). What special educators need to know about regular classes. *Educational Forum, 66,* 295–307.

Steedman, C. (1990). *Childhood, culture and class in Britain: Margaret Macmillan, 1860–1931.* New Brunswick, NJ: Rutgers University Press.

Strain, P., & Kerr, M. (1981). *Mainstreaming of children in schools: Research and programmatic issues.* New York: Academic Press.

Surr, J. (1992). Early childhood programs and the Americans with Disabilities Education Act (ADA). *Young Children, 47*(5), 18–21.

Zimiles, H. (1991). Diversity and change in young children: Some educational implications. In B. Spodek & O. N. Saracho (Eds.), *Issues in early childhood curriculum: Yearbook in early childhood education, Vol. 2.* (pp. 21–45). New York: Teachers College Press.

CHAPTER 2

Characteristics of Young Children with Diverse Educational Needs

CHAPTER OVERVIEW

This chapter describes:

1. Young children who are developmentally at risk. Educational strategies for working with them are briefly discussed.
2. The characteristics of gifted and talented young children. Educational strategies for working with them are briefly discussed
3. The characteristics of young children with the following disabilities:
   a. learning and developmental disabilities
   b. behavior disorders
   c. hearing impairments
   d. communication disorders
   e. physical and health impairments

   Educational strategies for working with these populations of children are briefly discussed.

All children have special educational needs and should be dealt with in a personal manner. There are, however, distinct groups of children with particular characteristics who require special educational adjustments in the regular classroom. These include children who are educationally or developmentally at risk, as well as gifted and talented children and those with disabilities. Seven categories of disabilities are discussed: behavior disorders, learning disabilities, mental retardation, visual impairment, hearing impairment, communication disorders, and physical and health impairments. This chapter describes the characteristics of these children and suggests general classroom modifications for their education. For convenience, each is presented as a separate category. Categories are of limited use in planning for children. Each child must be seen and treated as an individual.

CHILDREN AT RISK

Children at risk may be defined as those who have not been formally identified as having a disability, but who may be developing conditions that will limit their success in school or lead to disabilities. This can be the result of exposure to adverse genetic, biological, or environmental factors. Although many children who show evidence of risk factors never develop problems, others do develop disabilities. The term *at risk* implies only that children have been subjected to various prenatal (before birth), perinatal (at birth), or postnatal (after birth) risk factors that increase their chances for developing difficulties.

Children at risk are typically grouped into three categories: (1) those at *established risk,* (2) those at *biological risk,* and (3) those at *environmental risk* (Tjossem, 1976). Children at established risk have a diagnosed medical or genetic disorder that is well known and documented. Children with such genetic disorders as Down syndrome, for example, are considered at established risk. This disorder is known to produce mental retardation, deviant growth patterns, and classic physical characteristics (termed *stigmata*), especially in facial features.

Children at *biological risk* have prenatal, perinatal, or postnatal biological histories that signal potential problems. Maternal diabetes, mothers who contract German measles while pregnant, complications during labor, prematurity, low birthweight, or the accidental ingestion by the child of toxic substances all render a child at risk for developing a disability. Children at *environmental risk* are biologically or genetically normal but are classified as at risk because of adverse early life experiences.

Risk factors often occur in combination, interacting to increase the chances of delayed or aberrant development. A child who is identified as at risk due to biological factors may also be at risk because of environmental factors.

Several conditions occurring during the prenatal, perinatal, or postnatal stage of development can render a child's developmental future at risk. Among the more common are the following:

1. Children of mothers of low socioeconomic status who live in impoverished conditions.
2. Children of mothers under 15 or over 40.
3. Children of parents (mother or father) with a family history of congenital abnormalities.
4. Children of mothers who contract rubella (German measles) in the first three months of pregnancy.
5. Children of mothers with diabetes, toxemia, or high blood pressure.
6. Children of mothers who drink heavily during pregnancy.
7. Children whose mothers experience untreated RH blood incompatibility with them as infants.

8. Children of mothers who ingest drugs during pregnancy, such as thalidomide, LSD, heroin, morphine, methadone, cocaine, quinine, or thyroid drugs.
9. Children of mothers who smoke during pregnancy.
10. Children of mothers who receive inadequate nutrition during pregnancy.
11. Children who are premature (less than 37 weeks) or of low birthweight (under 5.5 pounds).
12. Children who have insufficient oxygen before, during, or immediately following birth.
13. Children who experience physical trauma during birth resulting in injury to the head, the brain or a vital organ.
14. Children who contract various postnatal diseases or infections, including meningitis and encephalitis.
15. Children who accidentally ingest toxic or poisonous substances.
16. Children who are victims of accidental or inflicted injury.
17. Children who receive poor postnatal nutrition.
18. Children from substandard or depriving environments characterized by:
    a. an absence of toys, educational materials, or other items that promote language development
    b. a loud, chaotic home where children learn to tune out stimulation
    c. homes where fewer adults are available to interact with children
    d. parents in economic despair
    e. parents who rely on punishment as the chief means for controlling behavior
    f. homes where parents are less likely to verbally interact with their children

The most effective treatment for children at risk is placement in a high-quality early-intervention program. The program should stress individualized education, language and cognitive stimulation, and opportunities for social interaction with adults and with peers.

It is estimated that more than 2.5 million children in the United States under age 6 are at risk for developing school difficulties or disabilities. Parents and teachers should be aware of the factors that place a child at risk. The early identification and treatment of these children can bring many of these conditions under control so potentially adverse outcomes are prevented or diminished in severity. It is important to note that the term *at risk* reflects a probability of problems' occurring; not all children with these characteristics develop problems.

A CHILD AT RISK

Randy, age 3, the son of Maria, age 16, lives in a low-income area with Maria's grandmother, her mother, and five aunts and uncles. Maria works days and attends night school completing her GED. She spends little time with Randy and admits that her son was not wanted. Maria's parents virtually ignore Randy. Randy was premature and weighed under 5 pounds at birth. He is now beginning to

> show delayed language development. Maria admits to having smoked and drunk heavily during pregnancy.
>
> Randy will enroll in the local Head Start program this fall. He will receive language therapy twice a week.

Preschool programs have been developed for children considered environmentally at risk since the 1960s. Research evidence demonstrates that such programs can have persistent and long-lasting effects. Such programs can help reduce the number of children who are assigned to special education classes and who may be retained in grade because of low achievement (Lazar, Darlington, Murray, Royce, & Snipper, 1982). An analysis of the social and economic costs of the consequence of being at risk and the expense of early childhood education for these children that was done by the High/Scope Foundation suggests that there is a 7-to-1 benefit ratio from such programs (Berrueta-Clement, Schweinhart, Barnett, Epstein, & Weikart, 1984). This has led many public school systems to adopt prekindergarten programs for children who are environmentally at risk.

Nancy Karweit (1993) compared different prekindergarten and kindergarten programs for at-risk children. Karweit, like Shepard and Smith (1989), finds no support for having children repeat kindergarten. In addition, she found benefits from attendance in all-day kindergarten for disadvantaged students, another way of characterizing children who are environmentally at risk. Karweit found that the benefits of all the programs were most pronounced immediately after completion of the program, but these benefits tended to wash out over time. No one program seemed superior to the others in regard to benefits. Although kindergarten effects were not conclusive, she does suggest that a systematic approach to kindergarten education will be effective for children of lower socioeconomic status, and that the systematic nature of the program may be more important than the program's philosophy. Although this survey provides some information upon which to make program decisions for young children who are environmentally at risk, it strongly suggests that more needs to be known before we can be optimally effective in educating these children.

GIFTED AND TALENTED CHILDREN

There has been increased interest among educators in identifying and serving young children with special gifts and talents. Among the reasons for this interest are the following:

1. The gifted and the talented represent the brightest and the best among us. In an increasingly competitive world, it is in our country's best interest to nurture their special skills.
2. Gifted and talented children, like other children, have a right to develop their skills fully. This can be achieved by providing services early in life.
3. Early identification and appropriate programming can help establish lifelong positive attitudes and habits toward learning.

4. Early identification will help parents ensure that their gifted child receives the most appropriate education.

Various definitions of the gifted and the talented have been provided by educators, but no single definition pleases all. A popular and widely quoted definition was offered by former U.S. Commissioner of Education Sidney Marland (1972):

> Gifted and talented children are those identified by professionally qualified persons who, by virtue of outstanding abilities, are capable of high performance. These are children who require differentiated educational programs and services beyond those normally provided by the regular program in order to realize their contribution to self and society. Children capable of high performance include those with demonstrated achievement and/or potential ability in any of the following areas: (1) general intellectual ability; (2) specific academic aptitude; (3) creative or productive thinking; (4) leadership ability; (5) the visual and performing arts; and (6) psychomotor ability. (p. 10)

This definition recognizes children with diverse talents. It is consistent with the concept of multiple intelligence suggested by Gardner (1983). Most schools, however, still place considerable emphasis on intelligence and achievement tests to identify gifted children. Such tests measure abilities that are critical to school performance, but they are not the only way to identify children's gifts. Research on a Head Start program showed that children this young may be particularly receptive to intervention strategies. It is assumed that the lack of such intervention may cause some preschool children never to qualify for programs for gifted children at the primary and secondary levels (Burke, 1989).

Academic aptitude can be determined in school-age children by achievement tests. But children who are creative or productive are best identified by their ability to generate innovative solutions to problems or create unique products. Students who excel in leadership are looked to by peers and adults to take charge of group activities. Students who excel in the visual and performing arts display artistic skills that may or may not match their general abilities. In most children, however, there is a positive relationship between intellectual giftedness and talent.

It is often difficult to identify gifts and talents in preschool children because children of this age are developing rapidly and their daily performance can vary. Several studies, however, have been able to identify gifts and talents in young children. Karnes (1983), for example, asserts that young children who are intellectually gifted, as a group, share several characteristics:

1. They tend to be socially and emotionally well adjusted.
2. They have longer attention spans and a more well developed vocabulary.
3. They are better at solving problems and engaging in abstract thinking.

Bloom (1982) suggests that children who are gifted and talented are able to learn new techniques, ideas, or processes rapidly, and are more competitive than average children. They also show a willingness to spend more time and make greater effort than others to achieve a high level or standard.

State funding for programs for children who are gifted and talented nationwide has increased since 1977, although most school systems are just beginning to be concerned with the needs of primary age students. Karnes, Shwedel, and Kemp (1985) found 113 programs for gifted children at the primary and preschool levels throughout the United States. O'Connell (1985) surveyed the Council of State Directors of Programs for the Gifted. The poll suggested the following program characteristics:

1. The intellectual domain is the central program model in 97 percent of the states.
2. Minimum program standards exist in 6 percent of the states.
3. Pull-out programs are found in 77 percent of the states; 33 percent of the states have in-class programs.
4. Accelerated programs are found in 31 percent of the states; 8 percent have enrichment programs; and 23 percent have other or merged alternatives (such as mentor, multiple alternatives, special content).

Most programs for the gifted center on the general intellectual and specific academic areas. These programs usually consist of acceleration of traditional content (e.g., mathematics, science, and social studies) and an enrichment component focusing on reasoning and creative thinking (Johnsen, 1986). The following list outlines behaviors that may indicate giftedness in young children.

Behaviors That May Indicate Giftedness in Young Children

Talent Area	Behavioral Indicators
Intellectual	Alert, observant, exceptional retention of material, curious, absorbed in activities, articulate, learns easily and readily, applies knowledge to practical situations, exceptional ability to solve problems.
Academic	
Reading:	Selects books frequently; advanced vocabulary and sentence structure; exceptional retention of symbols, letters, and words; demonstrates ability to read.
Mathematics:	Strong interest in counting, measuring, weighing, or ordering objects. Advanced understanding of mathematical relationships and symbols; performs simple subtraction and addition operations.
Science:	Examines and observes objects and events carefully. Exceptional skills in classifying. Long attention span, strong interest in science projects or experiments. Advanced understanding of cause and effect.

Creative	Observer, asks many questions, keen sense of humor, intense interest in self-selected activities, high energy, high productivity, independent, uses materials in multiple ways, has unusual ideas or makes original products.
Leadership	Readily adapts to new situations, sought out by other children as a play or work companion, self-confident, tends to direct activities, popular, interacts easily with adults and peers, takes initiative with peers.

Visual and Performing Arts

Art:	Strong interest in visual media; remembers visual objects in detail; spends much time drawing, painting, or modeling.
Music:	Demonstrates high interest in music, responds to the mood or character of music, repeats short rhythmic patterns with ease, sings in tune, identifies familiar songs from the rhythm alone, matches pitch of a model.

Efforts to educate preschool children who are gifted and talented are often limited to early admission to kindergarten. Occasionally these children also receive special educational services. In the primary grades, one or more basic delivery system may be used to educate the gifted and talented child (Gallagher, Weiss, Oglesby, & Thomas, 1983). The *enrichment classroom* involves a special program of study, beyond that normally offered in a regular classroom, for gifted students under the guidance of a specially trained educator. Special programming may be provided for gifted students in regular classrooms with the assistance of a specially trained *consultant teacher.* The *resource room pull out program* takes the child out of the classroom for short periods to receive instruction from a specialist. *Community mentor programs* provide gifted children with opportunities to interact with adults who have special knowledge in particular areas. *Independent study* allows gifted students to explore projects of special interest on their own under the supervision of a qualified teacher. The *special class placement* option groups gifted children together in a class. *Special schools* offer gifted students special programs in a segregated facility. Each of these options is designed to provide gifted students with an opportunity to interact with one another and receive an appropriate level of instruction. The curriculum in each program emphasizes the development of knowledge and the enhancement of creativity and problem-solving skills.

No two children who are gifted and talented are alike and, like all children, they must be dealt with as individuals.

A GIFTED CHILD

Lisa, 7, is an attractive, short, young girl who wears glasses and clean but not stylish clothes. Her IQ is above 140 and her academic work is consistently excellent. Lisa is popular with peers and adults and shows a special talent for music. She was walking at 11 months and talking at 16 months. Despite her visual impairment, Lisa is extremely adept at both fine motor and gross motor tasks. Lisa is exceptionally articulate, with an extensive vocabulary more like that of an adult than a child. She is conscientious and pours enormous energy into tasks to produce a high-quality product. Lisa also adapts well to children of varying levels of development.

Lisa's mother is a physician and her father a university professor. She is the firstborn of three children and her family situation is strong and stable. Her parents work closely with the school to provide Lisa with the most appropriate education possible.

The school is concerned as to how best to accommodate Lisa's educational needs. Because of her small physical stature, they are not considering promoting her beyond her current third-grade placement. At present, Lisa attends a special class for gifted children two days a week and is given academic work equivalent to a sixth-grade level. She participated in all class social and physical education activities and now serves as a tutor for fourth-grade mathematics.

Lisa's family is content with the school's efforts to meet her needs, but are very apprehensive about the future.

CHILDREN WITH DISABILITIES

This section describes the learning and behavioral characteristics of young children with disabilities. For convenience, each type of disability is presented as a separate category. Categories are of limited use, though, in planning for children who must be viewed and treated as individuals. Seven categories that closely parallel those presented in Public Law 94-142 are discussed: learning disabilities, behavior disorders, mental retardation, visual impairments, hearing impairments, communication disorders, and physical and health impairments.

Learning and Developmental Disabilities

The causes and definition of learning disabilities remain elusive. Some researchers suggest that learning disabilities are the result of brain dysfunction; others stress the importance of various genetic, environmental, or biochemical etiologies. All agree that learning disabilities vary from mild to severe. *Learning disabilities,* a catch-all term, describes a wide range of learning problems. The most widely accepted definition is provided in P.L. 94-142, the Education for All Handicapped Children Act: "The term *children with specific learning disabilities* means those children who have a disorder in one or more of the basic psychological processes involved in understanding or in using language, spoken or written, which disorder may manifest itself in an imperfect ability to listen, think, speak, read, write, spell, or do mathematical calculations." Most states include two additional criteria for learning disabilities: (1) Discrepancies must exist among specific abilities and achievement or between evidenced ability and achievement; and (2) the learning problem must be such that the child fails to learn through the instructional methods and materials used with most children and therefore requires specialized procedures for development.

Learning disabilities include conditions such as perceptual disabilities, brain injury, minimal brain dysfunction, dyslexia, and developmental aphasia. Not included are learning problems resulting from visual, hearing, or motor disabilities; mental retardation; or emotional disturbance. Nor are environmental, cultural, or economic conditions that place certain children at risk included. Among preschool children, a learning disability can reflect a child's imperfect ability to listen, understand, think, or speak. During the kindergarten and primary years, it is reflected in his or her imperfect ability to read, write, spell, or do arithmetic.

Symptoms of learning disabilities in young children include hyperactivity, perceptual-motor defects, general orientation deficits, disorders of attention, impulsivity, disorders of memory and conceptual thinking, and specific learning defects, especially in language. Identifying a child's learning disabilities requires eliminating other causes of the learning problem, such as mental retardation, cultural deprivation, poor teaching, or emotional disturbance.

Several different strategies have been developed to help children with learning disabilities. In *task or skill modification,* a skill is broken into simpler parts that are learned separately, then reintegrated. This strategy is based on the assumption that children learn simpler tasks more easily than complex ones. In *ability-to-process training,* the teacher focuses on correcting the deficit that seems to interfere with learning. Teachers may attempt to correct deficiencies in attention, memory, perception, thinking, or language.

Behavior analysis strategies for children who are learning disabled typically involve five steps: (1) *acquisition,* during which the teacher uses modeling, verbal directions, prompting, and reinforcement to teach a child to perform a task accurately; (2) *proficiency,* in which, following repeated practice, the child masters the task and is able to perform it quickly and automatically; (3) *maintenance,* a phase in which the child shows the ability to perform a task after some time; (4) *generalization,* during which the learner demonstrates the ability to transfer the skill or knowledge to a problem situation; and (5) *adaptation,* a stage in which the skill becomes part of the student's normal functioning. The behavior analysis approach assumes that learning difficulties are best dealt with when educational goals and objectives are translated into observable behaviors that are taught directly.

Cognitive intervention strategies emphasize the processes of learning rather than behavioral outcomes (Lerner, 1985). This approach teaches a set of strategies, termed *metacognition,* that help learners become aware of their own system of thinking. Examples of metacognitive strategies include *verbal rehearsal,* in which the child repeats rules for learning; *advanced organizers,* which mentally prepare the child for new learning; *self-monitoring,* which allows students to become aware of their mistakes; and *self-questioning,* a strategy to teach children to ask themselves questions to direct their learning in a systematic, logical fashion. These strategies have only recently been applied to teaching young children.

Although our knowledge of learning disabilities has increased, the absence of a clear definition of learning disabilities is still needed (Bryan, Bay, & Donahue, 1988).

A CHILD WITH LEARNING DISABILITY

Since infancy, Steve, age 3, was a mystery to his parents and others who knew him. He looked normal, with a healthy, robust body, sound ears, and what his aunt termed an intelligent look in his eyes. But Steve often was inattentive, was slow to develop language, appeared withdrawn, and often acted in an impulsive manner. He was uncoordinated compared with other children his age and had difficulty remembering things.

Steve's mother took Steve to a physician who tested and ruled out vision, hearing, and brain injury. After extensive testing, the local school psychologist concluded that Steve suffered from a learning disability. Steve had an auditory processing dysfunction; he had difficulty understanding and interpreting things he heard. The psychologist recommended placement in an integrated preschool program where a resource teacher worked with Steve for 1 hour daily. Steve spent the rest of the time with his normally developing peers who typically noticed nothing different about Steve. After 6 months, Steve became more attentive and less impulsive. He also made gains in his motor coordination skills as a result of work with an occupational therapist.

Behavior Disorders

Behavior disorders, sometimes called *emotional disturbances,* are deviations from age-appropriate behavior that seriously interfere with the child's own development or with the lives of others. Children with behavior disorders may be very aggressive or very withdrawn, very loud or very quiet, very euphoric or very depressed. According to Luebke, Epstein, and Cullinan (1987), aggression, anxiety, academic disability, and depression are types of behavior problems. The behavior of these children may appear strange in context and difficult to explain. Although educators do not agree about exactly what constitutes such a disability, behaviorally disordered children often exhibit behaviors that, although occasionally seen in most children, occur much more often in children with behavior disorders. These include self-destructive behaviors (such as head banging), temper tantrums, inability to tolerate frustration, moodiness and withdrawal, depression, difficulty in making friends, and school phobia (unfounded fear of going to school).

Emotional disorders are usually grouped into symptoms that disrupt states of consciousness (such as fear, worry, sadness, anxiety). Such states are experienced subjectively. They exist on a continuum (e.g., happy vs. depressed). They are related to physiological states, but they often have behavioral manifestations. At what point a symptom or a group of symptoms becomes an emotional disorder is based on the duration, intensity of feeling, and associated impairment (Boyle & Jones, 1985). The child who has occasional temper tantrums when frustrated is seldom a cause for concern; the child who has tantrums over minor frustrations several times a day may be cause for concern.

Psychological, environmental, and physiological causes have been associated with behavioral disorders. The psychological factors include frustration caused by delay of rewards or by conflict, and childhood bereavement caused by separation from or death of a loved one. Environmental factors include family influences, parental characteristics, and methods of child management used by parents and teachers. Physiological factors, including genetic factors, are also suspected to be possible causes of severe behavior disorders.

Federal and state education agencies have the responsibility for monitoring procedures used by local school districts to identify and appropriately serve behavior-disordered school-age pupils. Public Law 94-142 defined these children as having: (a) an inability to learn that is not a function intellectual, sensory, or health factors; (b) an inability to build or maintain satisfactory interpersonal relationships; (c) inappropriate behaviors and feelings under normal circumstances; (d) a general mood of unhappiness or depression; or (e) a tendency to develop physical symptoms of fear related to personal or school problems. The term *behavior disordered* includes children who are schizophrenic or autistic, but not children who are socially maladjusted, unless it is determined that they are seriously emotionally disturbed.

Some professionals feel that this definition of *seriously emotionally disturbed* fails to reflect the best thinking and professional input. The Executive Committee of the Council for Children with Behavioral Disorders (1987) suggested that the current definition does not provide a clear direction to the states and that services to behaviorally disordered students vary based on the state in which they reside.

In identifying legitimate behavior disorders in young children, several cautions must be observed:

1. Behavior considered normal in young children varies greatly. So-called normal children exhibit some of the same behaviors as disturbed children. Since no clear-cut standard exists, identifying true emotional disturbances can be difficult.
2. There are several behavior problems common to young children. These problems often are not cause for concern unless, of course, they persist over time.
3. Differences in the behavior of young children are partly due to differences in parents' child-rearing practices, expectations, and cultural values. Parents differ in the degree of permissiveness exercised with their child, in how children are permitted to express anger and frustration, in the type of discipline used, in behavioral and performance expectations, and in the extent to which they show warmth and physical affection to their child.
4. Many behavior disturbances exhibited by young children are transient in nature and are not likely to persist. Toilet training, transition into school, or transition from a half-day to a whole day of school are all examples of life events that can produce temporary behavior problems that, with time and a little understanding, will disappear. It is an injustice to label a child as disturbed because of temporary behavior problems.

Problem Behaviors Common among Young Children[1]

Problem	*Examples*
Aggressive and Antisocial Behaviors	Hitting, biting, throwing objects at others, hurting others, swearing, name-calling, not sharing, bribery, and stealing.
Disruptive Behaviors	Disrupting group time, leaving the classroom, running aimlessly around the classroom, shouting in the classroom, dropping objects to create noise.
Destructive Behaviors	Tearing books, breaking toys, wasting paper, destroying the work of others.
Emotional Behaviors	Crying, throwing tantrums, pouting, baby talk, thumb sucking, pants wetting, clinging, seeking attention, whining.
Social and School Problems	Nonparticipation, shyness, playing with only a single toy, talking infrequently, short attention span.
Enuresis	Repeated involuntary failure to control urination that occurs at least twice monthly and that is not due to physical disorders. This problem can occur during the day or at night.
Encopresis	Failure to control defecation, voluntarily or involuntarily, that occurs at least once a month and is not due to a physical disorder. Can occur during the day or at night.
Eating Behaviors	Finicky eating, overeating, messy eating.
Prolonged Mild Hyperactive Behaviors	Restless motor activity, short attention span, impulsiveness *and* distractibility. If these behaviors occur consistently, for long periods, the child should be referred for testing.

Despite the difficulties in identifying behavior disorders in young children, educators generally agree that the undesirable or inappropriate behaviors of behaviorally disordered children differ from those of normal children in three dimensions: (1) *severity*—the extremeness of the undesirable and inappropriate behavior; (2) *chronicity*—the length of time over which the undesirable and inappropriate behavior occurs; and (3) *context*—where and when undesirable and inappropriate behavior occurs. Teachers describe children with behavior disorders as those who easily become lost in a tangle of irrelevancies, distortions, unpleasantness, disorganization, and nonproductive activities. Behavioral disorders are usually grouped into symptoms representing socially undesirable patterns of behavior such as fighting, stealing, and lying. Such patterns of behavior are manifested externally. They usually

---

[1] These behaviors occur occasionally in most young children. When they occur consistently, they may indicate a more serious problem.

reflect deficient interpersonal competence or violation of age-appropriate social norms (Boyle & Jones, 1985).

Quay (1979) has classified children with behavior disorders into four groups: conduct disorders, anxious and withdrawn children, immature children, and socialized-aggressive children.

Children with *conduct disorders* defy authority; are hostile toward authority figures; are cruel, malicious, and assaultive; and appear to have few guilt feelings. *Anxious and withdrawn children* are shy, timid, seclusive, sensitive, submissive, overly dependent, and easily depressed. *Immature children* are inattentive, sluggish, lazy, preoccupied, reticent, and generally disinterested in school. *Socialized-aggressive children* exhibit some of the same behaviors as those with conduct disorders but include the more serious problems of stealing and, when older, belonging to gangs of juveniles.

Children exhibiting mild to moderate behavior disorders can be educated in the regular classroom. However, the regular teacher should receive advice, consultation, and help from special education teachers who work with the child within the classroom or in a resource room for part of the day. Children with severe disturbances may require special class placement, but with the increased emphasis in recent years on the normalization of children with disabilities and their placement in the least restrictive environment, more of these children are being included in regular class programs for all or a portion of the school day. Regular class placement for children with severe disturbances is especially found in early childhood programs (Strain, 1984).

The two most common forms of severe emotional disturbance among young children are autism and childhood schizophrenia. *Autism,* a condition believed to be present at birth, is first noticeable from $2\frac{1}{2}$ to 4 years of age. This condition is three times more common in boys than in girls. It manifests itself through a series of bizarre behaviors. These include self-destruction (e.g., head banging), self-stimulation (e.g., waving hands in front of face), aloofness, echolalia speech (mindlessly repeating what someone else has said), extremely delayed expressive language, an insensitivity to sound, and various stereotypical body movements such as spinning objects, rocking, whirling, shaking one's hand, or flapping arms and hands for extended periods of time. Although the precise causes of autism remain unknown, the prevailing view is that this condition is caused by an as-yet-undetected biological problem that occurs either in the prenatal or perinatal stage of development.

The symptoms of childhood schizophrenia include thought disorders, delusions, hallucinations, extreme changes in mood, withdrawal of interest in the environment, repetitious language unrelated to the situation, bizarre and repetitive movements, and evidence of normal and even exceptional intellectual skill. The onset of childhood schizophrenia is gradual beginning between the ages of 5 and 6 years. Childhood schizophrenia differs from autism in several ways: (1) Schizophrenic children are more likely than autistic children to engage in human contact; (2) the symptoms of autism appear in the first few years of life (even though it may not be formally diagnosed until later), whereas schizophrenia manifests itself following a period of seemingly normal development; (3) schizophrenic children often are sickly and undistinguished in physical appearance, whereas autistic children frequently are healthy and nice looking; (4) echolalia, common in autistic children, is uncommon among children suffering from schizophrenia; (5) autistic children show remarkable manual dexterity, whereas schizophrenic children, in contrast, frequently are unco-ordinated; and (6) the autistic child's language is severely impaired, whereas schizophrenic children display normal and even superior speech and language but often produce noncommunicative content.

Treatments for behavior disorders include drug therapy, family counseling, psychotherapy for children or their families, behavior modification, and other forms of psychological or psychoeducational interventions, not all of which can be imple-mented in the schools. When local schools are not equipped to provide such treatment for these children, outside agencies may be used. Teachers need to know how to help children adjust to the school and how to provide a responsive environment that meets their needs.

The psychodynamic and behavioral analysis approaches represent the two most common treatment strategies for young behaviorally disordered children. The psychodynamic approach views behavior disorders as the result of intrapsychic conflict. The emotional problems of adults are thought to stem primarily from childhood events, thus placing special emphasis on early experience and interven-tion. Treatment is aimed primarily at removing the underlying cause of behavioral deviance. One psychodynamically based treatment for young children is play therapy, described by Virginia Axline (1974).

Behavior analysis theory argues that all behavior is learned. The teacher's principal task is to rearrange the environment so that disordered behavior is weakened and appropriate behavior is strengthened. Initially, children may be placed into a segregated, manageable environment, then gradually integrated into the classroom. Teachers can learn behavior management strategies to help these children maintain appropriate behaviors; otherwise, such children might revert to their original condition. The chief technique in this procedure is reinforcement for appropriate behaviors.

Teachers who work with children who have behavior disorders must learn to understand them and to discover ways to deal with their behaviors. Teachers can analyze and alter the classroom setting to promote more positive aspects of the children's behavior. A crisis-intervention teacher or resource room teacher should become the classroom teacher's advisor, being on call on a long-term basis.

All young children exhibit some inappropriate behavior at some time. This may be especially true when a child first enters a nursery school, child-care center, or kindergarten class. In small amounts, for short periods of time, most of these behaviors are quite normal. It is only when a maladaptive behavior occurs week after week, with no sign of lessening, that the teacher should seek consultation.

A CHILD WITH A BEHAVIOR DISORDER

Jennifer King, 4, was described by her parents as highly distractible at home. She was described by her teacher as extremely overactive. From her first day at the child-care center, Jennifer refused to enter the classroom unless her mother was present. This attachment to her mother lasted throughout the year.

At times, Jennifer appeared to be out of control in the classroom. She had an unusually short attention span, would often stare into space, and would have outbursts of temper for no apparent reason. She would frequently leave her activity and wander aimlessly around the center. Requests to return to what she was supposed to be doing were ignored and physical restraint by the teacher resulted in tantrums. She rarely spoke to the teacher or the other children and played mostly alone. Her interactions with the other children were negative, involving fighting, kicking, and screaming.

Toward the end of the year, Jennifer's teacher, in an effort to prepare her for kindergarten, asked Jennifer's mother to wait in the hall rather than accompany her into the classroom. Jennifer reacted with a tantrum followed by whimpering that continued through the morning. After five days, Jennifer's teacher and mother agreed that Mrs. King should again accompany Jennifer into the classroom.

At the end of the year, noting Jennifer's many problems, Jennifer's teacher advised Mrs. King to seek special services for Jennifer in kindergarten next year.

Hearing Impairments

Individuals who are not able to hear sounds due to a malfunction of the ear or of the associated nerves have a hearing impairment. Such an impairment can be temporary or permanent, severe or mild. Myklebust (1964) has identified four variables to define and classify hearing impairment: degree of impairment, age of onset, cause, and physical origin. The degree of impairment and the age of onset have educational implications. As Streng and colleagues (1958) suggest:

> The child who is born with little or no hearing, or who has suffered the loss early in infancy before speech and language patterns are acquired, is said to be deaf. One who is born with normal hearing and reaches the age where he can produce and comprehend speech but subsequently loses his hearing is described as deafened. The hard of hearing are those with reduced hearing acuity either since birth or acquired at any time during life. (p. 9)

Defining and classifying hearing impairments, like visual impairments, is complicated. Hearing loss is generally defined along two dimensions: (1) intensity or loudness and (2) the frequency or pitch of sounds that can be heard. Intensity of sounds is measured in decibels (db), usually measured in the 0 to 120 db range. Hearing losses are stated in db levels. Frequency is measured in number of cycles per second and is expressed as hertz (Hz). For example, 1,000 Hz means that the soundwave vibrates 1,000 times per second. The higher the number of hertz, the higher the pitch of the sound. Although the human ear can hear sounds at frequencies between 20 Hz and 20,000 Hz, nearly all speech sounds occur between 500 Hz and 2,000 Hz. This is the frequency within which hearing impairments are usually defined.

Hearing loss is measured using a pure-tone audiometer. Typically, sounds are presented to each ear independently at varying decibel and frequency levels. The minimum decibel level at which the person can hear the sound is recorded for each frequency. For young children, there are testing procedures available that measure automatic body changes in response to these sounds. Minute changes in heart rate, for example, can be assessed to determine whether a subject is hearing a sound.

There are two major types of hearing losses. A *conductive hearing loss* involves a blockage or malformation that prevents sound waves from reaching the nerve fibers that transmit the impulses to the brain. Conductive losses often can be corrected by surgery or drug therapy. They often can be compensated for by use of hearing aids.

A *sensory–neural loss* involves damage to the sensors or nerve fibers that connect the inner ear to the hearing center in the brain. Sensory-neural losses can result from several hereditary and medical causes and generally are irreversible. Children with sensory–neural losses typically cannot use hearing aids. They must rely on other means of receiving auditory messages.

As with visual impairments, there is a difference between the legal and the educational definition of hearing loss. Hearing impairments are classified educationally by language learning, since language development is the primary restriction associated with hearing loss. Reynolds and Birch (1981) provide the following educational classification of hearing impairment:

> Children with little or no hearing in their first or second years do not learn language in the natural, informal way most children do. They can be regarded as educationally deaf. The hard-of-hearing children are those who have significant hearing losses, but who learn language in the usual way, though in some instances imperfectly. (p. 532)

This definition distinguishes between prelingual deafness, which occurs before language or speech has developed, and postlingual deafness, which occurs following the development of speech and language. When hearing becomes impaired, it makes a difference in the language and conceptual framework from which a child will operate.

Virtually all cases of moderate to severe hearing loss are discovered before children reach school age. Some mild hearing losses, though, are first noticed and reported by teachers. Among the behaviors that indicate a potential hearing problem are (1) difficulty in following directions, (2) turning the head to one side to listen, (3) inattentiveness, (4) hesitancy to participate in large groups, especially where a lot of talking takes place, (5) discrepancy between the observed ability of a child and test scores, (6) persistent colds accompanied by earaches, (7) problems in understanding speech after a cold subsides, and (8) stubborn, withdrawn behavior used to protect feelings of insecurity or isolation. A teacher who observes these factors, singly or in combination, should refer that child for testing.

The most pervasive effect of a hearing impairment in young children is delayed language and speech development (Northcott, 1978). Language is developed orally, and in the preschool years practically all communication takes place in the oral mode. Language involves receiving and sending messages. Both of these types of language activities are affected by hearing loss.

Infancy and early childhood are periods of phenomenal conceptual growth. The young child learns to identify many objects, actions, and feelings by learning that certain words stand for these things. Words are strung together into complex utterances according to a set of rules that are mastered before a child reaches school age. For a child with a hearing impairment, however, lack of normal aural reception serves as a major hindrance to language and concept development.

Related to the receptive language problems of children with hearing impairments are the difficulties they face in developing good expressive language or speech. The young child learns to speak by spontaneously babbling and vocalizing, hearing others, and gradually approximating speech sounds. Aural feedback on the child's own vocalizations and the ability to hear the speech of others are important in this process. Limitations in these abilities make speech development for young hearing-impaired children a difficult process.

Several studies have examined the impact of hearing losses on children's academic achievement. Deaf students are educationally delayed as much as 3 to 5 years. This deficit can increase with age (Trybus & Karchmer, 1977). Normally, educational delays are less apparent in arithmetic and spelling than in language-based academic subjects.

Studies on the emotional development of children with hearing impairments reveal a higher frequency of emotional problems compared with the hearing population. They also indicate a greater tendency on the part of children with hearing impairments to experience social isolation from other children, whether hearing impaired or not. Teachers must assist children who are hearing impaired in social situations. Both parents and teachers must work to help them understand the content of social exchanges. Children must not be allowed to become silent, passive observers; under such conditions, their social skills will never develop appropriately.

The two primary alternatives to hearing the speech of others developed for individuals who are deaf are speech reading and manual communication. In speech reading, a person who is deaf understands another person's speech by reading sounds from the movement of that person's lips, tongue, and face. The speaker needs no special code or communication system. Speech reading is not, however, an exact process. Many sounds have the same visual appearance, and some sounds cannot be seen at all. The efficient speech reader sees a portion of what would be heard, and fills in many sounds and words through contextual cues.

Manual communication, the second communication alternative for persons who are hearing impaired, uses sign language and fingerspelling to both send and receive messages. Several signing systems are currently used in the United States, and not all deaf and severely hearing impaired Americans make use of the same system. These systems, which have definite and pronounced differences, include American Sign Language, manual English, and signing exact English. Fingerspelling, the least ambiguous manual communication method, represents each letter and number. Most sign systems use fingerspelling for unfamiliar words or for words for which signs are not available.

Debate continues concerning which of these is the best system of communication. Supporters of speech reading argue that manual communication separates the person who is deaf from the hearing world. They further assert that allowing children who are deaf to sign dampens their enthusiasm for learning speech and speech reading. Advocates of manual systems stress that conceptual development is critical for children who are deaf. The early use of manual communication methods allows them to communicate more easily with others. They can also acquire more information about the world than can be gained through oral methods. Learning manual symbols also allows children to communicate with others who have hearing impairments. A third group of educators of deaf persons advocates using a total communication approach combining oral methods with manual communication.

Several technological devices can help persons with hearing impairments. The most well known is the hearing aid. All hearing aids have three basic components: a *microphone,* which, like a telephone mouthpiece, converts acoustic energy into electrical energy; a *receiver,* which transforms electrical energy into acoustical energy (as a telephone earpiece does); and an *amplifier* that enhances the signal level between the two. Hearing aids are widely used but have several limitations. They are effective only with individuals with conductive hearing losses. They are tiring to use. In addition, they often malfunction. Studies of hearing aids in schools (Kemker, McConnell, Logan, & Green, 1979) reveal that more than 50 percent of them operate poorly or not at all. Teachers must carefully monitor the operating condition of a child's hearing aid.

Major medical advances for persons who are hearing impaired have also been made in recent years. One such example is a cochlea implant—a device that consists of a microphone, sound processor, transmitter, receiver, and electrodes—that is placed in the inner ear to convert sound into electrical signals. This assists the deaf child to hear sounds.

Microcomputers, which are primarily visual in nature and responsive to touch, afford hearing-impaired students an opportunity to function at an equal level with their normally hearing peers. Computerized instruction also offers hearing-impaired students the opportunity for individualized instruction. Advances in captioned films and videos for the deaf also hold promising educational implications for the future.

The regular classroom needs to be modified for children who are hearing impaired. Unnecessary and confusing noises should be avoided. Speaking face to face with them and sitting them close to and facing the teacher during a discussion or other type of interaction is important. Teachers also must be prepared to support and promote the social behavior of children who are hearing impaired.

Children who are hearing impaired require special help to develop their communication skills. Speech reading, sign language, or a combination of these two approaches is necessary to develop these skills. A resource or consultant teacher is essential in helping classroom teachers work with these children.

A CHILD WITH A HEARING IMPAIRMENT

Martha, 5, has been diagnosed as having a moderate hearing loss that falls within the 40 to 50 decibel range on a pure-tone audiometer. She has difficulty hearing normal conversation unless the person is quite close; background noise may render speech unintelligible. Martha wears a hearing aid and is learning speech reading. She also has mild speech defects that include inaccurate pronunciation and atypical speech rhythm as well as abnormal intonation. Her vocabulary is limited compared with her hearing peers, and she is hesitant about speaking in class and participating in discussions.

Martha's hearing impairment was first noticed by her regular first-grade teacher. Among the telltale signs reported were (1) an odd position of the head while listening, favoring the right ear; (2) inattention during discussion; (3) repeatedly saying "Huh?" and asking for repetitions; and (4) asking classmates for directions. Martha's teacher suspected a hearing loss. She notified a school nurse who then contacted the audiologist.

Now Martha is always seated in the front of the room. The teacher and peers look directly at her while speaking. The teacher and peers speak loudly and distinctly to Martha. She has been assigned a buddy to help with directions and other verbal information. Martha receives one half hour of speech instruction twice weekly.

Communication Disorders

The two concepts, language and speech, are frequently confused and misused. Hallahan and Kauffman (1982) make the distinction as follows:

> Language is the communication of ideas through symbols that are used according to semantic and grammatical rules. Thus defined, language includes the sign language of the deaf (e.g., American Sign Language), tactual symbol systems (e.g., braille), and conventional written language. Speech is the behavior of forming and sequencing the sounds of oral language. (p. 224)

Language problems occur in oral, written, tactile, and gestural areas. Speech is an integral component of oral language. Oral language disabilities occur when individuals do not understand ideas that have been discussed with them or when they do not express themselves meaningfully (Hull & Hull, 1973).

Oral language can be analyzed into receptive and expressive factors. *Receptive language* involves the ability to receive and understand a message. *Expressive language* involves the ability to send a message. According to Perkins (1977), a deficiency in speech is evident when an individual's speech is "ungrammatical, unintelligible, culturally or personally unsatisfactory, or abusive of the speech mechanism" (p. 4). Unintelligibility and unsatisfactory quality of speech are subjective judgments; thus, defective speech depends on the listener.

Disorders in speech and language development are among the most common problems found in young children with disabilities. Such disorders may occur as a primary disability or as part of another condition, such as cerebral palsy or mental retardation. *Articulation disorders*—the production of defective, inconsistent, or incorrect speech sounds—are among the most frequently found problems in young children's speech. They account for 60 to 80 percent of all diagnosed speech disorders in young children and generally involve misarticulation of such sounds as *s, r, l, th,* and *sh*. Children with articulation disorders can exhibit several common types of errors. The first is *omission,* in which the child omits a sound, as in saying "at" for 'cat.' Another is *substitution,* in which the child recognizes appropriate sounds but uses the wrong one, as in saying "yeth" for 'yes.' A third is *distortion,* in which an attempt to approximate the correct sound is distorted. A fourth type of error is *addition,* in which the child improperly adds a sound to a word, as in saying "on-un the table."

Stuttering—in which the normal flow and rhythm of speech are disturbed by oscillations, fixations, repetitions, or prolongations of sounds, syllables, words, or phrases—is another common speech disorder in young children. Stuttering generally occurs intermittently in the child's flow of speech. The disfluency in the child's speech will vary with factors such as rhythm or rate or with linguistic factors such as initial sound, word length, grammatical function, and position in sentence.

Cluttering is a third speech disorder in young children. The characteristics of cluttering include excessively fast speech, disorganized sentence structure, garbled syllables and sounds, and excessive repetitions.

In addition to these speech problems, several voice or speech production disorders are also found in young children. They include hypernasality (in which excessive nasal emissions are made during speech), hyponasality (a failure to produce adequate nasal sounds), pitch levels that are too high or too low, speech that is too loud or too soft, and monotone (a lack of variation in vocal pitch or loudness). These voice or phonation disorders occur less frequently than the other speech problems.

Delayed verbal communication is also a common language disorder found in young children. In such a case, the child does not acquire speech or oral language at the predicted normal time or with a standard degree of accuracy. Delayed verbal communication can be present even when the child's articulation and speech production are normal for his or her age.

Inadequate communication skills can create several problems for the young child. They can interfere with social interactions. With limited communication skills, children are less able to negotiate their needs. They are also less able to apply their ideas with peers by making suggestions, posing questions, or engaging in dialogues that direct or mediate play activities. For the same reasons, communication deficiencies also can interfere with the child's ability to establish quality interpersonal relationships. This also can contribute to the development of a negative self-image on the part of the child with communicative disorders. Thus, early intervention with these children is of utmost importance.

Some therapeutic procedures used with young children who have language disorders include rewarding only gestures that are accompanied by utterance, encouraging verbal imitative behavior through appropriate reinforcement, and parallel talk by which children are helped to verbalize their thoughts. Regardless of the speech or language disorder found in young children, significant adults (e.g., teacher, parents, grandparents) must not give undue attention to the problem, since that can increase anxiety and compound the child's difficulty.

Several language instruction techniques have been successfully applied to young children with communicative disorders. *Functional language training* teaches children to apply language in relevant social situations as opposed to teaching them sounds, words, or sentences in an isolated situation outside the classroom. Similarly, *ecological language instruction* teaches children to use language in a variety of environmental contexts. The focus is on promoting transfer of skills to different settings where the skills are relevant. *Alternative modes of language,* including sign language, communication boards, and electronically presented symbol systems, are also encouraged for children with serious impairments.

In recent years, *infant intervention* has been emphasized. This approach places emphasis on developing prelinguistic language (e.g., gestures and basic concept training) for children who are considered at risk for developing language problems.

Although speech and language therapists are the primary intervention agents with children who have speech and language disorders, regular classroom teachers play a vital role in promoting children's language development. They can provide a variety of rich and successful language experiences with a continuous interaction among children with and without disabilities. Children require sufficient opportunities to produce speech communications and to receive rewards for their efforts, though their achievements may seem small. Teachers should avoid making them too self-conscious or too defeatist as they try to communicate with others. The classroom teacher alone will probably not be able to assist children with serious impairments. These types of problems will require specialized assistance from a highly trained speech and language therapist.

A CHILD WITH A COMMUNICATION DISORDER

Max, 6, has poor articulation (producing inaccurate speech sounds) and nonfluency (stuttering and halting speech) that interfere with communication, attract unfavorable attention, and have led to a poor self-image. Max's articulation problems are thought to be the result of habitual baby talk from his parents and should be easily corrected. His nonfluency problem appears to be caused by emotional problems and may be harder to correct.

Max receives help with his articulation problems from a speech and language therapist for one half hour, three times weekly. Max's teacher is trying to develop a climate of tolerance and acceptance for his disability among his classmates. She has discussed Max's disability with them, encouraging them to show no reaction when Max stutters or misarticulates and to accept him as they would any other student.

Physical and Health Impairments

Children with physical and health impairments have functional restrictions in relation to their physical ability (e.g., hand use, trunk control, mobility, strength, stamina). These conditions interfere with school attendance or learning since special services, such as training, equipment, materials, or facilities, are required. Both physical and health impairments can create obstacles to normal functioning in the classroom. In addition, these impairments can result in social isolation, potential disruptions in interpersonal relationships, the child's increased level of dependence on adults, and various emotional side effects stemming from repeated physical illness.

These deviations in physique or functioning can create behavioral inadequacies or restrictions within particular environments. A person in a wheelchair (a disability in most environments) can function appropriately in many situations when sitting for a long time is required. This individual is not disabled under these circumstances, nor does he or she have a disabled mind. Among the more common physical and health impairments that teachers are apt to see in young children are spina bifida, cerebral palsy, sickle cell anemia, muscular dystrophy, and epilepsy.

Spina bifida is a condition in which the spinal cord is not fully developed and has an opening that prevents complete protection of the cord. There are three major types of spina bifida. In myelomeningocele, the spinal cord protrudes through the gap in the vertebrae of the spine forming a sac-like structure that contains nerve roots and portions of the spinal cord. Myelomeningocele normally results in some paralysis of the lower limbs and trunk. Meningocele is virtually the same as myelomeningocele except that the protrusion or sac contains only the coverings of the spinal column. Normally, no neurological impairment occurs. Myelomeningocele occurs from four to five times more often than meningocele. Spina bifida occulta, the least severe form of spina bifida, occurs when the back arches of the vertebrae fail to develop. A bony defect results that is identifiable only by a growth of hair covering the area of the deformity.

These forms of spina bifida can produce neurological and motor impairment, the loss of bowel and bladder control, bone deformities (especially in feet, legs, and hips), and hydrocephalus (a collection of spinal fluid in the brain that leads to an enlarged head and often requires the surgical implantation of a shunt or tube into the brain to allow proper blood circulation and drainage of fluid). Hydrocephalus, which occurs in 90 to 95 percent of children with myelomeningocele, can result in mental retardation and seizures if left untreated.

Cerebral palsy, one of the most common orthopedic impairments found in children, is a neuromuscular disability. It is the result of injury to the brain before, during, or after birth. This disability, which occurs in an estimated 7 of every 100,000 births, actually encompasses a group of disorders resulting in motor difficulties that vary from mild involvement while walking, to self-help and communication problems, to total incapacitation. In mild cases of cerebral palsy, students have little or no difficulty succeeding in integrated classrooms. They may appear awkward or clumsy, or they may talk more slowly than other children, but when teachers and peers are sensitive to the condition, essentially normal activity is possible. Children with moderate cases also are often placed in regular classrooms, since the medical condition usually has no direct effect on the learning capabilities of the student. Even children with severe cases of cerebral palsy, often accompanied by other disabilities such as retardation, are now routinely being placed in regular class settings.

The three types of cerebral palsy most frequently encountered by teachers are (1) spasticity, which results in muscular tightness and difficulty in movement of limbs; (2) athetosis, which involves uncontrollable rhythmic movement in the muscles; and (3) ataxia, which entails muscular incoordination and loss of balance. Cerebral palsy is also described in terms of the limbs affected by the condition. In monoplegia, a rare form of cerebral palsy, one limb is affected. In hemiplegia, the arm and leg on one side are affected. Paraplegia affects the legs only. Triplegia affects three limbs, normally both legs and an arm. Quadriplegia affects all four limbs.

Sickle cell anemia is a genetic disorder that is found predominantly in African

Americans. It results in distortion and malfunction of the red blood cells, reducing the body's supply of oxygen and resulting in severe pain. During sickle cell crises, the pain often is so severe it cannot be relieved, even after the child has been hospitalized and given pain-killing drugs. The educational implications of sickle cell anemia relate to frequency of hospitalization and school absence as well as the occasional debilitating effects of the disease.

Muscular dystrophy is a progressive degeneration of the voluntary muscles of the arms and legs that results in increasing muscular weakness and incoordination as children grow older. Strong healthy muscle tissue is gradually replaced by fat and fibrous tissue resulting in general weakness and increased difficulties in movement. The disease is caused by a sex-linked recessive gene transmitted by the unaffected mother to her sons. Occasionally, the disease occurs in girls and is then thought to be transmitted through a recessive gene inherited from both parents.

Symptoms of the disease may appear in children as young as 3 years of age and include a general appearance of awkwardness and clumsiness, walking on tiptoes (the result of weakness in the muscles that pull the foot up), postural abnormalities (sway back with protrusion of the abdomen), severe curvature of the spine, and various skeletal deformities.

There often are temporary periods of remission. However, the general course of this progressive disease is downhill as students gradually lose their ability to walk and perform other physical functions. Most children are in wheelchairs by age 10, and death routinely occurs in the late teens or early 20s. This is the result of weakening heart muscles or weakness in breathing muscles that increases the risks of lethal lung infections.

Epilepsy is a disorder of the brain that results in occasional periods of abnormal changes in electrical brain potentials that trigger later seizures. The two major types of seizures associated with epilepsy are *petit mal* seizures, characterized by momentary loss of consciousness that is either unnoticed or mistaken for a lapse of attention, and *grand mal* seizures that involve a more extended loss of consciousness, accompanied by convulsive movements lasting several minutes. Seizure patterns vary, with some children experiencing a single seizure without recurrence and others experiencing recurring seizures of varying frequency.

The problems associated with orthopedic and health impairments that affect a child's educational opportunities occur in the communication, mobility, self-help, and social interaction domains. Many young children with orthopedic impairments also have associated speech problems. The combination of poor manual dexterity and unintelligible speech often results in such children's being able to share only a small part of their knowledge. For these children, receptive language frequently is more advanced than expressive language, and teachers may assume that children know less than they actually do. When children cannot communicate verbally or in writing, alternative communication systems such as signing or communication boards are available. Communication boards are flat pieces of cardboard, wood, or plastic on which letters, words, numerals, or pictures are mounted. Children can send messages by pointing to letters and common words on the board. Communication is not impaired if alternative ways to communicate are found; often this is done successfully with the only limitation being the form in which the message is sent.

Another common barrier for young, orthopedically impaired children is mobility—in the classroom, at school, and at home. Generally, such children's means of mobility are already determined by the time they get to school. It is the task of the teacher to adapt the school situation so locomotion is possible. Only experience can determine how a classroom should be arranged to accommodate a child in a wheelchair. The teacher should expect that not all problems of mobility can be solved before an orthopedically impaired child arrives at school. Initial flexibility is probably the best strategy for successful adaptation of the school setting to the mobility patterns of the child.

Some children with physical disabilities do not have control over normal self-help activities such as toileting, dressing, and eating. These children must learn to let others know how to help them. Teachers must guard against overprotecting them. The goal should always be maximum independence in activities. Information from parents or school specialists often can be helpful in determining the child's level of self-help skills.

Other health impairments that regular class teachers may encounter, though with less frequency, include

1. *Heart conditions*—Impairments resulting from malformations, mechanical problems, or injuries to heart muscles or vessels.
2. *Tuberculosis*—A bacterial infection, usually in the lungs, that can affect the organs, skin, heart, and bones.
3. *Leukemia*—A serious, often fatal disease of the blood marked by an increase in white blood cells and resulting in progressive deterioration of the body.
4. *Bronchial asthma*—A condition in which bronchial tubes become constricted and excess mucus is produced that obstructs breathing and produces spasms in the bronchial musculature. An attack of bronchial asthma may occur because of an allergy, too much physical exertion, or an emotional reaction. Teachers must help such children with bronchial asthma avoid contact with known or suspected allergens (e.g., pollen, fabrics, animal hair), protect them from overexertion, monitor their medication, know what to do in case of attack, and communicate with parents and professionals about the child's medical management.
5. *Diabetes*—A metabolic disorder in which the body is unable to use carbohydrates because the pancreas fails to secrete adequate insulin. This leads to an abnormally high sugar concentration in the blood and urine. Teachers need to help the child follow the required medical regimen (e.g., diet, injections) and be aware of emergency procedures to use in case of severe insulin reaction or diabetic coma.
6. *Rheumatic fever*—A disease, caused by a streptococcal infection, that is characterized by acute inflammation of the joints, abdominal pain, nosebleeds, skin rash, and fever. Rheumatic fever can damage the heart by scarring its valves and tissues.
7. *Hemophilia*—A hereditary condition, found primarily in males, in which the blood fails to clot following an injury. This results in profuse internal

or external bleeding. Even slight injuries can cause severe bleeding. Activities of hemophiliac children must be closely monitored.

8. *Lead poisoning*—A condition caused by large ingestions of lead primarily due to swallowing paint chips or chewing lead toys or other objects. Lead poisoning can result in impairment of the nervous system and muscle deterioration.

9. *Cystic fibrosis*—This genetic condition involves a generalized dysfunction of the exocrine glands that results in an abnormally thick, gluey mucus being secreted into the pancreas, lungs, and other body organs. Mucus in the pancreas blocks the various ducts to the intestines, preventing pancreatic secretions from reaching the intestines. This mucus interferes with digestion (causing malnutrition) and, if it enters the lungs, can cause breathing difficulties and damage of lung tissue. Children with cystic fibrosis cough frequently because of lung congestion and have an increased risk for respiratory infections or pneumonia. Affected children have frequent and large bowel movements because of alterations in digestive functions, a condition that also creates intestinal gas resulting in a protruded abdomen. These children also may have large chests due to hyperinflated lungs. Physical therapy and multiple medications are the treatments of choice for this condition. Cystic fibrosis generally is fatal, and children with it have a relatively short life expectancy.

Readers interested in learning more about health impairments are encouraged to consult Bharani and Hyde (1974), Chutorian and Myers (1974), Cobb (1973), and Connor (1975).

Because of their problems and the tendency for children who are developing normally to avoid those with physical limitations, many young children who are orthopedically impaired experience social isolation in school. Sometimes it takes longer to carry on a conversation with a child who has a speech problem, and many youngsters are not willing to take the time. Sometimes the presence of a person with a physical disability creates discomfort in another person. In addition, students often express a frustration in not knowing what to say to a child with a physical impairment. Without some teacher attention, a child with an orthopedic disability can be isolated in a classroom. With encouragement, solid friendships can be formed between young children who are physically impaired and their able-bodied peers (Lee & Walker, 1980). An important factor in promoting the social acceptance of these children is to analyze the classroom and to make any necessary modifications for them to function as competently and independently as possible. Teachers also need to design learning experiences and movement activities that are within their capabilities.

ORTHOPEDIC IMPAIRMENT—A CHILD WITH CEREBRAL PALSY

Pam, 5, has a mild case of spastic cerebral palsy caused at birth by anoxia (lack of oxygen). It results in muscle tightness and difficulty in moving her limbs. Her disability is most evident in walking, self-help, and communication skills. She appears awkward or clumsy and talks more slowly than other children. Her medical condition does not, however, have any direct effect on her learning capabilities.

In school, Pam works on the same tasks as her peers with some slight modification and is considered a bright student. Pam is popular, due in part to the teacher's preparation of her class peers through discussion. Pam's teacher often comments that there are several principles that guide her work with cerebral palsied children: (1) When students have unintelligible speech, it should be assumed that they know more than they are telling you. (2) The teacher should not hesitate to ask a student with poor speech to repeat a statement or to paraphrase a statement to see if it was heard correctly. (3) The student should be given ample time to answer questions. (4) Students should be encouraged to be as independent as possible in completing all self-help skills and activities. (5) The teacher should encourage peer relationships and support the cerebral palsied student in attempts to initiate peer interaction.

CHILDREN SUFFERING THE EFFECTS OF SUBSTANCE ABUSE

Social and educational agencies are beginning to observe the impact of the effects of substance abuse on children entering their programs. Most particular is the consequence of the cocaine abuse of parents, both during pregnancy and afterward. Although "crack babies" and the consequences of withdrawal after birth have been described by doctors and nurses, little is known about the long-term consequences of prenatal cocaine exposure or the effects of environmental conditions associated with maternal cocaine abuse on children. The Winter 1992 *Social Policy Report* of the Society of Research on Child Development has summarized what is known and has made recommendations for social policy.

Prenatal cocaine exposure has been associated with increased probabilities of premature birth, low birthweight, and small head circumference. It may also be linked to higher risk of physical malformation, symptoms of drug withdrawal, and increased difficulties in orientation. There may be long-term adverse effects on intellectual, social, and psychological functioning. Language development, as well as socioemotional and intellectual development, may be affected in the long term, yet more research is needed to identify the particular consequences of such a state. Children of addicted mothers may face environmental risks, including poverty, maternal depression, and, possibly, physical and emotional neglect (Hawley and Disney, 1992).

A number of local, state, and federal programs have been developed to address the problems noted here. Many of these programs focus on preventing or treating maternal addiction. Unfortunately, there are few programs available at present that deal with the developmental and educational needs of the child. Although teachers and social service practitioners report serious learning and behavioral problems in these children, it is unclear to what extent these children will suffer long-term effects. Recommendations are that these children be assessed and receive treatment as children with disabilities. Probably the best suggestion is for teachers to deal with behavioral and educational symptoms in the classrooms, and to work with whatever social programs are available to provide help for parents of these children.

SUMMARY

This chapter has described the characteristics of three groups of learners with exceptional educational needs—children at risk, gifted and talented children, and children with disabilities. Although these conditions were presented separately, teachers frequently encounter children with more than one disability in the classroom. In addition, children with disabilities may also may be gifted or talented in a certain area. A combination of disabilities and other conditions tends to complicate diagnosis and create problems in remediation.

Labeling children in the classroom is not as important as describing their educational strengths and needs. As a matter of fact, labels often do more harm than good. Each child's particular disabilities and strengths should be considered in designing an individualized program. We can easily stereotype children and prevent them from being considered as individuals. Stigmas are often attached to children who are identified as having disabilities or who are considered at-risk children. Many educators are concerned that labels create an expectation for low learning that becomes a self-fulfilling prophecy. Once children are placed in an educational track—no matter how informal or whether it is positive or negative—it becomes difficult to change them to a different track.

REFERENCES

Axline, V. (1974). *Play therapy.* New York: Ballantine Books.

Berrueta-Clement, J. R., Schweinhart, L. J., Barnett, W. S., Epstein, A. S., & Weikart, D. P. (1984). *Changed lives: The effects of the Perry Preschool Program on youths through age 19.* Ypsilanti, MI: High/Scope.

Bharani, S. N., & Hyde, J. S. (1976). Chronic asthma and the school. *Journal of School Health, 46,* 24–36.

Bloom, B. (1982). The role of gifts and markers in the development of talent. *Exceptional Children, 48,* 510–522.

Boyle, M. H., & Jones, S. C. (1985). Selecting measures of emotional and behavioral disorders of childhood for use in general populations. *Journal of Child Psychology and Psychiatry, 26*(1), 137–159.

Bryan, T., Bay, M., & Donahue, M. (1988). Implications of the learning disabilities definition for the regular education initiative. *Journal of Learning Disabilities, 21*(1), 23–28.

Burke, L. (1989). Identifying and serving the young gifted: A program for reaching classroom teachers. *Gifted Child Today, 12*(4), 10–12.

Chutorian, A. M., & Meyers, S. J. (1974). *Diseases of the muscle. The child with disabling illness: Principles of rehabilitation.* Philadelphia: Saunders.

Cobb, A. B. (1973). *Medical and psychological aspects of disability.* Springfield, IL: Charles C Thomas.

Connor, F. P. (1975). The education of children with crippling and chronic medical conditions. In W. M. Cruikshank and G. O. Johnson (Eds.), *Education of exceptional children and youth* (3rd ed., pp. 352–465). Englewood Cliffs, NJ: Prentice-Hall.

Executive Committee of the Council for Children with Behavioral Disorders. (1987). Position paper on definition and identification of students with behavioral disorders. *Behavioral Disorders, 13*(1), 9–19.

Gallagher, J., Weiss, P., Oglesby, K., & Thomas T. (1983). *The status of gifted/talented education: United States survey of needs, practices and policies.* Los Angeles: National/State Leadership Training Institute on the Gifted and Talented.

Gardner, H. (1983). *Frames of mind.* New York: Basic Books.

Hallahan, D. P., & Kauffman, J. M. (1982). *Exceptional children: Introduction to special education.* Englewood Cliffs, NJ: Prentice-Hall.

Hawley, T. L., & Disney, E. R. (1992). Crack's children: The consequences of maternal cocaine abuse. *Social Policy Report, Society for Research in Child Development, 6*(4), 1–22.

Hull, F. M. & Hull, M. E. (1973). Children with oral communication disabilities. In L. M. Dunn (Ed.), *Exceptional children in the schools.* New York: Holt, Rinehart, & Winston.

Johnsen, S. (1986). Who are the gifted: A dilemma in search of a solution. *Education of the Visually Handicapped, 18*(2), 54–70.

Karnes, M. B. (1983). The challenge. In M. B. Karnes (Ed.), *The underserved: Our young gifted children.* Reston, VA: The Council for Exceptional Children.

Karnes, M. B., Shwedel, A. M., & Kemp, P. B. (1985). Preschool: Programming for the young gifted child: Maximizing the potential of the young gifted child. *Roeper Review, 7*(4), 204–208.

Karweit, N. (1993). Effective preschool and kindergarten programs for students at risk. In B. Spodek (Ed.), *Handbook of research on the education of young children* (pp. 305–341). New York: Macmillan.

Kemker, F., McConnell, F., Logan, S., & Green, B. (1979). A field study of children's learning aids in a school environment. *Language, Speech and Training Services in the Schools, 10,* 47–53.

Lazar, I., Darlington, R. B., Murray, H., Royce, J., & Snipper, A. (1982). (Lasting effects of early education: A report from the Consortium for Longitudinal Studies. *Monograph of the Society for Research in Child Development, 47* (2–3, Serial No. 195).

Lee. R. C., & Walker, J. (1980). *Social interactions among physically handicapped preschoolers and their normally developing peers.* Paper presented at the annual meeting of the American Educational Research Association.

Lerner, J. (1985). *Learning disabilities: Theories, diagnosis and teaching strategies* (4th ed.). Boston: Houghton-Mifflin.

Luebke, J., Epstein, M. H., & Cullinan, D. (1987). First- and second-order factor analyses of the Behavior Problem Checklist with behaviorally disordered pupils. *Behavioral Disorders, 12*(3), 193–197.

Marland, S. (1972). *Education of the gifted and talented.* Report to the Congress of the United States by the U.S. Commissioner of Education. Washington, DC: U.S. Government Printing Office.

Myklebust, H. R. (1964). *Psychology of deafness: Sensory deprivation, learning, and adjustment.* New York: Grune & Stratton.

Northcott, W. H. (1978). Integrating the preprimary child: An examination of the process, product and rationale. In M. J. Guralnick (Ed.), *Early intervention and the integration of handicapped and non-handicapped children* (pp. 189–245). Baltimore: University Park Press.

O'Connell, P. (1985). *The state of the state's gifted and talented education: The council of state directors of programs of the gifted.* Augusta, ME: Maine Department of Education and Cultural Services.

Perkins, W. P. (1977). *Speech pathology: An applied science* (2nd ed.). St. Louis: Mosby.

Quay, H. (1979). Classification. In H. Quay and J. Werry (Eds.), *Psychopathological disorders of childhood* (2nd ed.). New York: Wiley.

Reynolds, M. C., & Birch, J. W. (1981). *Teaching exceptional children in all America's schools:*

A first course for teachers and principals (rev. ed.). Reston, VA: Council for Exceptional Children.

Shepard, L. A., & Smith, M. L. (Eds.) (1989). *Flunking grades: Research and policies on retention.* New York: Falmer.

Strain, P. S. (1984). Efficacy research with young handicapped children: A critique of the status quo. *Journal of the Division of Early Childhood, 9,* 4–10.

Streng, A., Fitch, W. T., Hedgecock, L. P., Phillips, J. W., & Carrell, J. A. (1958). *Hearing therapy for children* (rev. ed.). New York: Grune & Stratton.

Tjossem, T. M. (1976). *Intervention strategies for high risk infants and young children.* Baltimore: University Park Press.

Trybus, R. J., & Karchmer, J. A. (1977). School achievement scores of hearing impaired children: National data on achievement status and growth patterns. *American Annals of the Deaf, 112,* 62–69.

PART TWO

Planning, Organizing, and Collaborating to Deal with Individual Differences

CHAPTER 3

Identifying the Educational Needs of Young Children

CHAPTER OVERVIEW

This chapter discusses:

1. Casefinding methods.
2. Screening procedures to be used with children before school.
3. Screening procedures to be used with children already enrolled in school.
4. Screening instruments that can be used with young children.

Since 1975 the Child Find Mandate of P.L. 94-142 directed states to locate, identify, and evaluate children with disabilities. As a result, most states have implemented some type of preschool or early school screening program to facilitate locating and identifying these children (Gracey, Azzara, & Rheinherz, 1984). The Education of the Handicapped Act amendments of 1986 (P.L. 99-457) extended the requirement to educate children from birth through age 5 with disabilities and increased the need for preschool screening. The law has created a need to reevaluate existing strategies for screening and assessment of children at risk and children with disabilities and has also introduced new dimensions to the screening process (Katz, 1989).

Preschool screening is an initial procedure to identify children from the general population who may have special education needs, or have psychoeducational problems. Screening typically includes outreach procedures to advise and encourage participation, means to identify at risk children, and decision making concerning the children's need for further evaluation or intervention programs (Ysseldyke, Thurlow, & O'Sullivan, 1987).

Early identification is concerned with screening infants and preschool children in order to discover those likely to be "at risk" of experiencing school problems at a later time. The assumption is that school-related problems can be alleviated if treatment is initiated prior to school entrance (Mercer, Algozzine, & Trifiletti, 1988).

The early identification process enables educators to discover children who have disabilities and to understand each child's specific abilities and weaknesses. Finding children not yet enrolled in school who may have disabilities is called *casefinding.* Casefinding usually involves recording the name of each child to be screened, the names of their parents, and their address and telephone number.

Children with disabilities may already be in school and their conditions may not have been identified. Children's performance or behavior may suggest to the teacher that they have a disabling condition. These children, as well as those identified in the casefinding process, need to be screened. If a possible disability is identified, they should be put through a more elaborate diagnostic procedure. Screening usually involves limited testing or observation to identify those children who are not developing according to normal patterns. Diagnosis is a more complete educational evaluation of a child's skills and deficits for purposes of referring the child to an intervention program or, if necessary, designing an individual program for the child. Thus, a child with a disability is located, screened, and diagnosed before intervention is provided. This chapter discusses these three areas as they apply to the regular early childhood teacher.

CASEFINDING

Casefinding, the first step in identification, includes procedures to locate preschool children for screening. Parents, social agencies, and physicians are asked to refer children for screening. Regardless of the method used to locate children, it is important to institute a record-keeping procedure to ensure that the data on each child screened are maintained by the school system. The record system should be compatible with school records, whether maintained by computer or by hand.

Casefinding Methods

Locating young children who have actual or potential disabilities can be difficult. Preschool children normally are not found in one setting in a community. The actual casefinding process depends on the characteristics of the community, the types of resources available, and the nature of the target population. Four principal methods are used: agency referrals, media announcements, school records, and community surveys.

Agency Referrals.   The most common means of referring children with disabilities to preschool programs is through public agencies. Such agencies include public schools, health services, welfare and social services, preschools, mental health facilities, speech and language clinics, diagnostic clinics, and various community agencies. These include those supported by Easter Seals, United Cerebral Palsy, Crippled Children, and the Association for Retarded Children. Agencies should be made aware of programs, and their assistance requested in referring cases. Contact with an agency or service can be made through personal visits, by phone, or by letter. An exact description of the population to be served as well as the range of services to be provided should be furnished to each agency along with the name of a contact person, the telephone number of the school doing the screening, and a supply of referral forms.

Unfortunately, only a small percentage of children who are eligible for special programs are identified through agencies and services, and these are children whose disability usually is obvious. A broader approach must be used to identify and provide services for children with mild to moderate disabilities.

Media Announcements.   A second means of locating children is through media announcements. The announcement should give the time, place, and purpose of preschool screening and the name and telephone number of a contact person. Announcements should be carefully worded and publicity campaigns carefully organized in relation to the target audience. Information can be disseminated by television, radio, newspapers, or mass mailings. Bulletin board notices posted in churches, synagogues, laundromats, supermarkets, beauty parlors, barber shops, and libraries are also helpful, as are announcements at PTA meetings and meetings of civic organizations.

Media announcements educate the community, especially parents, about the purpose for and importance of early identification and intervention. Care should be taken not to alarm or confuse parents. Parents should be provided with reassurance and a clear explanation of the identification procedures and the range of services that will be available.

Media publicity should stress the importance of early intervention and emphasize that, because disabilities are sometimes subtle, it is a wise preventive measure for parents of all children to have their children screened. Announcements of screening sessions should be encouraging and positive in tone; they also should be accurate. The publicity should not imply that all children who receive help at an early age will have no problems in school.

Publicity must also assure parents that their rights and those of their children will be carefully protected. Before any testing is done, for instance, parents must be given the opportunity to read and sign consent forms. Parents must also be assured that unless they consent, no test information will be shared with any other person or agency. These procedures represent the law, and the rights of all individuals involved must be carefully preserved.

School Records.   Many schools ask parents to list the names of younger children in the family when they register their school-age children. A review of these records can reveal from 50 to 60 percent of the children eligible for screening (Feshbach, Adelman, & Williamson, 1974). Announcements of screening sessions sent home to parents of school-age children can also help locate the names of friends or neighbors who have preschool children.

Community Surveys. A fourth method used to locate children for screening is to survey the community. In addition to locating children to be screened for disabilities, survey information provides valuable data for school administrators to use in future educational planning. A survey can also help develop community interest in and support for the local school system by involving a large segment of the population in a common action. Community surveys can be conducted through house-to-house canvassing, telephone campaigns, and canvassing through schoolchildren.

The most effective of the three approaches is a house-to-house campaign (Feshbach, Adelman, & Williamson, 1974). House-to-house canvassing provides the interviewer with an opportunity to acquire developmental data on children by questioning parents about prenatal and birth history, the age at which the children first walked and talked, and so on. The interviewer, who may have the opportunity to observe and talk to the child in an informal setting, can provide parents with information on programs and services, answer questions, and discuss their concerns. The interview may also provide an opportune time to make an appointment for parents to take the child in for screening.

A telephone campaign can be useful in communities where at least 90 percent of the homes have telephones. Again, the most economical method is to use volunteers. A community can also be canvassed by sending forms home with school-age children and with children in day-care, preschool, and Head Start centers. Using these forms, parents can provide information on other young children in their families. These latter two methods, although less time-consuming and costly than a door-to-door campaign, are not as effective because they rely heavily on the initiative of parents.

Organizing the Location Team

When a method of finding children has been chosen, a staff must be selected and trained to locate them. The location team should be headed by someone who knows the community and who has contacts in public service agencies.

Locating children requires the involvement of many individuals in a coordinated effort. One individual should serve as the team leader, whose responsibilities include recruiting, training, and coordinating the activities of others. Other members of the team may include the staff of a cooperating school, paid professionals, and volunteers from the community. It is important to recruit volunteers, as casefinding methods such as house-to-house canvassing can be costly, diverting funds from the cost of providing services if volunteers are not used. Volunteers can be found through volunteer clearinghouses, senior citizen groups, or community service groups. College students, especially those in education or child development, or parent groups in local schools can be tapped for volunteers.

In any plan for locating children, procedures must be developed to ensure that data are recorded completely, tactfully, and, above all, accurately. As soon as location data are complete, screening may begin.

SCREENING

Teachers need to identify problems in a child that are beyond those found with regular classroom children. When screening indicates a disability, the teacher should request the assistance of a specialist for additional assessment. Both teacher and specialist can discuss specific difficulties and plan a program for the child. The teacher can make observations to develop a list of problems to provide a focus for the assessment. The list may consist of a series of questions and the specialist's responses. Spodek, Saracho, and Davis (1991) offer the following questions as examples for a physical therapist:

1. What is the extent of the child's impairment?
2. How will the child's leg movements affect his or her other skills (such as walking)?
3. What type of skills will the child be able to perform?
4. What types of activities should be planned for this child?
5. Who should be involved in working with this child?
6. What precautions need to be taken to safeguard the child?

Screening consists of brief, low-cost procedures to identify children who may have problems (Lichtenstein & Ireton, 1984; Paget & Nagle, 1986). The "at-risk" children identified tend to be those who significantly deviate from "normal" ranges but may not be considered disabled. Since screening procedures do not require extensive or in-depth assessment, the process is susceptible to mistakes. A child may be identified as "at risk" when no significant problem exists, or a child who has a potential problem may fail to be identified (Paget & Nagle, 1986). A more intensive and complete assessment follows for children identified through the screening process as possibly having a disability.

There are generally two types of screening situations: (1) screening groups of children before they enter school and (2) screening children in school. In the first instance, preschool children are taken to a center to be screened for possible disabilities. This normally follows the location process previously described. In the second case, children whom the teacher suspects may be handicapped are observed and tested.

SCREENING CHILDREN BEFORE ENTRANCE IN SCHOOL

This technique generally involves screening preschool children at a central location to identify those with possible disabilities. Teachers working in integrated preschools or in programs for young children with disabilities may be called upon to coordinate the screening process. The teacher's responsibility may include selecting and arranging a screening site, a screening team, and screening devices.

The Screening Site

A screening site must be large enough to accommodate the anticipated number of children. Screening devices have different space requirements and sites must provide adequate space for the use of specific instruments. For the process described here, minimum dimensions for a screening site are 25 feet by 50 feet. A list of potential screening sites can be developed. The following information should be collected for each: address of the site; name and telephone number of the administrator of the site; size and floor plan of the site; list of available furniture, including tables, chairs, and room dividers; list of persons to contact for help in the community; and local media to contact for publicity.

The Screening Team

Members of a screening team must understand the purposes of the screening procedure and be able to establish and maintain good relations with parents and with the community at large. Typically, a screening team will include one greeter, two hearing and vision screeners, a speech and language clinician, a parent interviewer, and an early childhood professional (preferably one experienced in working with young children with disabilities). If available, a social worker may be used to interview parents as well as to assess children's social–emotional development. A specialist in learning disabilities might also be included. Such a staff can screen 60 or more children a day.

The screening team leader may be a classroom teacher who has organizational ability and good interpersonal skills. The leader's major responsibilities are to make local arrangements at the screening site and to be available during screening to answer questions that arise. Additionally, in advance of screening, the team leader must (1) visit potential sites and select the most appropriate location, (2) estimate the number of children to be screened, (3) determine the size of the screening team, (4) complete publicity arrangements, (5) ensure that all necessary materials are available, and (6) make certain that team members have been trained.

The screening team should be trained before screening begins. During training, each member's role should be explained, procedures to be followed during test day should be presented and discussed, and all assessment tools and materials should be reviewed. Members should be familiar enough with one another's responsibilities to be able to assume a different role on a moment's notice. A person well acquainted with the screening process and well known in the community can serve as the greeter, making parents feel welcome, introducing the child to the child interviewer and the parent to the parent interviewer, and making certain that the child is properly registered. The parent interviewer develops rapport with the parents, helps them complete forms assessing their children's development, and interviews them to collect any pertinent information not included on the forms (e.g., the child's current state of health), recording all information accurately.

The child interviewer administers age-level tasks; observes and notes the child's social and emotional development, hearing and vision ability, and general physical development; and encourages the child's active participation in the interview and in

other screening activities. The child interviewer must be able to observe and accurately record the many different responses and characteristics of young children and must be able to relate well to them. Paraprofessionals or nondegree child workers can be trained to administer most screening instruments efficiently and effectively (Lillie, 1977).

Speech and expressive-language screening is usually conducted by a speech clinician with the aid of the child interviewer. The role of the speech clinician is to conduct the actual screening, to train paraprofessionals, and to evaluate the data collected. Both the speech clinician and paraprofessionals should be able to relate well to children; elicit verbal output samples in a number of ways and record this information accurately; assess children's ability to comprehend words, sentences, and concepts; distinguish between correct and incorrect phoneme production; and identify aberrant rhythm and vocal patterns. The speech clinician must also be available for follow-up evaluation of children.

One hearing and vision team, consisting of two hearing and vision screeners, is needed for every three to five interviewers. In many states, trained hearing and vision teams, public health nurses, or speech clinicians are available through federally or state-funded programs or through public health agencies or other organizations. If professionals are not available, paraprofessionals must be trained by local personnel who meet appropriate state certification and other standards. Desirable characteristics of hearing and vision screeners include the ability to work as part of a team and to work well with young children.

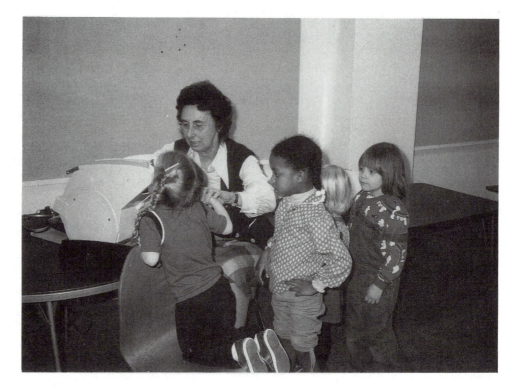

It may also be helpful to have one or two volunteers available to make parents comfortable, provide coffee, give children refreshments, and attend to siblings while parents are completing the initial forms.

Although preschool screening is discussed here, some schools also screen children just prior to school entry. Such screening is intended as a signal for the use of more extensive diagnostic services (see chapter 4), yet it is sometimes used to deny children kindergarten entrance, encouraging parents to keep their children home for an extra year, or to place children in a two-year kindergarten sequence prior to first grade (Gnezda & Bolig, 1988). Such procedures are a distortion of the screening process.

Screening Devices

One of the most important decisions made by teachers is what instrument(s) to use in screening. Instruments should be able to be given by trained volunteers or parapro-fessionals with minimal supervision since few screening programs provide an all-professional team. A comprehensive screening instrument should assess all major developmental areas such as speech and language development, gross and fine motor development, social development, and the development of self-help skills. Instruments should reflect the language or dialect spoken by the children who are being screened and experiences with which the children are familiar. Instruments also need to be valid, providing information about the problems they are designed to screen; reliable, producing approximately the same results each time they are used; and practical so that they can be administered without too much difficulty or cost.

Screening devices for preschool children need improvement. The most frequent problems with them are insufficient longitudinal validation, the confounding of screening and outcome assessments, and inadequate assessment of the predictive utility of the screening device (Satz & Fletcher, 1988). Reviews of research have identified the magnitude of these issues. Miller and Sprong (1986) concluded that two of four instruments on language and articulation studies met insufficient criteria for clinical use. Also, validity was based on simple correlations, providing no information on subject identification into predicted and outcome group members, a problem that many researchers (e.g., Mann & Liberman, 1984) do not recognize. In spite of these problems, studies indicate that early identification is a viable process.

Because of the problem of false positives and negatives in screening, children may be misidentified. Children who are identified as having disabilities may be stigmatized. Despite these difficulties, current screening processes are better than no screening effort at all. Without early screening, children may wait for months or years before assessment and intervention can begin, and such delays may be harmful in terms of their augmenting effects on disabilities.

In recent years, a number of early screening devices have been developed. A description of some of the screening instruments used to identify mildly to moderately impaired young children is provided at the end of this chapter. Before selecting an instrument to use, the teacher should review it carefully to determine whether it is practical to administer, score, and interpret and whether it is suitable for the child and the situation.

SCREENING CHILDREN IN THE CLASSROOM

Many disabilities can be identified through screening procedures like those described for preschool children. Other disabling conditions, however, often are not evident until the child is in school. Few adults are better qualified than classroom teachers to help identify potential disabilities in young children. Teachers have been trained to work with and observe young children. They see each child for long periods of time and in varied situations, whereas other professionals see the children in only limited situations (e.g., an office or clinic) in which they may be ill-at-ease. Teachers also see each child in relation to a number of other children of similar age and interests, which allows them to judge the range of normalcy.

Throughout the school day, teachers have many opportunities to note strengths and to spot problems in children. The variety of structured and unstructured tasks found in the classroom provide multiple opportunities for social and verbal interactions as well as large and small motor activities and give teachers a chance to monitor children's development. When screening children, teachers must select an efficient and organized way to describe what behavior(s) each child engages in.

Observation records, checklists, structured interviews, and rating scales are the most common approaches to educational screening in the classroom. These approaches are also used for assessment.

Observation Records

Keeping observation records involves writing down everything the child does for certain periods of time or during certain activities. Its purpose is to produce as complete a description as possible of what the child does in specified settings. Wright (1960) suggests:

> Begin reporting each observed sequence with a description of the scene, the actors, and the ongoing action. Report thoroughly in everyday language. Describe the situation and the child's actions as fully as possible. This includes everything the child says and does, and also everything said and done to him. Do not substitute interpretations that generalize about behavior or descriptions of behavior, but add such interpretations when they point to possibilities of fact that might otherwise be missed. Segregate every interpretation by some device as indentation or bracketing. Straight reporting must be left to stand out. (pp. 84–85)

Observation records are used as a way of gathering information about a situation Observers look at and listen to what is happening, then record it accurately. They record brief accounts of a situation. Factual descriptions of incidents, behaviors, or events provide illustrations of the different classroom situations. The following guidelines can be followed in recording anecdotes (Spodek, Saracho, & Davis, 1991):

1. Background information, such as the child's name and the date, time, and setting in which the event occurs, is recorded.
2. Descriptions of specific events as well as children's reactions, actions, and comments are carefully noted.
3. The range of observation records identify unanticipated behaviors by describing specific situations and emphasizing selected behaviors.
4. Observations are systematically analyzed to identify patterns in young children's behavior.

When making such records, notes taken on the scene of observation can be in improvised shorthand to be enlarged upon in writing after the observation period. A co-worker might read through the account and question the observer when the account is unclear. When long records are made, observers can work in rotation to minimize fatigue.

Regardless of the procedures employed, some common elements are found in anecdotal recording techniques. First, a time sequence, reported as large units of time (e.g., 10:00–10:50 A.M.) or multiple time samples (e.g., 9:00–9:03 A.M.; 9:07–9:10 A.M.), should be given. Second, specific child actions should be noted. Third, anecdotal records should be narrative descriptions of behaviors that are plain and easy to read.

Figure 3.1 is an example of an anecdotal record completed by the teacher on a child suspected of having a behavioral disorder.

Teachers might employ this technique to observe a large range of child actions and to attempt to pinpoint specific problems. Direct observation, however, may be

Child's name: Tom Maltin   Age: 3 yrs, 4 months   Sex: Male

Date: January 25, 1994   Time: 9:15–9:30 am

Setting: Outdoor free play

Observer: <u>Pablo Villarreal</u>   Observation No: <u>4</u>

Record exactly what you observe under observations and record any interpretations under interpretations.

Observations	Interpretations
Tommy is playing by himself in a sandbox in a play yard in which other children are playing. Tommy is far away from the other children. The teacher is standing roughly halfway between him and the others. Tommy leaves the sandbox and walks over to climb the monkey bars. No other children are at the monkey bars. Tommy shouts to the teacher, saying, "Miss Garza, watch me." Tommy climbs to the top of the apparatus and shouts, "Look how high I am!" The teacher nods at him. Another child then begins to climb the apparatus. Tommy, seeing this, cries, "My monkey bars, you can't play!" He then climbs down and runs over to a tree, again demanding that the teacher watch him. This time the teacher ignores him, and Tommy runs to the sandbox where he sits down and quietly begins to cry.	

FIGURE 3.1   An anecdotal record

difficult for some classroom teachers, since a teacher cannot concurrently give instruction and take such comprehensive notes. Thus, this technique may be more appropriate for other observers such as a resource teacher, teacher's aide, volunteer, or school psychologist.

Checklists

Checklists provide teachers with the maximum of observer structuring and allow a quick and efficient examination of a wide range of behaviors. Behaviors to be noticed are established at the time the checklist is constructed, and the observer checks those items on the checklist that are descriptive of the particular child.

Checklists generally assess the child in the areas of language, preacademic, motor, social, visual, hearing, and general health development. Typically, a list of behaviors is provided for each developmental area, and the teacher simply records whether $(+)$ or not $(-)$ the child engages in specific behaviors (see Figure 3.2, a screening checklist for social development reported by Allen, Rieke, Smitriev, &

I. *Interactions with adults. Does the child characteristically, week after week:*
1. resist separation from parents? ____ Yes ____ No ____ Sometimes
2. shy away from or act overly wary of new adults? ____ Yes ____ No ____ Sometimes
3. display an excessive number of attention-getting behaviors? ____ Yes ____ No ____ Sometimes
4. manipulate adults through such tactics as dawdling, lavish displays of affection, nearly inaudible voice level, tantrums? ____ Yes ____ No ____ Sometimes
5. refuse to accept adult help when obviously in need of it? ____ Yes ____ No ____ Sometimes

II. *Interactions with other children. Does the child characteristically, week after week:*
1. engage only in solitary or parallel play? ____ Yes ____ No ____ Sometimes
2. avoid certain children? ____ Yes ____ No ____ Sometimes
3. disrupt other children's play? ____ Yes ____ No ____ Sometimes
4. flit from one play group to another, seldom settling in for any length of time? ____ Yes ____ No ____ Sometimes
5. depend on grabbing, hitting, name calling, tantrums, or retreat to resolve conflict situations? ____ Yes ____ No ____ Sometimes
6. engage in self-stimulatory behaviors such as incessant thumb sucking, body rocking, head banging, self-directed monologues, unprovoked outbursts of shrieking, or hysterical laughing? ____ Yes ____ No ____ Sometimes

FIGURE 3.2   Sample checklist

Hayden, 1972). Similar behaviors are presented in other checklists, such as Figure 3.3, for different developmental areas.

The warning signs appearing on any checklist are not, of course, exhaustive. Items on checklists serve primarily to stimulate thinking about each child and lead to further planned observations. Checklists can provide an early warning sign that further assessment may be needed. Such measures can lead to better identification of potential disabilities in young children at a time when intervention is likely to be most effective.

Structured Interviews

A typical comprehensive assessment includes more than observation and rating scales. Behavioral assessment can also include structured interviews with relevant family members and the child who is being screened. Behavioral clinicians can conduct structured interviews during the initial assessment. The interview can provide (1) relevant data about the child, (2) information about specific situations of the problem behavior, (3) relevant information concerning the environmental stimuli related to the problem behavior, and (4) appraisal of the methods that have previously been tested, as well as recognizing contingencies to be used during treatment (Gross, 1984). The interview is probably the most widely used method of information gathering regarding the social-emotional behavior of young children. Usually, caregivers, parents, child-care workers, and teachers are interviewed; how-

Visual and hearing development			
Does the child appear to:			
have eye movements that are jerky or uncoordinated?	___ Yes	___ No	___ Sometimes
have difficulty seeing objects?	___ Yes	___ No	___ Sometimes
consistently favor one ear?	___ Yes	___ No	___ Sometimes
ignore, confuse, or not follow directions?	___ Yes	___ No	___ Sometimes

General health			
Does the child seem to:			
have an excessive number of colds?	___ Yes	___ No	___ Sometimes
have frequent absences because of illness?	___ Yes	___ No	___ Sometimes
have frequent discharge from eyes?	___ Yes	___ No	___ Sometimes
ears?	___ Yes	___ No	___ Sometimes
nose?	___ Yes	___ No	___ Sometimes

Language			
Does the child:			
use just two- and three-word phrases to ask for what he or she wants?	___ Yes	___ No	___ Sometimes
seem to have difficulty following directions?	___ Yes	___ No	___ Sometimes
respond to questions with inappropriate answers?	___ Yes	___ No	___ Sometimes
seem to talk too softly or too loudly?	___ Yes	___ No	___ Sometimes
seem to have difficulty articulating words?	___ Yes	___ No	___ Sometimes

Motor			
Does the child:			
appear clumsy or shaky when using one or both hands?	___ Yes	___ No	___ Sometimes
appear to move one side of the body differently than the other side when walking or running?	___ Yes	___ No	___ Sometimes
seem to fear or not be able to use stairs, climbing equipment, or tricycles?	___ Yes	___ No	___ Sometimes
stumble often or appear awkward?	___ Yes	___ No	___ Sometimes

FIGURE 3.3   Developmental checklist

ever, children can also be interviewed, although usually in a less formal and extensive manner (Martin, 1986). Interviews with children younger than 6 years old must first be conducted with the parents. Both an interview with the child alone and a complete family interview should follow the interview with the parents (Rosenberg, Wilson, & Legenhausen, 1989).

Rating Scales

Rating scales call for observer interpretation of behavior. In completing a rating scale, the observer must make a judgment about the presence, absence, or extent of certain characteristics. The observer may be required either to assign a numerical value on a scale to a specific trait such as dependence or simply to mark the appropriate word describing the frequency of a given behavior.

Rating scales frequently have been used to screen young children with potential learning problems. Most scales are fairly accurate for predicting school success or failure. Haring and Ridgeway (1967), for instance, concluded that kindergarten teacher ratings were effective predictors of learning problems in children. Similarly, in an informal study, Rochford (1970) noted that 95 percent of the children who later developed learning problems were identified as early as kindergarten by teachers using rating scales. Keogh and Smith (1970) found teacher ratings to be consistently significant when correlated with achievement scores in the second grade.

Rosenberg, Wilson, and Legenhausen, (1989) suggest that rating scales can easily help measure or identify children's behaviors both before and after treatment. They have suggested using the Connors Parent and Teacher Rating Scales (Connors, 1969, 1970) to measure hyperactivity in young children. Rosenberg and colleagues recommend using the Connors scales with young children.

Several classroom rating scales have been reported in the early education literature. Some of them are widely respected.

The Rhode Island Pupil Identification Scale (Novak, Bonaventura, & Merenda, 1972) is used to identify young children with learning problems. The scale, comprising 40 items reflecting behaviors associated with school failure, is in two parts. Part I consists of 21 items describing behaviors that are readily observable in the classroom; Part II consists of 19 items that evaluate a child's written work. Each item is rated on a 5-point scale. The scale was standardized on a representative sample of 800 kindergarten through second-grade children. Test-retest reliability scores were high (range 0.755 to 0.988), and most teachers described the scale as useful in helping to systematize classroom observations. Teachers also reported liking its conciseness, brevity, and relatively simple administration and interpretation.

The Pupil Rating Scale (Myklebust, 1971) helps identify young children with learning disabilities. Classroom teachers rate children in auditory comprehension, spoken language, orientation, motor coordination, and personal-social behavior. Each rating is based on a 5-point scale of behavioral description, with a 3 being the average rating, 1 and 2 below average, and 4 and 5 above average. Scores are derived by adding the numbers circled by the teacher. The scale, standardized on over 2,000 children, also provides for analysis of specific items or areas of behavior.

In addition to teacher rating scales, parents are sometimes asked to complete questionnaires regarding their children. The results are subsequently used as further indicators of the child's development. Parents are a good source of information to facilitate the task of identifying young children who are at risk. Parents can provide helpful information about various aspects of the general living condition of the family. Properly designed questions can provide insight concerning the quality of environment as it relates to the child's development. Since parents are the primary caretakers who observe their children in a variety of contexts and situations, their consultation can be valuable during the initial screening (Green & Payne, 1988).

The Parent Readiness Evaluation (Ahr, 1968), for instance, is used to screen children, ages 3–9. This scale, which requires parents to administer several verbal and performance subtests, assesses general information, memory for words, reproduction of numbers, and knowledge of syntax and grammar.

Similarly, *The School Readiness Survey* (Jordan & Massey, 1969) asks parents to screen child performance in the areas of number concepts, discrimination of forms, color naming, symbol matching, speaking vocabulary, listening vocabulary, and general information.

Despite their general effectiveness, rating scales suffer from some inherent weaknesses. The characteristics or traits being rated often are ambiguous. What one person may judge to be dependent behavior, another may not. Another potential problem is the "halo" effect: When raters feel positive toward an individual, they tend to rate that person high on positive attributes and to play down negative traits. (To help reduce the halo effect, teachers can rate all students on the same item before moving on to the next.) Finally, some teachers tend to avoid extremes when rating children, giving every child an average rating. This tendency precludes identification of children who deviate from the group. In general, rating scales that include more precise definitions of the traits rated are preferable.

Whatever classroom screening procedure teachers use—observation records, checklists, interviews, or rating scales—caution must be observed in interpreting the results:

1. Screening data should not be used to make a diagnosis of any disorder. A premature diagnosis can be as damaging as failing to recognize a problem and can cause unnecessary hardship for both the child and his or her family.

2. Some behaviors are not what they appear to be. For example, a child who is constantly jumping out of his or her chair or pushing to the front of the group may be considered to have a behavior disorder. This, however, may be the child's attempt to bring things into closer eye or ear range because of a vision or hearing problem.

3. In deciding whether or not a child's behaviors are normal, the customs of the family or community in which that child lives must be considered. Since these may be different from those of the teacher, he or she must decide whether the behavior in question interferes with the child's ability to learn.

4. The degree, rather than the kind, of potentially disabling condition should be considered. Most inappropriate behaviors such as crying, whining, sulking, or disobeying may be seen at some time in every child. Ordinarily, these actions are not cause for alarm unless they occur excessively; are used almost exclusively instead of other, more appropriate actions; and interfere with the child's healthy participation in various learning experiences.

MAKING REFERRALS

After screening data have been carefully considered, the teacher may wish to refer a child for further diagnostic testing. A referral represents a statement of concern about a student. In schools with special services, the referral is often the initial basis of communication between the classroom and special education teachers. Most schools have standard referral forms for teachers to use. Typically, these forms are clear, concise, and easy to complete. If necessary, the classroom teacher can seek help from special education teachers when filling out these forms. The following four items are found in most referral forms:

1. *Statement of the child's problem.* The teacher is asked to write a specific statement about the child's problem. For example: "Bobby consistently

refuses to join in group activities, seldom has positive interactions with others, and often is the subject of his classmates' ridicule, which makes him cry." In stating a child's problem, teachers should simply describe the behavior and avoid making inferences as to why the child behaves in a certain way.

2. *Specific comments on learning strengths.* These are descriptive comments that place an emphasis on the positive aspects of the learner's behavior; they can provide valuable ideas for programming.

3. *Documentary evidence.* Teachers should carefully present screening data gathered from various instruments to support the need for further diagnostic testing.

4. *Identifying information.* This includes the child's age, birthdate, date of referral, and any contacts the teacher has had with parents.

Screening is different from diagnosis. Screening procedures should provide a quick, effective way to assess each child. Screening is a rapid and cost-effective process and may not require professional interpretation, which can be managed with the diagnostic assessments of those children who have been identified in the original screening to determine who is likely to need remedial intervention (Satz & Fletcher, 1988). Parents need to consent to any referrals for diagnosis that are made.

DIAGNOSIS

Diagnostic assessment is a follow-up assessment of children who have been identified during the screening process as having potential problems. The assessment level is comprehensive, generally using norm-referenced, standardized instruments. Diagnostic testing is done primarily to discover the presence or absence of a problem, to verify the child's strengths and weaknesses, and to select the types of services and interventions needed to meet that individual child's needs (Paget & Nagle, 1986).

Diagnostic assessment usually assists in establishing eligibility for placing the child in a special program. It can also assist in selecting and designing intervention and treatment recommendations. Because preschoolers vary in their rate of development, continuous assessment may be needed (Paget & Nagle, 1986).

Diagnosis is a more complete evaluation of a child's skills and deficits conducted by a multidisciplinary team. There are two principal objectives in diagnosis: (1) to confirm or disconfirm the existence of a problem serious enough to require special programming and (2) to gather enough information about a child's disability to make an intelligent decision on the least restrictive and most appropriate placement for the child.

Diagnosis typically involves gathering developmental information on (1) social history, (2) physical examination, (3) neurological examination, (4) psychological examination, (5) speech and language examination, (6) hearing examination, (7) vision examination, and (8) educational examination (Cross & Goin, 1977). A social history is usually obtained through interviews conducted with the family by a social worker. In the interviews, information is gathered about the child's behavior in the home, ways in which the parents deal with the child's problems, the parents' feeling and attitudes about the child, and the overall impact of the child with a disability on the family.

The physical examination, conducted by a pediatrician, is designed to provide a picture of the child's general health at present, a review of medical history, and any information about any physical defects that may be present. Neurological examinations are most often administered by neurologists to children suspected of having learning disabilities. A neurological examination provides specific information about any central nervous system impairment. It also can reveal brain damage and detect the possibility of seizures or other malfunctioning.

Psychological examinations, conducted by school psychologists, may involve both (1) standardized tests to assess general intellectual and academic achievement, general aptitude, and specific academic achievement and (2) projective tests to determine the nature of a child's emotional responses. Such tests typically measure the child's performance against normative standards.

Speech and language examinations, generally administered by a speech pathologist, are designed to assess articulation, fluency, and voice problems as well as the child's ability to understand or use words and language. Speech problems make up a large proportion of the disabilities identified in the early years. Several different tests are used to identify speech and language disabilities. They include hearing, visual, and educational examinations.

Hearing examinations consist of audiometric tests administered by audiologists or public health workers to determine if any type of hearing impairment exists. Visual examinations, which are conducted by an ophthalmologist or public health worker, are designed to detect visual impairment. An educational examination, conducted by the classroom teacher, involves a diagnostic assessment to determine the child's learning style and abilities, both in general academic achievement and in specific content areas.

When diagnostic testing has been completed, the results can be brought together to form an accurate picture of the child's condition. To prevent misinterpretation of the results, each piece of information must be carefully evaluated in light of other results that have been gathered by people with expertise in the various areas and by people who know the child intimately. Parents should be involved in this process. All findings must be explored in order to place the child in an appropriate program. This is done in the team or multidisciplinary conference. This conference and the teacher's responsibilities are discussed in chapter 5.

SUMMARY

Identifying disabilities in children is an important part of the teacher's job. Some evidence suggests that careful early childhood evaluation procedures are effective in identifying even children with mild disabilities. The many alternatives for screening and diagnosing behavior presented in this chapter should be closely examined to match each child to the most appropriate technique.

Teachers must exercise special care in using screening data. They should not use these data to make a formal diagnosis or to label children. Screening data should not be used to raise parental anxiety by reporting that there is something wrong with a child; rather, screening data should be used to seek additional, more intensive assessment for the child.

The increase in early-intervention services resulting from P.L. 99-457 will require an expansion in strategies for early screening of children at risk and children with disabilities. The screening process, as mandated by P.L. 99-457, defies the traditional screening procedures that have been used. Although some traditional screening tools probably will continue to be appropriate to use under the new law, new screening strategies must be developed. Additional instruments that offer information on progressive facets of children's performance will be needed if the process is going to be responsible and committed to the children and their families (Katz, 1989).

SCREENING INSTRUMENTS

Title: The ABC Inventory
Authors: N. Adair & G. Blesett
Publisher: Research Concepts, Muskegon, MI, 1965
Age Range: 3.6 to 6.6 years
General Description: The ABC Inventory is designed to identify children who are likely to fail in preschool or kindergarten or who are not likely to be ready for first grade. The inventory, which can be administered to individuals or groups, usually by a trained diagnostician, takes about 9 minutes to administer and includes items related to drawing, copying, folding, counting, memory, general information, colors, size concepts, and time concepts. The manual reports extensive reliability studies and research on its effectiveness.

Title: Battelle Developmental Inventory (BDI)
Authors: J. Newborg, J. Stock, L. Wnek, J. Guidubaldi, & J. Suinicki
Publisher: DLM/Teaching Resources, Allen, TX, 1984
Age Range: Birth to 8 years
General Description: The BDI is an inventory designed to identify children with special needs from birth to age 8. It consists of five domains of assessment: personal–social, adaptive, motor, communication, and cognitive. The test recommends variations to administer to children with different disabilities and yields a percentile rank, z-score, t-score, age equivalent, normal curve equivalent, and a deviation quotient (a standard score with a mean of 100 and a standard deviation of 15). The inventory also includes a screening test of items from the full scale.

Title: Battelle Developmental Inventory (BDI) Screening Test
Authors: J. Newborg, J. Stock, L. Wnek, J. Guidubaldi, & J. Suinicki
Publisher: DLM/Teaching Resources, Allen, TX, 1984
Age Range: Birth to 8 years
General Description: The BDI Screening Test is a 96-item instrument designed to identify children with special needs from birth to age 8. Twenty (2 from each age level of the BDI) of its items are incorporated into 3 of its domains (personal–social, adaptive, and motor); 18 items are integrated into its other 2 domains (communication and cognitive). Separate scores are provided for receptive communication, expressive communication, tool communication, gross motor, fine motor, and total motor components, although a total score can also be obtained. The BDI screening test overall yields 10 scores with cutoff points at 1.0,

1.28, 1.50, 1.65, and 2.33 standard deviations below the mean. Each component also has age equivalents.

McLean, McCormick, Baird, and Mayfield (1987) investigated the validity and reliability of the BDI Screening Test with a population of children under 6 years of age. They concluded that its concurrent validity must be studied further. Since the BDI full scale has been favorably reviewed to assess young children with disabilities (McLean, McCormick, Brudger, & Brudger, 1987; Mott, Fewell, Lewis, Meisels, Shonkoff, & Simeonsson, 1986; Robinson, Rose, & Jackson, 1986), it is essential that those programs that use the BDI employ a corresponding screener. The McLean, McCormick, Baird, and Mayfield data suggest that presently the BDI remains considerably untested and results must be used with caution.

Title: Brigance Preschool Screen
Author: A.A. Brigance
Publisher: Curriculum Associates, North Bellerica, MA, 1990
Age Range: 3 to 4 years
General Description: The Brigance is used to assess children's basic skills and behavior to determine if they should be referred for comprehensive evaluation. It contains 11 subtests at each of its two levels, covering personal data, identifying objects and body parts, visual motor and gross motor skills, color and number concepts, building a tower with blocks, repeating sentences, picture vocabulary, and plurals. There are advanced items in a supplementary section as well. Because it only takes about 15 minutes to administer and can be administered by a teacher or aide with little training, it is widely used to screen large numbers of children.

Title: The Comprehensive Identification Process (CIP)
Author: R. R. Zehrbach
Publisher: Scholastic Testing Service, Inc., Bensenville, IL, 1976
Age Range: 2.6 to 5.6 years
General Description: The CIP is designed to facilitate casefinding and screening of children. The CIP, which can be administered to groups, is designed primarily for individuals and takes 30 to 40 minutes per child. The CIP has been standardized on more than 1,000 children and screens children using items from standardized instruments in eight areas: cognitive–verbal, fine motor, gross motor, speech and expressive language, social–affective, hearing, vision, and medical history. The test can be administered by either a teacher or a specially trained nonprofessional.

Title: Cooperative Preschool Inventory (CPI)
Author: B. M. Caldwell
Publisher: Cooperative Tests and Services, Educational Testing Service, Princeton, NJ, 1970
Age Range: 3 to 6 years
General Description: The CPI provides a measure of achievement in areas regarded as necessary for success in school. The instrument, which can be administered in 10 to 15 minutes by a trained parent or teacher, consists of 64 items, scored as either right or wrong, grouped into the following areas: concept activation, sensory, personal–social responsiveness, and associated vocabulary. The number of correct responses is converted to a percentile rank for differing chronological ages.

The test was standardized on 1,500 children from 150 Head Start classes nationwide. It is generally recognized by experts as a good screening tool, easy to administer and score, and particularly relevant for disadvantaged preschool populations.

Title: Del Rio Language Screening Test
Authors: A. Toronto & D. Leourman
Publisher: National Educational Publishers, Inc., Austin, TX, 1975
Age Range: 3.0 to 6.11 years

General Description: The Del Rio Language Screening Test is a language screening measure given in both Spanish and English. It is appropriate for English-speaking Anglo Americans, predominantly Spanish-speaking Mexican–American children, and predominantly English-speaking Mexican–American children. The instrument, developed to fulfill the need for special education programs for Spanish-speaking children in the Southwest, consists of five separate subtests, each of which may be used alone or in combination with others. The Del Rio has been standardized on 384 children, and adequate validity and reliability data have been established.

Title: Denver Developmental Screening Test (DDST)—Revised

Authors: W. K. Frankenburg, J. B. Dodds, & A. Fandal

Publisher: Denver Developmental Materials, Ladoca Project and Publishing, Inc., Denver, CO, 1975

Age Range: 1 month to 6 years

General Description: The DDST is perhaps the most widely used screening device to aid in the early detection of delayed development in children. The test consists of 105 items grouped in four sections—personal–social, gross motor, fine motor, and language. The number of items administered varies according to the age of the child. Each test item is represented on the test form by a horizontal bar along the age continuum to indicate the ages at which 25, 50, 75, and 90 percent of the children in the standardization sample passed an item. Each section of the test is continued until the level of development is identified when the child fails any item that 90 percent of the children normally can pass at a younger age.

The DDST, which can be administered by a teacher or a specially trained nonprofessional, has been standardized on over 1,000 children between 1 month and 6.4 years, with separate norms for gender and socioeconomic status. Reliability and validity data reported in the literature reveal generally favorable results, although the test was standardized on a limited regional sample with very few minority children. The DDST is considered to be an excellent screening device that is relatively simple to administer and interpret without special training in psychological testing. The accompanying manual provides very concise directions for scoring and interpreting responses.

Title: Developmental Indicators for the Assessment of Learning (DIAL)

Authors: C. Mardell & D. Goldenberg

Publisher: DIAL, Inc., Highland Park, IL, 1975

Age Range: 2.5 to 5.5 years

General Description: The DIAL is a prekindergarten screening test designed to identify children with potential learning problems in four developmental skill areas: Motor, fine motor, concepts, and communication are assessed with seven items each. DIAL takes approximately 20 to 30 minutes per child and is individually administered by a five-person team of professionals or paraprofessionals. The screening area is arranged into four stations plus a play and registration area. Cutoff points are provided at 3-month intervals, and results indicate whether children are "OK," need to be rescreened, or need a complete diagnostic evaluation. The manual reports extensive validity and reliability data standardized on a stratified sample of 4,356 children.

Title: Eliot-Pearson Screening Profile (EPSP)

Authors: S. J. Meisels & M. S. Wiske

Publisher: Eliot-Pearson Department of Child Study, Medford, MA, 1976

Age Range: 4 to 6 years

General Description: The EPSP provides a brief and easy developmental survey of the perceptual, motor, and language domains. The survey, which can be given by teachers or trained nonprofessionals, takes approximately 15 minutes to administer. Several test items from the EPSP have been taken directly from standardized tests. Although the EPSP has been trial-tested on more than 2,000 children, there is no evidence that this sample adequately represented cross sections of society. Additionally, reliability and validity measures are still incomplete.

Title: Meeting Street School Screening Test (MSSST)
Authors: P. Hainsworth & E. M. Siqueland
Publisher: Meeting Street School, East Providence, RI, 1969
Age Range: 5.0 to 7.5 years
General Description: The MSSST is an individually administered screening test designed to detect problems in the motor, visual, perceptual, and language domains. The 20-minute test, which may be administered by trained teachers, psychologists, physicians, or nonprofessionals, was standardized on 500 kindergarten and first-grade children selected from a cross section of the U.S. population. Norms are presented at half-year intervals, and extensive reliability and validity data are reported.

Title: Metropolitan Readiness Test
Authors: G. Hildreth, N. Griffiths, & M. McGauvran
Publisher: The Psychological Corporation, Atlanta, GA, 1976
Age Range: 5 to 7 years
General Description: The Metropolitan Readiness Test is among the most popular batteries currently used in kindergartens and primary grades. It contains seven subtests: meaning, listening, comprehension, perceptual recognition of similarities, recognition of lowercase letters, number knowledge, and copying-assessing skills that contribute to first-grade readiness. The test, which ordinarily is given at the end of kindergarten or the beginning of the first grade, requires children to be able to write but requires little special training for administration and scoring. Norms are based upon a nationwide sample of beginning first-graders, and reliability and predictive validity data are sound.

Title: Northwestern Syntax Screening Test (NSST)
Author: L. Lee
Publisher: Northwestern University Press, Evanston, IL, 1960
Age Range: 3 to 8 years
General Description: The NSST assesses initial deficits in both expressive and receptive use of syntax. The test, which takes approximately 20 minutes per individual to administer and is administered by a trained diagnostician, consists of a series of pictures designed to screen a child's comprehension and production abilities. Norms on the NSST are based upon 242 children between 3 and 8 years old. The NSST is widely used and respected by speech and language therapists.

Title: Preschool Screening System (PSS)
Authors: P. Hainsworth & R. Hainsworth
Publisher: First Step Publications, Pawtucket, RI, 1973
Age Range: 3.0 to 5.4 years
General Description: The PSS is an individual and group-administered test that consists of a child test and a parent questionnaire. The PSS, which takes from 15 to 25 minutes to administer, screens information-processing skills in language and visual–motor and gross motor skills. The parent questionnaire, also taking 15 to 25 minutes to administer, includes items regarding behavioral characteristics of the child's skills and behavior at home as well as a short medical and developmental history.

Normative data were collected on the PSS over a 2-year period on 600 children, and reliability and validity information are adequate. The PSS can be administered by any experienced examiner or trained technician or by a volunteer or paraprofessional supervised by an experienced technician.

Title: Slosson Intelligence Test (SIT)

Author: R. L. Slosson

Publisher: Western Psychological Services, Los Angeles, CA, 1963

Age Range: 4 years to adulthood

General Description: The SIT is a simple individual screening instrument administered by either a teacher or a trained diagnostician. It consists of vocabulary, memory, reasoning, and motor items. Validity and reliability data for children under 4 are minimal; however, such data are adequate for individuals 4 through adulthood. The instrument consists of one or two items per age level (reported in 6-month intervals), and items for the very young are given orally and require oral or simple motor responses. The SIT yields an IQ score that correlates well with the Stanford-Binet.

Title: The Vane Kindergarten Test (VKT)

Author: J. R. Vane

Publisher: Clinical Psychology Publishing Co., Brandon, VT, 1968

Age Range: 4.0 to 6.5 years

General Description: The VKT is a brief screening measure designed to detect problems in school readiness in vocabulary, perceptual motor, and draw-a-man tasks. It is individually administered by a trained psychologist and takes from 25 to 40 minutes. The vocabulary and perceptual motor tasks were standardized on 1,000 children and the draw-a-man tasks on 400 children representing a cross section of the population in the northeastern United States. Thus, the VKT contains adequate reliability and validity data.

REFERENCES

Ahr, A. E. (1968). *Parent readiness evaluation of preschoolers.* Skokie, IL: Priority Innovations.

Allen, K. E., Rieke, J., Smitriev, V., & Hayden, A. H. (1972). Early warning: Observation as a tool for recognizing potential handicaps in young children. *Educational Horizons, 50*(2), 43–55.

Connors, C. K. (1969). A teacher rating scale for use in drug studies with children. *American Journal of Psychiatry, 126,* 152–156.

Connors, C. K. (1970). Symptom patterns in hyperkinetic, neurotic, and normal children. *Child Development, 41,* 667–682.

Cross, L., & Goin, K. (Eds.) (1977). *Identifying handicapped children: A guide to casefinding, screening, diagnosis, assessment and evaluation.* New York: Walker and Company.

Feshbach, S., Adelman, H., & Williamson, W. F. (1974). Early identification of children with high risk of reading failure. *Journal of Learning Disabilities, 7,* 639–644.

Gnezda, M. T., & Bolig, R. (1988). A national survey of public school testing of prekindergarten and kindergarten children. Washington, DC: National Forum on the Future of Children and Families, National Research Council.

Gracey, C. A., Azzara, C. V., & Rheinherz, H. (1984). Screening revisited: A survey of U.S. requirements. *The Journal of Special Education, 18*(2), 101–107.

Green, H. G., & Payne, L. J. (1988). The usefulness of information gathered from parents in the identification of young children with handicaps: A review and discussion. *Early Child Development and Care, 30,* 181–186.

Gross, A. M. (1984). Behavioral interviewing. In T. Olendick & M. Hersen (Eds.), *Child behavioral assessments* (pp. 61–69). New York: Pergamon Press.

Haring, N. G., & Ridgeway, R. (1967). Early identification of children with learning disabilities. *Exceptional Children, 33,* 387–395.

Jordan, F. L., & Massey, J. (1969). *School Readiness Survey.* (2nd ed.). Palo Alto, CA: Consulting Psychologists Press.

Katz, K. S. (1989). Strategies for infant assessment: Implications of P.L. 99–457. *Topics in Early Childhood Special Education, 9*(3), 99–199.

Keogh, B. K., & Smith, C. (1970). Early identification of educationally high potential and high-risk children. *Journal of School Psychology, 8,* 285–290.

Lichtenstein, R., & Ireton, H. (1984). *Preschool screening.* Orlando: Grune & Stratton.

Lillie, D. L. (1977). Screening. In L. Cross and K. Goin (Eds.), *Identifying handicapped children: A guide to casefinding, screening, diagnosis, assessment and evaluation.* New York: Walker and Company.

McLean, M., McCormick, K., Baird, S., & Mayfield, P. (1987). Concurrent validity of the Battelle Developmental Inventory Screening Test. *Diagnostic, 13*(1), 10–20.

McLean, M., McCormick, K., Brudger, M., & Brudger, N. (1987). An investigation of the validity and reliability of the Battelle Developmental Inventory with a population of children younger than 30 months with identified handicapped conditions. *Journal of the Division for Early Childhood, 11,* 238–246.

Mann, V. A., & Liberman, I. Y. (1984). Phonological awareness and verbal short-term memory. *Journal of Learning Disabilities 17,* 592–599.

Martin, R. P. (1986). Assessment of the social and emotional functioning of preschool children. *School Psychology Review, 15*(2), 216–232.

Mercer, C. D., Algozzine, B., & Trifiletti, J. (1988). Early identification—an analysis of the research. *Learning Disability Quarterly, 11,* 176–188.

Miller, L. J., & Sprong, T. A. (1986). Psychometric and qualitative comparison of four preschool screening instruments. *Journal of Learning Disabilities, 19,* 480–484.

Mott, S., Fewell, R., Lewis, M., Meisels, S., Shonkoff, J., & Simeonsson, R. (1986). Methods for assessing child and family outcomes in early childhood special education programs. Some views from the field. *Topics in Early Childhood Special Education, 6,* 1–5.

Myklebust, L. R. (1971). *The pupil rating scale: Screening for learning disabilities.* New York: Grune and Stratton.

Novak, H. S., Bonaventura, E., and Merenda, P. F. (1972). *Manual to accompany, Rhode Island pupil identification scale.* Providence, RI: Authors.

Paget, K. D., & Nagle, R. J. (1986). A conceptual model of preschool assessment. *School Psychology Review, 15*(2), 154–165.

Robinson, C., Rose, J., & Jackson, B. (1986). Multidomain assessment instruments. *Diagnostic, 11,* 135–153.

Rochford, T. (1970). Identification of preschool children with potential learning problems. In R. Roger (Ed.), *Preschool programming of children with disabilities.* Springfield, IL: Charles C. Thomas.

Rosenberg, M. S., Wilson, R. J., & Legenhausen, E. (1989). The assessment of hyperactivity in preschool populations: A multidisciplinary perspective. *Topics in Early Childhood Special Education, 9*(1), 90–105.

Satz, P., & Fletcher, J. M. (1988). Early identification of learning disabled children: An old problem revisited. *Journal of Consulting and Clinical Psychology, 56*(6), 824–829.

Spodek, B., Saracho, O. N., & Davis, M. D. (1991). *Foundations of early childhood education: Teaching three-, four-, and five-year-old children.* Englewood Cliffs, NJ: Prentice-Hall.

Wright, H. F. (1960). Observational child study. In P. H. Mussen (Ed.), *Handbook of research method in child development.* New York: Wiley.

Ysseldyke, J. E., Thurlow, M. L., & O'Sullivan, P. J. (1987). The impact of screening and referral practices in early childhood special education: Policy considerations and research directions. *The Journal of Special Education, 21*(2), 85–96.

CHAPTER 4

Assessing Young Children

CHAPTER OVERVIEW

This chapter describes:

1. Concerns about assessing young children.
2. Forms of direct observation that can be used for assessment.
3. Assessment inventories and sociometric techniques.
4. Standardized and nonstandardized tests.
5. Ways of recording assessment information.
6. Assessment instruments.

Educational assessment is an important part of program development. It is particularly important in designing an individualized education program for children with disabilities. "Assessment is a process that involves the systematic collection and interpretations of a wide variety of information on which to base instructional/ intervention decisions and when appropriate, classification or placement decisions. Assessment is primarily a problem-solving process" (Gearheart & Gearheart, 1990, pp. 3–4). Assessment generally involves the systematic observation and analysis of a child's abilities and deficits. Initial assessment provides teachers with a starting point for educational programming. Ongoing assessment helps evaluate the effectiveness of current instruction and suggests new directions for educational plans.

Assessment is usually conducted by the teacher with the help of others— paraprofessionals, parents, and frequently ancillary personnel such as speech and language therapists or school psychologists. The attributes measured may include language, motor, perceptual, social, self-help, and cognitive skills, and in some instances, math and reading skills or readiness.

Program development for children with disabilities involves five general steps: (1) determining the educational goals for the program, (2) determining the child's functional level in relation to each of these goals, (3) designing and implementing an educational program, (4) periodically reassessing the child's progress, and (5) continuing the present plan or devising new strategies to achieve the goals.

To carry out these tasks, classroom teachers must be familiar with various information gathering and evaluation techniques. These include observation techniques, assessment inventories, formal and informal tests, and portfolio reviews, as well as techniques for recording the information and making judgments.

All assessment involves some type of observation. It may involve observing a written response on an assignment, observing behavior in specially designed situations, observing behavior in a highly controlled test situation, or observing reactions and behavior that occur naturally during routine classroom activities. Each kind of observation has its own advantages and disadvantages and provides different information.

Teachers need to be concerned with the validity, reliability, and practicality of the assessment techniques available to them. A joint committee of the American Educational Research Association, American Psychological Association, and National Council on Measurement in Education (1985) define validity as "the most important consideration in test evaluation" (p. 9). *Validity* concerns the extent to which a technique assesses what it is supposed to assess. To be valid, a reading readiness test should be related to a child's abilities to benefit from reading instruction and should predict the child's success in learning to read. A test of intelligence that requires a child to read or to follow extensive verbal directions may actually be testing language ability and may not be a valid indicator of intelligence.

All tests must be assessed for validity for the purposes for which it is being considered or used. A test may be highly valid for one purpose but useless for another. Using a test for a purpose for which it is not valid is worse than doing no assessment at all. If it is not valid, the results are not meaningful (Gearheart & Gearheart, 1990). Thus, a screening test may be valid for its own purposes; it cannot be considered valid as a readiness test or as a test of development. Similarly, a test of development is not valid for use as a readiness test. Too often, screening and readiness tests have been used to deny children entrance into kindergarten or to recommend that children be enrolled in a 2-year kindergarten program, postponing entrance to first grade for an additional year. These tests, which may be valid for their original purposes, are not valid for these purposes, nor are the decisions that are made based upon those tests. In addition, the standards for test validity need to be related to the uses to which the tests are put. Thus tests that have lesser consequences, for example screening tests that require additional assessment before decisions are made or instructional tests that teachers use in class, do not require the standards of validity that "high-stakes tests"—that is, tests where the consequences are serious—require (Shepard & Graue, 1993).

Reliability indicates the stability or consistency that characterizes a means of measuring behavior. It relates to the consistency in acquiring the same observation or score when repeatedly assessing the same behavior, attribute, or ability (Gearheart & Gearheart, 1990). Sometimes chance will so influence a child's score on a test, for example, that repeated testing yields very different results. Such a test is unreliable. Sometimes young children's characteristics are so changeable that it is difficult to find a reliable measure. A test that is valid but not reliable would not be useful to a teacher.

Practicality relates to the ability of the teacher to use the assessment technique with ease and the ability to use the results of that assessment. Some techniques, such as direct observation, may be too time-consuming to be practical for a teacher in a self-contained classroom. Other techniques may require skills beyond those expected of a teacher. Thus, giving a Wechsler Intelligence Test to a child is impractical unless there is a psychologist available to administer it. In addition, such a test will not prove helpful to teachers except in the broadest way.

There are four principal techniques used by teachers to assess child behavior in the classroom: direct observation, assessment inventories, standardized tests, and informal tests.

OBSERVATION

Observational methods have been developed to respond to the limited measures in examining interactions. Observations can be conducted at home, in a classroom, in a clinic, or in a laboratory. They provide a systematic way to either quantify specific behaviors or provide a rich description of interactions (Barnard & Kelly, 1991).

Direct observation involves systematically watching and recording children's behavior as it occurs. Many behaviors of young children that cannot be assessed by tests or other indirect methods are easily assessed by observation. These include showing respect, cooperation, levels of dramatic play, or increases in sentence speaking. Such observation also allows teachers to assess such variables as group participation and responsiveness, individual performance in group situations, attitudes toward school work, student-teacher interactions, and the effectiveness of different teaching methods and materials. Direct observation provides teachers with an immediate view of performance in natural settings.

Because direct observation leaves the natural scheme of things intact, it is seen as an appropriate measurement technique by most early childhood educators (Goodwin & Driscoll, 1980). Observations help focus teacher attention on what actually happens rather than allowing them to rely on impressions or subjective judgments. Young children are open and relatively unchanged or little bothered by being observed. They are less likely to camouflage or alter their behavior when observed than are older children or adults. By comparison, a formal test instrument elicits unusual or new behaviors from young children and often signals them to alter their behavior in accordance with the new situation (Lowenbraun & Affleck, 1976).

Teachers and others who work with young children are in a unique position to collect observational data on their students. Because of their daily association with children in familiar settings, teachers are able to observe children's performance for extended periods of time. With a little training and practice, teachers can learn to observe children's behavior objectively and precisely. In order to engage in direct observation, teachers need to regularly allocate time for it, keeping themselves free from other teaching responsibilities for that time.

A number of different direct and indirect forms of observation techniques can be used by teachers. These direct forms include specimen records, event records, duration records, time sampling, event sampling, placheck (planned activity check), student participation charts, media, and portfolios of children's work samples. Indirect forms include anecdotal records, checklists, and rating scales. These can be used in combination. Indirect forms of observation, which don't require the observer to record all behaviors, often include teacher impressions and require teachers to make judgments. This is less the case with the more direct forms. Indirect forms of observation were discussed in chapter 3. Direct forms are discussed here.

Direct Observation

Direct observations should be systematically recorded to note the child's strengths and weaknesses in specific skill areas and should be used as a continuous measure of student progress. A brief overview of observational techniques follows. Readers wishing more detailed information are encouraged to read more extensive works by Almy and Genishi (1979), Boehm and Weinberg (1987), Irwin and Bushnell (1980), Goodwin and Driscoll (1980), Salvia and Ysseldyke (1985), and Sattler (1981).

Specimen Records. Specimen records, which are the fullest accounts of children's behavior, are obtained when a teacher follows a single child for a period of time and records everything that happens to that child or that is done. Such a record provides a complete picture of a child, and the manner and context in which the child functions. The teacher can read over these records a number of times, each time abstracting the information that is most useful for a particular purpose. Patterns of behavior will stand out and a sense of the child will be projected.

Although such complete observations are rich in information, teachers seldom collect them. They require the teacher's total attention for relatively long periods of time, and most teachers find the demands of classroom teaching too great to allow them to withdraw from interactions with the rest of the children for the required periods of time. Sometimes teacher's aides, student teachers, volunteers, or other personnel might be available to relieve the teacher to observe or to collect such records themselves.

Guidelines for Collecting Observational Data
1. *Be specific in the language you use.* Describe specifically what you see in ways that others will be able to visualize. Be precise and descriptive in your language, using adverbs and adjectives that characterize what you see. Try to leave out judgments and inferences. If you are using a category system, define your categories ahead of time. Try to label your categories in ways that others will understand. Try to establish categories

that are mutually exclusive so you do not have to make a judgment as to which category to check during an observation.

2. *Describe the setting in which the child is observed.* The setting includes date, time of day, classroom activity, work assignment, and people and materials involved during the observation. Awareness of any or all of these items may help the teacher understand what sets off certain behaviors in children who are under study.

3. *Understand the purpose underlying the observation.* If you are observing to identify the antecedents of a problem, focus on times that will highlight the problem. If a child is having academic problems, observe when academics are being taught. Observing a child during free-play periods might not help you understand the way that child approaches academics.

4. *Obtain as much information as is practical and necessary.* How many observations you make, how long they are, when you make them, and how you make them depend on your purposes, as well as what is possible for you. If a child manifests behavioral problems, sample that child's behavior in a number of physical and social settings at different times of the day. This will help determine if this is a general problem, a problem with a single child or a single activity, or a problem that occurs only at a certain time. This sort of information can help in coming up with solutions that might work for you.

5. *Experiment with different procedures and forms.* It is a good idea to practice various observational techniques several times before actually collecting data.

6. *Check reliability.* If at all possible, have another person observe the same student at the same time and compare records. The degree to which two observers agree can serve as an index of reliability.

7. *Be as unobtrusive as possible.* Try to be matter-of-fact in your observations. Be as inconspicuous as possible in watching a child and recording behavior.

Duration Recording

Duration recordings help the teacher determine how much time a child spends in a particular activity or behavior. The amount of time a child spends doing his or her work and the length of time a preschooler engages in isolate, parallel, or cooperative play are examples of types of activities best assessed by duration recording. To record these child behaviors, a watch or clock can be used. During a given observation period the teacher simple notes the time a behavior or activity starts and when it stops, and then records the length of time between these two points. A teacher might, for instance, observe a child during free play for 5 days for 15 minutes each day (a total of 75 minutes), recording the duration of isolate play and totaling the amount each day. The data might appear as follows:

Duration Recording

Day (observe 15 minutes each day)	Total minutes spent in isolate play
1	7
2	14
3	11
4	8
5	12
	Total = 52 minutes

The time spent in isolated play can be translated into a percentage of total observation time:

$$\frac{\text{duration of isolate play}}{\text{total observation time}} = \frac{52 \text{ min.}}{75 \text{ min.}} \times 100 = 69\%$$

Duration recording can be time-consuming for the observer, but it can be used efficiently when the teacher is assisted by a special class teacher or an aide.

Time Sampling

Time sampling (see Figure 4.1) determines the degree to which a behavior occurs by observing and recording the incidence of that behavior at specific time intervals. The assumption is that the behavior occurs when the child is not observed in approximately the same degree as during the times observed. To sample behavior this way, a period of time is set for observation and is broken down into equal intervals with observations made at the end of each interval. A 30-minute period may be sampled by

FIGURE 4.1   Time sampling*

Ms. Bell wishes to determine the degree to which a child interacts socially with others during the play period. The 30-minute play period would be divided into 10 3-minute segments with observations made at 3-minute intervals. If the child is observed interacting with another child, Ms. Bell enters a plus (+). If the child is not interacting, she enters a minus (−). The record might look like this:

	−	+	+	−	+	+	−	−	+	+
minutes	3	6	9	12	15	18	21	24	27	30

These data reveal that the child was observed interacting 60 percent of the time the observer sampled the behavior.

---

* Time sampling is useful for observing frequent behaviors, since it does not require constant attention. Teachers can engage in other instructional activities, observing only at the end of each interval.

BOX 4.1   Event Sample

Mr. West has two boys in his second-grade class who often talk to one another. Mr. West is interested in recording the talk between the boys before he intervenes to reduce it. During several 15-minute work sessions, the number of verbal interactions between the boys is tallied. Mr. West defines talking as any time either boy speaks to the other. Thus, if one boy speaks to the other and the other replies, two interactions are recorded. Using this definition, Mr. West can now count the number of times these boys talk to one another.

---

dividing it into ten 3-minute segments, with the teacher observing very briefly at the end of each segment. The ten observations would then represent a sample of behavior for the entire 30-minute period.

Event Sampling

A teacher might wish to note how often during an extended period a particular behavior occurs for a child. Rather than sample over time, the teacher might note each time that behavior occurs. This is called *event sampling* (see Box 4.1). For example, a teacher who wants to know the extent of independent reading that occurs in class might set up a chart that lists the names of each child in the class. Columns are then assigned for each type of reading behavior, such as going to the reading area, reading alone, and reading with a group of children. The teacher can then put a tally mark in the appropriate column next to a particular child's name whenever a reading behavior is observed. Such a chart might look like this:

Child	*Goes to reading area*	*Reads alone*	*Reads with others*
_____	_____	_____	_____
_____	_____	_____	_____
_____	_____	_____	_____

Wrist golf counters, hand tally digital counters, or simple tally marks written on a piece of paper can also be used to keep track of how often a child performs a skill. Event recording is most often used with behaviors that occur quite frequently (see Box 4.1). When used regularly, this form of recording helps teachers notice small improvements in a child's behavior. The advantages to using event recording are its simplicity and its minimal interference with ongoing teaching.

Placheck

Placheck (planned activity check) (see Box 4.2) is a recording technique for teachers interested in observing groups of young children (Risley, 1971; Hall, 1974). In using placheck:

BOX 4.2   Placheck

Ms. Beck, the first-grade teacher, wants to check on what portion of her students are working on a math assignment during a 30-minute period.

Every 10 minutes, she quickly counts how many are working on the assignment. She had already counted the number of pupils present (20). During the first 10-minute period she finds that 10 of the 20 are working; during the second, 15 of the 20 are working, and during the third, 8 of the 20. These findings translate into 50 percent, 75 percent, and 40 percent, respectively.

---

1. The teacher selects and defines the child behavior(s) to be recorded in a group of children in a specific area.
2. At given intervals (e.g., every 8 minutes) the teacher counts, as quickly as possible, the number of children engaged in the behavior(s) and then records the total(s).
3. Next, the teacher counts and records how many individuals are in the area.
4. The number of children present in the area is then divided by the number of children engaged in the behavior, and this quotient is multiplied by 100 to find the percentage of those engaged in the behavior. This is illustrated in the following formula:

$$\frac{\text{number of children engaged in an activity}}{\text{number of children engaged in the area}} \times 100 = \% \text{ of children engaged in that activity}$$

Sample Participation Chart

In this procedure for observing several students simultaneously (see Figure 4.2), the names of the pupils are listed in a column with a space beside each name in which to record the sequence and frequency of his or her participation in group activities or discussions. Each child's participations are then totaled and compared with the number of participations of the others in the group. A teacher who is concerned that a small number of students dominate a certain activity area in the room might use the participation chart to test that hypothesis. Cartwright and Cartwright (1974) provide additional discussion and illustrations of the use of participation charts.

Media

Electronic media can be used to augment the paper-and-pencil techniques teachers use in their classrooms. A child or group of children can be videotaped or audiotaped while engaging in different activities. The teacher can use the tapes to capture ongoing behavior for analysis at a later date. When tapes are saved, comparisons can be made among those taken at different times. This technique, although often costly

Observer:	Mr. Garcia	
Activity:	Working in the block building area	
Time:	Activity time for a week	

Children	Tally	Total number of times observed in area
Carol	~~HHT~~ ~~HHT~~ ~~HHT~~ ~~HHT~~ /	21
Bob	~~HHT~~ ~~HHT~~ ~~HHT~~ ~~HHT~~	20
Ted		0
Alice	/ / / /	4
Mickey		0
Betty	/ / / /	4

FIGURE 4.2 Sample participation chart

and time-consuming, can be valuable for studying child behavior if the equipment is available and if there are people available to tape the class. The teacher can then take time to review the tapes and abstract material from them when children are not present. Teachers need to be aware that busy classrooms are noisy places. Because we are able to focus our attention, we tend to eliminate extraneous noise or movement as we watch and listen. Recordings of ongoing classroom events cannot eliminate the business of the classroom, so teachers may need to listen to and observe their recordings several times before they can make out what is actually happening.

Children's photographs may be taken by teachers or classroom aides during different activities over a period of time. The teacher can collect these and analyze the children's expressions, activities, and interactions with others. But there are dangers in making inferences when the context of a photo may not be recalled. Expressions are difficult to interpret, and the same expression in a child's face may be judged differently in different contexts. Photographs are best used in combination with other procedures such as anecdotal reports.

In collecting observations through media, as with other collections of observations, one must be aware of what is being sampled. If only the highlights of class activities are collected rather than the day-to-day activities, teachers need to be aware and need to make others aware that the collection is not representative of what normally transpires in the classroom.

Portfolios

Samples of children's work, including stories they have written, penmanship samples, or art products, may be used to assess a child's progress when teachers periodically select samples of the child's work, store them, and then look back over the work to determine whether or not the child is making progress. Such collections of children's work are called *portfolios.* Each piece of children's work should be labeled with the date and circumstance of its production. The works may be collected in folders similar to the portfolios artists use for their work. The collection of children's work must be done consistently. There should be consistency in the criteria used to select products to include in the portfolio. If a teacher collects the children's best painting for each week, the collection will represent the child's best efforts. If the teacher randomly selects children's stories each week, then that collection will represent the child's average work.

Products that lie flat, such as a piece of paper, are easy to collect and store. Teachers also need to document work that is not so easy to store or that is elusive. Block structures or clay work can be photographed. A child's verbal story can be tape-recorded. Children's performances can be videotaped. If the actual product cannot be recorded in this way, teachers can describe them in writing. These collections are invaluable in assessing children's products. However, care must be taken in interpreting these products just as in interpreting other products of evaluation.

ASSESSMENT INVENTORIES

Assessment inventories consist of statements of developmentally sequenced behaviors in areas of gross motor, fine motor, cognitive, communication, preacademic, and self-help skills that have been developed for use with children with specific disabilities, such as Down Syndrome, emotional disturbance, and learning disabilities. The items included in the inventories are derived from one or more of three principal sources: (1) standardized tests such as the Stanford-Binet Test of Intelligence or the Illinois Test of Psycholinguistic Abilities (ITPA), (2) observations of young children in classroom settings by practicing teachers and educational experts, and (3) developmental guidelines such as those compiled by Gesell and Ilg (1949). The process typically involves teachers' watching and then checking those items that are most descriptive of the child's present performance level. Table 4.1 contains a sample inventory.

In spite of their widespread use, assessment inventories tend to have a number of problems. Often the test maker fails to provide data to back claims that items are developmentally sequenced. In addition, the instrument may not have been tested with large, representative samples of children. Teachers and administrators must be aware that unless the authors of an assessment inventory explicitly report data on standardization, the developmental nature of the assessment tool is in question. Another problem related to use of these inventories is that their authors sometimes fail to report reliability data. For example, the inventory may be constructed in such a way that two observers cannot be certain that they are viewing the same behavior. Or accompanying instructions may be too vague to convey exactly what is to be observed. Thus, instructional decisions made by two professionals observing the same behaviors may differ because it is unclear what is to be observed.

Another shortcoming concerns inappropriate use of screening devices. Many program developers use screening devices for assessment purposes. However, screening devices are gross measures designed to detect the possibility of a disability; they are not specific enough to be used in assessment. The purpose for which a test was designed must govern its use.

TABLE 4.1   A sample preschool assessment inventory*

	Gross Motor Skills	Fine Motor Skills	Preacademic Skills	Self-Help Skills
36–48 months	Walks on a line. Balances on 1 foot for 5 seconds. Uses slides without assistance. Rides trike.	Traces diamond. Imitates cross. Copies circle. Places small pegs in pegboard.	Points to 6 base colors. Rote counts to 3. Counts 2 objects and tells how many. Does 7-piece puzzle.	Pours well from pitcher. Spreads with knife. Buttons and unbuttons clothing. Uses toilet independently.
48–60 months	Walks backward heel-toe. Bends from waist with knees extended to pick things up. Walks up and down steps alone.	Traces triangle. Copies cross. Copies square. Prints a few capital letters.	Names 6 basic colors. Names circles, squares, triangles. Rote counts to 10. Matches and sorts objects by texture.	Cuts food with knife. Laces shoes. Knows own name/city/street.
60–72 months	Walks a balance beam. Can cover 2–3 yards hopping. Turns somersault. Jumps from 12 inches landing on toes.	Copies triangle. Copies first name. Prints some numbers. Cuts out simple shapes.	Names some letters. Names some numerals. Counts 6 objects and tells how many. Copies block design.	

*Adapted from the Preschool Profile, University of Washington.

Finally, many assessment inventories are not detailed enough for use with young children with disabilities. This would cause the child's initial level of functioning to be recorded inaccurately, and small but significant levels of progress would not be detected.

In spite of these problems, assessment inventories are popular and teachers should be familiar with the most commonly used inventories. An annotated list of such inventories is provided at the end of this chapter.

SOCIOMETRICS

Sociometric techniques measure social relations by using peer ratings of their classmates' social behavior. Peer nominations are commonly used: Children are asked to name up to three classmates with whom they would like to participate in an activity (e.g., playing together or attending a party). Children are also asked to name those with whom they would not like to spend time. The positive and negative nominations are added up to identify each child's social status.

Children may also be asked to rate the peers whom they would like to work with, play with, or sit by. Scores are then totaled for each child; the lower the overall rating, the less popular a child is. In a typical scale, a rating of 1 means that a child is not liked, a 2 that he or she is liked a little, and a 3 that he or she is liked a lot. Faces with frowns, neutral expressions, and smiles may be used with children who cannot read.

Recently, researchers have developed more refined social status classifications (Coie, Dodge, & Coppotelli, 1982; French & Waas, 1985). French and Waas designed five social status categories by applying criteria such as popular (high—"liked most"; low—"liked least"), rejected (high—"liked least"; low—"liked most"), and average. Teachers and parents rated rejected children as displaying more behavior problems than popular, average, and neglected children. Coie et al. reported that peers perceived popular children as prosocial, rejected children as disruptive and aggressive, neglected children as shy, and controversial children as both prosocial and disruptive. Dubow and Cappas (1987) used a peer nomination procedure with third-to-fifth graders who were then identified as one of five social status types (popular, rejected, neglected, controversial, average). Status group differences among teachers' reports, peers' reports, and children's self-reports of adjustment were gathered.

Children's self-reports of adjustment are consistent with teachers' and peers' reports: Rejected children rate themselves as lowest in adjustment (Dubow & Cappas, 1987). Some researchers have suggested problems with this type of study. They suggest that the use of "liked least" peer nominations can negatively influence children's subsequent interactions with their peers (Dubow & Cappas, 1987). However, Hayvren and Hymel (1984) did not support these results, and different techniques for classifying rejected children are available (Asher & Dodge, 1986).

Many sociometric instruments offer a valuable way of measuring the children's social impact on those around them. A review of the literature by Asher and Hymel (1981) suggests that sociometric instruments are reliable and valid measures of a child's overall social competence. Peer ratings usually are considered the most obvious measure of the social validity of social skills training (Dodge & Murphy, 1984). However, sociometric measures are restricted if they are used independent of other measures, because they cannot indicate the specific behaviors that contributed to the change in peer acceptance (Hughes & Sullivan, 1988). Sociometrics are useful mainly with children in kindergarten or above. Other measures should be used below the kindergarten level since younger children's behavior often is not consistent with their ratings.

Sociometrics uses a rating scale to assess the degree to which individuals are accepted within a group. Most sociometric scales are simple to construct and administer. The most common sociometric technique used with young children is peer nomination (Wallace & Larsen, 1978). Typically, children are presented with a hypothetical situation (e.g., a birthday party) and asked to choose one or more classmates they would like to play with, sit next to, eat lunch with, or carry out any other prescribed activity with. Children may be asked to nominate one child, a group of children, or an ordered set of children. Teachers may also ask children to identify persons they least like. Among the questions children are likely to be asked are:

1. Which classmate(s) do you most like (or least like) to play with?
2. Which children get you into trouble?
3. Which child would you most like (or least like) to sit next to at your birthday party?
4. Which children do you think are bossy?

Sociometrics has most often been used in early childhood classes to test a child's popularity within a group (Asher, Oden, & Gottman, 1978).

STANDARDIZED TESTS

Standardized tests consist of a fixed set of items that are carefully designed to assess a particular defined area of achievement. Specific instructions are utilized to administer and score the tests. Also, standard criteria are developed at a national level for these tests according to the average scores of massive numbers of individuals who are comparable to those taking the test. Such standard criteria or norms permit teachers to contrast an individual's test score with those of a representative group who have been administered the same test, allowing the teachers to make judgments about that child's performance in relation to other children's achievement. Standardized tests present a national frame of reference in assessing an individual's achievement. The content and procedures that are founded for such tests are also standardized. An identical test is administered the same way to all individuals in different geographic areas, so comparisons are considered valid (Spodek, Saracho, & Davis, 1991).

Standardized tests are norm-referenced tests. The scoring is based on the norms established by administering the test to a representative sample of children and then creating scores based on that sample. Norm-referenced tests allow comparisons of test scores from one group to another. However, such tests have limited educational value for use with young children, especially with populations that do not lie within the norming sample, because they are designed to be administered following standard procedures. Such procedures might have to be modified for children with disabilities (Salvia & Ysseldyke, 1985).

Standardized tests do serve two useful purposes, however. Their test scores are helpful in obtaining services or funds, which frequently require evidence of the child's performance or status on some scale. In addition, a good standardized test administered by a well-trained or experienced examiner can provide information on the child in comparison to same-aged peers. For instructional purposes, however, informal tests, naturalistic observation, or assessment inventories may be more valuable to the teacher.

Standardized tests currently in use in the field of early education are designed to measure a number of traits including intelligence, achievement, affective development, personality, and language development. These tests are widely used with young children. Over the past decade, however, there has been growing disillusionment with traditional standardized test procedures and increasing documentation of their shortcomings, particularly with young children. A discussion of standardized instruments for young children can be found in Goodwin and Goodwin (1993).

INFORMAL TESTS

Another method of generating knowledge about children is through *informal testing*. Such tests are criterion-referenced tests, in which the scores are determined by the degree to which a student achieves a criterion of success in learning. One cannot

Ask the child to read the words and sentences orally. Record the child's exact pronunciations.

CVC* words	dip	hip	kit	mix
CCVC words	brim	flip	skid	thin
CVCC words	dish	fist	hint	lick
Words in sentences	Dick and Pip will go on the ship.			

*C = consonant, V = vowel.

FIGURE 4.3   Specific skill test: decoding words with short vowels

compare informal test scores from one class with scores from another class, because such informal tests are based on what has been taught to children in a specific class. The typical arithmetic or spelling test that a primary teacher might give weekly is such a test. Teachers use the information from such test scores to plan and modify the instructional program (Spodek, Saracho, & Davis, 1991).

Informal tests are a way of observing children's performance on day-to-day instructional tasks. These techniques are used most frequently for assessing academic skills. For instance, a teacher who administers and scores a spelling, math, or reading test is engaging in informal assessment. Informal assessment tools include teacher-made skill tests and teacher-made placement tests.

Skill Tests

Skill tests are designed to measure academic skills, such as writing numbers, spelling words, stating multiplication facts, or using punctuation in sentences. Typically, the teacher presents an activity or structures a situation that requires the child to perform the desired skill and then informally assesses the child's ability to perform it. For example, a teacher who gives a student a worksheet with a series of 20 sentences, each requiring a period, question mark, or exclamation point, can tell how competent the student is in using punctuation skills. Skill tests can be administered throughout the school year prior to initiating instruction in a certain area or upon its completion. Figures 4.3 and 4.4 present two examples of skill tests.

Placement Tests

Commercially or teacher-made *placement tests* determine at what level a child should begin some form of instruction by sampling skills and tasks from a curriculum that is graduated in difficulty. These tests typically present samples of items in the

FIGURE 4.4   Specific skill test: dividing one-digit divisors into two-digit dividends, without remainders

Row 1	4⟌24	5⟌35	7⟌49
Row 2	5⟌25	10⟌50	8⟌32
Row 3	8⟌72	8⟌64	7⟌56

order in which they are presented in the curriculum itself. If the curriculum has been sequenced from least to most complex, the sampling of tasks should indicate where the child is having difficulty, thus indicating where the child should begin work.

To create a placement test, the teacher may go through a set of graduated curriculum materials selecting a sample of tasks for each different step presented in those materials. To increase the usefulness of such a test, some teachers present test items in the same sequence as they appear in the curriculum. For example, a teacher interested in designing a placement test for a spelling book might select every fifth word from each list found in the three spelling levels at which the child is performing. The child is then asked to spell these words until he or she experiences failure. The teacher examines the words spelled, determines the point at which the child began missing words, and determines a placement point for spelling.

The same technique can be used for placement in a mathematics book. The teacher selects the mathematics texts for grade 1, 2, or 3 and then systematically extracts items that sample the skills presented in the material. However, since many commercial materials focus on more than one skill area for a specific academic subject, a mathematics book might include work in the areas of computation, problem solving, money, time, and geometry. Skills may vary widely across these different strands; thus, separate placement points in a time-telling sequence, a subtraction sequence, a money sequence, and a problem-solving sequence might be necessary.

Informal assessment devices such as those described above can be used to evaluate a child's performance in any instructional area. In addition to teacher-made skill and placement tests, situations or tasks can be structured to determine how a child deals with problem-solving situations. Piagetian conservation tasks or an obstacle course set up to observe how the child handles his or her body, crosses his or her midline, or balances on a walking beam are other examples of this type of assessment.

RECORDING ASSESSMENT DATA

There are a number of ways to record assessment data. They may be recorded in the form collected, percentages of correct responses can be computed and recorded, or graphs may be developed from the data. Whatever method of recording is selected, it should be easy to maintain and appropriate to the type of data collected and the skill measured. It should also communicate effectively to those using the information.

Raw Data

For some skills only the raw data—that is, the information as it is collected—need be recorded. The teacher may, for instance, keep a simple daily record of the number of occurrences of a skill or behavior such as talking out in class, sharing appropriately with others, hitting other children, and so on. A simple tally sheet might be appropriate for counting the number of occurrences of a skill or behavior (see Figure 4.5). Raw data might also record the number of correct and incorrect responses for a specific skill. For instance, a teacher might give a child 10 story problems to solve each

Date	Number of instances of sharing	
9/5	/ / / /	4
9/6	/ / /	3
9/7	_HHT_	5
9/8	/ / /	3
9/11	/	1
9/12	/ /	2

FIGURE 4.5   Tally sheet

day. By keeping the number of problems constant, the teacher could record the correct and incorrect responses daily. A possible format for recording the raw data is illustrated in Figure 4.6

Computed Data

To make raw data collected in assessment easier to compare over time, the teacher might wish to compute percentages correct from the data. This may involve calculating percentages of correct and incorrect responses or the rate of their occurrence within a specified time period. The teacher might note, for example, that when given 30 sentences, Susan correctly used punctuation in 24 of them. This represents 80 percent of the items. Figure 4.7 provides an example of a data-recording device using computed data.

Graphs

Graphs often are the most efficient and effective way to display assessment information. The graph illustrates in a visual manner the changes in a child's performance over time. Graphs can be used to help teachers make instructional decisions and communicate effectively to parents and other professionals. Graphs are particularly useful because of the number of dimensions that can be recorded and the many ways the devices can be used. These include:

1. The number of correct or incorrect responses.
2. The frequency of a skill.

FIGURE 4.6   Record of correct and incorrect responses on a spelling test

Date	Spelling list #	Correct responses	Incorrect responses
9/6	1	7	8
9/8	2	9	6
9/8	3	12	3
9/11	4	4	11
9/2	5	5	10

Name: Bob J

Step on sequence	Date	Skill area: Multiplication Percentage
1 digit × 2 digits	1/3	82
1 digit × 3 digits	1/24	88
1 digit × 4 digits	2/7	84
2 digits × 2 digits	2/21	90

FIGURE 4.7 Example of data-recording device using percentage scores

3. The number of responses per specified time interval.
4. The percentage of accuracy of the behavior.
5. The amount of time or duration in which a behavior occurred.

Standard graphic arrangements employ two axes drawn at right angles—a horizontal axis (*X* axis) and a vertical axis (*Y* axis). Usually the units of measurement are amount of the skill or behavior (frequency, rate, percentage, proportion, duration) for the *Y* axis and units of time (minutes, sessions, days, weeks) for the *X* axis.

Noncumulative graphs are constructed by plotting the amount of the skill (*Y* axis) at the intersection of the time section (*X* axis) and then, after the points have been placed, connecting them by a line. For example, a teacher may be concerned with a student who fails to share with others during 29 play periods. For five consecutive days, the teacher records the number of sharing instances and finds that there were 7, 9, 3, 6, and 5 occurrences respectively. Figure 4.8 is a graphic presentation of the sharing. Developmental guidelines require observing children in natural settings only. A complete evaluation of the child may take several weeks.

FIGURE 4.8 Noncumulative graph

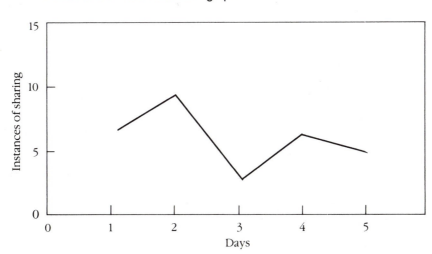

Frequently, teachers will want to present multiple classes of assessment data on the same graph. This is usually accomplished by using different symbols to represent different skills, persons, or settings. For instance, a teacher may be interested in representing the sharing, smiling, and positive talking behaviors of the same student on the same graph over a five-day period. The same strategy might be used to graph assessment data for different settings.

SUMMARY

This chapter has examined assessment of young children in integrated settings, specifying various techniques for collecting and recording assessment data. The purpose of assessment is to determine a child's skills and deficits in order to select a starting point for instruction and to evaluate the effectiveness of ongoing instruction. Effective assessment should occur regularly over time.

Assessment information should feed into instructional programming. The results of that assessment should be used to develop individualized educational programs (IEPs) and to evaluate their effectiveness. Instruments that are used by teachers to assess children, their capabilities, and their achievement need to be carefully matched to the goals and values of the classroom program. An annotated list of assessment instruments is presented in this chapter. Some of these are designed for general use, and others were created in relation to a specific program. Teachers should be aware of the purposes of any assessment instruments they select to find those that match their particular program.

ASSESSMENT INSTRUMENTS

The following is a selection of assessment instruments that may be used with young children. Teachers should check test manuals to determine the validity and reliability data generated for each instrument as well as to determine if the instruments would prove practical for them.

Title: Assessment-Programming Guide for Infants and Preschoolers
Author: W. Umansky
Publisher: Developmental Services, Columbus, OH, 1974
Age Range: Birth to 72 months
General Description: This instrument is designed to help teachers determine the needs of a child through systematic observation and to provide guidelines for planning a program to fit the child's specific needs. A child is assessed in five areas—motor, perceptual–motor, language, self-help, and social–personal—with items often listed under several different areas. The test is well standardized on children both with and without disabilities. It consists primarily of developmental guidelines and requires observing children in natural settings only. A complete evaluation of the child may take several weeks.
Title: Basic Concept Inventory
Author: S. Engelmann

Publisher: Follett Publishing Co., Chicago, IL, 1967

Age Range: 3 to 10 years

General Description: This test provides a comprehensive checklist of basic concepts (e.g., sentence comprehension, pattern awareness) that are needed to succeed in first grade. It is a criterion-referenced, individually administered test intended primarily for at-risk preschool and kindergarten children, slow learners, and emotionally disturbed or mentally retarded children. The instrument may be used as a basis for either remedial instruction or diagnostic evaluation.

Title: Basic School Skills Inventory-Diagnostic (BSSI-D)

Authors: D. D. Hammill & J. E. Leigh

Publisher: Pro-Ed, Austin, TX, 1983

Age Range: 4 to 7.5 years

General Description: The BSSI-D is a norm-referenced instrument used to assess readiness skills. It consists of 110 items to assess six domains: daily living skills, spoken language, reading readiness, writing readiness, math readiness, and classroom behavior. It is individually administered and varies in time for administration.

Title: Batelle Development Inventory (BDI)

Authors: J. Newborg, J. Stock, L. Wnek, J. Guidubaldi, & J. Suinicki

Publisher: DLM/Teaching Resources, Allen, TX, 1984

Age Range: Birth to 8 years

General Description: The BDI is an assessment instrument that is individually administered to children. It collects assessment information through structured settings, direct observation, and interviews with parents and teachers. The test can be modified for children with disabilities. The domains of cognitive, motor, adaptive, personal–social, and communication generate 30 profile scores on the child's strengths and deficiencies. It can be administered in 1 or 2 hours and generates standard scores, percentile ranks, and age equivalents.

Title: Bayley Scales of Infant Development (BSID)

Author: N. Bayley

Publisher: Psychological Corp., San Antonio, TX, 1984

Age Range: Birth to 2.5 years

General Description: The BSID comprises two scales (mental and motor scales) that are individually administered. It has 30 behavior ratings to assess body control, coordination of large muscles, manipulative skills of the hands and fingers, sensory-perceptual acuities, sensory discrimination, memory, learning and problem-solving ability, beginnings of verbal communication, and evidence of the ability to develop generalizations and classifications.

Title: Behavioral-Developmental Profile

Authors: M. Donahue, A. Keiser, L. Smith, J. D. Montgomery, U. L. Roecker, & M. F. Walden

Publisher: The Marshalltown Project, Marshalltown, IA, 1975

Age Range: Birth to 6 years

General Description: This profile assesses skills in the language, cognitive, fine and gross motor, personal–social, self-help, and cognitive areas. These developmental areas are collapsed into communication, motor, and social abilities. A total of 327 items are grouped into age categories with 1-month segments for the first 12 months, 3-month segments for 12 to 24 months, 6-month segments for 24 to 36 months, and 12-month segments for 36 to 72 months.

Each item is briefly stated in behavioral terms, and an individually administered direct test is used. Test items are based on patterns of "normal" child development. The profile is used with a score sheet that identifies a success level, an emergent level, and a level indicating that the child is unable to perform. The test can be administered by a teacher or other trained professional.

Title: Bender Visual Motor Gestalt Test (commonly known as the Bender Gestalt Test)
Author: L. Bender
Publisher: American Orthopsychiatric Assn., Albany, NY, 1938
Age Range: 4 years and up
General Description: The Bender Visual Motor Gestalt Test is used to detect visual perceptual difficulties as well as the possible presence of brain damage. Designed for individuals ages 4 and up, it consists of eight designs that are copied by the child under standard conditions and is scored according to errors in reproduction.

Title: Boehm Test of Basic Concepts (BTBC)
Author: A. E. Boehm
Publisher: Psychological Corp., Atlanta, GA, 1971
Age Range: Approximately 4.5 to 7 years
General Description: The BTBC measures mastery of concepts in the areas of quantity, number, space, and time, and other areas considered important for achievement in the first years of school (K–2). This test is individually administered; it takes 15 to 20 minutes to administer each of two test booklets. The test may be given in one or two sessions. No special training is required to administer the test, and percentile norms by grade and socioeconomic level are provided.

Title: Boehm Test of Basic Concepts-Preschool (BTBC-P)
Author: A. E. Boehm
Publisher: Psychological Corp., San Antonio, TX, 1986
Age Range: 3 to 5 years
General Description: The BTBC-P measures mastery of concepts in the areas of quantity, number, space, and time, and other areas considered important for achievement relating to children 5 to 7 years of age. It is individually administered (10 to 15 minutes). The BTBC-P assesses 26 relational concepts, requires only a pointing response, and gives percentile age bands for 3, 3.5, 4, 4.5, and 5 years.

Title: Bunks' Behavior Rating Scale (BBRS) (preschool and kindergarten edition)
Author: L. Bunks
Publisher: Western Psychological Services, Los Angeles, CA, 1977
Age Range: 3 to 6 years
General Description: The BBRS is designed to record behavioral or learning disorders indicative of organic brain dysfunction. There are 105 items, clustered into 18 groupings, that are rated by the teacher on a 5-point scale indicating the degree to which each identified behavior is present in the child. Among the behaviors assessed are self-blame, anxiety, impulse control, anger control, sense of identity, aggressiveness, and social conformity. The scores for each subscale are recorded on a profile sheet and then plotted on a horizontal number line. The number line is divided into three sections—not significant, significant, very significant—indicating the degree of the problem. Having each child rated by several observers in several situations increases the validity of the instrument. The examiner may be anyone who knows the child well (e.g., parents, teachers, or aides). The instrument has been standardized on a large number of children.

Title: California Preschool Social Competency Scale (CPSCS)
Authors: S. Levine, M. Freeman, & M. Lewis
Publisher: Consulting Psychologists Press, Palo Alto, CA, 1969
Age Range: 2.5 to 5.5 years
General Description: This scale, designed for observing in the preschool classroom, measures the adequacy of preschoolers' interpersonal behavior and the extent to which they assume social responsibility and independence. It consists of 30 items representative of critical behaviors in the young child's social functioning. The child is observed over time in

a variety of situations and ratings are based on the child's typical performance. The statements within each item are ordered by level of competence and numbered cumulatively from 1 through 4. The rater, after determining the appropriate level, circles the number representing the rating for that item. A child rated 4 is presumed to be able to perform at all previous levels on that item. Total raw scores are converted to a percentile score by reference to the appropriate table of norms, and can be graphed on the back of the scale booklet.

The scale has been standardized on a representative sample of children. The CPSCS is easy to administer and, because it directly measures performance on a task in a natural setting, is useful as a criterion measure of the effectiveness of social interventions.

Title: Carolina Developmental Profile

Authors: D. L. Lillie & G. L. Harbin

Publisher: Kaplan School Supply Corp., Winston-Salem, NC, 1975

Age Range: 2 to 5 years

General Description: This profile is a criterion-referenced behavior checklist designed for use with the Developmental Task Instructional System developed by the same authors. The goal of the combined system is to prepare children for formal academic instruction in the early elementary school years. It focuses on six areas: gross motor, fine motor, visual perception, reasoning, receptive language, and expressive language. Items are sequenced within the developmental area, and a task number, task description, and developmental age are assigned to each item. If the child completes the task, the teacher checks "can do"; if not, "cannot do" is checked. The test, which is easy to administer and score, should be given in a large room over several different sessions. All visual materials are included in the profile, but additional materials such as blocks, balls, and scissors must be gathered before administering. Performance criteria for each item are easily interpreted, but there are only five items for each age in each area, providing somewhat limited information.

Title: Catell Infant Intelligence Scale (CIIS)

Author: P. Catell

Publisher: Psychological Corp., San Antonio, TX, 1969

Age Range: 3 to 30 months

General Description: The CIIS is an individually administered supplement of the Stanford-Binet Intelligence Scale for younger children. According to the child's age, tasks are culled for administration to obtain mental age and IQ scores. Administration time requires 20 to 30 minutes.

Title: CIRCUS

Authors: A. Scarvia, G. Bogatz, A. Draper, G. Tangeblut, W. Sedwell, N. Ward, & A. Yates

Publisher: Educational Testing Service, Princeton, NJ, 1974

Age Range: 4 to 6 years

General Description: CIRCUS measures the instructional needs of children in order to plan individualized educational programs. CIRCUS consists of 17 instruments, 5 of which are devoted to language. There are also measures of qualitative understanding, visual discrimination, perceptual–motor coordination, letter and numeral recognition, sound discrimination, visual and associative memory, and problem solving. Three instruments, which must be completed by the teacher, are also included: one for classroom activities, one for test-taking behavior, and one that surveys the child's educational environment. CIRCUS may be administered by a teacher to groups of children, and users may select those instruments that fit their needs.

Title: Cognitive Abilities Scale (CAS)

Author: S. Bradley-Johnson

Publisher: Pro-Ed, Austin, TX, 1987

Age Range: 2 to 3 years

General Description: The CAS assesses cognitive developmental skills regarding language, imitation, memory, reading, mathematics, and handwriting. It contains 88 items and measures the overall nonverbal performance for those children who will not talk or who have unintelligible speech.

Title: Criterion-Referenced Placement Test
Author: G. Cast
Publisher: MAPPS project, Exceptional Child Center, Logan, UT, 1975
Age Range: Birth to 5 years
General Description: This test assesses children's entry-level skills in receptive and expressive language and motor development. The instrument is designed for use with the Curriculum and Monitoring System (CAMS). The test items were developed from the sequenced objectives in CAMS and may be administered by anyone who works with young children. It takes 20 to 25 minutes to administer.

Title: Development Profile II
Authors: G. D. Alpern & M. S. Shearer
Publisher: Psychological Development Publications, Aspen, CO, 1981
Age Range: Birth to 12 years
General Description: Development Profile II is designed to help teachers construct individual curriculum prescriptions for children. It contains 217 items arranged into five scales and ordered into four age levels. The profile is administered in an interview by an adult rater who knows the child well. It can be administered in 20 to 40 minutes by a trained examiner, and explicit and easily understood directions are included in the manual. The standardization sample consisted of 3,008 subjects randomly selected to represent all socioeconomic and cultural sections of the population. The test manual provides detailed discussion regarding test construction, item analysis, and standardization procedures. The instrument generally involves parent input, which can be very valuable.

Title: Developmental Therapy Objective Rating Form (DTORF)
Author: M. Wood
Publisher: University Park Press, Baltimore, MD, 1972
Age Range: Approximately 3 to 8 years
General Description: The DTORF contains 144 carefully sequenced objectives in four areas—behavior, communication, socialization, and academics—used to indicate both developmental milestones already achieved and criteria for grouping as well as to provide a basis for planning. The rating form takes 36 minutes to administer and is generally completed by a team of professionals who know the child well. The DTORF was originally designed for emotionally disturbed children at the Rutland Center Model in Athens, Georgia.

Title: Frostig Developmental Test of Visual Perception
Author: M. Frostig
Publisher: Consulting Psychologists Press, Palo Alto, CA, 1961
Age Range: 4 years and up
General Description: The Frostig test measures five perceptual skills—eye–motor coordination, figure-ground perception, constancy of shape, position in space, and spatial relationship—via a paper-and-pencil test for young children. Norms starting at age 4 are used to compute a perceptual quotient. Remedial activities and programs related to test results are also provided.

Title: Developmental Test of Visual Perception (DTVP)
Authors: M. Frostig, W. Lefever, & R. B. Whittlesey
Publisher: Consulting Psychologists Press, Palo Alto, CA, 1966

Age Range: 3 to 8 years

General Description: This test measures five perceptual skills—eye–hand coordination, figure-ground perception, form constancy, position in space, and spatial relations. The DTVP is administered in a group, and raw scores for each subtest are converted to perceptual age scores.

Title: Goldman–Fristoe Test of Auditory Discrimination

Authors: R. Goldman, M. Fristoe, & R. Woodcock

Publisher: American Guidance Service, Circle Pines, MN, 1970

Age Range: 3 years and up

General Description: This test assesses the listener's ability to distinguish among common speech sounds under both quiet and distracting noise conditions. The format includes a series of test plates containing four drawings and a prerecorded audiotape. The child responds to a stimulus word by pointing to one of four pictures simultaneously presented on the plate. Subtests include the auditory selection attention test, the diagnostic auditory discrimination test, the auditory memory test, and the sound symbol test.

The test was standardized on 745 subjects from which percentile norms by age level were developed for children to 6 years, 2 months old. Items were constructed on everyday tasks, and educators and speech clinicians view the test as sound.

Title: Goodman Lock Box (GLB)

Author: J. Goodman

Publisher: Stoelting Co., Chicago, IL, 1981

Age Range: 2.5 to 5.5 years

General Description: The GLB is a systematic instrument that records observations of play activities to obtain scores on competence, organization, and aimless actions. It is a nonverbal instrument and requires 6.5 minutes of observation.

Title: The Houston Test for Language Development

Author: M. Crabtree

Publisher: Houston Test Co., Houston, TX 1963

Age Range: Part I: 6 months to 3 years; Part II: 3 to 6 years

General Description: This test is designed to assess language development skills in children. These include self-identity, vocabulary, body parts and gestures, communicative behavior, counting objects, geometric designs and drawings, and sentence length. The test takes 30 to 60 minutes and is administered by a speech clinician.

Title: Indiana Preschool Developmental Scale (IPDS)

Authors: B. Bateman, J. Henn, J. Wilke, R. Wilson, C. Muslin, & W. Bragg

Publisher: Developmental Training Center, Bloomington, IN, 1976

Age Range: Birth to 6 years.

General Description: The IPDS provides a profile of 300 items describing the level of the child's functioning in the motor, personal autonomy, communication, and preacademic areas. It is designed to help teachers formulate for the child a program to be implemented by either the teacher or the parent. The IPDS is a criterion-referenced instrument with corresponding curriculum objectives for each item. It provides alternative equivalent response modes for children with visual impairments, hearing impairments, physical/multiple disabilities, and visual-auditory disabilities.

The IPDS is administered and scored by the teacher. A 5-point rating scale is provided for each item. In general, the items are similar to those on other profiles and the information related to the assessment procedures is clearly presented and well organized.

Title: Kindergarten Evaluation of Learning Potential (KELP)

Authors: J. A. Wilson & M. C. Robeck

Publisher: Webster Division, McGraw-Hill, St. Louis, MO, 1967

Age Range: 5 to 7 years

General Description: KELP is designed to predict success in the early grades based on kindergarten learning. Items include color identification, head design, bolt board, number boards, safety signs, writing one's name, and social interaction. Items from KELP are taught by the teacher, who observes and records the learning of the tasks over the kindergarten year. Classroom materials, teaching tips, and summary retention tests are available. Test scores have been correlated with Stanford-Binet scores, and the manual reports surveys by teachers who have used KELP.

Title: Learning Accomplishments Profile—Revised (LAP-R)

Author: D. LeMay, P. Griffin, & A. R. Sanford

Publisher: Kaplan School Supply, Lewisville, NC, 1981

Age Range: Birth to 6 years

General Description: The LAP-R is designed to provide a criterion-referenced record of a child's skills. It enables the teacher to identify learning objectives, measure progress through changes in the rate of development, and provide information relevant to student learning. LAP-R measures the child's development in six areas: gross motor, fine motor, social, self-help, cognitive, and language. The items, stated in behavioral terms, were extracted from instruments widely used in the field. The scoring sheet restates each item and the developmental age or age range. Usually the classroom teachers as examiners record the assessment date and the child's achievement for each item. A comments column can be used to record data regarding criteria, materials, or problems. LAP-R is administered over a period of days and actually in a series of steps. Long-range and short-term objectives are developed. Teaching effectiveness is assessed. Teachers may need to modify some of the items to fit the needs of more moderately impaired children.

Title: Minnesota Preschool Scale

Authors: F. Goodenough, K. Maurer, & M.J. Van Wagener

Publisher: American Guidance Service, Circle Pines, MN, 1940

Age Range: 6 months to 6 years

General Description: The Minnesota Preschool Scale is designed to assess the mental abilities of young children. The scale consists of 26 verbal and nonverbal items. The test can be individually administered by a trained professional in approximately 30 minutes, and scoring procedures can be completed with a minimum of difficulty. Testing procedures are well described, as are standardization procedures and norm groups.

Title: Peabody Individual Achievement Test

Authors: L. M. Dunn & F. Markward

Publisher: American Guidance Service, Circle Pines, MN, 1970

Age Range: 5 years and up

General Description: This is an individually administered measure of mathematics, reading, spelling, and general information. The test, which requires 30 to 40 minutes to administer, yields six scores—mathematics, reading recognition, reading comprehension, spelling, general information, and a total—all of which have norms presented as grade equivalents, percentile ranks, and standard scores. The test requires only oral or pointing responses. The manual reports extensive reliability and validity data as well as a detailed description of standardization procedures and norm groups.

Title: Peabody Picture Vocabulary Test—Revised (PPVT-R)

Author: L. M. Dunn

Publisher: American Guidance Service, Circle Pines, MN, 1981

Age Range: 2.5 to 18 years

General Description: The PPVT-R provides an estimate of verbal intelligence by measuring the child's hearing vocabulary. It has two forms and assesses receptive language. It requires verbal or nonverbal responses. It is an individually administered criterion-referenced test administered by a testing professional and requiring from 10 to 15 minutes. This test provides a measure of only one aspect of intelligence—receptive vocabulary. It provides adaptations for nonreaders and slow readers, speech impaired, cerebral palsied, partially sighted, and perceptually impaired children.

Title: Portage Guide to Early Education (revised edition)
Authors: S. Bluma, M. Shearer, A. Frohman, & J. Hilliard
Publisher: The Portage Project, Portage, WI, 1976
Age Range: Birth to 6 years
General Description: The Portage Guide was designed to help educators assess child behavior and plan curriculum goals. This criterion-referenced instrument contains three parts: (1) a checklist of 580 items sequentially arranged in five behavioral areas—socialization, language, self-help, cognitive, and motor, (2) a card file listing possible methods of teaching related to these behaviors, and (3) a manual of directions. Skills listed on the checklist are behaviorally stated, and the child may be assessed by an individual with minimal training. Children are assessed in a variety of settings so that a representative sample of their behavior is taken.

Title: Preschool Attainment Record (PAR) (research edition)
Author: E. Doll
Publisher: American Guidance Service, Circle Pines, MN, 1966
Age Range: Birth to 7 years
General Description: The PAR is an expansion of the Vineland Social Maturity Scale designed to measure the physical, social, mental, and language attainments of young children. The record includes eight areas: development–ambulation, manipulation, rapport, communication, responsibility, information, ideation, and creativity. There is one item for each area per 6-month interval. The test is individually administered by a professional in 20 to 30 minutes.

Title: Primary Mental Abilities Test (PMAT)
Author: T. G. Thurstone
Publisher: Science Research Associates, Chicago, IL, 1963
Age Range: 5 to 6 years
General Description: The PMAT is designed to provide multifactored and general measures of intelligence. The instrument consists of five tests—verbal meaning, number facility, reasoning, perceptual speed, and spatial relations. It takes a little over an hour to administer and may be given to small groups. The perceptual speed test is timed. The test is given from a test booklet (no other materials are required), and mental age equivalents for each part and for the total test are given.

Title: Scale of Social Development (SSD)
Author: J. J. Venn, T. S. Serwatka, & A. Anthony
Publisher: Pro-Ed, Austin, TX, 1987
Age Range: Birth to 6 years
General Description: The SSD assesses three skill clusters: participates/socializes, investigates/identifies, and prefers/complies. It can be used to assess the progress of deaf children or those with multiple disabilities.

Title: School Readiness Test (SRT)
Author: O. F. Anderhalter
Publisher: Scholastic Testing Service, Bensenville, IL, 1989
Age Range: 5 to 6 years

General Description: The SRT indicates the student's readiness level for formal instruction in seven domains: word recognition, identification of letters, visual discrimination, comprehension, interpretation, handwriting readiness, and number readiness. The test requires 60 minutes to administer; its direction manual provides instructions in English and Spanish.

Title: Skills Inventory
Authors: D. Brown, V. Simmons, & J. Methvin
Publisher: Jackson County Education Service District, Medford, OR, 1978
Age Range: Birth to 6 years
General Description: The Skills Inventory provides a criterion-referenced assessment and curriculum guide for children with visual deficits. It contains 693 skills and serves three purposes: (1) to assess the child's developmental level in cognition, language, self-help, socialization, fine motor, and gross motor domains; (2) to select appropriate teaching goals; and (3) to record the child's acquisition of new skills. The test is individually administered, preferably by a school psychologist, but no data on testing time are provided. Scoring procedures are well described and easily implemented. This is one of the few comprehensive checklists available for visually impaired children.

Title: Stanford Early School Achievement Test (SESAT)
Authors: R. Madden & E. F. Gardner
Publisher: The Psychological Corporation, Atlanta, GA, 1970
Age Range: 5 to 6 years
General Description: The SESAT measures cognitive abilities upon entrance into kindergarten or first grade. Subtests include the environment (social and natural environments, social science, natural science), mathematics (conservation of number, space, volume, counting, measurement, numeration, classification, simple operations), letters and sounds, and aural comprehension. The test is group-administered in five sessions. Groups of 5 to 6 children per assistant are recommended for beginning kindergartners, and groups of 15 per assistant for older children. The test takes approximately 90 minutes to administer over several sessions.

Title: Test of Early Reading Ability (TERA)
Author: D. K. Reid, W. P. Hresko, & D. D. Hammill
Publisher: Pro-Ed, Austin, TX, 1981
Age Range: 3 to 8 years
General Description: The TERA assesses children's reading ability in three domains: knowledge of the alphabet, comprehension, and the conventions of reading. This 50-item test is individually administered.

Title: Test of Relational Concepts (TRC)
Authors: N. K. Edmonston & N. L. Thane
Publisher: Pro-Ed, Austin, TX, 1988
Age Range: 3 to 8 years
General Description: The TRC assesses 56 concepts in spatial, temporal, and quantitative words and dimensional adjectives. It is individually administered in 15 minutes.

Table 4.2 summarizes the assessment instruments that teachers may use with young children.

TABLE 4.2 Tests in early childhood education

Title	Age Range	Author	Publisher
Assessment-Programming Guide for Infants and Preschoolers	0–6 years	Umansky	Developmental Services
Basic Concept Inventory	3–10 years	Engelmann	Follett
Basic School Skills Inventory-Diagnostic	4–7.5 years	Hammill & Leigh	Pro-Ed
Batelle Development Inventory	0–8 years	Newborg, Stock, Wnek, Guidubaldi, & Suinicki	DLM/Teaching Resources
Bayley Scales of Infant Development	2–30 months	Bayley	Psychological Corp.
Behavioral-Developmental Profile	0–6 years	Donahue, Keiser, Smith, Montgomery, Roecker, & Walden	Marshalltown Project
Bender Gestalt Test	4 years and up	Bender	American Orthopsychiatric Assn.
Boehm Test of Basic Concepts	4.5–7 years	Boehm	Psychological Corp.
Boehm Test of Basic Concepts-Preschool	3–5 years	Boehm	Psychological Corp.
Bunks' Behavior Rating Scale	3–6 years	Bunks	Western Psychological
California Preschool Social Competency Scale	2.5–5.5 years	Levine, Freeman, & Lewis	Consulting Psychologists
Carolina Developmental Profile	2–5 years	Lillie & Harbin	Kaplan School Supply
Catell Infant Intelligence Scale	3–30 months	Catell	Psychological Corp.
CIRCUS	4–6 years	Scarvia, Bogatz, Draper, Tangeblut, Sedwell, Ward, & Yates	ETS
Cognitive Abilities Scale	2–3 years	Bradley-Johnson	Pro-Ed
Criterion-Referenced Placement Test	0–5 years	Cast	MAPPS Project, Exceptional Child Center
Development Profile II	0–12 years	Alpern & Shearer	Psychological Development
Developmental Therapy Objective Rating Form	3–8 years	Wood	University Park
Frostig Developmental Test of Visual Perception	4 years and up	Frostig	Consulting Psychologists
Developmental Test of Visual Perception	3–8 years	Frostig, Lefever, & Whittlesey	Consulting Psychologists
Goldman–Fristoe Test of Auditory Discrimination	3 years and up	Goldman, Fristoe, & Woodcock	American Guidance

(continued)

TABLE 4.2   Continued

Title	Age Range	Author	Publisher
Goodman Lock Box	2.5–5.5 years	Goodman	Stoelting
Houston Test for Language Development	Pt. I: 6–36 months; Pt. II: 3–6 years	Crabtree	Houston Test
Indiana Preschool Developmental Scale	0–6 years	Bateman, Henn, Wilke, Wilson, Muslin, & Bragg	Developmental Training Center
Kindergarten Evaluation of Learning Potential	5–7 years	Wilson & Robeck	Webster Division, McGraw-Hill
Learning Accomplishments Profile—Revised	0–6 years	LeMay, Griffin, & Sanford	Kaplan School Supply
Minnesota Preschool Scale	6 months–6 years	Goodenough, Maurer, & Van Wagener	American Guidance Service
Peabody Individual Achievement Test	5 years and up	Dunn & Markward	American Guidance Service
Peabody Picture Vocabulary Test—Revised	2.5–18 years	Dunn	American Guidance Service
Portage Guide to Early Education	0–6 years	Bluma, Shearer, Frohman, & Hilliard	Portage Project
Preschool Attainment Record	0–7 years	Doll	American Guidance Service
Primary Mental Abilities Test	5–6 years	Thurstone	Science Research Associates
Scale of Social Development	0–6 years	Venn, Serwatka, & Anthony	Pro-Ed
School Readiness Test	5–6 years	Anderhalter	Scholastic Testing Service
Skills Inventory	0–6 years	Brown, Simmons, & Methvin	Jackson County Education Service District
Stanford Early School Achievement Test	5–6 years	Madden & Gardner	Psychological Corp.
Test of Early Reading Ability	3–8 years	Reid, Hreskó, & Hammill	Pro-Ed
Test of Relational Concepts	3–8 years	Edmonston & Thane	Pro-Ed

REFERENCES

Almy, M., & Genishi, C. (1979). *Ways of studying children: An observational manual for early childhood teachers* (rev. ed.). New York: Teachers College Press.

American Educational Research Association, American Psychological Association, & National Council on Measurement in Education (joint committee) (1985). *Standards for educational and psychological testing.* Washington, DC: American Psychological Association.

Asher, S. R., & Dodge, K. A. (1986). Identifying children who are rejected by their peers. *Developmental Psychology, 22,* 444–449.

Asher, S. R., & Hymel, S. (1981). Children's social competence in peer relations: Sociometric and behavioral assessment. In J. D. Wine & M. D. Smye (Eds.), *Social competence* (pp. 125–157). New York: Guilford.

Asher, S. R., Oden, S. L., & Gottman, J. M. (1978). Children's friendships in school settings. In L. G. Katz (Ed.), *Current topics in early childhood education,* Vol. 1 (pp. 33–61). Norwood, NJ.: Ablex.

Barnard, K. E., & Kelly, J. F. (1991). Assessment of parent–child interaction. In S. J. Meisels & J. P. Shonkoff (Eds.), *Handbook of early childhood intervention* (pp. 278–302). New York: Cambridge University Press.

Boehm, A. E., & Weinberg, R. A. (1987). *The classroom observer: A guide for developing observation skills* (2nd ed.). New York: Teachers College Press.

Cartwright, C. A., & Cartwright, G. P. (1974). *Developing observation skills.* New York: McGraw-Hill.

Coie, J. D., Dodge, K. A., & Coppotelli, H. (1982). Dimensions and types of social status: A cross-age perspective. *Developmental Psychology, 18,* 557–570.

Dodge, K. A., & Murphy, R. R. (1984). The assessment of social competence in adolescents. In M. P. Karoly & J. J. Steffen (Eds.), *Adolescent behavior disorders: Foundations and contemporary concerns,* Vol. 3 (pp. 61–96). Lexington, MA: Lexington Books.

Dubow, E. F., & Cappas, C. L. (1987). Peer social status and reports of children's adjustment by their teachers, by their peers, and by their self-ratings. *Journal of School Psychology, 26,* 69–75.

French, D. C., & Waas, G. A. (1985). Behavior problems of peer-neglected and peer-rejected elementary-age children: Parent and peer perspectives. *Child Development, 56,* 246–252.

Gearheart, C., & Gearheart, B. (1990). *Introduction to special education assessment: Principles and practices.* Denver: Love.

Gesell, A., & Ilg, F. L. (1949). *Child development: An introduction to the study of human growth.* New York: Harper.

Goodwin, W. L., & Driscoll, L. D. (1980). *Handbook for measurement and evaluation in early childhood education.* San Francisco: Jossey-Bass.

Goodwin, W. L., & Goodwin, L. D. (1993). Young children and measurement: Standardized and nonstandardized instruments in early childhood education. In B. Spodek (Ed.), *Handbook of research on the education of young children* (pp. 441–463). New York: Macmillan

Hall, R. V. (1974). *Behavior modification: The measurement of behavior* (rev. ed.). Lawrence, KS: H and H Enterprises.

Irwin, D. M., & Bushnell, M. M. (1980). *Observational strategies for child study.* New York: Holt, Rinehart & Winston.

Lowenbraun, S., & Affleck, J. Q. (1976). *Teaching mildly handicapped children in regular classes.* Columbus, OH: Merrill.

Preschool profile. (Unpublished). Model Preschool Center for Handicapped Children, Child Development and Mental Retardation Center, University of Washington, Seattle.

Risley, T. R. (1971). Spontaneous language in the preschool environment. In J. Stanley (Ed.), *Research on curriculums for pre-schools.* Baltimore: Johns Hopkins University Press.

Salvia, J., & Ysseldyke, J. E. (1985). *Assessment in special and remedial education* (3rd ed.). Boston: Houghton Mifflin.

Sattler, J. M. (1981). *Assessment of children's intelligence and special abilities* (2nd ed.). Boston: Allyn & Bacon.

Shepard, L. A., & Graue, M. E. (1993). The morass of school readiness screening: Research on test use and test validity. In B. Spodek (Ed.), *Handbook of research on the education of young children* (pp. 293–305). New York: Macmillan.

Spodek, B., Saracho, O. N., & Davis, M. D. (1991). *Foundations of early childhood education: Teaching three-, four-, and five-year-old children.* Englewood Cliffs, NJ: Prentice-Hall.

Wallace, G., & Larsen, S. (1978). *Educational assessment of learning problems: Testing for teaching.* Boston: Allyn & Bacon.

CHAPTER 5

Developing Individualized Educational Programs

CHAPTER OVERVIEW

This chapter describes:

1. The Individualized Educational Program (IEP).
2. Stages in the development of IEPs.
3. The contents of IEPs.
4. Sample IEPs.

Until recently, regular classroom teachers played a minor role in designing educational programs for children with disabilities. Administrators, psychologists, and special educators often excluded them from decisions regarding placement and programming of these children even though these children were educated in integrated classes (Strickland & Turnbull, 1982). Since the enactment of Public Law 94-142, classroom teachers have been required to be active in developing individualized educational programs (IEPs) for children with special needs who are integrated into regular classes. These are also required of gifted children in some states. An IEP must be created for each student who has a disability or needs special education programming and placement (Schulz, Carpenter, & Turnbull, 1984). Early childhood educators working in integrated classrooms must be familiar with their requirements. It should be noted that for children ages 3–5, an individualized family service plan (IFSP) may be developed instead of an IEP. This plan would include more extensive services, but it must include the elements of an IEP.

The IEP is a management system for planning and implementing educational services for up to a year. It is designed in response to the assessment of the child who has a disability (Henry & Flynt, 1990). It is a written statement about the objectives, content, implementation, and evaluation of a child's educational program (White & Haring, 1980). Individualized educational programs are required by law to determine that children with disabilities are provided with an education that is appropriate to their needs and abilities. The IEP states the educational objectives proposed for the child, how they are to be attained, and how the results will be evaluated. It is jointly arrived at by a team of educators.

This chapter provides an overview of individualized educational programs, what they are, who develops them, how they are developed, and what information they contain. The reader interested in more information on IEPs might consult Morgan (1981), Siders and Whorton (1982), Strickland and Turnbull (1982), and Tymitz-Wolf (1981).

THE IEP TEAM

An IEP is developed by a multidisciplinary team consisting of individuals from different professional disciplines. These include the child's teacher, the special education teacher, an evaluation specialist, and other ancillary personnel. Each brings a different set of professional competencies and perspectives to the assessment and planning for the child's needs. It also includes the child's parent(s) or guardian(s) and the child (when appropriate). Each member of this team—known as the child study, or IEP, team—plays a unique role in formulating the IEP.

The IEP team may be chaired by the building principal, a special educator, the classroom teacher, or another member of the team. The chair schedules and presides over the IEP conference, advises parents of their rights, calls upon individual staff members to present and discuss assessment data, and presents the school's recommendations for programming. The chair also sees that the basic components of the IEP are stated in writing and that the completed IEP is signed by all team members, including the parents.

The child's teacher(s) is anyone who has provided or will be providing direct instruction to the child. Normally, this includes both the child's regular and the special class teacher. Their responsibilities include describing the child's classroom performance, explaining to parents the various techniques that will be used, and answering any questions about what will occur in the classroom.

The teacher also can help to prepare the parents for the IEP meeting by explaining the purposes of the IEP and the IEP conference, reviewing the events that will occur, discussing with parents their rights and responsibilities, and mentioning questions parents might be asked. Such questions might include:

- What are the most important skills for your child to learn?
- Are there problems for your child at home that might be addressed at school?
- What methods have you found effective in rewarding and punishing your child?

By receiving questions ahead of time, parents can think about the comments they wish to make at the IEP conference.

Parents must be informed of and should agree to all actions concerning their child, including referral of the child to the child study team. If parents disagree with the IEP, an appeals procedure must be followed. The team must try to find a time and place to meet that is convenient for the parents. If neither parent can attend, the team is expected to involve parents in other ways. Telephone calls, including conference calls, can be used. The team must keep a record of its attempts to arrange meetings and see that the parents are informed of the outcomes of meetings they do not attend.

At the IEP conference, parents should be encouraged to take an active role in designing their child's program. They should be made to feel comfortable and be asked to express their views about the child's curriculum and educational services. Parents should be prepared to describe their child's out-of-school behavior, to participate in making placement decisions, and to specify what type of responsibility they are willing to assume in implementing the IEP.

IEP conferences provide parents and teachers with opportunities to share knowledge and contribute to the development of a suitable and practical plan for the child with a disability. Teachers can encourage and inform parents before the IEP meeting by

1. Encouraging parents to develop and write a list of questions about issues to be addressed.

2. Requesting (a week or 2 in advance) parents to establish short- and long-term goals for their child.
3. Involving parents in prioritizing goals for the year.
4. Asking parents to report at the IEP meeting their child's behaviors at home in relation to following directions, completing home assignments, and socialization skills.
5. Asking parents to identify effective motivations at home and to describe the child's learning in the home.
6. Making sure that parents understand the educational goals that have been established for the child with a disability and the procedures to achieve these goals.
7. Setting a possible follow-up meeting with a member of the professional staff to clarify for the parent any confusion. (Green, 1988)

The family and the school should have common goals. They should work together to help children with disabilities learn, grow, develop, and utilize their

TABLE 5.1 Ancillary personnel and their responsibilities on the IEP team

Personnel	Responsibilities
Evaluation Specialist/ School Psychologist	Administers and interprets developmental and diagnostic tests; makes observations of child in the classroom.
Speech and Language Therapist	Evaluates and treats language disorders as well as disorders of articulation, voice or fluency; serves as resource consultant to teacher.
Physical Therapist	Evaluates and treats physical disabilities involving gross motor movements; frequently designs programs for gross motor development or to provide exercise fitting the child's needs.
Occupational Therapist	Evaluates and treats disorders involving fine motor movements, especially those associated with the self-help skills (buttoning, zipping, and tying) and skills related to writing.
Audiologist	Identifies hearing impairments; tests and quantifies loss of air and bone conduction, and determines whether referral to an otologist (physician who treats the ear) is indicated for a hearing aid or for medical treatment.
School Nurse	Evaluates a variety of minor health problems; refers more serious problems to appropriate medical specialists.
Social Worker	Investigates homes and neighborhoods; prepares summaries of cases served by other social agencies; assists in acquiring social and personal data.
Physician	Diagnoses, treats, and refers health problems as well as organic-based problems, including vision and hearing problems, nutritional deficiencies, and organic brain damage.
Special Class Teachers	Remediate areas of exceptionality such as mental retardation or learning disabilities; consult with regular class teachers on educational methods and materials.
Regular Class Teachers	Describes the child's classroom performance; prepares parents for IEP meeting; provides plans for integrating the child into the class.

capacity to be happy, healthy, and productive individuals. This process can be the most productive and rewarding in helping children with disabilities (Green, 1988).

When appropriate, *the child* should be included in the team meetings. Although this is not a practical option for younger children, children in junior or senior high school do occasionally participate.

The evaluation specialist, often the school psychologist, is generally called upon to report on and interpret psychological evaluations (including standardized tests) of individual children and to make recommendations to the team based on these evaluations.

Ancillary staff are auxiliary personnel who are included on the team when the child has a disability that requires the services of a particular specialist. If a child has difficulties in speech or language, for example, a specialist in communications disorders should be included in the team. If the child is blind, a mobility instructor might be included. If the child has a physical disability, a physical or occupational therapist, or both, should be on the team. Other staff members who may be involved include curriculum specialists, audiologists, ophthalmologists, social workers, guidance counselors, medical and health personnel, and representatives of community agencies (such as Easter Seals) that serve persons with disabilities. Table 5.1 summarizes the responsibilities of each member of the ancillary staff in helping to formulate the IEP.

The IEP is the product of a team effort, with individuals with different specific concerns and different perspectives jointly working in the interests of the child. Team members usually agree about the nature of the child's problem and the most appropriate education program for the child. When disagreements arise, a team member has the option of writing a dissenting opinion to be appended to the IEP.

STAGES IN DEVELOPING THE IEP

Usually, the team develops the IEP in the stages shown in Figure 5.1.

Referral

This first stage of referral occurs when the parents, teachers, principal, physician, or other ancillary personnel request that a child they suspect has a disability be assessed. The referral process is initiated by a representative of the local educational agency, who informs the parents and then helps select and organize the IEP team. The team meets to review the referral and, when appropriate, interviews the referral agent about the nature of the child's problem, when it occurs, and what (if any) strategies have been tried to remediate it.

Preliminary Diagnostic Screening

This next stage provides data on the history of the referred student. Information may come from the child's cumulative school record and from interviews with parents, teachers, and other personnel who are knowledgeable about the child's educational, psychological, emotional, social, and physical status. After reviewing the student's

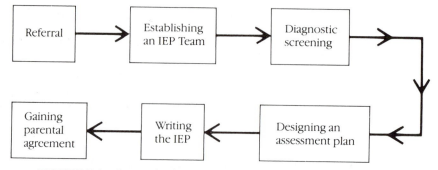

FIGURE 5.1   Stages in developing an IEP

history, the IEP team decides to either accept or reject the referral. If the referral is accepted, written parent permission is obtained for the assessment.

Assessment Plan

This plan must be designed and administered based on the information obtained in the preliminary screening. The plan may involve administering standardized tests or more informal inventories in areas such as self-help skills; general readiness; perceptual capabilities; or reading, language, and social skills. It also may involve classroom observations. Before the IEP meeting, a representative of the school must meet with the parents to present, interpret, and discuss the assessment data collected. If, based on all available information (see Table 5.2), the team decides that special education services are advisable, they proceed to the final stage—writing the IEP.

TABLE 5.2   Sources and uses of information for developing an IEP*

Sources	Use
1. Referral Forms	Help form hypotheses on child's problem and determine other kinds of information needed.
2. School Records	Provide information on student's education history and whether or not there are recurring problems in student's background.
3. Standardized Tests (norm-referenced)	Tell how child compares with other children in areas such as development and achievement.
4. Criterion-Referenced tests	Assess child's level of accomplishment in relation to a set of goals, without reference to accomplishments of other children.
5. Observation	Provides a picture of child characteristics and behaviors (e.g., social interaction) in the classroom or other environments.
6. Interviews with Parents or Guardians	Provide information on child's behavior in settings other than the school.
7. Work samples	Provide samples of child's performance.

*Chapter 4, on assessment, discusses each source in detail.

Writing the IEP

The IEP may be written in two steps. First, staff members who work with the child meet to exchange information and to write a preliminary draft of the IEP. This draft is then presented to the parents for discussion, revision, and their approval at the IEP meeting.

Responsibility for writing the IEP customarily falls upon the IEP committee chair with help from other team members, Teachers and specialists usually identify specific long- and short-term goals and related treatment plans. Different forms are used by different state and local educational agencies for recording them. However, the IEP must contain written statements of (1) the child's present levels of performance and of annual goals and short-term objectives; (2) the special education and related services to be provided; (3) the extent to which the child will participate in regular education programs; (4) the objective criteria by which progress on the IEP will be measured; (5) a justification for the child's educational placement; and (6) written parent approval. Two sample IEPs are presented at the end of this chapter.

CONTENTS OF THE IEP

The *statements of present levels of performance* describe the child's current educational achievement in relation to actual school performance as observed by teachers as well as test results. The IEP team reviews current assessment data, summarizes the child's present functional level, and identifies areas in which instruction is needed.

In the example provided in Box 5.1, the description of present educational performance was written in clear, concise language. The instruments or processes used in evaluation were identified. Other examples of statements describing the present levels of performance of a young child with a disability are:

- Bob read 85 percent of the Dolch Sight Word List at the first-grade level.
- Ellen can read silently at a 1.1 grade level, demonstrating good comprehension when answering oral questions concerning facts, the main idea, and sequencing of events; but she has poor comprehension when answering questions requiring her to draw inferences.
- Teacher observations show that Marie seldom interacts positively with other children during free play in the classroom or outdoors.
- Based on the Peabody Individual Achievement Test (PIAT), Edward is functioning approximately 1 year below grade placement in listening comprehension, word recognition and analysis, hearing sounds in words, and phonic spelling of words.
- Samuel's cursive handwriting is often illegible. He has problems with letter formation and spacing and reveals habitual reversals of *b* and *d* and inversions of *m* and *w*.

Once team members are satisfied with the statements of present levels of performance, they proceed to write the annual goals. An *annual goal* describes what

---

BOX 5.1   Sample Statement of Present Levels of Performance

Tom, a third-grade student, is experiencing mild learning problems and, based on a case evaluation and referral, is considered eligible for special education and related services. At the IEP conference, Tom's evaluators and teachers bring samples of his classwork and test scores. The team, including Tom's parents, generate the following statements describing his present levels of performance:

1. Tom reads at the beginning first-grade level as measured by the Metropolitan Achievement Test and the Dolch Sight Word List. Results of an informal reading inventory administered by his teacher showed that Tom read a first-grade reader at less than 10 words per minute and comprehended approximately 30 percent of what he read.

2. An arithmetic test showed that Tom's computational skills were average for a third-grader but, because of reading problems, he had considerable difficulty in completing story problems.

3. Tom's daily school work indicates that his penmanship is almost illegible.

4. Teacher observation records show that Tom is often out of his seat, talks out a great deal, and is generally off-task during work periods.

Tom's planners at the IEP conference identified the following general educational needs: (a) to improve reading fluency and comprehension, (b) to increase accuracy in solving story problems in math, (c) to increase legibility of his penmanship, (d) to decrease the number of talk-outs and out-of-seat related tasks.

---

the individual is expected to learn by the end of a school year. These goals, written for each area of disability, should be based on the child's present performance levels and should represent a reasonable estimate of how well the child might be expected to progress in the new program. Priorities for annual goals should also be established according to the student's most immediate needs. The number of goals developed depends upon the student's chronological and mental age, the amount of instructional time devoted to each area, and the priority needs of the student.

In the hypothetical case of Tom, cited earlier, five educational needs were identified. His IEP team might translate these needs into the following annual goals, in order of importance:

By year's end, Tom should

1. Be reading on at least a beginning second-grade level at a rate of 30

words per minute with fewer than 2 words per minute incorrect and at an 80 percent comprehension level.

2. Be able to compute at least three different types of story problems.

3. Be able to legibly write all upper- and lowercase cursive letters in isolation and, if possible, connected writing.

4. Stay in his seat for at least 60 percent of assigned work periods.

5. Raise his hand 80 percent of the time before speaking during assigned work periods.

6. Spend at least 80 percent of assigned work periods working on school-related tasks.

Goal statements do not define exact instructional tasks. Instead, they furnish long-range direction for an individual's program development. One problem in writing an annual goal is in deciding how narrow or broad the goal should be. The aim should be to identify and group related skills into clusters. For example, a kindergartener working on self-help skills would have an annual goal stating that he or she will be able to put on inner and outer clothing rather than three separate goals such as the ability to put on (1) a coat, (2) a hat, and (3) shoes. Table 5.3 provides several other examples illustrating how to combine related skills into a single annual goal.

In writing annual goals, the team should recognize that goal-setting is a complex process. It involves making predictions about children who may not progress in the normal manner and about whose progress we have little knowledge to guide us. For these reasons, annual goals are viewed as an estimate of where a child might be at the end of a year. Local educational agencies seldom are held accountable if the child does not achieve the projected goals.

Long-term goals and services dealing with the affective needs of children with disabilities are easy to develop. Short-term objectives are more difficult. For instance,

TABLE 5.3 Combining related skills into annual goals

Skill Area	Related Skills	Goal
Academics	Write lowercase cursive letters Write uppercase cursive letters Form whole words	Child will write all lower- and uppercase letters in cursive and use them in connected writing.
Motor	Draw triangles with pencil Draw circles with crayon Draw squares with pen Color pictures Cut out pictures Paste pictures	Child will be able to draw common geometric shapes, (e.g., triangle, circle, square) with pencil, crayon, and pen; use crayon to color pictures; cut them out; and paste them up.
Social	Interact appropriately with boys Interact appropriately with girls Interact appropriately with regular class teacher Interact appropriately with special class teacher Interact appropriately with parents	Child will interact appropriately with peers, teachers, and parents.

it is simpler to identify low self-esteem, peer relations, and self-discipline as difficult areas and to design general long-term goals to alleviate these concerns. Interpreting these general goals and services into a specific plan becomes difficult (Fairchild, 1985).

Short-term instructional objectives describe the program steps that the child will take toward the performance level required by the annual goal. These usually are established by the classroom teacher. Objectives usually are written and sequenced, from simple to complex, for each goal. Short-term objectives describe what a child might be expected to achieve in 1 or 2 months. Shorter or longer intervals are acceptable as long as there is progress toward the objectives and the goal.

For Tom, who had an annual goal of computing three types of story problems, the IEP team might recommend the following short-term objectives:

> ***Goal:*** To compute 3 types of story problems.
> ***Short-Term Objectives***
> 1. Given a worksheet with story problems yielding equations such as $2 + 3 = N$, $9 - 6 = N$, $4 + 7 = N$, Tom will compute 20 problems with 90 percent accuracy for 3 consecutive days.
> 2. Given a worksheet with story problems yielding equations such as $2 + N = 5$, $2 - N = 1$, $7 + N = 100$, Tom will compute 25 problems with 90 percent accuracy for 3 consecutive days.
> 3. Given a worksheet with story problems yielding equations such as $N + 6 = 9$, $N - 7 = 10$, $N + 1 = 16$, Tom will compute 30 problems with 90 percent accuracy for 3 consecutive days.
> 4. Given a worksheet with all three types of story problems—$2 + 3 = N$, $2 + N = 5$, $N + 3 = 7$—Tom will compute 20 problems with 90 percent accuracy for 3 consecutive days.

Short-term objectives should be written in clear, concise, and observable terms. Verbs such as *list, solve, point, write, say,* or *compute* are preferred. They are explicit about how the learner will demonstrate having reached a goal. In addition, many state regulations require that short-term objectives include at least four components—a learner; an observable, measurable skill; conditions under which the skill will be performed; and a standard or criterion—as in these examples:

- Given five types of paragraphs, each containing five declarative sentences with no punctuation marks (*condition*), Tom (*the learner*) will correctly place a period at the end of each sentence (*skill*) with 90 percent accuracy (*criterion*).

- Given a worksheet containing 20 two-digit subtraction problems with renaming (*condition*), Jenny (*the learner*) will compute all problems (*skill*) with at least 90 percent accuracy (*criterion*).

- Craig (*the learner*) will correctly put on and tie his shoes (*skill*) with 90 percent accuracy (*criterion*) when they are placed before him by his teacher (*condition*).

In writing short-term objectives, team members can draw on a variety of sources including commercial materials, school district curriculum guides, and textbook skill charts. Generally these sources offer objectives in specific skill areas—math, reading, or language—that are arranged in levels of increasing complexity. Assessment instruments for determining entry and progress on the curriculum also can be included. The IEP team can adapt these sequences and objectives to meet the needs of the individual.

A computer can help create and maintain an exhaustive list of short- and long-term objectives. Gore and Vance (1983) describe a computer program that stores thousands of goals and objectives on a single diskette. The program offers unlimited resources for keeping track of objectives. It relieves teachers of the ordeal of typing out selected student objectives. The software can store and retrieve 9,000 annual goals or short-term objectives per diskette. The menu identifies 24 curricular areas, developed by local staff members and reflecting the curricular area, age levels, and instruction to be provided. Areas include speech therapy, physical therapy, and vocational skills. "Goal and Objective Entry Forms" and a printed list of goals and objectives in developmental sequences are available to teachers. The computer program prints three copies of the designated goals and objectives within the IEP framework. An IEP can include up to 35 goals and 350 short-term objectives. The teacher can use the IEP for review and discussion with the students' parents. If commercial materials or curriculum guides are unavailable or are inadequate to assist the team in writing and sequencing objectives, the team can develop their own. The aim is to break goals into smaller steps, arrange the steps in logical order, and then write each step as a short-term objective.

A statement of special education and related services needed to achieve each objective must be listed in the IEP. The planners should note the type of special education service, the extent to which it is needed, the setting that will best provide the needed support, how much time will be provided, and who will provide the service.

Special media and materials not routinely used in regular classrooms must be listed on the IEP next to the short-term instructional objectives for which they will be used. Examples include hearing aids, low-vision aids, prosthetic devices or adaptive equipment, special transportation, or special instructional materials such as Language Masters or audiotapes. It is helpful to list these materials by name, author, publisher, and level and to indicate the dates on which the materials will be used. A brief comment on the potential effectiveness of the materials also may be included.

The projected dates for initiation and termination of special education services are also included. This helps to prevent children with disabilities from having to wait to receive services. By recording the anticipated duration of services, the team is better able to assess individual progress and to set realistic aims for children in future years. The school system also will be better able to determine when openings will occur in existing programs and when services will be available. Because students may progress faster or slower than anticipated, statements of duration of services—like annual goals—are viewed as estimates.

The nature of the student's participation in regular education must be spelled out in the IEP. This statement, reported as the percentage of time (or number of hours) to be spent in the regular classroom, serves to emphasize the importance of placement in the least restrictive environment and the importance of helping the child maintain as much contact as possible with peers who do not have disabilities. Activities such as recess and lunch, as well as academic instruction, should be included. The team should be careful, however, to list only those activities in which planned, meaningful interaction will occur. The following is a sample statement:

"Joan, age 7, will attend social studies, art, and physical education classes with regular class peers for three hours daily."

Appropriate objective criteria and a schedule for evaluating progress must be included to ensure that progress is being made and to determine whether the IEP should be revised. The method and criteria to be used to evaluate progress must also be specified in the IEP. Progress on annual goals and short-term objectives should be reviewed at least annually (preferably at shorter intervals), and should address the following questions:

1. Is the educational placement still appropriate?
2. Are the same ancillary staff still necessary?
3. Are the deficits being remediated?
4. Are the recommended goals and procedures still appropriate?
5. Are assigned responsibilities of team members being carried out?
6. If the plan is not appropriate, are adjustments necessary?

If the team decides that major program revisions are required, they must obtain written parent permission for a new program. Besides specifying evaluating criteria, the team also must recommend and justify an educational placement for the child. This statement describes the child's placement and why it was selected, and states that the entire team (including the parents) agrees with the placement.

The components of the IEP should include:

1. *Current level of performance,* with documentation of entry-level skills and concepts used to set up goals and objectives.
2. *Annual goals* statement indicating the student's expected level of performance over a calendar year.
3. *Short-term objectives* that outline the steps between the student's current performance levels and the projected annual goals.
4. *Evaluation, procedures, criteria, and schedules* that are used at least annually to assess the student's achievement on the goals and short-term objectives.
5. *Documentation of special education placement and related services* in relation to the appropriate needs of the student according to current level of performance, annual goals, and short-term objectives.
6. *Extent of time in regular education programs,* which meets the legal requirement for the IEP of placing children with special needs in regular classes when appropriate, considering their educational needs.

7. *Dates of services,* including date for initiating services and the anticipated duration of these services. (Schulz, Carpenter, & Turnbull, 1984; Strickland & Turnbull, 1982).

After completing the IEP, the parents must agree to it in writing. IEP forms include a signature line on which parents or guardians indicate their approval. If parents disagree with the child's evaluation or program, including the IEP itself, the school must provide mechanisms for appeal, including impartial due process hearings.

A due process hearing is chaired by an impartial hearing officer who is not an employee of the school. Parents have a right to (1) be accompanied by a lawyer or other counselor, (2) present evidence, (3) confront and cross-examine witnesses, and (4) obtain a transcript of the hearing or a written decision by the hearing officer. If still dissatisfied, parents have a right to appeal to their state educational agency and, ultimately, to a federal or state court.

In addition to the specific items reviewed above, the IEP also should include basic biographical information (e.g., date of birth, sex, home address), the name and position of each person on the IEP team, meeting dates, and individual recommendations of team members who may disagree with the final IEP. Sample forms on which IEPs can be written are provided at the end of this chapter.

Gifted Students

An IEP also should be developed for gifted students. It should provide a valid rationale based on the best available knowledge concerning the characteristics of gifted and creative children. The IEP model for the gifted should incorporate the characteristics of the gifted as well as instructional and learning theories. Several assumptions underlie the IEP model for this population (Renzulli & Smith, 1988):

1. Gifted students can master the regular curriculum at a much faster pace and higher level of proficiency than their peers. Therefore, some alternative means must be provided for gifted students to use a variety of learning styles and different ability levels in covering basic material at different rates and forms.

2. Gifted students must be provided with opportunities to identify and pursue topics and areas of study that interest them. They should have opportunities to (a) explore a wider variety of potential interests, (b) identify common domains of special interest, (c) emphasize or frame problems within these domains, and (d) strive to use these self-selected problems in a way that looks like the method of a firsthand inquirer instead of a passive learner of a lesson.

3. The gifted students' IEPs should focus on their strengths. The major objective of the IEP is to identify both general and specific strengths in higher levels of thinking, creativity, and task commitment to provide them with opportunities to develop their strengths in unstructured learning situations.

The best way to implement an IEP for a gifted student is to use student advisement. The responsibilities of the advisor are to:

- Assess the student's present levels of scholastic development, individual interests, and learning styles.
- Review the program to determine if the student (a) has already mastered basic material, (b) is able to master the material through alternative arrangements, or (c) is able to substitute advanced-level experiences for regular curricular material.
- Arrange for alternative learning approaches.
- Assist the student in developing individual and small-group investigations (Renzulli & Smith, 1988).

SUMMARY

This chapter has described individualized educational programs, or IEPs. The IEP should be written by a child study team that includes the teacher, the parents or guardians, other personnel, and, in some instances, the child. It must spell out specific long- and short-range goals and objectives for the child, and how these will be accomplished and under what circumstances. It also must state specifically how the effectiveness of the program will be evaluated. Once the IEP is developed and approved, placement of the child has been made, and services have been initiated, instructional intervention in the mainstream can begin.

Turnbull and Winton (1984) report that most parents do not actively engage in the IEP process and that many professionals view the IEP process as worthless. The process is viewed as a necessary evil instead of an opportunity to design a functional and appropriate blueprint to assist the intervention process. Bricker (1988) suggests (1) that the IEP must genuinely involve the family and (2) that the IEP process should reflect a direct connection among the assessment information, IEP goals and objectives, intervention activities, and assessment.

The quality of IEPs depends on well-written, valid goals and objectives that can be understood by all involved. Differences in school personnel's knowledge, experiences, and ability to develop clear and appropriate goals and objectives may create an inconsistency in the quality of the IEPs (Gore & Vance, 1983). The expertise of all individuals involved in the IEP is essential in developing and maintaining IEP quality.

SAMPLE IEPs

IEP forms differ from state to state and, within states, from school district to school district. The following sample IEPs are included to give the teacher an idea of what such forms might be like, the kinds of information they might include, and the type of space constraints the teacher will have to deal with. The two IEPs included are copies of actual IEPs developed for two children of different ages, with different problems, and from different communities. They have been modified to eliminate any identifying information. They represent how teachers actually use IEPs, rather than of what an ideal IEP might look like.

IEP1   Division for exceptional children individualized educational program

(Attach assessment data)

Student's name: Aaron Anderson

Date of Birth: 6/25/88   Age: 4 yrs. 4 mos.

School: Adams   Grade: preschool   Class: Recommend integrated class

Current Services: Currently in nonintegrated ECH class

Program Level(s) Recommended: Integrated preschool class

Related Services: Speech therapy 2 times weekly; Orthopedic therapy one

day a week for a month to learn how to maneuver in corrective shoes.

I give consent for my child (named above) to receive program(s) and service(s) as described

_____
Signature

_____
Relationship to child

_____
Date

Date(s) of IEP Meeting(s): 10/18/92
Dates of IEP implementation From: 10/18/92
                           To: 5/18/93

IEP Development Team

Signatures	*Position*
_____	Chair
_____	D.E.C. Representative
_____	Referring Teacher
_____	Parent

(continued)

Formal testing and evaluation information

Test Used	Pre-Test Date	Post-Test Date	Tester	Comments
Alpern-Boll	8/18/92		Maxine Saul	
Chronological Age	4 yrs. 2 mos.			
Physical Age	3 yrs. 9 mos.			
Self-Help Age	5 yrs. 1 mo.			
Social Age	3 yrs. 4 mos.			
Academic Age	3 yrs. 0 mos.			
Communication Age	3 yrs. 11 mos.			

Present Level of Performance	Annual Goals	Short-Term Objectives	Evaluation Criteria	Projected Date of Mastery	Special Materials, Strategies, and/or Techniques
I) Cognitive A) Aaron (S) is able to imitate a *t* and *u* B) He is able to draw a diagonal line from corner to corner on a 4" square paper. C) He counts 10 objects in imitation and builds a bridge with 3 blocks in imitation.	I) Cognitive A) S will develop basic concepts of color, size, shape, and number.	I) Cognitive A) Given a choice of 5 colors, S will point to color named by teacher. B) When asked, S will rote count to 5. C) When asked, S will correctly identify big and little objects. D) Given a choice of 4 shapes, S will identify and name triangle, circle, and square.	80% accuracy 100% accuracy 100% accuracy 90% accuracy	5/93 3/93 2/93 4/93	
II) Self-help Aaron dresses himself, with some difficulty fastening. He buttons and unbuttons and zips and unzips when not requested to work the catch. He has good feeding skills and uses utensils well. He can prepare some of his own food (e.g., sandwich) and can go to the bathroom unaided, with some accidents at night.					

Present Level of Performance	Annual Goals	Short-Term Objectives	Evaluation Criteria	Projected Date of Mastery	Special Materials, Strategies, and/or Techniques
III) Motor A) In gross motor skills, S is able to jump from 8″ height, pedal a tricycle and turn corners, and bounce and catch a large ball. B) In fine motor skills, he cuts a 4″ line, grasps pencil and crayons in the proper way, and can screw together a threaded object.					
IV) Socialization. S has just completed two months in an ECH*/program and has thus had few opportunities for interaction with peers. He follows short, simple rules in adult directed games and will repeat rhymes, songs, or dances. S is also able to describe feelings about self such as mad, happy, and love.	A) S will develop associative and cooperative play skills B) S will increase attending skills.	A) S will play at a cooperative level with at least 1 other child for 15 minutes. B) S will learn to take turns. C) S will ask permission to use a toy that a peer is playing with. D) S will sit and attend to a task for 15 minutes.	Teacher Observation Teacher Observation Teacher Observation Teacher Observation	5/93 1/93 1/93 5/93	
V) Communication When requested, S can tell his full name, explain how common objects are used, and carry out a series of 3 directions. He also imitates much of the adult speech he hears.					

*Early Childhood Education for the Handicapped

IEP2 Individualized educational program

Date: 6/11/93

Name: Charlene Martin

Date of Birth: 12/10/84

School: Southview El.   Grade: 2

Parents Name: Mr. & Mrs. Henry Martin

Address: 2275 S. Washington Street

Phone: 555-8376

Personnel Attending Conferences (names)

Classroom Teacher: Ian Dower

Special Education Teacher: _____

Psychologist: _____

Speech & Language Specialist: Rose Wheeler

Social Worker: _____

Parent: Mr. & Mrs. Martin

Other: George Wall, OTR; Sandy Decker, PT

Present Levels of Performance
Reading: Second grade reader

Language Arts: Generally first

 grade

Math: First grade

Other: Charlene has Down Syndrome

Annual Goals
1. Improve articulation of sounds.
2. Improve auditory processing.
3. Improve expressive language skills.
4. Continue strengthening knees, hips, and ankles.
5. Continue improving balance.
6. Continue improving visual-motor skills.
7. Continue improving proximal joint stability.

Child's Strengths
Reading skills
Socialization skills

Child's Deficits
Body tone
Visual motor development
Articulation production in
   conversational speech
Auditory processing; expressive
   language

Participation in Regular Program
Areas of study   *Percentage of time*
regular multi-age   all day
primary class

Assessment Used

(continued)

Annual Goal	Specific Objectives	Methods	Comments
Expressive language	Encourage conversational interchange in spontaneous speech. Expand use of adjectives in phrases and sentences. Establish appropriate use of *is* and *are.* Increase expressive vocabulary. Reinforce appropriate use of pronouns (*he, she, they*) in sentences. Expand length of utterances in sentences to an average of 5 and 6 words. Establish the use of *who, what,* and *where* questions. Establish appropriate reversals of words in questions.		
Articulation	Reinforce correct production of /p/ /b/ /w/ /h/ in conjunction with clinician at Community Language Clinic.		
Auditory processing	Recall a four-stage command. Listen to questions and respond appropriately. Verbally relay incidents of the previous day and week. Comprehend categorization of items (food, clothing, animals, etc.).		
Improve balance	Balance on L or R foot, eyes open for 5 sec.	Ball Gymnastics Seated bounce Roll hips forward/back; roll hips L & R Hop on 1 foot walk straight line; various patterns	
Increase muscle strength Hip extension & abduction	Do 10 hip extensions and 10 hip abductions L and R.	Ball gymnastics; prone—airplanes	
Knee extension	Use #2 weight on ankle; do 10 extensions L and R seated, feet unsupported.	Side-lying leg lifts Floor exercises— prone and seated, feet unsupported— leg extensions	
Gross motor		Trike riding Jumping jacks Angels in the snow Run & kick ball Jump down from height	
Eye/hand coordination	Catch ball independently in various situations.	Ball handling (bounce, catch) Catch ball bounced 1' to either side Catch ball thrown 2–3' above head Imitate clapping— regular and irregular rhythms	

REFERENCES

Bricker, D. (1988). Commentary: The future of early childhood/special education. *Journal of the Division for Early Childhood, 12*(3), 276–278.

Fairchild, T. N. (1985). The school counselor's role as a team member: Participating in the developments of IEPs. *The School Counselor, 32*(5), 364–370.

Gore, W. V., & Vance, B. (1983). The micro meets the IEP. *Academic Therapy, 19*(1), 89–91.

Green, L. S. (1988). The parent-teacher partnership. *Academic Therapy, 24*(1), 89–94.

Henry, N. A., & Flynt, E. S. (1990). Rethinking special education referral: A procedural model. *Intervention in School and Clinic, 26*(1), 22–24.

Morgan, D. (1981). Characteristics of a quality IEP. *Education Unlimited,* 12–17.

Renzulli, J. S., & Smith, L. H. (1988). A practical model for designing individual educational programs (IEPs). *Gifted Child Today, 11*(1), 34–40.

Schulz, J. B., Carpenter, C. D., & Turnbull, A. (1984). *Mainstreaming exceptional students: A guide for classroom teachers.* Boston: Allyn & Bacon.

Siders, J. A., & Whorton, J. E. (1982). The relationship of individual ability and IEP goals. *Elementary School Guidance and Counselling, 16,* 187–193.

Strickland, B., & Turnbull, A. P. (1982). *Developing and implementing individualized education programs.* Columbus, OH: Merrill.

Turnbull, A., & Winton, P. (1984). Parent involvement policy and practice: Current research and implications for families of young, severely handicapped children. In J. Blacher (Ed.), *Severely handicapped young children and their families* (pp. 337–397). New York: Academic Press.

Tymitz-Wolf, B. (1981). Guidelines for assessing IEP goals and objectives. *Teaching Exceptional Children, 14,* 198–201.

White, O., & Haring, W. G. (1980). *Exceptional teaching.* Columbus, OH: Merrill.

CHAPTER 6

Working with Parents

CHAPTER OVERVIEW

This chapter discusses:

1. Family support programs.
2. The importance of home–school relations.
3. Parents' possible reactions to a child's disabilities.
4. Assumptions underlying parent involvement programs.
5. Patterns of parent involvement.
6. Ways of planning parent programs.
7. Ways of integrating parents of diverse children into programs.

Parent education has always been an important element in early childhood programs. Indeed, the history of parent education in the United States is intertwined with that of early childhood education. Early kindergartens included working with parents as well as activities for children, and one of the first nursery schools established in our country was a parent cooperative. This interrelationship of work with young children and work with families is rooted in the notion that families provide the primary context for the young child's development. Parents are also the child's first teachers. Indeed, programs for children below the age of three, especially those designed for children with disabilities or for children at risk, are usually home-based programs. These often address children through their parents.

The importance of parent involvement in the education of young children has been underscored in the many research and development programs designed since the 1960s for children of poor and minority group backgrounds. The Head Start and Follow Through programs that resulted from this work, as well as other federally funded programs, have mandated parent involvement as an integral element. This involvement often takes the form of parent education in which parents are helped to deepen their understanding of child development and develop new skills for educating and rearing their children. Parents also help in classrooms. And they have been brought into the decision-making process through the creation of parent advisory boards and other mechanisms that give parents a voice in determining their children's educational programs and in selecting staff.

It should be noted that the parent programs discussed here are not just for parents. In our society today, we find many children whose primary caregiver is not the parent. Grandparents, foster parents, and others who serve as the child's caregivers should all be involved with the school in some way, as long as they assume the function of parents for a child in the program.

Many different levels of parents programming are discussed in this chapter. Each level of programming involves parents to a different degree. These levels can be characterized as parent (and others in the family) support programs, parent participation programs, parent education programs, and programs designed to support communication between parents and teachers. (See Box 6.1.) Schools need to decide what degree of parent involvement they wish to support, and design their program accordingly.

FAMILY SUPPORT PROGRAMS

Recently, family support programs have emerged where the clients are the entire family, including the parents of the young children enrolled (Kagan, Powell, Weissbourd, & Zigler, 1987). These are community-based programs whose major purpose is to educate and support parents in their role as socializers and caregivers. Their services empower parents, and, instead of increasing their helplessness and dependence (Weissbourd & Kagan, 1990), promote their interdependence through parent

---

BOX 6.1   Levels of Parent Involvement

Level of Program	*Type of Activity*
Family Support Program	Parent as program client
	Systems approach
Parent Participation Program	Parent advisory board
	Parents as classroom volunteers
Parent Education Program	Parent meetings, workshops, seminars
Communication with Parents	Parent meetings, newsletters, bulletin boards
	Parent conferences, reports of children's progress

education and support groups, home visitation, drop-in services, warmlines and hotlines, information and referral, lending libraries, health/nutrition services, and child care when parents participate at the center.

Family support programs have become an important component in the array of early childhood programs (Weiss, 1990). Family systems theory provides the rationale for many of these programs. Families are seen as serving basic nurturing, economic, and educational functions. Each member of the family is linked to other members; they are influenced by and interact with each other. Families achieve a dynamic balance that addresses their needs and adapts to particular life circumstances. They are also embedded in larger social systems (McCollum & Maude, 1993).

This dynamic is recognized in the family provisions of Public Law 99-457, the Education of the Handicapped Act amendments. Section H of the act requires an Individualized Family Service Plan (IFSP) to be established when infants and toddlers are involved. The act gives evidence to the importance of families in work with young children with disabilities by requiring a Family Education Plan (FEP) for children below the age of 3. Family support programs, although not as extensive in their requirements as are requirements for older children, follow the same view of embedding the education of young children within work with families.

Four principles underlie service delivery in these family support programs:

1. The long-range goal of programs is prevention instead of treatment.
2. The parent instead of the child is the primary client.
3. Service delivery considers the parents' developmental characteristics.
4. Social support is considered a universal benefit to the individuals, particularly during life transitions (e.g., transition to parenthood, child's transition into school, transition for the new parent back to the world of work). (Weissbourd & Kagan, 1990)

Three such programs are described by Galinsky and Weissbourd (1992).

In teaching children with diverse educational needs, the teachers' work with parents needs to be underscored. Involving parents in decisions about the education of their children with disabilities has a legal base under P.L. 94-142, which requires that parents understand and approve the educational plans designed for their children. This suggests that teachers should spend more time on and give more attention to interpreting their programs to parents of all their children.

There are also significant moral and professional reasons for supporting a high level of parent involvement. This chapter discusses the importance of working with parents, describes some of the problems confronted by parents of children with disabilities, presents a rationale for parent programs, and describes the various types of programs that can be offered.

LINKING HOME AND SCHOOL

In most states all children above the age of 7 are required to attend school, and public funds are used to support those schools. The responsibility for school policy belongs to elected members of boards of education, who represent their community as a whole. Parents can also influence school policies. They can petition school administrators, school board members, and members of state legislatures. They can also educate the community as a whole about the needs of children in school.

Bronfenbrenner (1974) has suggested that involving the child's family is critical to the success of an intervention program. When parents are considered partners, the program's effects are reinforced and its achievement sustained beyond the end of the program. Parents can help their children apply what has been learned in school in a variety of settings, providing the child with opportunities to extend his or her learning (Marholin, Siegel, & Phillips, 1975; Stokes and Baer, 1977). The program's effects are likely to be severely limited without it.

Parents are the first teachers of their children. Their teaching is informal and often indirect, yet it is effective. This informal teaching, however, may not be enough for children with disabilities, who might need more explicit and more varied forms of instruction. These forms might not be discovered intuitively, and specific teaching strategies might have to be taught to these parents. Children with disabilities may continue to be the responsibility of their parents over a significantly longer period than do their normal counterparts (Shearer & Shearer, 1979). Thus, helping these parents learn skills for teaching their children can affect the learning process over an extended period of time.

By establishing a working relationship with parents, the school can improve communications and develop agreement about educational goals and ways to achieve these goals. This can make what happens to the child at home more consistent with what happens at school, limiting unnecessary conflict and confusion.

Lillie (1976) has identified four different dimensions of parent programs: (1) providing social and emotional support, (2) exchanging information, (3) improving parent–child interactions, and (4) having parents participate in the school's program. Each of these dimensions requires the attention of teachers who work with children.

Providing Social and Emotional Support

The three kinds of social support that have been investigated are informational, instrumental, and emotional (Cohen & Wills, 1985; House & Kahn, 1985). *Informational support* consists of sharing information and advising on ways to manage certain situations. Concrete help, gifts, and money are examples of *instrumental support. Emotional support* allows parents to feel that they are not alone in their concerns and that their efforts at working with their children are valued.

Social support for parents is important in linking home and school. Behavioral scientists studying social support have typically defined the structure of interest as the individual's social network (or circle of intimates). A social network refers to an individual's circle of intimate peers, or that group of friends, family, or workmates who are meaningful to the individual (Hall & Wellman, 1985). Network support varies directly with network size; larger networks are more supportive (Hall & Wellman, 1985; Vaux, 1988). Network density affects support utilization. Usually the more dense, or close-knit networks are more often used compared to less dense networks (Gottlieb & Pancer, 1988).

Relationships between types of social support and parenting behavior suggest that emotional support promotes parents' ability to be accessible and responsive to the child, regardless of the current life situations. For parents who are confronted by a challenge of stress (e.g., the transition to parenthood, a developmentally at-risk child, a temperamentally difficult infant), informational or instrumental support that directly relates to that specific stressor can promote performance, coping, and problem solving (Stevens, 1991).

Social support influences parenting behavior through social transmission of knowledge about parenting. This knowledge is transmitted from one member of the social network to another through exchanges of informational support, emotional support, and perhaps tangible aid or assistance.

Activities in a parent program can be designed to reduce anxieties caused by the family's emotional reactions to the child's disability and to make the family members feel better about themselves as a social unit. A similar need for support may exist in all family units, but the need often is more critical when a child has a disability.

Exchanging Information

In any educational program, information needs to be shared among parents and teachers. Parents can learn about their child's program and about the progress being made. Parents can also gain information about principles of child growth and development, and learn specific things they can do to help their child. Teachers, too, need to have information about the child's background and home behavior to improve their understanding of that child's school behavior. This information can be used to build a better educational program for each child. Many of the traditional school-parent meetings as well as parent conferences are designed to share information with parents. Indeed, this has probably been the most successful part of early childhood parent programs in most schools.

Improving Parent–Child Interactions

A range of approaches is available to help improve parent–child interactions. Some programs are designed to teach parents systematic, structured ways of working with their children (e.g., Becker, 1971; Linde & Kopp, 1974); others are designed to help parents develop insight into why their children behave the way they do (e.g., Ginott, 1965; Gordon, 1970). Still others provide experiences to support optimal interactions between parents and children (Gordon, Guinagh, & Jester, 1972; Sparling & Lewis, 1979).

Direct teaching is a mechanism whereby one caregiver tells another about something; points out a behavior, an event, or a phenomenon; and tells the other about its significance. In modeling, one caregiver shows another ways to work with the infant. Modeling may be intended or unintended. Finally, reinforcement refers to individuals' receiving positive praise, which may be verbal or nonverbal (candy, rewards, trips, activities, etc.). Coaching, interpreting, and evaluating are three additional strategies individuals use to teach others (Stevens, 1991). Coaching is direct and may be intrusive, but it usually communicates a desired adult behavior, urging the learner to do something or to behave in a certain way. Interpreting is usually indirect, is often less intrusive but no less instructive, and usually comments on the infant's behavior. Evaluating is also indirect. It includes comments about the physical atmosphere as well as about the adult's or the infant's behavior. All of these strategies can transmit knowledge about infants and about parenting.

Social learning theory has been used as a basis for helping parents improve their interactions with their children. Bandura's (1977) social learning theory helps us assume that network members influence the child-rearing beliefs and strategies of parents through modeling, teaching, and reinforcement. Stevens (1988) and Stevens and Bakeman (1990) found that these mechanisms influence the parenting behavior of young parents. They followed 15- to 17-year-old black teens, pregnant for the first time, from the last trimester of pregnancy to their infants' first birthday. They videotaped the play interaction of teen mother, infant, and grandmother, and transcribed the verbal behavior of participants. They examined exchanges such as those that probably naturally occur in the home, while grandmothers and mothers interact and when one adult talks with the other about some significant incident involving the infant.

Having Parents Participate in the School's Program

The final dimension of parent involvement relates to having parents engage in activities related to their child's program. They may participate in advisory groups, act as aides in the classroom, or become involved in making materials for the program.

There are definite benefits to be derived from this increased parent involvement. Parents can provide a pool of talent, often untapped, for the class. Many parents have special skills or knowledge related to their employment or hobbies, or have special backgrounds and interests. Parents can also supplement resources provided by the schools by donating materials such as wrapping paper, scraps of cloth, egg cartons, paper tubes, and other items found in the home. These can be used in a variety of classroom projects.

Parents can be aides and helpers in the classroom, either on a regular basis or for specific projects or excursions. Adding these adults to the classroom can allow greater individual attention to be given to children. In the classroom, parents can help work on projects, clean up, observe, and tutor children with special needs. Providing experiences with more and varied adults may help children who need to develop skills in interpersonal relations, which may be especially important to some children with disabilities.

Once parents know the program and feel good about it, they can become good public relations resources, providing information to the community at large about what is happening to children in school. They can also become effective advocates of the school program. In many cases parent advocacy has been directly responsible for altering policies and laws relating to children, especially those with disabilities, through the parents' work with school boards, advisory councils, and state and federal legislatures (Lillie, 1974).

Schools might develop parent programs containing only some of the four dimensions just mentioned. Given the availability of resources, schools and teachers might evolve a program using just one or two of these dimensions. Also, not all parents will become involved in all dimensions of a parent program that has been developed, nor will they all be involved to the same extent. Work and other considerations may limit the time they can give to the program, and the degree to which they can become involved in it. Teachers need to be as accepting of the abilities and needs of parents as they are of children. Teachers also need to understand that although parents of children with disabilities have the same concerns about their children as do all parents, they are faced with a different set of circumstances in being parents.

PARENTS' REACTIONS TO THEIR CHILDREN'S DISABILITIES

Teachers need to be sensitive to parents' reactions to their children's disabilities and to their levels of acceptance of their children's conditions. Parents differ in their reactions to their children's disabilities. Some accept the problem more easily than others, although the initial reaction may change as they live with their child. The range of parental reactions has been described by Gardner (1973), Love (1970), and others. Karnes and Lee (1980) have summarized these reactions into stages of denial, anger, guilt, blame, shame, overprotection, and adaptation.

Some parents of children with disabilities will *deny* the problem exists. The diagnostician's competence may be questioned and opinions of other experts sought. Parents may feel *anger* toward their child and themselves. If this happens, teachers should attempt to direct parents' hostile feelings into useful channels, such as working to benefit children with similar conditions.

Parents may feel burdened by *guilt* about "mistakes" they made that may have little to do with the child's condition. Parents may *blame* others for creating the condition, or the child's teacher and school for inappropriate education. Teachers should attempt to help parents see the reality of the situation.

Parents may feel *shame* about the birth of a child with a disability. Talking to other parents of children with disabilities can be helpful at this stage. Counseling may be the best strategy in this situation. Parents may *overprotect* their disabled child, limiting his or her opportunity to play with other children and encounter challenge. This prevents the child from developing in as normal a way as possible with other children and may be a further disability. Parents may have to be convinced to involve children with disabilities in educational programs and extracurricular activities.

Fortunately, in most cases parents accept their children's conditions and *adapt* to them. They develop positive attitudes toward themselves and their children. They are able to learn the skills needed to contribute to their children's futures.

ASSUMPTIONS UNDERLYING PARENT INVOLVEMENT PROGRAMS

In developing a parent involvement program, a teacher must assume the support of the school and its administration. There should be other persons in the school who are willing and able to help as well. The teacher must also assume both that he or she has or can develop the skills necessary to carry out the program and that the parents for whom the program is designed are able and willing to become involved and to learn from their involvement.

Most parents are sincerely interested in the education of their children and will work to promote that education. The onset of most parent involvement programs requires the most time from the professional staff, and the greatest amount of support and help must be given to the parents. Parents will generally find time to give to the program if teachers communicate their willingness to give of their time and energy and if a mutually agreeable schedule is established. If parents are to be expected to support the children, teachers must be willing to support parents.

In establishing programs of parent participation, teachers need to assess the parents' concerns for their children's education. Teachers need to be aware of the values of the community and whether those are the values held by the parents involved; and they must also discover the goals parents have established for their own children's education. When there is inconsistency or conflict between the goals and values of the parents and those of the teachers, there is little hope for cooperation. Sometimes apparent inconsistency is the result of misunderstandings or a lack of communication. Once the teacher has become aware that this has happened, lines of communication can be established and teachers can help parents understand what the school wants for their children. Improved communication may require increased effort and use of new resources, but it can be a vital basis for establishing parent cooperation.

When real differences exist between the values of the school and those of the home, programs of parent participation are more difficult. Parents may be unwilling to become involved in school activities and may feel uncomfortable in school settings. An adversarial relationship may develop between teachers and parents. In such cases it may be helpful to try to negotiate agreements between parents and children whereby schools begin to accept some of the values and goals of the parents in the hope that parents may become more understanding and more accepting of the school's point of view.

Parents must feel their participation will be worthwhile—both meeting their own needs, interests, and desires and supporting their children's learning and development. Using parents only for routine classroom cleaning tasks will lead them to feel they are not making a meaningful contribution to their children's education. Although this may ease the burden for the teacher, the parents learn little that they can use with their children; nor do their children benefit directly from their involvement. On the other hand, if parents are taught how to read stories to their children, to play educational games with them, or to carry on conversations with them—activities that are significant in extending the child's language—they are likely to feel more satisfied because they gain a sense of contributing directly to their children's learning.

Parents should be given specific tasks and shown how to engage in those tasks. They should also be shown how those tasks are related to the goals of the program and how those goals are in turn related to the needs of the children.

Teachers should show appreciation and enthusiasm for the contribution being made and provide parents with feedback on their own performance. Telling parents they have read a story particularly well or have successfully engaged a child in a difficult interaction will help the parents appreciate the contributions they are making. Feedback to parents should be positive and instructive. Parents will make errors in their work with children, especially in the beginning, and so they should also be told or shown, tactfully, how to improve.

Teachers' suggestions about how parents work with the children should be specific. Showing a parent exactly how to hold a book, where to sit in relation to a child or group of children, and how to ask particular questions about a story will be of greater help to parents than will telling them to be warm and responsive. The results of parents' work with children, and especially the progress shown by those children, should be pointed out regularly and consistently.

Parents come from different backgrounds, and thus have different values and conceptions of what is good and useful for children. They also have different views of what their role should be in relation to children. Not all parent activities will be of equal interest to all parents, nor will they all need to be involved in all the activities planned. Parents who cannot be involved in the classroom during the day because of work responsibilities can be involved in other ways. Even parents with little education can instruct children if they are shown what to do. Each contribution should be valued. Mutual trust and respect should provide the basis for a joint support for the child's continued learning and development.

PATTERNS OF PARENT INVOLVEMENT

Although the involvement of parents of children with disabilities will differ little from that of all other parents in the school, there will be some activities designed specifically for these parents. In all schools, teachers are expected to report to all parents about their children's progress. Parents may also be invited into the school periodically to view the program. Often schools have parent or parent-teacher associations that hold meetings during the school year and sponsor other parent activities. Schools may invite parents to view class performances or to share in various school observances. However, these limited forms of participation may not be enough to have an impact on the children's education. Only by a joint effort of parents and teachers can the optimum educational effect be achieved This means going beyond the traditional, limited role of the parent in school. Care should be taken, however, that these parents are not isolated from the rest of the school's parent group.

Sharing Information with Parents

Federal and state legislation requires that all parents have access to all information that the school has concerning their children. Teachers need to interpret this information to parents. Test scores, for example, mean little by themselves, but when test scores and records of observations of children in class are interpreted together, the parents can gain a full picture of how their child functions in school. Only when many different kinds of information are pooled—including teacher observations, test results, and the judgments of professionals—does a full picture evolve that can become the basis for educational plans and decisions. The typical report card is usually too general and nonspecific in its grading system to communicate the basis for educational decisions. Information should also be shared with parents through written reports and newsletters, as well as orally through regular parent conferences.

Written Reports.   Written reports can take a variety of forms; report cards are one of these. Typically, report cards are standardized forms used by the school to report pupil progress to parents. They are used in primary grade classes and in many kindergartens, but are seldom found in preschool programs. Report cards cover categories of academic learning (reading, language arts, music) as well as social behavior (getting along with others, sharing, cooperating). The cards are designed so that teachers can complete them for an entire class fairly quickly, since one must be completed for each child at regular intervals during the school year. Reports of children's progress may be reported with simply a letter grade (A, B, C, D) or a judgment of how a child meets a criterion (S = satisfactory, U = unsatisfactory).

Report cards, by their nature, deal with general expectations for an entire class. Since children with disabilities have learning expectations that are different in some ways from other children in a classroom, report cards alone are not adequate for sharing information with parents. Some supplementary written report, specifically related to the goals established in the child's individualized educational program, must also be provided. This could take the form of a checklist or a narrative letter, either of which might also be used with all the children in a class.

The *checklist* generally consists of items that are more specific to what is learned in a particular class than those on a report card. Statements of particular accomplishments can often be denoted by a simple mark in a column. Examples of observation checklists were presented in chapter 3. The reporting checklist is not much different in form. The actual content of a checklist can be determined by the individual teacher or school and can thus be designed to provide parents with a better idea of what each child is specifically accomplishing.

A *narrative letter* is another way of sharing written information with parents about their child. Letters can communicate the qualitative aspects of a child's work better than can report cards or checklists since letters can be used to describe activities more fully. Such a letter can describe a child's learning style and pattern of interaction with other children, as well as the books read or the materials used. Descriptions of specific incidents can be included. To save time, some teachers duplicate a letter describing activities of the whole class and supplement this with a few paragraphs specific to each child.

No one form of sharing information about individual children is totally satisfactory in all ways. The more specific and descriptive a report is, the more time it takes to complete. Teachers are often caught in a dilemma about which form to use. Compromises often need to be made. A combination of different types of individual reports may provide the best balance.

Report cards and individual letters to parents share specific information with individuals. *Newsletters,* on the other hand, can be used to share information of general interest with all parents. They can describe incidents and activities of the entire class that would be interesting to all.

A newsletter might be sent home at the end of each semester, each quarter, or each month. The frequency depends on how much time a teacher can devote to its production as well as how much help is available. Newsletters can describe special events (such as a field trip or the visit of a resource person) as well as ongoing activities of special interest (such as a cooking experience in a nutrition unit). They can include articles highlighting a particular staff member, describing her or his academic background and professional experience as well as personal information related to family, hobbies, or travel. Short vignettes describing individual children's products or activities can also be included, with care taken to mention each child at some time during the year. Notices of community or school activities, reports on articles or books that might be of interest to parents, information about community resources, and requests for materials or help for the classroom might round out the content of a newsletter.

Newsletters for integrated classrooms should be of interest to parents of children both with and without disabilities. They should be written in understandable language. Parents can often be used as resources in the publication of a newsletter, writing items, typing copy, and reproducing material.

Parent Conferences.   Many teachers share information with parents at parent conferences, either to substitute for written reports or to supplement them. Because parent conferences are a form of face-to-face contact, they often enhance positive communication. If messages are misunderstood by either party, questions can be asked and meanings can be clarified immediately. Also, a wide range of communication can be covered in a short time. Also, unlike written communication, there is dialogue between parents and teacher, so communication goes both ways.

In order for parent conferences to be effective, they must be carefully planned and implemented. The teacher should set up an agenda for the conference and bring together materials to be discussed with the parents. The conference agenda should be flexible, however, so concerns raised by parents and concerns that become evident to the teacher as a result of the conference dialogue can be discussed. The list below outlines several guidelines for successful parent-teacher conferences.

Guidelines for Parent-Teacher Conferences
Before the Conference
1. Identify the purposes for the conference (e.g., reporting, information sharing, problem solving).
2. Prepare an agenda.
3. Review the child's record.
4. Prepare specific materials to show parents (e.g., observation notes, test results, work samples).
5. Set a time for the conference that is convenient for all.
6. Invite both parents, if possible.
7. Find a comfortable, relaxing, quiet place for the conference.

During the Conference
8. Be friendly; establish a positive atmosphere.
9. Inform parents about the class program, schedule, and routines.
10. Make positive comments about the child; talk about strengths as well as problems.
11. Be specific about the problems you present.
12. Use language that parents can easily understand.
13. Provide opportunities for parents to speak as well as listen; be a good listener yourself.
14. Work cooperatively with parents on specific solutions and activities for the child; identify responsibilities.
15. Summarize the meeting, make sure you and the parents are clear about the next steps.

After the Conference
16. Make a brief record of the content the meeting.
17. Plan for follow-up.

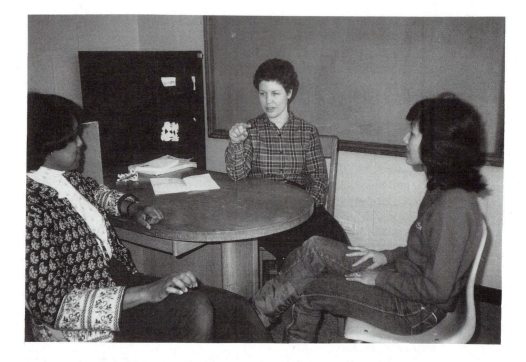

Conferences need to be followed up. A brief written record should be made of a parent conference, noting topics discussed, parent reactions, and any follow-up that needs to take place. It is helpful to involve both parents of a child in a conference, although this is not always possible and sometimes a child has only one parent. If, however, decisions are made that involve more than one parent, it is important that all those involved participate somehow in the decision. Sometimes telephone calls or letters can supplement parent conferences.

Other Ways of Sharing Information.   A range of other methods can be used for sharing information with parents. Schools often set up bulletin boards especially for parents. Notices of meetings or activities of interest to parents along with newspaper and magazine articles might be posted on them. Requests for help might also be posted there. Bulletin boards are relatively easy to set up and can be changed fairly often, since teachers do not have to develop what they put on them. Care should be taken that a parent bulletin board be placed where it can easily catch the attention of parents, that it be maintained attractively, and that its contents be changed regularly to keep it interesting.

If space is available in the school building, a separate room or alcove might be set aside as a parents' center. Such a center might contain comfortable chairs for parents to sit in, as well as firmer chairs and a table to facilitate work. The room might have a coffee pot going to encourage parents to spend some time there as well. This might be where the bulletin board is located. It also might have a small library, including magazines, flyers, pamphlets, and books of interest to parents. Some books that might be especially useful to parents of young children with disabilities are the following:

Becker, W. C. *Parents are teachers.* Champaign, IL: Research Press, 1971.

Bicklen, D. *Let our children go.* Syracuse, NY: Human Policy Press, 1974.

Braga, J., & Braga, L. *Children and adults.* Englewood Cliffs, NJ: Prentice-Hall, 1976.

Brehm, S. S. *Help your child: A parent's guide to mental health services.* Englewood Cliffs, NJ: Prentice-Hall, 1978.

Brown, D. S. *Developmental handicaps in babies and young children.* Springfield, IL: Charles C Thomas, 1972.

Buscaglia, L. *The disabled and their parents.* Thorofare, NJ: Charles B. Slack, 1975.

Croft, D. *Parents and teachers: A resource book for home, school, and community relations.* Belmont, CA: Wadsworth, 1979.

Fredericks, H. D., & Baldwin, V. *Isn't it time he outgrew it?* Springfield, IL: Charles C Thomas, 1976.

Isaacs, S. *Troubles of children and parents.* New York: Schocken, 1973.

Jeffree, D. M., & McConkey, R. *Let me speak.* New York: Taplinger, 1976.

Jeffree, D. M., McConkey, R., & Hewson, S. *Let me play.* New York: Taplinger, 1977.

Jeffree, D. M., & Skeffington, M. *Let me read.* London: Souvenir Press, 1980.

Jenkins, J. K., & McDonald, P. *Growing up equal: Activities and resources for parents and teachers of young children.* Englewood Cliffs, NJ: Prentice-Hall, 1979.

Leitch, S. M. *A child learns to speak: A guide for parents and teachers of preschool children.* Springfield, IL: Charles C Thomas, 1977.

Mopsik, S. I., & Agard, J. A. *An education handbook for parents of handicapped children.* Cambridge, MA: Abt Associates, 1979.

Patterson, F. G. *Families.* Champaign, IL: Research Press, 1975.

Wender, P. H. *The hyperactive child—A handbook for parents.* New York: Crown, 1973.

Additional opportunities to share information with parents are available through a range of informal contacts a parent might have with the school. Especially in nursery schools and child-care centers, parents may drop their children off in the morning and pick them up at the end of the school session. These short periods provide limited but useful opportunities for teachers to share information "on the fly." Teachers who plan so that one staff member is available to greet the children and send them off can spot particular parents with whom they might want to converse briefly and develop a short exchange. Such opportunities should not be overused, however, nor should they be seen as a substitute for parent conferences.

Telephone conversations and *brief notes* sent home with children also offer opportunities to share bits of information. Teachers should not overdo these either since, if they are used too often, parents may stop paying attention to the messages sent home.

Parent Education Programs

Teachers, often with the help of other school personnel, may be given the responsibility of developing a parent education program to help parents develop specific skills in educating their children with disabilities. To avoid reteaching skills they already have, the teacher must identify what parents already know about their child with a disability and about how to work with them.

Since parents have limited time and competing interests and their ability to commit themselves to a parent education program may be limited, the programs developed should be of relatively short duration. In establishing a program, the teacher should attempt to identify common interests and goals. Both parents and teachers should agree on the areas of parent education and on expected outcomes. Once goals are established and desired skills are clearly defined, parents should be taught as simply as possible. They should be shown what to do and given an opportunity to practice what they learn. It is important to provide feedback on parents' performance. Tell them what they are doing right; help them correct errors.

In working with parents, teachers should speak simply, avoiding educational jargon if possible. It is also helpful to run the program in the type of setting in which children and parents will operate, such as the child's home and the classroom.

Skills and activities that parents use at home should be consistent with the way in which the teacher works with the children in school. Open lines of communication can help parents and teachers know what each is doing and can create a consistent set of home-school learning expectations, activities, and environments. The list below outlines several guidelines for successful parent meetings.

Guidelines for Parent Meetings

Before the Meeting
1. Involve parents in planning the meeting.
2. Plan a convenient time for the meeting.
3. Find a comfortable, convenient place to meet.
4. Announce the topic and format of the meeting well in advance; inform parents of what they should bring.
5. Send out notices of the meeting, with return slips.
6. Follow up on parents who do not return slips.
7. Arrange for transportation and babysitters if necessary.
8. Check with parents about refreshments.

During the Meeting
9. Start and end the meeting on time.
10. Establish ground rules early (e.g., smoking, breaks, confidentiality).
11. Be flexible in following the agenda.
12. Vary program activities (e.g., discussion, role playing, lecture, film, games).
13. Provide opportunities for everyone to be involved in the discussion.
14. Allow some time for informal interaction at the end of the meeting.

After the Meeting
15. Make a brief record of what happened.
16. Plan for follow-up activities.

Parents as Program Advocates

Parents of children with disabilities have a special stake in the education of these children. They can become advocates of the programs in which their children are enrolled and involve themselves in public relations activities. Parents can talk about their children's programs to friends and neighbors within the community. Parents can also help run fundraising activities to purchase materials and equipment not provided by public funds. Parents can represent the school on local radio and television programs, provide press releases, or inform the local paper of activities that might be worthy of press coverage.

Parents of children with disabilities can also be effective advocates in the political arena, meeting with public officials, writing letters to legislators, and attending local school board meetings. They can testify at public hearings in support of specific programs. The parents' knowledge and commitment will serve to enhance their role in the area of public policy. Although parents must speak for themselves, they may need help in developing the skills needed to speak out in public. Teachers should not provide scripts for parents to use at hearings or in media presentations, however; the parents' own words usually are most effective. Rather, teachers should provide parents with the information they will need in their advocacy role, make parents aware of the opportunities that arise for establishing advocacy relations, and help parents develop the skills they may need.

Helping Parents Help Other Parents

Parents respond differently to the needs of their children. Often parents who discover that their children have disabilities suffer from a sense of isolation. This sense of isolation may be caused by the feeling that their children are different from other children and that their responses to their children are different from other parents' responses in similar situations. Knowing that others have had similar experiences and have responded in similar ways can do much to alleviate such feelings of isolation. Persons who have shared similar experiences are also better able to communicate with one another about similar inner thoughts and feelings. Such sharing—the basis for many self-help groups—can be the basis for establishing supportive relations among parents of children with disabilities. A parent of a child with a disability often can be an effective counselor to another such parent, providing emotional support and encouragement and sharing ways of dealing with practical problems.

Teachers can encourage parents to consult with one another by introducing parents to one another and by setting up parent meetings and discussion groups, which the teacher must take care not to dominate. Parents should be allowed to determine for themselves the content and purposes of these meetings and discussions, with the teacher providing mainly technical assistance. If the group or teacher desires, a school social worker might be recruited to provide insight and support to a group. As parents feel more comfortable about themselves, they will feel more comfortable about their children and the program the school provides for them.

Parents in the Classroom

The ways parents can be included in the activities of the classroom are usually limited only by the desire, willingness, and ability of the teacher to use other adults in the classroom and to supervise them. Most parents can learn the techniques needed to support children's programs, such as reading stories to children, helping in craft activities, or working with manipulative materials or paper-and-pencil activities. Parents with particular talents or hobbies may be invited to share these with the children as a special activity. Parents are a helpful and necessary addition on a field trip. They can also be used to observe and record children's behavior.

Parents may be volunteers or they may become part of the paid staff of early childhood programs. In terms of regular attendance and responsibility, more can be expected of a paid parent aide than of a volunteer participant. But parents will do many of the same things whether they are employed or volunteer their services.

Parents who are involved in classroom activities must be aware of classroom organization and routines and must know what will be expected of them. They should be given tasks that they are able to perform reasonably well. Individualizing the parents' involvement is just as important as individualizing the children's program.

Parents on Advisory Councils

Many federal programs, such as Head Start, require that parents serve on advisory councils to ensure that they have a role in educational decision making. Such councils can be effective in helping determine the nature of children's programs. The effectiveness of a council will depend to a great extent upon how the council is allowed to operate and the way in which school professionals deal with the council.

Successful advisory councils create conditions that allow parents to be effective members. Adequate information is provided so that parents have a basis for making decisions. The information given to parents is organized so that they can use it easily. Reports are written in language parents can understand, and statistical reports are summarized and interpreted. All reports are sent to parents well ahead of scheduled meetings so that they have time to read and think about the material.

Meetings should be scheduled when the majority of council members can attend. Whenever possible, a schedule of meetings should be established for the semester. Meetings should be long enough to allow discussion of all agenda items, or, when necessary, a series of meetings might be scheduled. Many parents cannot spend long evenings at a meeting, and few persons can be very effective decision makers working into the early hours of morning. Reports and proposals need to be given to the council well in advance of their deadlines so that the members will feel they have the ability to modify a request or report without scuttling a program. Minutes of all meetings should be kept and distributed soon after a meeting so that members can remember what transpired and make necessary corrections.

Most important, an advisory council should be taken seriously. Administrators and staff should heed the advice given, and when that advice cannot be followed, the council should be helped to understand why. If an advisory council is not listened to, its members will give up trying to be effective. They will stop coming to council meetings or they will attend but not offer suggestions or participate in discussions. At that point an advisory council exists in name only.

Parents have serious concerns about the education of their children. They see their children and their children's schools from a different vantage point than do professionals, and they have different interests at heart. An advisory council should advise, not determine a program, and not all of its suggestions will ever be implemented; but if advice is continually disregarded or manipulated by professionals, then the parents involved will feel disparaged and insulted. Relationships between parents and teachers are never completely without problems or differences of opinion. But when parents are respected and their contributions are valued—whether contributions to decisions or to classroom practice—then an effective partnership can be established between home and school that can serve the best interests of the children.

PLANNING AN EFFECTIVE PARENT PROGRAM

Working effectively with parents requires planning. A well-thought-through plan of action allows a teacher to identify goals and to gather and utilize resources so that optimum use can be made of the teacher's time and energy. Following are some elements of a good plan for parent participation.

Establishing Mutually Determined Goals

The first task in designing a parent program is to determine what goals are considered desirable by all parties: parents, administrators, and other professionals. Parents might want a program that helps them be better informed; administrators might want a program that gives the school public visibility; teachers might want parents to serve as classroom aides. All of these goals are legitimate and might be possible to some extent, but priorities must be established.

A variety of techniques can be used to identify desirable goals. The teacher could send questionnaires, interview people from each group, or call small group meetings to gain this information. The teacher should make it clear that although suggestions are being solicited, it might not be possible to address everyone's interests and that priorities need to be established. The final determination of goals, however, should reflect the concerns of all parties.

The final goals of the year's program might be varied. For a single program, the goals might include, for example:

- Helping parents become more effective in working with their own children.
- Improving communication between teachers and parents.
- Improving communication among parents.
- Helping parents develop better ways of managing their lives and the lives of their children at home.

Developing the Program

Program goals are generally stated in broad forms that must be translated into more specific objectives designed to move the parents toward these goals. In developing objectives, teachers need to identify the skills, attitudes, and understandings that will become the focus of the program. Given the focus of improving communication among parents at school, for example, the teacher needs to determine what activities will in fact improve that communication. This could include increasing the number of parent meetings held during the school year, increasing attendance at school meetings, increasing the number of parents who participate in meetings, or changing the quality of parent interactions at meetings. Each objective would move the program toward the same goal but would require the teacher to take a different line of action.

The teacher who can think of observable events that would indicate the achievement of an objective will be better able to judge whether that objective has been reached. Counting the number of meetings held, the number of persons attending meetings, the number of people speaking up at meetings, or the number and kinds of interactions between parents during meeting and comparing those figures with observations of the program during the previous year can help determine the degree to which the situation has changed.

Based on the program goals and objectives set, the teacher can begin to develop a set of program activities. The teacher needs to consider each activity in relation to the objective(s) it is designed to meet, determining who will do the activity, where it will be done, how it will be done, and for how long. He or she must gather the necessary material, identify the appropriate space, and schedule the time required to complete the activity.

Heward, Dardig, and Rossett (1979) have presented strategies that can be used in teaching parents of children with disabilities to deal with problems they encounter at home. The authors suggest using behavior management techniques in helping parents teach new behavior to their children, weaken the dysfunctional behavior that may exist, and increase their children's positive behaviors. Suggestions for adapting the home environment to the needs of their children and planning for future situations are also provided. An excellent resource directory is included.

EVALUATING PARENT PROGRAMS

Teachers must know how well they have been able to implement the programs they have planned and how effective the programs have been. This requires collecting information about the program from its inception and analyzing this information to make judgments about it. Program records can include simple descriptions of how program goals were identified, how objectives were generated, and how activities were planned and implemented, as well as what happened to those involved during the course of the program. Teachers need to assess the program while it is in process to allow modifications to be made early enough to make a difference. The information collected can also be used in planning programs in the future. The following list contains several questions that will help teachers evaluate their programs.

Questions for Program Evaluation

- Are methods of reaching parents successful?
- Could alternative methods be used to better advantage?
- Are materials required for the activities available when needed?
- What other sources of materials could be found?
- Is there adequate parent participation in the various sessions?
- How do parents respond to activities planned for them?
- Do the activities seem to make a difference?

Both formal and informal techniques can be used to gather information for evaluation. Although school personnel such as school psychologists or principals can help collect information, parents are the prime source of information about program outcomes. Judgments made about the program based on the information collected must be related to how well the program was implemented and the degree to which the program's goals and objectives were met. Problems that arise in implementing a program may result in limited outcomes. It may be that although the activities that were developed seemed to be good ways to achieve the goals and objectives, they were not as effective as the teacher thought they would be. It may also be, however, that the goals and objectives could not be achieved by any group of parents. Being sensitive to all dimensions of the program will allow the teacher to make the best analyses and judgments based upon the information available.

Parent programs are not ends in themselves, but are developed as another way of improving the child's education. To the extent that the child's education is improved, the parent program is successful. If it does not affect the education of the child, then the parent program, no matter how satisfying to those involved, cannot be considered successful. This indirect impact is hard to assess, since it may be hard to observe the difference teachers wish to make. Therefore, judgments about the impact of parent programs are difficult to make.

INCLUDING ALL PARENTS

Parents of children with disabilities represent only a minority of the children in a classroom. Although these parents, much like their children, have distinct needs that must be met in particular ways, they also need to be included in the program provided for all parents. The teacher's specialized program should not be so overwhelming that it keeps these parents from participating in more general activities. In addition, teachers have to respond to the concerns of parents of children without disabilities regarding the impact of mainstreaming on their children.

Most parents have had little contact with children with disabilities. Too often the lack of contact and the resulting absence of knowledge can create fears on the part of parents of normal children. The teacher will have to cope with both the ignorance and the fears of these parents. Parents may be afraid that including children with disabilities in a normal classroom will be harmful to their children. They may be concerned that children with a disability, especially if it is a behavior disorder, may physically hurt their children or that their children will begin to model the behavior of the children with disabilities, leading to inappropriate behavior and the possibility of arrested development. They may also be afraid that the time and attention the classroom teacher must give to a child with a disability will be time and attention taken away from their own children, causing their learning to suffer.

Teachers need to understand the sources of parental fears. Since one of these sources often is ignorance, teachers should help parents learn about the nature of disabilities in childhood. Parent meetings that deal with child development and the nature of children's disabilities can prove helpful. Teachers can use community resources, including spokespersons from various community organizations, in planning these meetings. It also helps to provide parents with simple articles or pamphlets describing the particular disabilities that are represented in the class.

Another way of allaying parents' fears is to have them see what is happening in the classroom. If a teacher can have an open-door policy, allowing parents to visit the class without a great deal of fuss or red tape, parents will find that many of their fears are groundless. Parents of normal children can also serve as resource persons in the classroom, working with children with disabilities and, through this activity, becoming aware of the nature of the disabilities.

A number of studies show the effects of social support on parents' child-rearing practices. Cotterell (1986) found that Australian mothers provided more stimulating home environments when these mothers received greater informational support about child rearing from social network members, lived in communities with more women at a similar stage in life, and received greater support from their husbands. Child-rearing information network (especially from relatives) promoted the mother's parenting abilities.

Parents of children with disabilities who have greater social support (either informational, emotional, practical, or tangible) use a more positive interactive behavior during free-play episodes. Mothers who received greater support were more encouraging and more attentive to their children, and assisted their children's engagement with objects (Dunst & Trivette, 1988).

Stevens (1988) studied social support relating to personal control and parenting behavior of parents of at-risk children. In this study, three groups of low-income mothers were targeted. Two of the three groups (black teens and white adults) showed that mothers' information and assistance with child-rearing problems from extended family members were predictive of more positive parenting behavior. Other studies (e.g., Weinraub & Wolf, 1983; 1987) showed that among both single- and two-parent families, middle-class Caucasian mothers who received more parenting support had a more positive interactive behavior with their preschool children. Parenting support referred to the degree to which mothers valued the parenting beliefs of their intimate associates and to the extent of parenting support received from groups and organizations. Their behaviors (interactive behavior with the child, maternal control, encouraging the child to act maturely, greater nurturance, and verbal and nonverbal communication) became more positive when they received more parenting support. These results were supported in a study (e.g., Crnic, Greenberg, Ragozin, Robinson, & Basham, 1983; Greenberg & Crnic, 1988) of white middle-class mothers. Mothers with more intimate support and more community support had a more positive effect in interaction with their infants. They enjoyed the interaction more, were more positively affected, and responded more.

A study of working-class Hispanic families (Feiring, Fox, Jaskir, & Lewis, 1987) showed that mothers receiving more *tangible* support from the father and from the social network were more proximal, provided more stimulating caregiving, and had less distal interaction. Such a proximal engagement with the infant can promote infant emotional and intellectual development (Bradley, Caldwell, & Rock, 1988).

Most of the studies indicate that social support to parents from network members provided the family system with substantial benefits, especially if the support affects the child-rearing enterprise. However, Zarling, Hirsch, and Landry (1988) did not find a relationship between new mothers' ratings of support (informational, emotional, or tangible) and maternal sensitivity to the infant at 6 months. Their measures of support may have been reflective of global social support and insensitive to the different support variations provided around the child-rearing enterprise. When informal social support benefits the individuals' performance, parent programs can assist them to construct and use these network relationships.

Children's special needs have in the past led to segregated programs. The move toward mainstreaming is an attempt to eliminate this segregation. The program that a teacher and school staff design for parents can either support or thwart integration. All parents of all children are concerned about what is happening to their children in the school. The parent program should help all parents move beyond concern for their children alone, understanding that what happens throughout the class, and indeed throughout the school, affects each child.

SUMMARY

Recent laws, especially Public Laws 94-142 and 99-457, have made parent involvement in the education of their children with disabilities mandatory. This concern for parent involvement should carry over to the parents of all children in the school, not only those with disabilities. All parents should feel that they are participating members on an educational team. This requires that all parents should be informed about what is happening to their children and should be involved, to the greatest degree possible, in educational decisions about their children and even in the implementation of those decisions. A long-term working relationship, built upon mutual trust and understanding, can result from an effective program of working with parents in the school.

Social support to parenting behavior and social transmission mechanisms provide guidance to develop family support programs. Stevens (1991) identifies two major implications: *First, family support programs should depend on group parent education strategies to strengthen families' informal social networks and to promote the social support that these networks provide.* Parents' social network relationships and the informational and emotional support they receive can strengthen their child-rearing abilities. Group parent education is an effective strategy in which parents of young children meet with other parents to discuss child-rearing and alternative strategies to interact with and raise children. Such group consultation strategies help parents to build more informal social networks.

Most parent education programs group according to similarity in their children's developmental periods. As a result, these ongoing groups offer an effective setting in which child-rearing information is closely related to the parents' specific concerns.

Middle-income parents enrolled in a two-year, group parent education program sponsored by the Minnesota Early Learning Design (MELD) were found to significantly develop more new friendships with other parents of young children than did parents who were not enrolled in such a parent support program. At the end of the second program year, the participants had more child development knowledge than did nonparticipants (Powell & Lief, 1990).

Second, family support programs should implement the mechanisms of transmission (modeling, coaching, interpreting, evaluating). Although there is no empirical research to support the value of these mechanisms for the social transmission of parenting, they seem to have some value. Family support programs can offer opportunities for groups of parents and children to participate in joint play activities. In these settings, these mechanisms can function most efficiently and parents can have the opportunity to observe each other use alternative play and teaching strategies with their children, and can participate in the strategies of coaching, interpreting, and evaluating. These interpreting and evaluating exchanges can encourage parents to (1) discuss child behavior and its meaning and (2) critique play materials and physical environmental stimuli. These settings facilitate group leaders or parent consultants to encourage mothers to consider alternative play and interactive strategies with their children and to use modeling to demonstrate a specific interactive strategy.

A strong parent program can help extend the learning of children with disabilities beyond the confines of the classroom. It can also help parents of children without disabilities understand how children with disabilities develop, learn, and function. Parents of children with disabilities have the right to know about and approve their children's educational program. Contact with these parents should begin early. Parents may have different reactions to the knowledge that their child has a disability. At different points in their own development, they may be willing and able to participate in the educational programs in different ways and in varying degrees. A range of program alternatives should be available to parents so a proper match can be made between what they can do and what the school offers. Teachers can share information with parents through conferences, newsletters, and informal contacts. They need to provide programs to help parents cope with their children's needs and extend their children's education. Parents need to be helped to become effective program advocates at various levels in the community and effective members of advisory councils. In addition, they need to be provided with a support system responsive to their needs. Parents should be provided opportunities to work in their children's classrooms. Teachers should work together with parents in establishing program goals, then develop activities to achieve these goals. Evaluating the program will help teachers improve it throughout the year as well as plan future parent programs.

REFERENCES

Bandura, A. (1977). *Social learning theory*. Englewood Cliffs, NJ: Prentice-Hall.

Becker, W. C. (1971). *Parents are teachers.* Champaign, IL: Research Press.

Bradley, R. H., Caldwell, B. M., & Rock, S. L. (1988). Home environment and school performance: A ten year follow-up and examination of three models of environmental action. *Child Development, 59*, 852–867.

Bronfenbrenner, U. (1974). *A report on longitudinal evaluations of preschool programs.* Vol. 2: *Is early intervention effective?* Washington, DC: Department of Health, Education, and Welfare.

Cohen, S., & Wills, T. A. (1985). Stress, social support and the buffering hypothesis. *Psychological Bulletin, 98,* 310–357.

Cotterell, J. L. (1986). Work and community influences on the quality of child rearing. *Child Development, 57,* 362–374.

Crnic, K. A., Greenberg, M. T., Ragozin, A. S., Robinson, N. M., & Basham, R. B. (1983). Effects of stress and social support on mothers and preterm and full-term infants. *Child Development, 54,* 209–217.

Dunst, C. J., & Trivette, C. M. (1988). A family systems model of early intervention with handicapped and developmentally at-risk children. In D. R. Powell (Ed.), *Parent education as early childhood intervention: Emerging directions in theory, research and practice* (pp. 131–180). Norwood, NJ: Ablex.

Feiring, C., Fox, N. A., Jaskir, J., & Lewis, M. (1987). The relation between social support, infant risk status, and mother–infant interaction. *Developmental Psychology, 23,* 400–405.

Galinsky, E., & Weissbourd, B. (1992). Family-centered child care. In B. Spodek & O. N. Saracho (Eds.), *Issues in child care. Yearbook in early childhood education,* Vol. 3 (pp. 47–65). New York: Teachers College Press.

Gardner, R. M. B. D. (1973). *The family book about minimal brain dysfunction.* New York: Jason and Son.

Ginott, H. (1965). *Between parent and child.* New York: Avon.

Gordon, I. J., Guinagh, B., & Jester, R. E. (1972). *Child learning through child play.* New York: St. Martin's Press.

Gordon, T. (1970). *Parent effectiveness training.* New York: Wyden.

Gottlieb, B. H., & Pancer, S. M. (1988). Social networks and the transition to parenthood. In G. Y. Michaels & W. Goldberg (Eds.), *The transition to parenthood: Current theory and research* (pp. 235–269). Cambridge, MA: Cambridge University Press.

Granovetter, M. (1974). *Getting a job.* Cambridge, MA: Harvard University Press.

Greenberg, M. T., & Crnic, K. A. (1988). Longitudinal predictors of developmental status and social interaction in premature and full-term infants at age two. *Child Development, 59*(3), 554–570.

Hall, A., & Wellman, B. (1985). Social networks and social support. In S. Cohen & S. L. Same (Eds.), *Social support and health* (pp. 23–42). Orlando: Academic Press.

Heward, W. L., Dardig, J. C., & Rossett, A. (1979). *Working with parents of handicapped children.* Columbus, OH: Merrill.

House, J. S. & Kahn, R. L. (1985). Measures and concepts of social support. In S. Cohen & S. L. Syme (Eds.), *Social support and health* (pp. 83–108). Orlando: Academic Press.

Kagan, S. L., Powell, D. R., Weissbourd, B., & Zigler, E. F. (Eds.) (1987). *America's family support programs.* New Haven: Yale University Press.

Karnes, M. B., & Lee, R. C. (1980). Involving parents in the education of their handicapped children: An essential component of an exemplary program. In M.J. Fine (Ed.), *Handbook on parent education.* New York: Academic Press.

Lillie, D. (1974). Dimensions in parent programs: An overview. In I. J. Grimm (Ed.), *Training parents to teach. Four models.* Chapel Hill, NC: Technical Assistance Development Systems.

Lillie, D. L. (1976). An overview of parent programs. In D. L. Lillie & P. L. Trohanis (Eds.), *Teaching parents to teach.* New York: Walker and Company.

Linde, T. F., & Kopp, T. (1974). *Training retarded babies and preschoolers.* Springfield, IL: Charles C Thomas.

Love, H. D. (1970). *Parental attitudes toward exceptional children.* Springfield, IL: Charles C Thomas.

McCollum, J. A., & Maude, S. P. (1993). Portrait of a changing field: Policy and practice in early childhood special education. In B. Spodek (Ed.), *Handbook of research on the education of young children* (pp. 352–371). New York: Macmillan.

Marholin, D., Siegel, L., & Phillips, D. (1975). Treatment and transfer: A search for empirical procedures. Unpublished. Urbana: University of Illinois.

Powell, D. R., & Lief, K. (1990, October). Information and social support in the transition to parenthood: A study of MELD. Paper presented at the biennial meeting of the Family Resource Coalition, Chicago.

Shearer, M. S., & Shearer, D. E. (1979). Parent involvement. In L. B. Jordan, A. H. Hayden, M. B. Karnes, & M. M. Wood (Eds.), *Early childhood education for exceptional children: A handbook of ideas and exemplary practices* (pp. 208–235). Reston, VA: Council for Exceptional Children.

Sparling, J., & Lewis, I. (1979). *Learning for the first three years.* New York: St. Martin's Press.

Stevens, J. H., Jr. (1988). Social support, locus of control, and parenting in three low-income groups: Black adults, white adults, and black teenagers. *Child Development, 59,* 635–642.

Stevens, J. H., Jr. (1991). Informal social support and parenting: Understanding the mechanisms of support. In B. Spodek & O. N. Saracho (Eds.), *Yearbook in early childhood education* (pp. 152–166). New York: Teachers College Press.

Stevens, J. H., Jr., & Bakeman, R. (1990, March). Continuity in parenting among black teen mothers and grandmothers. Paper presented at the biennial meeting of the Society for Research on Adolescence, Atlanta.

Stokes, T., & Baer, D. M. (1977). An implicit technology of generalization. *Journal of Applied Behavior Analysis, 17,* 349–367.

Vaux, A. (1988). *Social support: Theory, research, and intervention.* New York: Praeger.

Weinraub, M., & Wolf, B. M. (1983). Effects of stress and social supports on mother–child interactions in single- and two-parent families. *Child Development, 54,* 1297–1311.

Weinraub, M., & Wolf, B. (1987). Stress, social supports and parent–child interactions: Similarities and differences in single-parent and two-parent families. In C. F. Z. Boukydis (Ed.), *Research on support for parents and infants in the postnatal period* (pp. 114–138). Norwood, NJ: Ablex.

Weiss, H. B. (1990). State family support and education programs: Lessons from the pioneers. *American Journal of Orthopsychiatry, 59,* 32–48.

Weissbourd, B., & Kagan, S. L. (1990). Family support programs: Catalysts for change. *American Journal of Orthopsychiatry, 59,* 20–31.

Zarling, C. L., Hirsch, B. J., & Landry, S. (1988). Maternal social networks and mother–infant interactions in full term and very low birthweight, preterm infants. *Child Development, 59,* 178–185.

CHAPTER 7

Planning and Organizing for an Integrated Class

CHAPTER OVERVIEW

This chapter describes:

1. Strategies for developing teaching plans.
2. Ways to implement teaching plans.
3. Curriculum materials for children with special needs.
4. Ways of serving children with handicapping conditions.

Creating an integrated classroom that includes children with different abilities and disabilities has been recommended because it is believed that all children can learn best in these settings. All children should participate in the same activities and should be educated in the same manner to the greatest extent possible. To accomplish this, teachers need to identify and adjust those factors in their classrooms that may impede the progress of children with special needs. Teachers also need to continuously evaluate the performance of the children in their classes so that instruction can be modified to focus on changing student needs.

There are no special techniques or magical formulas for including children with disabilities in a classroom. No single method can be effective for all; each child and each classroom situation is truly unique.

PLANNING

Although the ways used to teach most children are effective with many children with disabilities, there are times when programs need to be modified to accommodate a child's needs. One approach to working with children with disabilities is to plan

prescriptively (Haring & Schiefelbusch, 1976; Laycock, 1980). This prescriptive planning may be useful for children with some disabilities, but it needs to be modified for regular classes. This approach has seven steps: (1) assessment, (2) setting objectives, (3) developing a plan, (4) selecting procedures, (5) implementing the program, (6) evaluating learner performance, and (7) revising the program. Many of these steps are the same as those described for developing an Individualized Educational Program (IEP) in chapter 5. The IEP is a written statement of the objectives, content, procedures, and evaluation of the educational program designed for a child with disabilities. IEPs are generally designed for long-range planning. The steps described here are applicable for short-term planning based upon the IEP and using much of the information already accumulated.

Assessment

Through an initial assessment, information is gathered to help the teacher identify what skills and content the child has or has not mastered in different areas of the curriculum. Teachers should review teacher reports; psychological reports; developmental, social, and educational histories; reports of other educational specialists; and possibly medical reports. The teacher might also wish to confer with the child's previous teachers, the parents or guardians, the guidance counselor, the school director or principal, the psychologist, the parent liaison worker or social worker, and the school nurse. Each person may have information that could supplement the information to be found in the school record.

After reviewing this information, the teacher should then gather information about the child's current abilities, using the techniques described in chapter 6. A number of different measures, including formal tests and observation techniques, should be used to provide a more representative picture of the child.

Setting Objectives

Based on the initial assessment, the teacher can specify instructional objectives to serve as intended outcomes. These objectives can relate to social skills or play behaviors as well as to academics. If written in behavioral terms, an instructional objective contains a statement of (1) the expected skills to be achieved, (2) the criterion for success in each skill, and (3) the conditions in which the student will be expected to perform each skill.

A simple objective may be achieved in a single teaching step, whereas a complex one may require a number of steps. Task analysis can be used to break down complex objectives into their component parts. Instruction can then be sequenced, moving from most simple to most complex. Teachers may develop a task analysis by (1) watching a child without a disability perform the task and then analyzing what is observed, (2) performing the task themselves and analyzing what they have done, (3) working backward from the final skills, or (4) brainstorming with colleagues as to the steps involved. Each step in the analysis should be described in specific terms and the teaching tasks should be of approximately equal difficulty. Teachers often find it helpful to work through a sequence of tasks themselves or to have the task analysis reviewed by a colleague in order to locate potential problems before working on it with a child.

Developing a Plan

An educational plan should describe the arrangements to be used to teach specific children or groups of children in a class. Formats for writing lesson plans vary, but most plans contain common elements. Plans can be written on index cards, on charts, or in a teacher's plan book. They can be posted in the room where learning activities will take place if more than one adult will be involved.

Elements of a Lesson Plan

Objectives: Specify learning areas and goals.

Setting: Describe the situation in which the lesson(s) will be taught (e.g., the number of other children included, the time of day, the other activities that will take place while the lesson is being taught).

Materials: Identify the resources needed and gather them ahead of time.

Procedures: Describe who or what will present the material, how it will be presented, and what teaching tactics might be used.

Evaluation: Describe methods to be used to assess outcomes.

SELECTING INSTRUCTIONAL PROCEDURES

Instructional procedures include both teaching techniques and instructional materials. There are a number of different teaching techniques that teachers can use with individuals, as needed. Some of the techniques that are used to encourage learning among children with disabilities are direct instruction, verbal instructions, modeling, manual guidance, prompting, fading, shaping, practicing, and generalizing.

Direct instruction involves a structured lesson to present skills or concepts directly to children (Gersten & Carnine, 1986; Gersten, Woodward, & Darch, 1986). Educators such as Benjamin Bloom (1981) assume that direct instruction is appropriate for at-risk students in the primary grades. Educators supporting Bloom's assumption argue that direct instruction assists students to develop competence in academic subjects, which will help them to benefit from any type of later instruction. Young students who feel competent may approach learning in a more positive way. Whereas educators such as Brophy and Good (1986) believe that teachers who use direct instruction can enhance academic growth, other educators have criticized this technique (e.g., Gersten & Carnine, 1986). Direct instruction may stifle students, and its effects may dissipate after students are left on their own. Schweinhart, Weikart, and Larner (1986) found that direct instruction in preschool did accelerate academic achievement during the elementary years; however, the children in the program with an early academic focus had difficulties in later life, especially in the social domain.

Less able learners may function better if lessons are broken down into a sequence of simplified units, and teachers or instructional materials exercise control over minute-to-minute activities and provide continuous feedback. However, this instructional strategy is not appropriate for more able learners (Snow, 1982, 1986; Snow & Lohman, 1984).

Verbal instructions such as "Place the pictures in the right order," "Begin each sentence with a capital letter," or "Match the object with the appropriate picture" tell children how to perform a task. These instructions should contain the information necessary to perform the required skill and should be given when the learner is attentive. There are times when verbal instructions alone are inadequate. Demonstrating a skill, perhaps while providing a verbal explanation, can be used along with other techniques.

The teacher may demonstrate a skill and then ask the child to imitate the performance. This is called *modeling.* Skills can be modeled by the teacher or other children, or a more permanent model can be provided through illustrations (e.g., copying the teacher's arrangement of colored blocks or copying a name from a printed name card). Modeling can occur directly, as when the teacher demonstrates a self-help skill, or less directly, as when the teacher shows a film, reads a story, or gives a puppet show. The child should be expected to pay attention while the skill is being modeled; the demonstration should be short and simple, and the model should be a valued individual.

In providing *manual guidance* the teacher physically guides the learner in performing a skill. Manual guidance is effective when children have difficulty in understanding directions or have motor deficits, as do children who are orthopedically impaired or who have cerebral palsy. It helps if children experience how it actually feels to accomplish the skill to be learned. For example, the teacher may stand behind a child, take the back of his hands, move his fingers to grasp the top of his trousers, and apply an upward pull to complete pulling up his trousers.

When using manual guidance, teachers should apply gentle, continuous pressure in guiding the child. If the child resists, stop for a moment to help him or her relax, or try some siple movement such as raising and lowering the child's arms. It is also important to give the child a verbal cue before beginning the guidance procedure, combining verbal instructions with manual guidance and encouraging the child to associate the two together. After a while, manual guidance can be gradually removed or limited to only a small part of the entire skill.

Prompts (or cues) signal the child to perform a certain skill in a particular situation. Verbal prompts are short statements—usually an abbreviated form of instruction—that tell children what to do. For instance, a teacher can prompt a child to move scissors correctly by saying "open–shut," or to build high block buildings by saying, "Steady it." Indirect verbal prompts are verbal statements or questions that imply a specific action. For instance, if a child is in a warm classroom wearing a heavy coat, the teacher might say, "Isn't it warm here?" or "Aren't heavy jackets for outside?" Gestural prompts are nonverbal signals such as pointing to, touching, or tapping the correct answer; waving hello or goodbye; or shaking one's head to indicate yes or no. Visual prompts, which are pictorial or symbolic cues, include such techniques as using books of exaggerated size to draw attention to the book area, or placing the correct choice in a discrimination task closest to the child.

Prompts should be gradually removed so that students can function under natural conditions. This is sometimes called *fading*. For example, beginning handwriting programs commonly require students to trace letters, then to write letters following a dotted line, then to write letters when only the beginning points are provided, and finally to write letters when no extra cues are provided.

Shaping is a procedure that builds on the successive approximation to some skill, for example, reinforcing a student for sitting in place for progressively longer periods of time. In shaping block building, a teacher might first encourage a child to place one block upon the other. Later the child might be encouraged to build enclosures; then more complex building could be encouraged. To shape legible writing, a teacher might begin by expecting a child to produce letters that approximate the correct form. Gradually, the teacher adjusts the criteria so that eventually only letters of the correct size, form, and slant are accepted.

Practice (or drill) involves the opportunity to perform a task repeatedly in order to increase the quality and fluency of a skill. For example, students can practice to increase their accuracy and speed in reading sight words or math facts.

Children should be helped to generalize (or transfer) the skills taught in one situation to other situations. Without such *generalization,* gains made in a classroom or treatment setting are of limited value. Many skills generalize naturally for most individuals without any emphasis placed on the process. A number of basic techniques to enhance transfer of training can be used. If children learn behaviors that will be rewarded by others, these will probably transfer. Teachers can also create behavior traps—situations that allow elements in the natural environment to support learning. Teaching in different settings and with different people involved is also effective.

Another method is to support incompatible behavior—that is, any behavior that is physically impossible to emit at the same time as an undesirable behavior.

IMPLEMENTING A PLAN

Just as no two teachers will plan the same way, so no two teachers will implement a plan in the same way. There are, however, some common elements in all teaching. The suggestions that follow for teaching young children with disabilities should prove useful.

Suggestions for Teaching Young Children with Disabilities

1. *Implement the plan as developed as much as possible.* Teachers often function spontaneously in a classroom. Nevertheless, they should use the plans they have developed even though modifications may be needed. If a plan has been well designed, it should allow for flexibility when translated into action.

2. *Be certain that the learner is attentive.* Some children with disabilities have difficulty concentrating on learning tasks for extended periods of time. Teachers must help such children stay on task. Having a variety of activities available by which to achieve the same goal often helps.

3. *Encourage constructive divergent thinking.* Constructive imagination is a worthwhile educational goal and may provide the foundation for adult creativity. Most young children are naturally creative. All children should be encouraged to develop productive divergent thinking skills.

4. *Offer opportunities for the child to make choices.* Children might be able to choose what is to be done, when it should be done, where it should be done, and sometimes whether or not it should be done. Teachers must, of course, monitor children's choices to be certain they are neither overwhelmed nor underchallenged.

5. *Be consistent.* Children generally learn better when they know what to expect. Clearly specifying the rules or standards for classroom behavior and the consequences for noncompliance with those standards helps avoid problems.

6. *Actively involve the child in learning tasks.* Young children, especially those with disabilities, need to be actively involved in learning. Give children opportunities to manipulate materials, ask questions, and engage in discussions, dramatic play, group investigations, and learning games.

7. *Observe the child closely.* The teacher must be observant of the child's approach to a task, watching for wavering of attention or any blocks to progress.

8. *Give specific feedback.* Provide information about the child's performance. The sooner feedback is provided and the more specific it is, the more learning will be facilitated.

9. *Support the child.* Support and reinforcement can increase desirable social skills in children as well as increase preacademic and academic performance.

Several current textbooks on early education for children with disabilities provide additional guidelines for working with these children, including those by Allen (1992); Cartwright, Cartwright, and Ward (1989); Cook, Tessier, and Armbruster (1987); Lerner, Mardell-Czudnowski, and Goldenberg (1987); Neisworth, Herb, Bagnato, Cartwright, and Laub (1980); Peterson (1987); Raver (1991), and Safford (1989).

Allocating Resources

In preparing to implement a plan, teachers first concern themselves to allocation resources and to organize their room and the day for instruction. Many prekindergarten and kindergarten teachers, along with some primary teachers, arrange their room into activity or learning centers, allowing children to choose from a number of activities during a work time. Schedules for these classes are organized into large blocks of time and children may move from activity to activity, rather than have specific periods when all children work on the same subject. Such an arrangement is especially useful in an integrated classroom where children with varying strengths and needs are working together.

Helping Children Follow Directions

Teachers give more than 200 directions daily. Attention and listening skills are important in helping students understand and follow directions. Teachers need to help their students understand and follow directions (Salend, 1990). Instructions should provide students with information concerning the task's rationale, content, type of assistance (e.g., aides, adults, peers), time of completion, format, and mode of evaluation. Teachers can list the materials they will need on a task card to help them complete the assignment (Cohen & de Bettencourt, 1988). Children need to know where and when to complete a task, and guidance must be provided about what they can do if they finish early (Salend, 1990).

Children should be given specific directions that are reviewed orally with visual aids, such as a chalkboard, overhead projector, or chart. Teachers need to simplify directions into brief meaningful statements for those students who continue to have difficulty following directions (Wallace, Cohen, & Polloway, 1987). Teachers should try to limit their directions to no more than two instructions at a time. The children can work on one part of the activity and check with the teacher before continuing to the next stage (Jones & Jones, 1990).

The *rebus system,* which uses simple pictures to depict certain words in a narrative, can help students understand written directions (Cohen & de Bettencourt, 1988). Recurring direction words and their corresponding rebus are placed conveniently in the classroom where all students are able to see it (see Figure 7.1).

Some children with disabilities have difficulty understanding instructions, manipulating materials, making decisions, and completing assigned tasks. Children with learning disabilities may not have mastered a strategy for allocating time among tasks

Written Directions	Pictorial Directions	Written Directions	Pictorial Directions
circle		read	
look		think	
listen		book	
write		mark	
cut		page	
color			

FIGURE 7.1   Sample of a rebus system

or designed sufficient time to complete tasks. These students need assistance in organizing content, materials, and time in a meaningful way. Shields and Heron (1989) described antecedent and consequence strategies that can be used to help children improve the organizational and time management skills they need. *Antecedent* strategies set the occasion for the students to become more organized, whereas *consequence* strategies reinforce demonstrated organizational skill. Antecedent strategies include assignment logs and charts, workstations, color coding materials, times, and guided notes (Heron, 1987). Consequence strategies include providing reinforcement and feedback, and maintaining home–school communication (Heron & Harris, 1987).

Evaluating the Program

Program evaluation should be planned along with the goals and objectives, curriculum, and instructional methodology. A program must have evidence of its effectiveness. Evaluation of overall program success requires

1. An assessment of the program's achievement of its overall goals, specifying the criteria that were used to assess the program's effectiveness; and
2. a description of assessment instruments and information used to assess the program's effectiveness. (Peterson, 1987)

Information should be collected on a regular basis to determine whether the instruction has been successful. If the information gathered at the end is similar to the initial assessment data, then conclusions concerning student learning can easily be made. Continuous observation and assessment of a child's performance helps the teacher determine the effectiveness of an instructional program and facilitates adapting the program to meet the child's changing needs.

Revising the Program

Any planned program, once implemented, requires some modification. In some cases, only minor refinements are needed; in others, the teacher must redesign the program. Adjustments are made based on evaluation of the program as it has been implemented.

ORGANIZING FOR INSTRUCTION

Although a good part of planning involves designing teaching and learning strategies, planning also deals with providing the resources needed to implement those strategies. The teacher must look at the basic resources in the classroom—time and space—and determine how best to use them since they are available only in limited quantity. Materials must be gathered and arranged. Furniture and basic equipment are generally provided from the start of the school year and seldom are augmented. These may need to be arranged in different ways at different times to serve different purposes. Adequate supplies and human resources must also be found. School resources can be supplemented: Parents can be asked to contribute materials, some of which they might otherwise discard, and volunteers and even the pupils themselves can supplement the teacher by helping to provide instruction. Provision of resources often must be planned well ahead of time and teachers must think about how best to use them.

Room Arrangements

The way teachers arrange the physical elements of a classroom can either support or interfere with their plans. Most classrooms have certain basic attributes that limit what can be done. The size of a room, its lighting, placement of windows, availability of water, and accessibility of bathroom facilities are things a teacher cannot change.

Rooms may also have permanent built-in storage areas, bulletin boards, and other things that also cannot be changed but that may be worked around.

Generally, schools provide basic classroom furniture including tables, chairs, desks, shelves, cabinets, and whatever else is considered essential. Painting easels, a phonograph, and a tape recorder may also be provided along with books, paper, art supplies, and physical education or climbing equipment. Preprimary classrooms generally have a good deal of play material and manipulatives as well. Teachers can supplement these basic supplies during the school year by ordering additional materials and by soliciting contributions from parents, businesses, and community groups. Unfortunately, teachers themselves are often forced to provide some of the resources not supplied by the school; those might include pictures, small rugs, pillows, soft furniture, plants, and even small animals.

Teachers of young children may not know ahead of time that a child with a disability will be enrolled in class or what that child will be like. Yet they must be ready to modify their teaching when such a child is enrolled or identified. The teacher needs to check the classroom to make sure it is adequate to serve that child's needs and that no unnecessary obstacles are present. Traffic patterns may need to be assessed so that free movement throughout the classroom is possible without some children interfering with the work of others. Access to stored supplies, water, cleanup supplies, and toilet facilities should also be checked. The teacher should also see that there is no unnecessary clutter in the room. Although clutter often is of minimal significance to normal children, it can be distracting to many children with disabilities. Visual clutter makes it difficult to focus on important visual elements; auditory

clutter may make it hard to hear significant sounds; and physical clutter may interfere with children's movements around the room.

Care should be taken to ensure that the room is safe and meets all children's needs. The room arrangement should be kept simple, especially at the beginning of the year. As the children get used to the room and learn to handle a more complex environment, the teacher can gradually increase the amount and range of materials provided and the number of activities available.

It is important that teachers and children establish and enforce safety rules. For example, crutches should be kept close to the child who needs them, and wheelchairs, crutches, canes, or other equipment must be kept out of traffic areas. In addition, children who are orthopedically or visually impaired may accidentally bump into things or people. A wheelchair can easily swing or roll to the wrong place. Running in the classroom should be prohibited; this will protect not only the visually impaired but all other children as well.

The availability of adequate light, the color of walls and equipment, and the sound-absorbing qualities of the room need to be carefully considered along with variety and flexibility. Storage space and locker facilities for personal belongings and classroom materials and equipment should be accessible to all children.

Placement of furniture and equipment that at first seemed good may prove to have certain disadvantages once a child with a disability becomes part of the class. Such children may, for example, need periods of isolation if social or sensory distractions keep them from successfully dealing with schoolwork. A change in furniture arrangement—using bookshelves to partially screen an area, for example—might provide a degree of isolation while allowing the teacher to easily supervise activities.

Sometimes furniture needs minor modification such as placing crutch tips on table legs so they will not slip. Sometimes furniture needs to be rearranged—for example, placing a desk for a child with a visual disability in a spot where there will be adequate light from a window or fixture without undue glare. And sometimes new furniture or equipment will need to be procured: perhaps a table high enough for a child in a wheelchair to use, or a tape recorder to be used primarily by a single child.

Outdoor spaces for large-muscle activity must be provided to meet the needs of all children. Equipment and activities should be adapted for children with disabilities to allow them to participate in as many outdoor activities as possible. Health and safety considerations are particularly important for those who are blind, deaf, physically disabled, or mildly retarded, and care should be taken to identify hazards and avoid possible accidents within and around the school.

Some children with orthopedic impairments, especially those with poor sitting balance, need special seating arrangements. A chair with arms or with sides high enough to protect the child from falling to either side might need to be used. A high-backed chair will support the child's trunk and keep the head upright. Some children may be unable to sit on the floor without support. A minimal amount of support can be provided by sitting them against a wall or removing the legs of a chair and using its seat and back on the floor.

Once a room has been set up, it is usually advisable to make as few basic changes as possible in the arrangement. Children who are visually impaired need to become oriented to a classroom when school starts and must be reoriented whenever changes are made; changing the room too often can be confusing. Continual rearrangement of space can also be distracting and may especially upset children with behavior disorders, who depend on the regularity of life to provide the necessary structure for their behavior.

Learning Centers

Many primary classes are organized with desks or tables set in rows or semicircles. This allows all the children to focus on the teacher and allows the teacher to supervise all of the children at the same time. Such an arrangement makes good sense when everyone in the classroom is doing the same thing at the same time under the teacher's direct supervision. In many prekindergartens, kindergartens, and primary classes in which programs are more individualized, however, teachers arrange their rooms into learning centers.

A learning center is a section of a room set aside for a particular kind of learning activity. It is at least partially segregated from other sections of the room so that children can work within the center with some degree of isolation. Learning centers support individualization. Different activities can take place in different centers with children working individually or in small groups on individual projects, functioning in their own styles and operating at their own paces. Learning centers often are helpful in mainstreaming children in a classroom since the child with a disability can work alongside other children without necessarily engaging in the same activity. Thus, learning centers allow classrooms to be child centered, rather than teacher centered; they help individualize learning and allow for independent, active participation of the children (Blake, 1977).

In prekindergarten and kindergarten classes, there may be a dramatic play center, a construction center, an arts and crafts center, a manipulative materials center, a library center, a music center, and a display center. The floor plan of a classroom depicted in Figure 7.2 contains such centers. In primary classes, with their more academic orientation, centers may be organized around subject matter areas: a math center, a reading and writing center, a science center, an arts center, and a social studies center. Learning centers can also focus on topics that cut across subject matter areas: an environmental studies center, a school newspaper center, or a center for studying the community.

Each center should be provided with the materials and resources necessary to support active learning. Adequate space should be provided as well. A block building center will contain wooden building blocks of varying sizes and shapes, along with toy cars, miniature people, and other accessories that enable children to construct multifaceted structures. A sociodramatic play center can contain dress-up clothes and props to support play around a specific theme. Providing food containers, a toy cash register, paper bags, and a few baskets will encourage supermarket play, and white aprons or jackets, wooden tongue depressors, a stethoscope, and the like could encourage hospital play.

Many centers are designed for open-ended activities, but they can also be designed so that more prescribed activities develop. A library center might have a

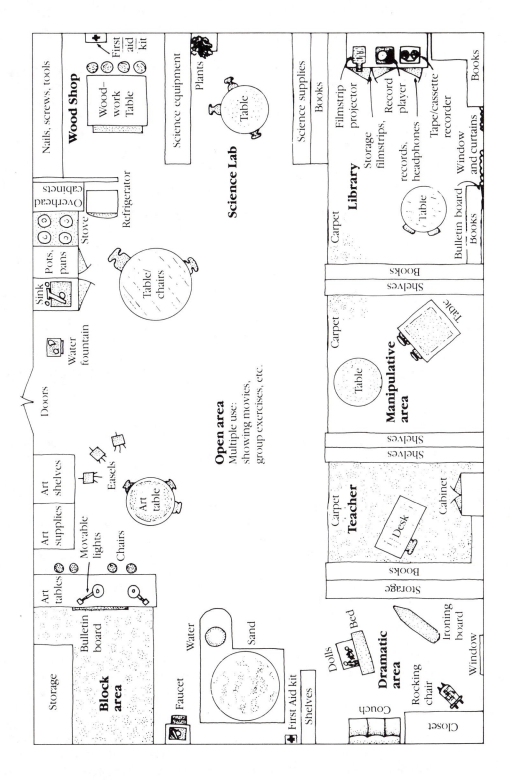

FIGURE 7.2 Floor plan for a classroom

variety of books in it to encourage children to read. It could also have a tape recorder or paper and pencils available for children to use to record their descriptions and comments about what they have read and to write short reports. A math center might have manipulative materials for counting and measuring, as well as sets of task cards upon which are written directions for specific activities in which children should engage. If children cannot read, the directions on the cards can consist of pictures or rebus writing, in which words and pictures are combined. No matter how directions are provided, the centers should be designed so that the learning activities engage children and so that some record can be made of children's activities and learning. Checklists such as those described in chapter 3 are useful for that.

Learning centers may be designed to help children develop skills, for discovery/ enrichment, to develop listening abilities, or to enhance creativity (Gearheart, Weishahn, & Gearhart, 1988). *Skill centers* permit students to practice skills in areas such as arithmetic computation facts, spelling, alphabetizing, and defining vocabulary. *Discovery/enrichment centers* use a variety of learning activities to expand students' knowledge in subjects such as science and mathematics. *Listening centers* are designed to provide students with instruction or recreation through listening activities. *Creativity centers* usually emphasize activities such as arts and crafts, music, creative writing, and poetry.

Salend (1990) offered the following guidelines for developing learning centers:

1. Identify students' academic levels, abilities, interests, and needs.
2. Determine related objectives.
3. Offer students several activities that permit them to explore new skills and practice previously acquired skills.
4. Develop appropriate materials that students can use independently or in small groups.
5. Teach students to work at learning centers.
6. Offer students directions that are easily understood and guides on the use of the materials and accompanying media.
7. Explain to students the appropriate times for using the center and the number of students that the center can accommodate at one time.
8. Monitor student progress and change materials and activities as students master new skills.

Activities should also be designed so that children can function with limited input from the teacher. When not otherwise engaged, the teacher can circulate among the various centers or focus on a group of children while others in the class are busy with their own independent activities. This means that materials should be readily accessible and that each center should be designed for easy cleanup. Keeping materials in tote trays or plastic shoeboxes is useful, as is marking shelves to show where each set of materials belongs. Children have to be given directions and practice in using learning centers when they begin. Teachers might want to start out with only one learning center at the beginning of the school year, then expand when children indicate they are capable of their independent use.

Instructional Materials

Instructional materials include manipulative materials, worksheets, reading or math textbooks, and play materials. Since most early childhood programs do not have an abundance of funds, materials must be purchased wisely. When choosing materials, teachers must consider learner characteristics, teachers concerns, and cost-effectiveness, such as those listed below.

Questions to Ask in Selecting Materials
Learner Characteristics
1. Is the material compatible with program objectives?
2. Is the material appropriate for the learner's interest, age, and grade level?
3. Does the material require prerequisite skills that the intended learner has?
4. Is the material compatible with the child's strengths and needs? For example, if the child learns best through auditory stimuli and responds best through verbal answers, does the material play to these strengths?
5. Is the specific medium of the material (e.g., activity cards, games, filmstrips) appropriate for the student?
6. Is the material well made and safe?
7. Is the material flexible, permitting self-pacing by the learner?
8. Is the material appropriate for learners at different skill levels?
9. Is the material attractive and relevant to the learner's interests and background?

Teacher Concerns
1. Does the material require specialized training and skills for the teacher to use it effectively?
2. Does the material fit within the existing classroom structure?
3. Are accompanying manuals or other support resources helpful?
4. Does the material include a suitable evaluation component?
5. Does the material demand too much teacher time for preparation, supervision, and evaluation?
6. Does the material portray any race, sex, or handicapping condition in a negative or stereotypical manner?

Cost-Effectiveness
1. Is there hidden cost in the material? Does the cost compare favorably to costs of similar materials on the market?
2. Is the material durable and likely to give reasonable service over time?
3. Can enough students benefit from the material to justify the expense involved?

If no appropriate commercial materials are available, the teacher might be able to adapt materials used in the past or construct his or her own materials.

Special Curriculum Materials

Many preschool curriculum packages are currently available. Details on each curriculum model, appropriate assessment instruments for each model, and evaluation techniques for each model are available (see Bagnato & Neisworth, 1981; Fewell & Kelly, 1983). Specific questions related to the decision-making process are

1. How must objects be combined?
2. How must teaching be done?
3. How must time be allocated?
4. Are activities child-initiated or adult-initiated?
5. Does learning occur mainly through child–environment and child–child interactions or teacher–child interactions?
6. Is the teacher or environment the major source of reinforcement? (Linder, 1983)

Regular and resource room special education teachers use a variety of curriculum materials, often commercially produced, to supplement the regular instructional material available in the classroom. Some of the more widely used programs for children with disabilities in integrated early education settings are presented here.

The *Portage Guide to Early Education* (Bluma et al., 1976) is a product of the Portage Project, a First Chance program begun in 1969 to train parents to teach their handicapped children in the home. The original target population was preschoolers (from birth to age 6) with disabilities who lived in rural areas of Wisconsin and would be educated at home. In 1976 the *Portage Guide* was expanded to accommodate children with disabilities in Head Start, kindergarten, and primary classes.

The *Portage Guide* consists of a developmental checklist of 450 skills in social, cognitive, language, self-help, and motor domains, and a set of curriculum cards (color-coded by domain) that match each skill. Each curriculum card describes the skill to be taught and suggests materials and activities to assist in teaching it. When a child has successfully learned a skill, the teacher presents the next skill on the developmental checklist. Activity charts describe the goals to be achieved, how often skills are to be practiced, and the types of rewards to be used.

LAP (Learning Accomplishments Profile) (Sanford, 1974), according to its developer, is suitable for both normal and developmentally delayed children. The curriculum was developed by the Chapel Hill Training Project at the University of North Carolina and consists of six skill domains—gross and fine motor, social, self-help, cognitive, and language skills.

LAP materials include two paperback books, the *Learning Accomplishments Profile* and the *Manual for Use of the Learning Accomplishments Profile,* that list a series of developmental behaviors, instructions for assessing and recording these behaviors, and lesson plans for 44 weeks of instruction. Also available is a *Planning Guide for Preschool Children,* an early LAP for children birth through 31 months, a book of learning activities for children 12 to 72 months, and a planning guide, based on Bloom's (1956) taxonomy of educational objectives, for preschoolers who are gifted. Both the *Portage Guide* and the LAP materials contain checklists that can be used for criterion-referenced evaluation.

DISTAR (Direct Instructional System for Teaching and Remediations) (Engle-mann et al., 1974) was developed to address the educational needs of children who are at risk of future educational failure because they lack language skills essential to success in school (Stallings & Stipek, 1986). It is a curriculum for teaching arithmetic, reading, and language skills. DISTAR provides a sequenced curriculum with intensive oral drill in verbal and logical patterns. The general instructional strategy is that of teaching a rule followed by application of that rule. A verbal formula is learned by rote and then applied to a series of analogous examples of increasing difficulty. The main characteristics of the DISTAR method are fast-paced instruction; reduced off-task behavior; a strong emphasis on verbal responses; carefully planned, small-step instructional units; and heavy work demands requiring children to concentrate for up to 20 minutes per lesson. DISTAR is a sequenced curriculum and a rigidly controlled instructional process that is taught using direct instruction.

In examining the combined use of direct instruction strategies and the language emphasis of the DISTAR reading program, Sexton (1989) found that DISTAR was a successful means to develop school-based language. However, the results of the effects of the DISTAR reading program in relation to language achievement have been inconclusive (Sexton, 1989).

GOAL (Game Oriented Activities for Learning) (Karnes, 1972, 1973) uses a psycholinguistic model (derived from the Illinois Test of Psycholinguistic Abilities) to guide language instruction. Since inadequate language skills represent one of the greatest problems for the young handicapped child, verbalizations in conjunction with manipulation of concrete materials are considered to be the most effective means of establishing new language responses. A game format (card packs; lotto games; models and miniatures; and sorting, matching, and classifying games) is used to create situations in which verbal responses can be made in a productive, meaningful context without resorting to rote learning. If a child is unable to make a verbal response, the teacher supplies an appropriate model. When the child begins to initiate personal responses, the teacher has an opportunity to correct, modify, and expand the verbalization. GOAL is designed to be used in three 20-minute structured periods throughout the schoolday.

Other special instructional programs include the following:

The RADEA Program (Walling, 1976) is designed to increase the adaptive behaviors of children between the developmental ages of birth and 7 years. The program concentrates on developing specific information-processing skills including auditory and visual perception, perceptual-motor, oral language, and functional living skills. Each area of the curriculum is analyzed into sequenced component tasks. Materials include a teacher's manual, task-activity cards, daily progress charts, individual progress profiles, test scoring sheets, picture cards, and recorded cassettes to use in auditory training.

Project PAR Sequential Curriculum for Early Learning (Cole & Stevenson, 1976) is designed primarily for children 4 to 6 years of age with minimal learning difficulties. The intent is to help prevent academic failure and to prepare the slow learner for successful placement in a regular mainstreamed classroom. PAR contains a card file of classroom activities and color-coded pages of activities designed to promote developmental skills in cognitive, physical, social, and emotional areas. The curriculum also comes with a comprehensive planning guide and an evaluation form that help facilitate record keeping.

School before Six: A Diagnostic Approach (Hodgen, Koetter, LaForie, McCord, & Schramm, 1974) focuses on the needs and strengths of children 3 to 5 years of age, in the language, socioemotional, gross, fine, and perceptual motor domains. A discussion is presented on problems typically shown by children in each domain along with a normal developmental sequence of skills. Diagnostic procedures, detailed directions for instructional tasks, simple recording forms, and suggestions for teaching are also provided.

The *COMP Curriculum and Activity Manual* (Willoughby-Hulb, Neisworth, Laub, Hunt, & Llewellyn, 1980) is a behaviorally based curriculum providing sequenced objectives for children from birth through age 5 in communication, self-care, motor, and problem-solving areas. Activities and teaching strategies for each objective are suggested, along with evaluation methods and forms for recording children's progress.

Curricular Programming for Young Handicapped Children—Project First Chance (Bos, 1980) covers five skill areas—body management, self-care, communication, preacademics, and socialization—for children with disabilities between $2\frac{1}{2}$ and $6\frac{1}{2}$ years of age who do not have severe visual or hearing impairments. Individual and group-oriented activities are presented by skill area. Each activity specifies a behavioral objective, prerequisite skills, and a description of teaching materials and recording procedures.

Learning Abilities: Diagnostic and Instructional Procedures for Specific Learning Disabilities (Adams et al., 1972) is designed for mainstreamed preschool and kindergarten children with learning disabilities, emotional disturbance, mental retardation, physical handicaps, hearing impairments, or language delays. The curriculum is designed to aid classroom teachers in identifying a child's strengths and in planning individualized instructional programs. Each program contains specific objectives, suggested classroom materials, suggested evaluation procedures, and progress record sheets.

The *Cognitively Oriented Curriculum* (Weikart, Rogers, Adcock, & McClelland, 1971) is a Piaget-based program for children 3 and 4 years of age of varying backgrounds. Activities are presented for each of four content areas—classification, seriation, temporal relations, and spatial relations. An introduction to Piagetian theory and an outline of developmental stages are included along with instructions for using the curriculum. An activity guide gives examples of activities organized according to levels of symbolization (concrete object level, index level, symbol level, and sign level) and levels of operation (motor level and verbal level).

An Experimental Curriculum for Young Mentally Retarded Children (Connor & Talbot, 1970) provides programming in seven areas of development—self-help, social, intellectual, manipulative, imaginative, creative expression, and motor skill areas—for preschool children who are educably mentally retarded. The curriculum guide presents objectives, teaching procedures, and activity ideas for each developmental area, all organized according to developmentally sequenced levels. Suggestions are also provided for programming in different settings.

The *Wabash Guide to Early Developmental Training* (Tilton, Liske, &

Bousland, 1977) covers the motor, cognitive, language, self-care, and number concepts skill areas for infants to school-age children. This curriculum contains sequenced objectives, record forms, equipment lists, and detailed descriptions of teaching strategies and activities.

Learning Language at Home (Karnes, 1977) is a parent-oriented curriculum for normal children 3 to 5 years of age or for children with disabilities at this developmental level. The intent is to train parents to use gamelike activities to interact with their children and support their language development. The activities, based on the Illinois Test of Psycholinguistic Abilities, are sequenced according to difficulty. Each activity contains an objective, a list of materials needed, a step-by-step procedure, and related criterion activities. Additional suggestions for stimulating language development and assessing child progress are described in an accompanying manual.

A range of other organized teacher materials is also available. Lerner, Mardell-Czudnowski, and Goldenberg (1987) provide an extensive listing of many of these, with brief descriptions of each. These are classified into the areas of perceptual–motor, concepts, communications, social-affective, and comprehensive learning materials.

Scheduling

The way activities are organized throughout the day may need to be modified when children with disabilities are integrated into a regular classroom. Since some of these children require more time to get set for learning tasks and to complete them than do their peers, the daily schedule needs to be flexible. If learning centers are established, as suggested above, then the day can be organized into large blocks of time during which children alternate among a number of different learning tasks. This avoids the problem of some children having to wait for others to complete a task before moving on to new work. It also allows children to get started on learning tasks at varying times during the day, which permits the teacher to use time more freely, working with children when they need help rather than ushering all of the children through activities together. The more flexible the teacher is with use of time, the more individualized the instruction can be, providing for the learning needs of all children in the class.

Cleanup may present problems in an integrated classroom, with some children needing special help or extra time. Children with disabilities may find it difficult to put materials away properly. Instruction and demonstrations in cleanup procedures often are helpful. Pairing a child with a disability with a child without disabilities at cleanup is also useful.

Classroom schedules should take into account the fact that some children with disabilities are removed from class for special instruction or therapy during the school day. It is often possible to arrange schedules so that these children are not removed from their regular class during times that the classroom teacher deems most important. This is especially important when a child is doing particularly well in learning activities, or during periods that support the greatest social integration within the class. Both the classroom teacher and the specialist have to be flexible in scheduling to provide the most appropriate educational programs.

Transitions

Transitions refer to times between different activities. During transition times, children usually put away the materials they are using for that particular activity and replace them with the set of materials they are going to use for the next activity. There is a period of "wait" time, which can make a difference between a pleasant, well-run day and a potentially unpleasant environmental chaos. Teachers need to plan transitions to keep a good management system in the classroom.

Teachers need to plan for the lapse of time between the end of one activity and beginning of another activity. This lapse occurs as a result of the need to clean up and put things away from one activity while preparing for the next. When a large-group activity is being organized, time may also be spent repeating directions, waiting for everyone to find the right materials, and getting the entire group's attention. The more transitions in a schedule, the less time is available for teaching (McCoy & Prehm, 1987).

During transition times, teachers need to establish a few simple rules. Let the students know the specific time for stopping one activity and for beginning the next. A verbal message may be sufficient, but an additional signal (such as the sound of a musical instrument) may be necessary when students are working in small groups. Some students may need additional help. A child with a hearing impairment may need

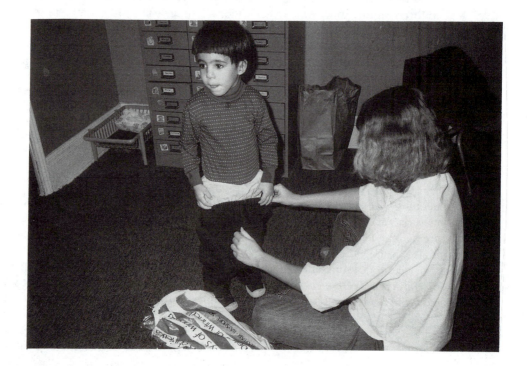

a more obvious clue to know that a transition is taking place. That child may need a slight tap on the shoulder or some physical signal to know that it is transition time. For the child who has insufficient language skills to understand the signal, teachers may need to model the elicited behavior.

Coordinating a Team Effort

When teachers become involved in educating children with disabilities, they must begin to become a part of a team. From the beginning of the identification process, the classroom teacher must team up with others on behalf of all children. Identification and assessment strategies require competencies far beyond those of the typical teacher. In fact, no one person can provide all the services necessary for working with children with disabilities. Only by pooling knowledge and skills can the quest for the most appropriate education for these children come to fruition. In addition, the due process requirements of such programs specify that parents as well as children be involved in decision making and in implementing the educational program.

The actual membership of a team may vary from school to school. The school administrator—whether principal or director—may serve as captain of the team, identifying appropriate team members, coordinating the efforts of all, providing the backup to facilitate the team effort; or he or she may serve in a less active role. In addition, a range of specialists might be involved: psychologists, social workers, speech and language specialists, health professionals, special educators, social workers, parent-liaison workers, and others who might have a contribution to make.

Each person on the team will see the child's problem from his or her own perspective. The specialized knowledge that allows each person to contribute to the team also provides the perspective from which the child is seen and the diagnosis is made.

Early childhood education has always been an interdisciplinary field with a commitment to the education of the whole child. An understanding of the child as a complete human being is basic to a program concerned with each area of development and learning. Classroom teachers should not be intimidated by the specialized knowledge that other team members may bring to the school setting. Each specialist has in-depth knowledge about a limited field, yet each lacks the perspective that the generalist teacher can bring. It is the teacher who has a sense of the whole child and who sees the way the child functions in a variety of situations, under different challenges, and in different social and physical settings. The understanding that comes from this total knowledge must temper any judgment that arises from knowledge of any single attribute of the child. The classroom teacher makes a major contribution in any decisions that the team arrives at concerning the most appropriate educational program for a child with disabilities.

The team continues to work on behalf of the child with disabilities well beyond the point when an individualized educational program (IEP) is developed, although not every member of the team will maintain the same level of involvement. Although the classroom teacher may have primary responsibility for that child's education, it is important that communication continue between teacher and specialists so that the efforts of all can be well coordinated. A special educator may also serve as a resource person to the teacher, making suggestions regarding instructional strategies, helping the teacher collect information on learning and behavior, providing supplementary material, and responding to requests the teacher might make. The resource teacher might also help with referrals for services beyond those available in the school.

Along with the positive benefits of working as a team, there are costs. Teachers who work within a team can feel they lose some of their autonomy and flexibility of action. Decisions are not made by them alone: They must consult with others, justify their positions, and possibly make compromises. In addition, the process of communication requires time for team members to speak with one another, to plan together, and to record their actions. Conflicts can arise and will require attention if they are to be resolved. The leadership qualities of the school administrator may be tested in these situations, as he or she responds to a need to provide additional resources, to use interpersonal skills to clear up differences, and generally to facilitate the work of all involved while protecting the integrity of each team member.

Even with the involvement of many people, classroom teachers may feel that the burden and responsibility for the child with a disability is primarily theirs. In a way this is true, because in the long run, what happens between these children, their peers, and their teachers in the regular classroom during the day will have the greatest impact on that child's education. Teaching continues to be a lonely profession, but there are things that can be done to make it less lonely. Teachers can look for others to assume some of the teaching tasks in the classroom. When teacher's aides or assistants are available, they can share some of the burden; volunteers can also help, and many teachers have found that other children in the class can assume some of the responsibilities for instructing the children.

SERVING CHILDREN WITH DISABILITIES

In many public schools, children with disabilities are served in resource rooms and regular classes. Research on academic achievement compares full-time special class placement with either full regular class placement or resource room models (Madden & Slavin, 1983). Affleck, Madge, Adams, and Lowenbraun's (1988) reviewed the literature concerning this and found no significant difference in academic achievement between educable mentally retarded children who received daily part-time instruction in a self-contained classroom and those who were placed in a regular class full time. They also found no significant differences in achievement among elementary school age students with learning disabilities in integrated classrooms and those in resource rooms. Children with behavioral disorders in resource room programs gained significantly in reading and math achievement. Current research comparing resource room students with students in an integrated classroom indicated favorable academic and social effects for the integrated class (Wang & Birch, 1984a, 1984b).

Resource rooms provide children with disabilities with individual or small-group instruction in a special room outfitted for that purpose (Jenkins & Mayhall, 1973; Reger, 1973; Lilly, 1979). The emphasis is on teaching specific skills, either academic or behavioral, that the student needs. Thus, children are based in the regular class with their age mates and leave only for certain periods of the school day for specific lessons.

Schools generally use one of three variations on the resource room model: noncategorical, categorical, and itinerant. In *noncategorical resource rooms,* which are the most widely used, children are provided with programs based on individual need. In this approach, a single instructional group could include children with cerebral palsy, with behavior disorders, with mental retardation, and with learning disabilities who have the same instructional needs. This model, according to Hammill and Wiederhold (1973), has at least three advantages: (1) the children do not have to be transported to a school that has an appropriate categorical class, (2) a greater number of children can be served daily than can be served in a self-contained class, and (3) close communication is promoted between resource teachers and regular class teachers. The *categorical resource room* operates in the same way as the noncategorical resource room except that to qualify for placement, the child must fit into a specific group and be identified, for example, as being mentally retarded, emotionally disturbed, or learning disabled.

In the *itinerant resource program* variation, the resource teacher is not based in any one school but travels among a number of schools. Such a teacher may visit from 20 to 50 children in as many as seven or eight different schools or a regular basis. The major advantage to this approach lies in the mobility of the teacher, which makes it effective in rural areas and with preschools that have small enrollments. It does have its problems, however. Since itinerant resource teachers are not based in any school, they may have difficulty being fully accepted by the staff in the schools they visit. In addition, much time is spent in transit, and transporting materials from school to school may be a problem (McCarthy, 1971).

Resource consultant teachers may function in resource rooms—categorical or noncategorical—or as itinerant teachers. They are usually certified special education teachers who perform a variety of administrative, consultative, and direct-instructional functions. Within the resource room, the resource teacher typically tests children to identify needs and then develops appropriate objectives, strategies, and methods for meeting those needs. With the assistance of an instructional aide, this teacher also provides direct teaching to children, usually in basic skill areas.

Outside the resource room, resource teachers act as advisors to regular classroom teachers, assisting in planning and implementing the children's programs. They may help teachers adapt or develop materials, or they may suggest commercially available materials. They also work jointly with classroom teachers to determine instructional objectives, teaching-learning procedures, and standards of acceptable performance by the handicapped in the mainstreamed classroom. With this type of help, most regular class teachers can provide successful learning opportunities for handicapped children.

Scheduling is a major problem for both resource and regular class teachers. It is not always possible to schedule students into a resource room for academic instruction when their classmates are receiving similar instruction. As a result, both the resource and regular class teacher must address these important questions:

1. When during the day can children be scheduled for instruction in the resource room?

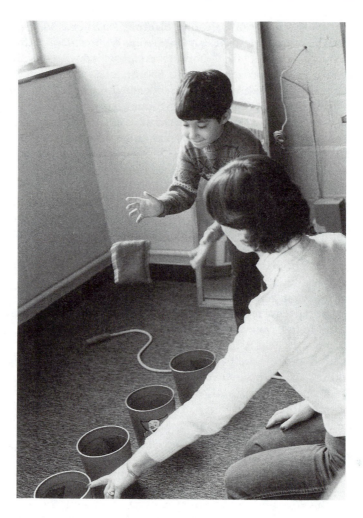

2. Which regular class activities will students miss while attending the resource room?
3. What are the consequences of attending the resource room for instruction in academics?

Such scheduling issues are best resolved when classroom and resource teachers plan collaboratively. Any method for providing service will be greatly enhanced by a spirit of coordination, cooperation, and communication among professionals.

Resource Room's Cost Effectiveness

The number of students receiving special education services is determined by the money that is available in the budget (Roddy, 1984). An unprecedented number of students have been identified as having disabilities during the past decade (Gerber,

1984). The increase in these educational costs has led policymakers to search for alternative approaches to expensive pull-out programs (Affleck et al., 1988).

These concerns have forced educators to redefine special education services and to search for alternative ways to deliver services. Many have suggested that regular educators be responsible for the education of children with mild or moderate disabilities. Affleck et al. (1988) found that the integrated classroom was more cost-effective than the resource room while achieving similar results. Lilly (1982a) emphasized the worth of regular education as valuable for all children. Lilly (1982b) claimed, "Some of the most exciting current work in special education has to do with what I have called 'rediscovery of the regular curriculum' " (p. 61). Edgar and Hayden (1982) also believe that regular educators should assume the major responsibility for the education of children with mild disabilities. Although such a placement seems an attractive option, the rights of children with disabilities must be protected in such a move (Affleck et al., 1988).

PEER TUTORING

When a teacher is alone with a class of a children, there is a limit to the number of interactions that are possible with individuals and small groups. Using peer tutors can provide children with disabilities with more instructional time than a teacher could provide alone, thus increasing the individualization in a classroom.

Young children can effectively teach tasks involving simple skills or activities that can be learned through modeling or imitation. Academic learnings that are simple to understand and that contain a sequence of objectives as well as many nonacademic learnings can be taught by peer tutors. Having a child read to another or to a group or having a child help another child count objects might help provide the young child with an understanding of the process of grouping and counting or of what is involved in gaining meanings from the printed page. The following list shows ways in which peers can function as tutors.

Areas in Which Young Peers Can Function as Tutors
- Teaching appropriate social behavior.
- Teaching initiation of positive social interactions.
- Teaching appropriate use of classroom materials.
- Teaching play behaviors.
- Teaching identification, discrimination, and labeling of colors, shapes, and simple quantities.
- Teaching speech patterns.
- Teaching basic letter-sound associations.
- Teaching simple sight vocabulary.
- Teaching appropriate responses to oral reading.
- Teaching spelling of simple words.
- Teaching basic computational facts.

Tutors should be selected because they wish to act as tutors; they should volunteer rather than be assigned. In part, a child's wanting to be a tutor grows out of the relationship the teacher has with the children in the class. Children will want to tutor for a teacher who is warm and supportive. A good way to solicit volunteers for tutoring is to hold a short meeting with the class describing the tutoring program and providing examples of the kinds of activities involved in tutoring. Then the children could be invited to volunteer. Their decisions will thus be based on some understanding of what is expected of them. Even then, some children who volunteer may wish to withdraw along the way. This should be allowed.

Training tutors before they begin to work with children with disabilities anticipates difficulties and saves much time later. The training will vary depending upon the ability level of the tutors and the tasks expected of them. In informal tutoring, training is less extensive, perhaps requiring only brief instructions as to what is expected. In primary classrooms, for example, children may be paired off and given flash cards with addition or multiplication facts written on them. These children may only be told to teach each other the facts on the cards. Other tasks require more elaborate training.

Tutors may be trained in small-group sessions initially, with individual training sessions provided later. Figure 7.3 is an example of a program for training peer tutors.

In supervising tutors, the teacher circulates around the classroom, observing the interactions that take place, providing encouragement and praise, giving tutors instructional tips, and tutoring occasionally to provide a positive model. Praising tutors for good work is important. The teacher maintains responsibility for the teaching situations and should be available to deal immediately with problems and requests for help.

Objective:	To train a child without disabilities to initiate positive social contacts with isolate peers with disabilities.
Setting:	Small training room near the child's classroom.
Procedures:	1. The teacher tells the nondisabled child that he or she is going to learn how to help the teacher by getting a certain child to play. The teacher indicates that asking children to play a game is what they will practice first.
	2. The teacher models and explains how to play the game.
	3. The tutor role-plays and explains how to play the game.
	4. During the role-playing activity, the teacher corrects the child's behavior and praises his or her efforts.
	5. The teacher instructs the tutor that it is also important to give children toys to play with.
	6. The teacher models how to approach a child and give him or her a toy.
	7. The tutor role-plays this procedure.
	8. During the role-playing, the teacher corrects the child's behavior and praises his or her efforts.
	9. The teacher models steps 2 and 6 with the isolate child while the tutor observes.
	10. The tutor conducts steps 2 and 6 with the isolate child as the teacher observes and provides corrective feedback and praise.
	11. The tutor conducts training while the teacher occasionally watches.

FIGURE 7.3 Program for training children without disabilities to initiate social contacts with isolate peers

The tutors' skills also need to be continually improved. Teachers should check on learning problems that may go unnoticed, occasionally asking a student to read a page, respond to a set of flash cards, or perform some other task related to the tutorial. With this information the teacher can plan alternative procedures that could correct observed problems. A teacher can pick up problems before they become too distracting and can deal with them as necessary.

As tutors become more proficient, the teacher can supervise less directly, circulating through the room less frequently and paying less attention to specifics. But teachers should resist the temptation to decrease the amount of supervision prematurely. Direct supervision should be withdrawn tentatively, with the teacher increasing involvement if children appear to be having difficulty. Telling tutors how to behave is never enough. The teacher must continually model the behaviors tutors are to emulate and constantly offer praise as the tutors engage in instructional activities with children. The teacher must be concerned with being the kind of teacher he or she wishes the tutors to become.

Teachers can confer briefly with the tutor after each tutoring session or at the end of the day. Such conferences allow the teacher both to gain information from the tutor and to discuss the child's progress and provide additional feedback for the tutor. Conferences are also a good time to discuss and plan new strategies with the tutor. Readers interested in learning more about peer tutoring are encouraged to consult Gartner, Kohler, and Riesman (1972); and Guralnick (1978).

SUMMARY

Integrating children with disabilities into a regular classroom requires a great deal of thought and effort. Planning an individual program may have to be more systematic than is customary, with modifications made in the room arrangement and schedule of the class as well as in the activities planned. The teacher will become a member of a multidisciplinary team concerned with the total education of the child with a disability. A resource room might be used to augment regular classroom instruction. Teachers must learn to use all resources available to them, including those that other children in the classroom provide. It is only through optimal use of all resources that the most appropriate educational experience can be provided for a child with a disability in an integrated setting. In the process of planning and implementing the plan, not only will the learning of the child with a disability be enhanced, but the learning of all those involved, adults as well as children, will benefit.

In planning activities for children with disabilities, it is important that we do not overdo the need to focus on specific needs and disabilities. A disabling condition may require teaching very specific skills and concepts in isolation. However, only by embedding these skills in the ongoing activities of the class and integrating learning will children with disabilities become capable of living as normal a life as possible. Thus, teachers need to conceive of the school experience as a totality and focus on integrated experiences for all children.

REFERENCES

Adams, A. H., et al. (1972). *Learning abilities: Diagnostic and instructional procedures for specific learning disabilities.* New York: Macmillan.

Affleck, J. Q., Madge, S., Adams, A., & Lowenbraun, S. (1988). Integrated classroom versus resource model: Academic viability and effectiveness. *Exceptional Children, 54*(4), 339–348.

Allen, K. E. (1992). *Mainstreaming in early childhood education* (2nd ed). Albany, NY: Delmar.

Bagnato, S. J., & Neisworth, J. T. (1981). *Linking developmental assessment and curricula.* Rockville, MD: Aspen Systems Corporation.

Blake, H. E. (1977). *Creating a learning-centered classroom.* New York: Hart.

Bloom, B. S. (Ed.) (1956). *Taxonomy of educational objectives.* Handbook I: *The cognitive domain.* New York: McKay.

Bloom, B. S. (1981). *All children learning: A primer for parents, teachers, and other educators.* New York: McGraw-Hill.

Bluma, S., et al. (1976). *Portage guide to early education* (rev. ed.). Portage, WI: Cooperative Educational Service Agency, No. 12.

Bos, D. (1980). *Curricular programming for young handicapped children: Project First Chance.* Tempe: Arizona State University.

Brophy, J., & Good, T. L. (1986). Teacher behavior and student achievement. In M. C. Wittrock (Ed.), *Handbook of research on teaching* (pp. 328–375). New York: Macmillan.

Cartwright, G. P., Cartwright, C. A., & Ward, M. E. (1989). *Educating special learners.* Belmont, CA: Wadsworth.

Cohen, S. B., & de Bettencourt, L. (1988). Teaching children to be independent learners: A step by step strategy. In E. L. Meyen, G. A. Vergason, & R. J. Whelan (Eds.), *Effective instructional strategies for exceptional children* (pp. 319–334). Denver: Love.

Cole, K. J., & Stevenson, A. H. (1976). *Project PAR sequential curriculum for early learning.* Saginaw, MI: Saginaw County Child Development Centers.

Connor, F. P., & Talbot, M. E. (1970). *An experimental program for young mentally retarded children.* New York: Teachers College Press.

Cook, R. E., Tessier, A., & Armbruster, V. B. (1987). *Adapting early childhood curricula for children with special needs.* Columbus, OH: Merrill.

Edgar, E. E., & Hayden, A. H. (1982). Who are the children special education should serve and how many children are there? Unpublished manuscript, University of Washington, Seattle.

Englemann, S. et al. (1974). *DISTAR,* Chicago: Science Research Associates.

Fewell, R. D., & Kelly, J. F. (1983). Curriculum for young handicapped children. In S. G. Garwood (Ed.), *Educating young handicapped children.* Rockville, MD: Aspen Systems Corporation.

Gartner, A., Kohler, M. M., & Riesman, F. (1972). *Children teach children.* New York: Harper & Row.

Gearheart, B. R., Weishahn, M. W., & Gearhart, C. J. (1988). *The exceptional student in the regular classroom* (4th ed.). Columbus, OH: Merrill.

Gerber, M. M. (1984). The Department of Education's Sixth Annual Report to Congress on PL 94–142: Is Congress getting the full story? *Exceptional Children, 51*(3), 209–224.

Gersten, R., & Carnine, D. (1986). Direct instruction in reading comprehension. *Educational Leadership, 43*(7), 70–77.

Gersten, R., Woodward, J., & Darch, C. (1986). Direct instruction: A research-based approach to curriculum design and teaching. *Exceptional Children, 53*(1), 17–31.

Guralnick, M. J. (Ed.) (1978). *Early intervention and the integration of handicapped and nonhandicapped children.* Baltimore: University Park Press.

Hammill, D. D., & Wiederhold, J. L. (1973). *The resource room: Rationale and implementation.* Philadelphia: Journal of Special Education Press.

Haring, N. G., & Schiefelbusch, R. L. (1976). *Teaching special children.* New York: McGraw–Hill.

Heron, T. E. (1987). *Developing organizational skills for LD students with attention deficit disorder.* Paper presented to the Ohio Council for Learning Disabilities Mid-Winter Conference, Columbus.

Heron, T. E., & Harris, K. C. (1987). *The educational consultant: Helping professionals, parents, and mainstreamed parents.* Austin, TX: PRO ED.

Hodgen, L., Koetter, J., LaForie, B., McCord, S., & Schramm, D. (1974). *School before six: A diagnostic approach.* St. Louis: CEMREL.

Jenkins, J., & Mayhall, W. (1973). Describing resource teacher programs. *Exceptional Children, 40,* 35–36.

Jones, V. F., & Jones, L. S. (1990). *Comprehensive classroom management: Creating positive learning environments* (3rd ed.). Boston: Allyn & Bacon.

Karnes, M. B. (1972, 1973). *Game oriented activities for learning (GOAL).* New York: Milton Bradley.

Karnes, M. B. (1977). *Learning language at home.* Reston, VA: The Council for Exceptional Children.

Laycock, V. K. (1980). *Prescriptive programming in the mainstream.* In J. W. Schifani, R. M. Anderson, & S. J. Odle (Eds.), *Implementing learning in the least restrictive environment: Handicapped children in the mainstream.* Baltimore: University Park Press.

Lerner, J., Mardell-Czudnowski, C. M., & Goldenberg, D. (1987). *Special education for the early years* (2nd ed). Englewood Cliffs, NJ: Prentice-Hall.

Lilly, M. S. (Ed.) (1979). *Children with exceptional needs: A survey of special education.* New York: Holt, Rinehart & Winston.

Lilly, M. S. (1982a). *Divestiture in special education: A personal point of view.* Paper presented to the Presidents' Roundtable, Council for Exceptional Children International Convention, Houston.

Lilly, M. S. (1982b). The education of mildly handicapped children and implications for teacher education. In M. C. Reynolds (Ed.), *The future of mainstreaming: Next steps in teacher education* (pp. 52–64). Reston, VA: Council for Exceptional Children.

Linder, T. W. (1983). *Early childhood special education: Program development and administration.* Baltimore: Paul H. Brookes.

McCarthy, J. (1971). Providing services in the public schools for children with learning disabilities. In D. Hammill & W. Bartel (Eds.), *Educational perspectives in learning disabilities* (pp. 279–291). New York: Wiley.

McCoy, K. M., & Prehm, H. J. (1987). *Teaching mainstreamed students.* Denver: Love.

Madden, N. A., & Slavin, R. E. (1983). Mainstreaming students with mild handicaps: Academic and social outcomes. *Review of Educational Research, 53,* 519–569.

Neisworth, J. T., Herb, S. J., Bagnato, S. J., Cartwright, C. A., & Laub, K. W. (1980). *Individualized education for preschool exceptional children.* Germantown, MD: Aspen Systems.

Peterson, N. L. (1987). *Early intervention for handicapped and at-risk children.* Denver: Love.

Raver, S. A. (1991). *Strategies for teaching at-risk and handicapped infants and toddlers: A transdisciplinary approach.* New York: Macmillan.

Reger, R. (1973). What is a resource room? *Journal of Learning Disabilities, 10,* 609–614.

Roddy, E. A. (1984). When are resource rooms going to share in the declining enrollment trend? Another look at mainstreaming. *Journal of Learning Disabilities, 16*(1), 26–27.

Safford, P. L. (1989). *Integrated teaching in early childhood.* White Plains, NY: Longman.

Salend, S. J. (1990). *Effective mainstreaming.* New York: Macmillan.

Sanford, A. (1974). *Learning accomplishments profile.* Winston-Salem, NC: Kaplan School Supply.

Schweinhart, L. J., Weikart, D. P., & Larner, M. B. (1986). Consequences of three preschool curriculum models through age 15. *Early Childhood Research Quarterly, 1*(1), 15–45.

Sexton, C. W. (1989). Effectiveness of DISTAR Reading I program in developing first graders' language skills. *Journal of Educational Research, 82*(5), 289–293.

Shields, J. M., & Heron, T. E. (1989, Winter). Teaching organizational skills to students with learning disabilities. *Teaching Exceptional Children,* 8–13.

Snow, R. E. (1982). Education and intelligence. In R. J. Sternberg (Ed.), *Handbook of human intelligence* (pp. 493–585). New York: Cambridge University Press.

Snow, R. E. (1986). Individual differences and the design of educational programs. *American Psychologist, 41,* 1029–1039.

Snow, R. E., & Lohman, D. F. (1984). Toward a theory of cognitive aptitude for learning from instruction. *Journal of Educational Psychology, 76,* 347–376.

Stallings, J., & Stipek, D. (1986). Research on early childhood and elementary school teaching programs. In M. C. Wittrock (Ed.), *Handbook of research on teaching* (pp. 727–753). New York: Macmillan.

Tilton, J. T., Liske, L. M., & Bousland, S. R. (1977). *Wabash guide to early developmental training.* Boston: Allyn & Bacon.

Wallace, G., Cohen, S. B., & Polloway, E. A. (1987). *Language arts: Teaching exceptional students.* Austin, TX: PRO-ED.

Walling, J. (1976). *The RADEA program.* Dallas, TX: Melton Book Co.

Wang, M. S., & Birch, J. W. (1984a). Effective special education in regular classes. *Exceptional Children, 50,* 391–398.

Wang, M. S., & Birch, J. W. (1984b). Comparison of a full-time mainstreaming program and resource room approach. *Exceptional Children, 51,* 33–40.

Weikart, D. P., Rogers, L., Adcock, C., & McClelland, D. (1971). *The cognitively oriented curriculum.* Ypsilanti, MI: High/Scope.

Willoughby-Hulb, S. H., Neisworth, J. T., Laub, K. W., Hunt, F., & Llewellyn, E. (1980). *COMP curriculum and activity manual.* University Park: The Pennsylvania State University.

CHAPTER 8

Supporting Social Learning

CHAPTER OVERVIEW

This chapter discusses:

1. Social integration and its importance to a child's development.
2. Social withdrawal, its symptoms and possible causes, and the short- and long-term impact of social isolation on a child.
3. Ways of measuring social interaction in the classroom.
4. Strategies for promoting social interaction.
5. The teacher's and peers' influence in establishing a positive classroom climate.
6. Strategies for managing behavior problems of young children.
7. Drug treatment for behavior problems in young children.

Social integration refers to children and teachers working together in a classroom. Positive social integration is an important educational objective, especially with children of widely differing abilities. As a result of social integration, children can learn cognitive, social, and language skills from each other; recognize and value the uniqueness of others; expand friendships; gain status, acceptance, and security; and enhance their own self-confidence, learning to deal with new situations. Simply placing children of differing abilities together in the same setting will not guarantee social integration. This must be actively guided and promoted. It is important that classroom teachers know the factors that influence and the strategies that enhance positive social integration.

THE BENEFITS OF INTEGRATION

Developing positive social interactions in the early years is extremely important. The types of relationships that young children develop will affect their later academic performance, their feelings about themselves, their attitudes toward others, and the social patterns they will adopt. Teachers can prevent behavior problems before they arise and support optimum social growth by identifying and helping socially unskilled children.

Several scholars have documented the importance of peer relations to children's development. Piaget (1935), for example, asserted that peer interactions improve the cognitive development of preschoolers, providing them with alternative perspectives in problem-solving situations. Rubenstein and Howes (1979) found that the play of toddlers is more complex when they play with others. Guralnick (1981) noted that social interaction with other children improves communication skills as children adjust the complexity of their language to fit the cognitive level of the listener. Hartup (1983) demonstrated that peer exchanges teach children to share, to respond appropriately to aggression, and to develop appropriate sex-role behaviors. Murray (1972) and Perret-Clemont (1980) showed that gains in cognitive skills result from social exchanges with more competent peers.

Early social relations also set the stage for developing friendships, providing young children with their first opportunities to share affection with someone outside their family. Friendships also teach children the value of loyalty and the ability to respond to the needs of others. In summary, positive social integration helps children develop the social skills to initiate and sustain peer relations that are vital to children's psychological well-being.

SOCIALLY WITHDRAWN CHILDREN

Some children do not interact well with peers, or remain isolated. These children, called social isolates, socially unskilled, or socially withdrawn, are often described as not talkative, not likely to initiate play with peers, or unresponsive to the social initiations of others, or as those who stand on the edge of activities.

Several studies have documented the long-term consequences of social withdrawal. These children are likely to develop mental health problems later in life (Cowen, Pederson, Babijian, Izzo, & Trost, 1973), to drop out of school (Ulman, 1957), and to be identified as juvenile problems (Roff, Sells, & Golden, 1972). Kohn (1977) found that socially withdrawn preschoolers remain that way through the first 5 years of school and perform more poorly academically.

Several theories have been used to explain the cause of social withdrawal. Psychoanalysts believe that this withdrawal is rooted in early mother-child relationships and that children who are emotionally deprived at home, not having established close relationships with their mothers, develop feelings of inadequacy and a sense of distrust that interferes with their social relations (Erikson, 1963). The suggested treatment is designed to first establish trust between the child and a therapist and then to expand that trust to others.

Applied behavior analysts argue that social withdrawal occurs either because the socially withdrawn child has not developed the skills to initiate or respond appropriately to peers, or has not received adequate reinforcement from peer interaction and thus chooses not to use these skills. Treatment focuses on enhancing the child's social skill repertoire and in educating the child regarding the positive, naturally occurring reinforcers associated with social interaction.

Social learning theory (Bandura, 1971) views social withdrawal as a function of the environment; the behavior of the child; and personal characteristics, such as the child's cognitive state, affective state, or memory of past experiences. Since changes in one factor can impact on the others, treatment must take into account all of these factors to alter withdrawn behavior.

The *cognitive problem-solving perspective* suggests that socially withdrawn children lack the social knowledge for establishing peer relations or for conducting social interactions—knowledge about how to make friends, resolve conflicts, play games, take turns, or initiate or respond to social interactions. The suggested treatment is to identify the individual's social skill deficits and teach him or her the needed skills (Strain, 1985).

A number of strategies exist for helping withdrawn children, most of which are useful for promoting interactions among all young children. Almost any child can be withdrawn; it is easy to overlook these children because they seldom disrupt the classroom. But we need to attend to their needs in a sensitive, caring manner.

MEASURING SOCIAL INTERACTION

In order to become more aware of the quality of social interactions in their classrooms, teachers can evaluate social interaction by using sociometrics, by measuring children's rate of interaction, and by using rating scales. These procedures are discussed here.

Sociometrics

Sociometric techniques measure social relations by using peer ratings of their classmates' social behavior. Peer nominations are commonly used: Children are asked to name up to three classmates with whom they would like to participate in an activity (e.g., playing together or attending a party). Children are also asked to name those with whom they would not like to spend time. The positive and negative nominations are added up to identify each child's social status. Sociometric techniques are more fully discussed in chapter 4.

Rate of Interaction Measures

A child's social interactions with peers can be assessed through direct observation and recording of specific social behaviors (Lamb, Suomi, & Stephenson, 1979). These interactions are reported by rate of interaction per minute, total frequency of social interaction during a period of time, or the percentage of timed intervals in which interactions occur. Teachers can collect such information on their children periodically. These and other observational strategies are discussed in chapter 3.

Rating Scales

Teachers or parents can rank a child or a group of children on a variety of social characteristics, including quality of verbal interactions, general level of popularity, and overall quality of social behavior. The SAMPLE (Social Assessment Manual for Preschool Level) assessment manual (Greenwood, Todd, Walker, & Hops, 1978) is an example of a rating measure of social interaction. Such measures are easy to administer and are relatively accurate in characterizing classroom peer interactions.

Measuring the level and quality of classroom peer interactions can have many benefits. It allows teachers to determine whether a particular child or group of children need to improve their relations with others.

STRATEGIES FOR PROMOTING PEER INTERACTION

A number of social skill training strategies have been developed recently that employ both adult-directed and peer-directed interventions. These include both adult-directed strategies and child-directed strategies.

Adult-Directed Strategies

Adult Reinforcement.   Teachers can provide social reinforcement through verbal praise or by giving children attention following a social exchange. Each is an effective technique for promoting positive social interaction. Reinforcement can be given for sharing, smiling, beginning an interaction, responding to someone else's interaction, or extending or sustaining an existing interaction. Teachers must be careful that the praise or attention does not disrupt or interfere with ongoing social exchanges. In addition, the reinforcement should be given periodically and in a varied manner to sustain its effects. Teachers should also be aware that adult attention or praise may not be reinforcing for some children.

Play Therapy.   In play therapy (Axline, 1969b), individual treatment sessions are conducted in a clinical setting using play materials. The therapist follows the child's lead, focusing on activities and topics of interest to the child. Play therapy helps the child to express conflicts and concerns that cannot be articulated verbally and to build a relationship of trust and acceptance that will allow the child to develop a more constructive and happier life. Some studies (e.g., Cox, 1963; Seeman, Barry, & Ellenwood, 1964) have demonstrated that play therapy can enhance a child's popularity among his peers and improve the overall quality of the child's interactions.

Trostle (1988) presents a model of child-centered group play based on Axline's (1969a) model of play therapy. This included ancillary-guided sessions, using guidance counselors or similar professionals to guide children's play once or twice a month; teacher-guided individual sessions, where the teacher would work with the child in a separate area of the room while an aide or parent works with the other children; or teacher-guided simultaneous sessions, where small groups of children work with nondirective toys simultaneously in various areas of the room. This technique can contribute to children's self-control, free-play abilities, and social acceptance.

Adult Models.   Modeling, showing someone how to do something, can enhance children's social abilities. Often, a teacher needs only to show a child how to behave in various social situations, such as initiating a social interaction ("Let's play in the doll area") or sustaining an ongoing interaction ("Let's build a block house, only this time with two kitchens"). Adult models tend not to be as effective as peer models.

Verbal Instructions.   Verbal instructions involve offering suggestions, telling, or explaining to children what is expected of them in various social situations. Verbal instructions are mostly used together with other techniques, such as positive reinforcement or modeling.

Social Coaching.   Social coaching can teach interaction skills and reduce disruptive behavior, such as childhood aggression. Coaching has been used with aggressive as well as with normal children. Coaching includes three components: (1) Children are taught strategies for playing with others through verbal discussion and role playing. (2) They are then given opportunities to rehearse these skills with peers. (3) Afterwards, they use the strategies in natural social situations and report back about how effective the strategies are (Ladd, 1981).

Peer-Directed Strategies

Peer-directed interactions involve teaching a child or group of children to engage in various social behaviors in order to promote the social interaction abilities of their socially less skillful peers. Children rather than adults become training agents, more closely resembling the natural process of social skill acquisition. Peer tutors for social skill training should be volunteers who attend school regularly, who already display positive social behavior toward other children, and who can follow adult directions. Strategies for training tutors are presented in chapter 7.

Other peer-directed interventions include putting children in close proximity to one another, prompting and reinforcing, getting other children to initiate social encounters, helping children to accept the initiation of another, having other children serve as models, and placing the child in a classroom manager role.

Placing a socially competent child next to a child with social problems and asking him or her to play with the target child should be linked with encouraging the target child to play with others and showing that child how to play. This *proximity strategy* facilitates the natural transmission of social skills.

Socially skillful children can learn to *prompt and reinforce* the social behaviors of others. Prompts may consist of invitations ("Come play with me"); reinforcement consists of praise after the interaction ("Thank you, I enjoyed playing with you"). Prompts and reinforcement are more effective when used jointly.

Socially competent children can be taught to direct social overtures to other children, asking a child to play, giving a child a toy, offering physical assistance, or suggesting a play idea. The teacher can rehearse the children in various initiation strategies and support them in being persistent in their efforts to engage the other children in social interactions. Social tutors can also be trained to *accept the initiation of others,* responding appropriately to social overtures from a child who has been prompted to initiate an interaction.

Peer Modeling.   Peer modeling has been widely used to teach social skills to children. Two types of models are used, including (1) live models with children observing the behaviors of their socially adept peers in the classroom, and (2) symbolic models with children observing the social behaviors of models on a videotape or film. Live models should be children who are popular and who enjoy high social status in the classroom to increase the chances that the model will be watched and imitated by others. The teacher should call children's attention to the model's behavior and publicly reinforce what the model is doing. The teacher should also employ more than one model.

Using a *classroom manager role* (Saitamo, Maneady, & Shook, 1987) involves selecting a socially unpopular child as class leader or manager during popular and visible classroom activities. Each child can serve as a manager and, on occasion, the teacher might use co-managers, pairing up children to work cooperatively on certain activities.

Teachers can use these strategies to promote social interaction. Teachers should practice these strategies until they feel comfortable with them. Each will be effective with some children, but not with others. Additional strategies for promoting interaction are presented in chapter 9.

ESTABLISHING A CLIMATE CONDUCIVE TO SOCIAL INTEGRATION

Two factors play an important role in establishing a classroom conducive to social integration: teacher influence and peer influence.

Teacher Influence

The teacher is the most important factor in determining how children feel about school, themselves, and each other, and in how much progress they make. Teachers also influence the extent to which children of diverse abilities are accepted by one another. Brophy and Putnam (1979) have identified a number of attributes of effective teachers. They should be liked by their students, and be cheerful, friendly, emotionally mature, sincere, and well adjusted. They should be able to stay calm in a crisis, listen to children without becoming authoritarian or defensive, avoid conflicts, and maintain a problem-solving orientation in their classrooms. Such teachers can use a variety of techniques to effectively manage their classes.

The impact of the teacher's behavior on the classroom has been demonstrated in a number of studies (Peterson & Walberg, 1979; Rosenshine & Stevens, 1986; Walberg, 1986). The characteristics of teachers that are conducive to a healthy social classroom climate include positive self-concept, positive behavior, understanding, planning, and knowledge about behavior problems and solutions to use.

Teacher's Self-Concept. Although most research has focused on the relationship of the child's self-concept to development, some writers (e.g., Clark & Peterson, 1986) have directed their attention toward the relationship of the teacher's self-concept to the child's social development. Jersild (1965) asserts that the personal problems of teachers can interfere with their classroom performance and can influence their pupils. Combs (1965) found that effective teachers are distinguished by their positive attitudes toward themselves and others. He noted the importance of fostering positive self-concepts among teachers and asserted that the attitude of teachers toward themselves and others enhances the self-concept of their pupils. Moreover, teachers with positive attitudes toward themselves promote a positive classroom atmosphere, whereas those with negative attitudes toward themselves promote negative feelings among pupils (Karnes & Lee, 1979).

Teacher's Positive Behavior. People who feel good have a positive effect on others; those around them usually begin to show some of the same feelings. If teachers are positive and enthusiastic, their students will be positive and enthusiastic. Negative teacher attitudes and behavior often make them passive, withdrawn, and even fearful. In addition, a teacher's expectations can influence students' academic achievement and social behavior. If a teacher has low expectations for a child, these expectations may result in a self-fulfilling prophecy—the student may perform poorly (Brophy & Good, 1986; Rosenthal & Jacobson, 1968).

The teacher's behavior and expectations also influence the child's self-esteem. Through interactions with significant persons in their lives—family members, peers, and teachers—children begin to reflect how they are valued as people (Maccoby, 1980). Adults who demonstrate warmth, respect, empathy, and acceptance are far more likely to nurture positive self-images in children (Gecas, Colonico, & Thomas, 1974). Positive attitudes and expectations for all children, but especially for those who differ from normal developmental patterns, must be combined with praise, support, and encouragement. By emphasizing children's good points, teachers can build their students' confidence and their persistence in completing more difficult learning tasks.

Teacher's Understanding. Teachers in an integrated classroom must be sensitive to differences in their students' abilities and to conflicts or misunderstandings that can result from them. The negative stereotypes and prejudices that even young children can develop are dangerous in the classroom. Teachers communicate important attitudinal messages to students about individual differences. Students quickly learn whether or not the teacher favors high achieving students or feels respect or disdain for those who have special problems. The teacher's attitude also sets a tone for child–child relationships (Macmillan, Jones, & Meyers, 1976).

By gathering information in school and in the child's home, teachers can gain a better understanding of their children and of the differences that exist among them. They can use this knowledge to design appropriate programs for all children. An accepting atmosphere promotes integration while providing an optimum setting for the social growth of the entire class. It will also provide a model of understanding.

Knowledge of Behavior Problems.   Behavior problems can arise even in the most carefully planned social environment. Teachers must be able to recognize and cope with them. Children with diverse needs may act in ways that interfere with, prohibit, or compete with school-related activities and useful social and work skills. To maintain a positive social climate, regular classroom teachers must know what type of problem behaviors to expect and how to deal with them.

Spodek (1985) has identified the following guidelines to help teachers develop an approach to discipline:

1. Children should know the behaviors expected of them.
2. Children should be told why rules are in effect.
3. Children should have opportunities to observe and practice proper behavior.
4. Behavior expected of children should be possible of them.
5. Children cannot be expected to behave properly at all times.
6. Teachers should behave with consistency toward the children in their class.

These guidelines, which are important for all children in an integrated classroom, represent the basis for avoiding behavior problems. A later section of this chapter examines specific techniques to use when behavior problems arise.

Peer Influence

Young children learn a great deal from one another. They learn to see themselves as leaders, as followers, or as isolates. When they are accepted and liked by peers, children gain confidence and self-assurance and perform better in school. Uncertain or partial acceptance, on the other hand, produces anxiety and self-doubt. Students who are totally rejected can experience trauma, act out aggressively, or withdraw into apathy or fantasy.

The extent to which children are affected by their peers depends on their age, maturity, social skills, ethnic background, and disability. Preschool-age children, for example, tend not to be as strongly influenced by their peer group as are older children. Home and adult praise are more important to them than is peer approval. Beginning in the primary years, the effect of peers increases (Winkler, 1975). In any case, physically disabled children at any age tend to be less well accepted by peers.

Considering the impact that children's peers have on their social and academic development, teachers in integrated settings must learn to understand and to use the classroom social environment. A teacher can increase the chances for healthy social interaction among children in integrated early childhood settings. Being sensitive to peer norms and values, understanding peer roles and relationships, and making peers aware of differing abilities are all important in this regard.

Peer Norms and Values.   In any class of children, a system of norms and values exists that defines what will be accepted and admired. Children want to be popular and accepted by their peers. If they perceive that activities such as participating in class, cooperating with the teacher, or accepting differences in others is approved, they will conform to these standards. Peer support for these behaviors can be effective in motivating individual children.

Teachers can explain the importance of cooperation and sharing, helping children understand that all individuals, however different their abilities and personalities, still deserve the respect of all. Teachers should model appropriate social responses and reinforce children for appropriate behavior.

Knowledge of Differing Abilities

All students require information about the abilities and backgrounds of the children with whom they learn. Children need to know the specific effects that exceptional conditions have on their classmates and on themselves. Children will be curious about these differences and may have misconceptions about those who are different, possibly perceiving a child with cerebral palsy as sick or perhaps retarded. To support an integrated environment, children must learn about one another.

Several strategies exist for helping children learn about the differing abilities and backgrounds of their peers. Teaching units may be developed to emphasize the abilities of children who are gifted or have disabilities, or learning centers devoted to various topics can be provided. These centers may teach children about different forms of communication (e.g., signing, Braille, communication boards) or books can be provided that address the needs of persons with disabilities.

One of the most effective strategies for teaching children about one another is classroom discussion. A teacher may invite a resource person to speak about a topic, or a discussion may begin spontaneously as a result of an incident that occurs in the class. Discussions convey information and impressions. In conducting classroom discussions, the students who are the focus of discussion should feel comfortable about being the center of attention. Respect for the student should be maintained at all times, and problems or concerns should be dealt with in a direct yet sensitive manner.

Simulations can also increase children's knowledge of their peers. One student can assume the role of another. For example, a nondisabled child might spend a day or a portion of a day in a wheelchair. Puppetry is another form of simulation. Puppets with disabilities, for example, can be an effective strategy for changing the attitudes of young children without disabilities toward those with disabilities (Aiello, 1976). When planning such activities, teachers should emphasize the similarities as well as differences that exist among different children.

MANAGING PROBLEM BEHAVIORS

From time to time, teachers in integrated early childhood programs are confronted with students who exhibit a wide variety of problem behaviors. These problems arise despite their best efforts to create a supportive social climate and to promote positive social interactions. These behaviors may be exhibited by almost any child in the classroom.

Several strategies are available for dealing with classroom behavior problems. These are rooted in different personality theories, including behavior analysis theory, psychodynamic theory, and ecological psychology. In recent years, the use of drug therapy also has been suggested.

Behavior Analysis Techniques

Psychologists and educators have developed a variety of techniques that have been used in working with children with disabilities and that can be adapted to an integrated classroom. The most useful ones are presented here.

Positive Reinforcement.   Positive reinforcement for appropriate behavior is a widely used and easily implemented technique. A reinforcer (a positive event such as a smile, approval, recognition, a good grade, or affection) is given following a positive behavior. Many materials or events can serve as reinforcers, but not all children will find the same thing reinforcing. Whatever is used should be something valued by the child, whether an edible reinforcer (e.g., small amounts of candy, cookies, or fruit), a toy or other small inexpensive object, or an activity. Social reinforcers including praise, attention, and affection can also be used. When activities are used as reinforcers, a token economy (described below) may be established. Material or activity reinforcers can have educational value in themselves. Whatever reinforcers are selected, teachers should be careful to use them for a limited time only, reducing their use to allow appropriate behaviors to provide their own satisfactions.

Extinction.   Extinction, a method for weakening inappropriate or disruptive behavior, involves ignoring behavior. This is useful when a child is unlikely to be reinforced by peers for a behavior or when a teacher's attention is a more powerful source of reinforcement than that provided by peers. Teachers need to be aware that extinction procedures generally take time to be effective, and that sometimes ignoring a behavior actually makes the behavior worse before it becomes better. Since some behaviors are harmful and cannot be ignored, this technique cannot always be used. Extinction is more effective when used in combination with positive reinforcement for appropriate behavior.

Time-Out.   Time-out refers to withdrawing a child from a group situation to a less reinforcing environment for a brief period of time as a response to inappropriate behavior (Brantner & Doherty, 1983). A child may be removed from activities but remain in the classroom; the child is required to sit at the periphery of an activity and observe the appropriate social behavior of others. In the most restrictive form of time-out, the child is removed from the classroom. This represents a last resort and should be avoided if possible.

In using time-out, a teacher should (1) provide clear, concisely worded reasons to explain why a child has been placed in time-out, (2) give the child one or two warnings before administering time-out, and (3) keep time-out brief (no more than 3 to 5 minutes).

Since time-out is a form of punishment, it can produce undesirable effects. Some children will resist time-out and respond to it by acting out, either verbally or physically. Other children may cry or become withdrawn, avoiding contact with the teacher or with peers. Time-out should be used carefully and judiciously. Asking a child to behave appropriately, explaining why appropriate behavior is important, and then reinforcing the desirable social response may be more effective than time-out (Martin & Pear, 1978).

Token Economy Systems.   Token economy systems are used when immediately available reinforcers cannot maintain appropriate classroom behavior (Kazdin, 1982). Tokens are exchanged for other reinforcers, such as a toy or an activity. There are six essential steps to using a token economy system: (1) specify what behaviors will earn tokens; (2) develop a menu specifying what the tokens will buy; (3) set prices and wages: how many tokens are earned by each goal behavior and what each activity, privilege, or object costs in tokens; (4) use tokens that can readily be given, are handy, and will cause minimum interference; (5) establish the value of tokens through instruction ("This token is given for good work"); and (6) keep a record of the point each child earns and spends each day.

A token system also must eventually be removed so that the children learn to respond to natural reinforcers, such as praise and approval. Cooper, Heron, and Howard (1987) suggest five general guidelines for removing token systems:

1. Present tokens paired with social approval with the approval presented first, followed by the token.
2. Gradually increase the number of behaviors required to earn a token.
3. Gradually decrease the length of time the token economy is in effect.
4. Gradually decrease the number of activities and privileges that serve as back-up reinforcers.
5. Gradually fade the physical evidence of tokens.

Although tokens can be effective in maintaining appropriate classroom behavior, there are several problems with using them, including the problem of removal and the amount of teacher time it takes to implement. Records must be kept and tokens dispersed, and children must be carefully monitored.

Contingency Contracts.   Contingency contracts involve an agreement between the teacher and the child that specifies the relationship between the child's behavior and the consequences that will follow (Homme, 1977). This procedure, used principally in the primary grades, is effective with children who have difficulty associating a behavior with its consequences. A contingency contract defines the task, when it will be completed, how it will be completed, the reinforcers to be earned, the penalty for noncompliance with the contract, and a bonus that can be earned for good work.

There are several advantages to contingency contracting. When a child has some input, performance may improve. Moreover, contingencies are not as likely to be aversive since the child negotiates for them. In addition, contracts are flexible and can be renegotiated and revised to fit the needs of the individual. Contracts also provide a way to structure a relationship between individuals. They can help children understand the impact of their behavior on others. A child has to understand the nature of a contract for this to be used, however.

Group contingencies can also be developed with the entire class (Gresham, 1985). In such cases, a single individual, a small group, or the entire class can earn consequences.

Self-Management.   In recent years there has been increasing interest in teaching children to control their own behavior through self-management programs. Self-management involves five steps: (1) self-selecting and defining the target behavior, (2) self-observing and recording the behavior, (3) selecting the behavior change procedures, (4) implementing the procedures, and (5) evaluating the program.

Self-management allows self-reinforcement of behaviors that the teacher might not notice and therefore would not reinforce. Students who manage their own behavior can contribute to the operation of a more efficient classroom, allowing the teacher more time to focus on teaching. In addition, some behaviors, such as positive self-statements, can only be managed through self-control. Some students perform better under self-management than under teacher-managed programs. Self-management is widely recognized as one of the ultimate goals of education. As John Dewey (1939) wrote, "The ideal aim of education and formal schooling is the creation of self-control." (p. 30)

Verbal Instructions.   Verbal instructions involve telling or explaining to children what is expected of them. Such instructions should be simple and easily understood by the children. Although verbal instructions alone can be effective in changing behavior, they generally are used with other techniques.

Shaping.   Shaping involves changing behavior gradually through a series of successive approximations. The teacher first waits until the child's behavior somewhat approximates the behavior to be learned or prompts such behavior. When an approximation to the desired behavior is manifest, the teacher reinforces it. As the child's behavior further approaches the desired behavior, he or she is again reinforced. This shaping process continues until the new behavior is learned.

Response Cost.   In response cost, a negative behavior results in the loss of reinforcing events (Sulzer & Mayer, 1972). Loss of a specified amount of recess or gym time for undesirable classroom behavior is an example of response cost. This is a form of punishment that teachers should try to avoid if possible, since rewards generally are more effective.

Psychodynamic Approaches

The approaches described above focus on children's behavior; psychodynamic approaches focus on the presumed underlying causes of that behavior. Dreikurs (1968), for example, suggested that children misbehave for one of four reasons: (1) to gain attention, (2) to display power, or (3) to display a deficiency in order to either seek special services or (4) be exempted from certain expectations. Teachers need to find out why children misbehave. The last of these reasons suggests that a misbehavior may be a call for help from a child and needs to be treated differently from a misbehavior that results from other causes.

Dreikurs suggests that teachers use *logical consequences* rather than punishment or reinforcement to deal with misbehavior. These express the reality of the social order, involve no moral judgments, and are concerned only with present circumstances. For children who deliberately create a mess, for example, the consequence might be that they stay and clean up, possibly missing a valued activity. The children should also be told why a particular consequence has been selected.

Often the negative feelings children have are not given legitimate outlet in school and are expressed in negative behavior. Legitimizing these feelings and helping children cope with them, as well as providing children with skills for expressing their feelings verbally rather than behaviorally, can lessen disruptive behavior in a classroom. The teacher should make clear that although the child's feelings are understood, the negative behavior associated with them cannot be permitted. Group meetings can be used to deal with children's feelings about having a child with a disability in class. This can lessen the fear and ignorance that may occur, eliminate stereotyping, and help children deal directly with issues that confront them.

The group process might also be used to deal with problems of social behavior. A number of programs have been designed to aid early childhood teachers in helping their children deal with personal feelings and concerns. These include *DUSO— Revised: Developing Understanding of Self and Others* (Dinkmeyer, 1982), *Dimensions of Personality* (1972), *First Things—Values* (1972), and *Methods in Human Development* (Bessell & Palomares, 1970). Martorella (1975) compared these four in terms of basic teaching used, basic affective themes addressed, and key student and teacher roles.

The *DUSO-1* program is designed for kindergarten and primary grades. It includes storybooks, recordings, posters, activity cards, role-playing cards, discussion cards, and props and puppets, along with a teacher's manual. It is designed to help children understand themselves, their feelings, and the feelings of others, and to comprehend the interdependence of the group. Teachers are expected to read stories, lead discussion groups, and help children engage in role-playing and puppet dramatizations. The materials are designed to help children understand social and emotional behavior and develop desirable behavior responses.

Dimensions of Personality is a primary grade program that makes use of student and teacher manuals, activity sheets, and ditto masters. Children participate in group discussions and work on individual exercises. The function of this program is to develop social competencies, including skills in working with groups, and to build positive self-concepts.

The *First Things—Values* program consists of a set of records or cassettes, filmstrips, and teachers' manuals. Moral dilemmas are posed to children through audiovisual presentations. These are related to truth, fairness, rules, promises, and notions of right and wrong. Children are asked to take a position related to one of these dilemmas and provide a rationale for that position. The material is built on Kohlberg's concept of stages in moral development (see Turiel, 1973).

Methods in Human Development provides materials for children as young as age 4. The program focuses around "Magic Circle" activities in which children participate in group process discussions, with the teacher functioning as group leader, discussion stimulator and clarifier, and rule enforcer. The program is designed to improve communication in the group, develop children's self-concepts, and improve personal self-control.

Each of these programs can aid teachers in dealing with the social climate of the class—helping children become better aware of their own feelings and the feelings of others and develop a more positive sense of self—and providing a medium wherein class difficulties can be discussed and possible solutions explored. In each of the programs, the teacher functions as a discussion leader as well as an observer of social conditions in the classroom. The teacher may also serve as a diagnostician and behavior reinforcer. Teachers may review the programs and select the one that conforms to their views of how social behavior is best modified in the class and how children's social development is best supported. Whichever program is selected, it is important that what occurs within the program is supported in the social life of the class.

Ecological Approaches

Another approach to dealing with behavior problems in early childhood classrooms is to look for ways to modify the environment to diminish the possibility of conflict. Swap (1974) views many of the problems that emotionally disturbed children have in school as resulting from the fact that they are still resolving conflicts associated with earlier developmental stages. Because the classroom environment often is designed for children with greater emotional maturity, the regular classroom setting contributes to social conflict and behavioral problems for those children. Teachers need to become careful observers of their children, capable of judging their emotions as well as their academic maturity. Modifying academic requirements, varying work space, using different kinds of groupings, and matching instructional materials to the capabilities of the students can help reduce inappropriate behaviors.

Kounin (1970) also views discipline and classroom management from an ecological point of view. His studies on the "ripple effect" demonstrated that the way a teacher corrects one student's behavior influences the behavior of the other students in class. This seems especially so with young children. He also found that the teacher's awareness of classroom processes is conveyed to students and contributes to their effectiveness as classroom managers. Thus, teachers with "eyes in the back of their heads," who are able to attend to a range of activities and are aware of the goings-on in the classroom, are most effective in managing the group process.

Similarly, an alert teacher can establish an adequate flow of classroom activities, pacing them properly for the children, maintaining the momentum of the activities, and attending to the need for proper transitions. Activities for all children, including children with disabilities, need to be varied and challenging, and should help them feel they are making academic progress. By using the social, physical, and academic elements of the classroom environment to meet the educational needs of all the children, teachers can avoid using more manipulative and direct forms of discipline and punishment.

Each of the techniques reviewed here can be effective, either singly or in combination, in dealing with the behavior problems of young exceptional children. Teachers need to select techniques that are consistent with their educational philosophy and their approach to classroom teaching.

DRUG THERAPY

The past several years have witnessed a dramatic increase in the use of psychotropic drugs, particularly stimulants, as interventions for changing children's behavior. Teachers in integrated early childhood programs may encounter children who take some medication to control behavior. Psychotropic drugs are prescribed by a physician to affect a child's mood, thought processes, or behaviors. Teachers are most likely to encounter stimulants given to hyperactive children. The most common of these—Ritalin, Dexedrine, and Cylert—are prescribed in over 97 percent of the cases in which drug treatment is used to alter a hyperactive child's behavior.

The principal impact of stimulants is to depress the activity level of children, the opposite of how stimulants affect adults. Studies with hyperactive children show that stimulants depress activity level during highly structured activities but appear to have little or no effect during less structured activities. Stimulants have been reported to improve interpersonal relationships between children and their teachers, parents, and peers, as well as to reduce the number of classroom behavior problems.

Studies show that stimulants have virtually no positive impact on hyperactive children's school achievement (Gadow, 1986). Hyperactive children who are taking prescribed stimulants are no more likely than those who are not taking medication to make measurable academic gains. Stimulants can produce relatively mild but still undesirable physiological side-effects, including insomnia, mild loss of appetite, mood changes that can give the appearance of depression, some involuntary muscle movement known as tics (e.g., eye flinching), increases in nail biting, and minor effects such as stomach aches, mild nausea, irritability, and increased talkativeness. If taken over time, stimulants can create an "amphetamine look" characterized by a pale, pinched, serious facial expression and dark hollows under the eyes (Barkley, 1981). In addition, long-term use of stimulants can retard physical growth, though the child will return to normal growth patterns once the stimulants are discontinued.

Most hyperactive children take between 10 and 20 milligrams of a stimulant per day. These stimulants require approximately 30 minutes to take effect and last for about 3 to 4 hours; time-released capsules last for as long as 12 hours. Children generally are given a dose in the morning and at noon, with some receiving an additional dose in the evening to help them sleep. The average duration of drug therapy is 39 months, though some children take drugs for as little as 3 months and others for a lifetime.

Physicians and educators are raising concerns about the growing use of stimulants. Barkley (1981) has suggested the following guidelines to assist in making decisions about whether hyperactive children should be given stimulants to control behavior:

1. Consider the age of the child. Drug treatment is not recommended for children under 4 years of age, except in unusually severe cases.
2. Use drugs only after other therapies to modify hyperactive behavior have been tried.
3. Consider the child's family situation. Can the family afford medication? Are the parents sufficiently intelligent to supervise the use of medication? Are the parents antidrug? Is there a delinquent sibling or drug-abusing parent in the household?
4. Does the hyperactive child have any history of tics (involuntary muscle movements), psychosis, or thought disorders? If so, stimulants are contraindicated.
5. Is the child anxious, fearful, or likely to complain of psychosomatic disturbances? If so, stimulants again are contraindicated.
6. Does the physician have the time to monitor medications properly?
7. Has the child had an adequate physical and psychological evaluation?

The growing medical and legal concerns over the use of drugs to alter children's behavior and the need for more information about such drugs' long-term effects guarantees that drug therapy will be a controversial issue for years to come.

SUMMARY

Social integration is important to a young child's long-term development. Social isolation can have long-term effects on children. Teachers need to be aware of the social interaction in their classrooms and the problems that children might have in their social relations. Teachers can use a variety of strategies for promoting social interaction. They can develop a positive classroom climate, using a number of ways for managing behavior problems of young children and utilizing other children as well as themselves as positive sources of influence. A number of programs to help teachers are available.

APPENDIX A

Social Skill Programs

Several social skill training programs have been developed over the past several years by university and commercial publishers make use of both adult- and peer-directed interventions. Some of these are discussed here.

PEERS (Procedures for Establishing Effective Relationship Skills) (Hops, Guild, Fleischman, Paine, Street, Walker, & Greenwood, 1978) is a program for teaching social interaction skills to preschoolers consisting of four principal components: (1) direct social skill training procedures that can be used by both adults and peers to teach such social behaviors as social initiations, appropriately receiving the initiation of another, and learning how to sustain and extend interactions; (2) cooperative game activities for teaching social skills; (3) a point system for rewarding appropriate behaviors during recess; and (4) a child implemented self-report program for social progress.

SCIPPY (Social Competency Intervention Package for Preschool Youngsters) (Day, Powell, Dy-Linn, & Stowitschek, 1982) is a program for socially withdrawn preschoolers that contains procedures for selecting social activities for training purposes, for teaching social skills, for training tutors, and for gradually eliminating teacher prompts. This program promotes social interaction among diverse children, including those with disabilities, those who are at risk, and those who have no disabilities.

Spivak and Shure (1974) provided a set of procedures for teaching social problem-solving skills. This treatment consists of a series of scripted lessons, formal games to teach language and social problem-solving concepts, and strategies for teaching children to resolve their own social problems.

The Integrated Preschool Curriculum (Odom, Bender, Stein, Doran, Houden, McInnes, Gilbert, Deklyen, Speltz, & Jenkins, 1984) teaches social tutors to direct social initiations to socially less adept peers. The curriculum includes scripted lessons for training tutors, suggested role-play activities, and direct instructional strategies for promoting "good playing" with peers. Tutors are trained to suggest play ideas, to promote sharing, and to reinforce appropriate behaviors. Activity cards describing play activities designed to set the context for interaction are also provided.

LEAP (Learning Experience—An Alternative Program for Preschoolers and Parents) (Strain, 1984) incorporates peer-instruction across developmental areas. This program offers peer instruction to promote social interactions in three forms: (1) peers as participants in group-oriented contingencies, (2) peers as behavioral models, and (3) peers as direct agents of training. This program is effective in developing social skills among lower functioning students.

Skillstreaming the Elementary School Child: A Guide for Teaching Prosocial Skills (McGinnis & Goldstein, 1984) contains a number of practical guides for teaching prosocial skills that has been especially useful in primary-level classrooms. Checklists are provided for classroom survival skills, friendship-making skills, skills for dealing with feelings, skill alternatives to aggression, and skills for dealing with stress. Skill packages offer teachers activities for enhancing social interaction.

APPENDIX B

Additional Resources

The following books and periodicals will further enrich the teacher's knowledge of social learning in the early years.

1. Kostelnik, M. J., Stein, L. C., Whiren, A. P., & Soderman, A. K. (1988). *Guiding children's social development*. Cincinnati, OH: South-Western Publishing Company.

This text contains a number of practical guidelines and strategies for addressing such common social concerns as building positive relationships through nonverbal communication, promoting children's self-awareness and self-esteem, responding to children's emotions, enhancing children's play, fostering self-discipline in children, handling children's aggressive behavior, helping children cope with stress, supporting children's development in sensitive areas, supporting children's friendships, promoting social behavior, and teaching children to make judgments.

2. Essa, E. (1985). *A practical guide to solving preschool behavior problems*. Albany: Delmar.

This book uses a case-study format to present strategies for dealing with the following behavior problems of young children: aggressive and antisocial behaviors, disruptive behaviors, destructive behaviors, emotional and dependent behaviors, eating behaviors, multiple problem behaviors, and problems related to participation in social and school activities.

3. Garwood, S. G. (Ed) (1987). *Social policy and young handicapped preschool children*. Austin, TX: PRO Ed.

This edition of the *Topics in Early Childhood Special Education* periodical contains a number of articles arguing for the development of programmatic specialties related to the social education of young children with exceptional educational needs.

4. Schneider, B. H., Rubin, K. H., & Ledingham, J. E. (1985). *Children's peer relations: Issues in assessment and intervention*. New York: Springer-Verlag.

This book includes a number of articles that review current research on the treatment of socially unskilled children. Separate chapters are provided on social competence, on assessing social withdrawal, and on developing social intervention procedures for socially isolated children and adolescents.

5. Meisels, S. J. (Ed.) (1986). *Mainstreaming handicapped children: Outcomes, controversies, and new directions*. Hillsdale, NJ: Erlbaum.

This book contains information on policy and practical strategies related to mainstreaming students with exceptional educational needs. Although the book focuses on mainstreaming across grades, selected chapters are especially useful for early education teachers.

REFERENCES

Aiello, B. (1976). Especially for special educators: A sense of our own history. *Exceptional Children, 42,* 244–252.

Axline, V. M. (1969a). *Play therapy* (rev. ed.). New York: Ballantine Books.

Axline, V. M. (1969b). Play therapy procedures and results. In H. Dupont (Ed.), *Educating emotionally disturbed children*. New York: Holt, Rinehart & Winston.

Bandura, A. (1971). Psychotherapy based on modeling principles. In A. Bergin and S. L. Garfield (Eds.), *Handbook of psychotherapy and behavior change* (pp. 653–708). New York: Wiley.

Barkley, R. A. (1981). *Hyperactive children: A handbook for diagnosis and treatment*. New York: Guilford Press.

Bessell, H., & Palomares, U. (1970). *Methods in human development*. San Diego: Human Development Training Institute.

Brantner, J. P., & Doherty, M. A. (1983). A review of timeout: A conceptual and methodological analysis. In S. Axelrod and J. Apsche (Eds.), *The effects of punishment on human behavior* (pp. 87–132). New York: Academic Press.

Brophy, J. E., & Good, T. L. (1986). Teacher behavior and student achievement. In M. C. Wittrock (Ed.), *Handbook of research on teaching* (3rd ed.) (pp. 328–375). New York: Macmillan.

Brophy, J. E., & Putnam, J. G. (1979). Classroom management in the elementary grades. In D. L. Duke (Ed.), *Classroom management. 78th Yearbook of the National Society for Education* (pp. 182–216). Chicago: University of Chicago Press.

Clark, C., & Peterson, D. (1986). Teachers' thought processes. In M. C. Wittrock (Ed.), *Handbook of research on teaching* (3rd ed.) (pp. 255–296). New York: Macmillan.

Combs, A. W. (1965). *The professional education of teachers: A perceptual view of teacher preparation*. Boston: Allyn & Bacon.

Cooper, J. O., Heron, T., & Howard, W. L. (1987). *Applied behavior analysis*. Columbus, OH: Merrill.

Cowen, E. L., Pederson, A., Babijian, H., Izzo, L. D., & Trost, M. A. (1973). A long-term follow-up of early detected vulnerable children. *Journal of Consulting and Clinical Psychology, 41*, 438–446.

Cox, F. N. (1963). Sociometric status and individual adjustment before and after play therapy. *Journal of Abnormal and Social Psychology, 48*, 364–366.

Day, R., Powell, T., Dy-Linn, E., & Stowitschek, J. (1982). An evaluation of the effects of a social interaction training package on mentally handicapped preschool children. *Education and Training of the Mentally Handicapped, 17*, 125–130.

Dewey, J. (1939). *Experience and education*. New York: Macmillan.

Dimensions of personality. (1972). Dayton, OH: Pflaum/Standard.

Dinkmeyer, D. (1982). *DUSO–Revised: Developing understanding of self and others*. Circle Pines, MN: American Guidance Service.

Dreikurs, R. (1968). *Psychology in the classroom* (2nd ed.). New York: Harper & Row.

Erikson, E. (1963). *Childhood and society*. New York: Norton.

First things-values. (1972). Pleasantville, NY: Guidance Associates.

Gadow, K. D. (1986). *Children on medication*. Vol. 1: *Hyperactivity, learning disabilities, and mental retardation*. San Diego: College-Hill Press.

Gecas, V., Colonico, J. M., & Thomas, D. L. (1974). The development of self-concept in the child: Mirror theory versus model theory. *Journal of Social Psychology, 92,* 466–482.

Greenwood, C. R., Todd, N. M., Walker, H. M., & Hops, H. (1978). *Social assessment manual for preschool level* (SAMPLE). Eugene: CORBE (Center at Oregon for Research in the Behavioral Education of the Handicapped).

Gresham, F. M. (1982). Misguided mainstreaming: The case for social skills training with handicapped children. *Exceptional Children, 48*, 422–433.

Greshman, F. M. (1985). Social validity in the assessment of children's social skills: Establishing standards for social competency. *Journal of Psychoeducational Assessment, 1*, 299–307.

Gresham, F. M. (1986a). Conceptual issues in the assessment of social competence in children. In P. Strain, M. Guralnick, & H. Walker (Eds.), *Children's social behavior: Development, assessment, and modification* (pp. 143–179). Orlando: Academic Press.

Gresham, F. M. (1986b). Conceptual and definitional issues in the assessment of children's social skills: Implications for classification and training. *Journal of Clinical Child Psychology, 15*, 3–15.

Gresham, F. M., & Elliott, S. N. (1984). Assessment and classification of children's social skills: A review of methods and issues. *School Psychology Review, 13*, 392–401.

Gresham, F. M., & Lemanek, K. L. (1983). Social skills: A review of cognitive-behavioral training procedures with children. *Journal of Developmental Psychology, 4*, 239–261.

Gresham, F. M., & Reschly, D. J. (1987). Dimensions of social competence: Method factors in the assessment of adaptive behavior, social skills, and peer acceptance. *Journal of School Psychology, 26*, 367–381.

Guralnick, M. J. (1981). Peer influences on development of communicative competence. In P. Strain (Ed.), *The utilization of peers as behavior change agents* (pp. 31–68). New York: Plenum.

Hartup, W. W. (1983). Peer relations. In M. Heatherington (Ed.), *Handbook of child psychology,* Vol. 4 (pp. 103–196). New York: Wiley.

Homme, L. (1977). *How to use contingency contracting in the classroom.* Champaign, IL: Research Press.

Hops, A., Guild, T. J., Fleischman, D. H., Paine, S. C., Street, A., Walker, H. M., & Greenwood, C. R. (1978). *PEERS* (Procedures for Establishing Effective Relationship Skills). Eugene: CORBE (Center at Oregon for Research in the Behavioral Education of the Handicapped).

Jersild, A. T. (1965). Voice of the self. *NEA Journal, 54*, 23–25.

Karnes, M. B., & Lee, R. C. (1979). *Early childhood education: What research says to teachers.* Reston, VA: Council for Exceptional Children.

Kazdin, A. E. (1982). The token economy: A decade later. *Journal of Applied Behavior Analysis, 15*, 431–445.

Kohn, M. (1977). *Social competence, symptoms and underachievement in childhood: A longitudinal perspective.* Washington, DC: Winston.

Kounin, J. (1970). *Discipline and group management in classrooms.* New York: Holt, Rinehart & Winston.

Ladd, G. W. (1981). Effectiveness of a social learning method for enhancing children's social interactions and peer acceptance. *Child Development, 52*, 171–178.

Lamb, M. E., Suomi, S. J., & Stephenson, G. R. (1979). *Social interaction analysis: Methodological issues.* Madison: University of Wisconsin Press.

Maccoby, E. E. (1980), *Social development psychological growth and the parent-child relationship.* New York: Harcourt, Brace, Jovanovich.

McGinnis, E., & Goldstein, A. P. (1984). *Skillstreaming the elementary school child: A guide for teaching prosocial skills.* Champaign, IL: Research Press.

Macmillan, D. L., Jones, R. L., & Meyers, C. E. (1976). Mainstreaming the mildly retarded: Some questions, cautions and guidelines. *Mental Retardation, 14*, 3–10.

Martin, G., & Pear, J. (1978). *Behavior modification: What it is and how to do it.* Englewood Cliffs, NJ: Prentice-Hall.

Martorella, P. H. (1975). Selected early childhood affective learning programs: An analysis of theories, structure and consistency. *Young Children, 30*(4), 289–301.

Murray, F. (1972). The acquisition of conservation through social interaction. *Developmental Psychology, 6*, 1–6.

Odom, S. L., Bender, M., Stein, M., Doran, L., Houden, P., McInnes, M., Gilbert, M., Deklyen, M., Speltz, M., & Jenkins, J. (1984). *Integrated preschool curriculum.* Seattle: University of Washington.

Perret-Clemont, A. N. (1980). Social interaction and cognitive development in children. *European Monographs in Social Psychology*, No. 19. London: Academic Press.

Peterson, P. L., & Walberg, H. G. (1979). *Research on teaching: Concepts, findings and implications.* Berkeley, CA: McCutchan.

Piaget, J. (1935). *The language and thought of the child.* London: Routledge and Kegan Paul.

Roff, M., Sells, S. B., & Golden, M. M. (1972). *Social adjustment and personality development in children*. Minneapolis: University of Minnesota Press.

Rosenshine, B., & Stevens, R. (1986). Teaching functions. In M. C. Wittrock (Ed.), *Handbook of research on teaching* (3rd ed.) (pp. 376–391). New York: Macmillan.

Rosenthal, R., & Jacobson, L. (1968). Teacher expectations for the disadvantaged. *Scientific American*, 218–219.

Rubenstein, J. L., & Howes, C. (1979). Caregiving and infant behavior in day care and in homes. *Developmental Psychology, 15*, 1–24.

Saitamo, D. M., Maneady, L., & Shook, G. (1987). The effects of a classroom manager role on the social status and social interaction patterns of withdrawn kindergarten students. Unpublished. Pittsburgh: University of Pittsburgh.

Seeman, J., Barry, E., & Ellenwood, C. (1964). Interpersonal assessment of play therapy outcome. *Psychotherapy: Theory, research and practice, 1*, 64–66.

Spivak, G., & Shure, M. B. (1974). *Social adjustment of young children: A cognitive approach to solving real-life problems*. San Francisco: Jossey-Bass.

Spodek, B. (1985). *Teaching in the early years* (3rd ed.). Englewood Cliffs, NJ: Prentice-Hall.

Spodek, B., Lee, R. C., & Saracho, D. (1983). Mainstreaming handicapped children in the preschool. In S. Kilmer (Ed.), *Advances in early education and day care*, Vol. 3 (pp. 107–122). Greenwich, CT: JAI Press.

Strain, P. S. (1984). Social behavior patterns of handicapped and non-handicapped-developmentally disabled friend pairs in mainstream preschools. *Analysis and Interventions in Developmental Disabilities, 4*, 15–28.

Strain, P. S. (1985). Programmatic research on peers as intervention agents. In B. H. Schneider, K. H. Rubin, & J. E. Ledingham (Eds.), *Children's peer relations: Issues in assessment and intervention* (pp. 193–205). New York: Springer-Verlag.

Sulzer, B., & Mayer, G. R. (1972). *Behavior modification procedures for school personnel*. Hinsdale, IL: Dryden Press.

Swap, S. M. (1974). Disturbing classroom behaviors: A developmental and ecological view. *Exceptional Children, 41*, 163–172.

Trostle, S. L. (1988). The effects of child-centered play sessions on social-emotional growth of three- to six-year-old bilingual Puerto Rican children. *Journal of Research in Childhood Education, 3*(2), 93–106.

Turiel, E. (1973). Stage transition in moral development. In R. Travers (Ed.), *Second handbook of research on teaching* (pp. 732–758). Chicago: Rand McNally.

Ulman, C. A. (1957). Teachers, peers and tests as predictors of adjustment. *Journal of Educational Psychology, 48*, 257–267.

Walberg, H. J. (1986). Syntheses of research on teaching. In M. C. Wittrock (Ed.), *Handbook of research on teaching* (3rd ed.) (pp. 214–229). New York: Macmillan.

Winkler, D. R. (1975). Educational achievement and school peer group composition. *Journal of Human Resources, 10*, 189–204.

PART THREE

Modifying Classroom Programs for Individual Children

CHAPTER 9

Using Educational Play

CHAPTER OVERVIEW

This chapter discusses:

1. The role of play in educating young children.
2. The different theories of play.
3. The importance of play in the education of diverse children.
4. The different types of educational play.
5. Ways of adapting educational play to meet the needs of diverse children.

Play has always been an important part of early childhood programs. All areas of development are influenced by play—social, emotional, physical, and cognitive. Play gives children an opportunity to express their ideas and feelings as well as to symbolize and test their knowledge of the world. Children with disabilities need this opportunity as much as do normal children. Although much of the education of these children is concerned with providing direct support for academic and preacademic learning, play should not be denied its rightful place in their education. In fact, an integrated classroom provides the ideal support for play-learning activities.

Play is a form of behavior that is intrinsically motivated. It is performed for its own sake, and is conducted in a relaxed way to produce positive effects. Play is free from concern with end products. Interference with the spontaneity of play can destroy its essential character. Spodek, Saracho, and Davis (1991) provide the following criteria for play:

1. Play is motivated by the satisfaction gained from the activity. It is not governed by basic needs or drives, or by social demands.

2. Players are concerned with activities more than with goals. Goals are self-imposed, and the behavior of the players is spontaneous.
3. Play occurs with familiar objects or following the exploration of unfamiliar objects. Children supply their own meanings to play activities and control the activity themselves.
4. Play activities can be nonliteral.
5. Play is free from the rules imposed from the outside, and the rules that do exist can be changed by the players.
6. Play requires the active engagement of the players.

These criteria can be useful in understanding play. Unfortunately, is not always clear why people play and particularly why *children* play.

Play is an essential activity for young children. Through play, young children develop a wide range of verbal and nonverbal communication skills. They also learn about their playmates' feelings and attitudes, and learn to accept their classmates' points of view (Saracho, 1985). The socialization aspect of play helps them learn to get along with others. Play helps young children learn about their social world as they play different roles, express their ideas and feelings, and negotiate social relationships with their peers. Play also helps them to gain information, developing and testing ideas to expand their knowledge (Spodek & Saracho, 1988).

Children's play must be planned to offer a supporting environment, making sure that enough materials and equipment are available, extending the children's play, and encouraging positive relations among children. This chapter presents various theories of play and discusses the importance of play in the education of all young children. It also contains suggestions for adapting educational play—including manipulative play, physical play, dramatic play, and games—for children with disabilities.

THE ROLE OF PLAY

The term *play* is used in many ways. Sometimes play means a dramatic performance or a person making music with an instrument. Play also describes people's "kidding around." A pun can be interpreted as a play on words. Since the word *play* is used in many forms, its definition creates problems in understanding play (Spodek & Saracho, 1988).

The three major contemporary theories of play are the psychoanalytic, constructivist, and arousal-seeking theories. Understanding these theories can help teachers generate guidelines for the different types of educational play (manipulative play, physical play, dramatic play, and games).

Psychoanalytic Theory

The psychoanalytic theory of play evolved from the work of Sigmund Freud and his followers. It has been modified since it was originally developed. Children's play is viewed as intrinsically motivated, with playful acts intended to reduce accumulated tension and to provide pleasure. According to Freud, play serves two functions. First, it is a vehicle children use to master their own thoughts and actions. Children's active participation or passive observation controls their internalized thought processes and their voluntary physical movements.

Activity, the second role of play, is related to the individual's socioemotional development. Pain or unpleasantness tends to affect social relationships and interpersonal exchanges. Play activities and exploration help children understand painful situations and substitute pleasurable feelings for unpleasant ones. Play involves interpreting situations, including symbolic elements related to people and objects in the present and past. Children express their feelings through play behavior (Wehman & Abramson, 1976).

Play therapy, based on psychoanalytic theory, is a psychological treatment that has been used extensively with emotionally disturbed children. It permits children to naturally express themselves and to act out feelings of tension, fear, and insecurity. The therapist uses play to help children control their feelings and become more secure. The play therapist's responsibility is to draw out the children's feelings through play while communicating at their level (Axline, 1974). Teachers should not engage in play therapy themselves, but they can use the play process to help them understand children's feelings and to help children cope with the world around them.

Constructivist Theory

The constructivist theory of play is based to a great extent on Piaget's work. This theory suggests that children construct knowledge as they gain information about the world through the dual processes of assimilation and accommodation. *Assimilation* allows children to gather information from the world and use the action patterns they already have to solve present problems. *Accommodation* allows children to adjust their internal understandings to new ideas. When assimilation assumes primacy over accommodation—which occurs in childhood—spontaneous play occurs. Play permits the two processes to interact, allowing children to create an *equilibrium,* or balance, between the ideas they have and the information they collect (Fein & Schwartz, 1982).

According to Piaget (1962), there are three developmental stages of play: sensory-motor play, symbolic play, and games with rules. The stages evolves in a sequential order and the mental structures of each are progressively integrated into later stages. For example, playing games with rules occurs after symbolic play, which occurs after sensory-motor play. As a new stage of play develops, the previous stages become subsumed into it, though it is always accessible to the child or adult.

In the first stage of play, children's repetitive actions are the focus of physical activity. In the second stage, make-believe or symbolic play evolves. This stage begins at about age 18 months and continues until about age 7. In symbolic play any object can stand for any other object. For example, wooden boxes can be used to represent cars and trucks.

The final stage of play, games with rules, starts at about age 7. It is characterized by children's activity based on social convention and interaction. As games with rules become established, practice play and symbolic play diminish. Examples of games with rules include checkers, chess, and card games.

By observing children's play, teachers can identify their level of play development and can intervene appropriately. Such interventions include changing the play setting, adding different materials, raising questions of the children, or stepping in momentarily to direct the play toward educational goals, then stepping out of the play situation. Teachers must be sure that children's play is not distorted by these interventions. If the children become oriented to reality and authority, then the activity is no longer play.

Recent years have seen the development of what has been called a post-Piagetian perspective on children's cognitive development. Much of this approach is rooted in the theoretical work of L. S. Vygotsky, who was a contemporary of Piaget and died at an early age in 1934. His book, *Thought and Language* (1962), although it has been available in English for over 30 years, has received increasing attention recently. A second book, *Mind in Society* (1978), was compiled from his writings after his death.

Although Vygotsky viewed knowledge as constructed by the individual, he saw it as a collective act imbedded in a sociohistorical context. Unlike in Piagetian theory, which considers cognitive development as preceding learning, Vygotsky viewed learning as a precursor to cognitive development. The key here is that learning can take place a bit beyond a child's level of development if some sort of aid is provided in a cultural context. Vygotsky referred to this area where learning takes place as the *zone of proximal development*. Vygotsky conceived of children's play as being in the zone of proximal development. That is, children use play to help them make sense of the world and as a support for intellectual development.

Arousal-Seeking Theory

The arousal-seeking theory is based on the assumption that people play to maintain an optimal arousal level. Ellis (1973) suggested that people constantly strive for sensory variation. If sensory input remains constant, individuals cannot pay attention to it for very long. If little information is available, individuals search for additional stimulation. If there is too much information available, individuals avoid stimulation. Play can be used to mediate the amount of information available to the child.

RESEARCH ON PLAY WITH YOUNG CHILDREN OF DIVERSE NEEDS

Play is typically seen as a central activity in most traditional early childhood programs. It is not always given the same central role in special programs. This situation is changing, however.

Children with Disabilities

The play of children with disabilities has attracted the attention of educators in recent years. Educational play can improve children's performance in language, motor, cognitive, and social skills (Strain, Cooke, & Appolloni, 1976; Wehman, 1977). It can positively influence their adaptive behavior. It also can positively influence their ability to adapt to different situations. Tremblay, Strain, Hendrickson, and Shores

(1981) examined two categories of play-initiations (assisting and sharing) and found that play leads to reciprocal social exchanges among young children. Hendrickson, Gable, Hester, and Strain (1985) later found that both assisting and sharing were effective in gaining desired child responses. These results demonstrate the positive influence that classmates may have on their socially withdrawn peers. Initiating and maintaining reciprocal social exchanges between young children with severe disabilities and children with no disabilities demonstrate the positive effects of direct intervention on socially withdrawn children (Strain & Fox, 1981).

Children with disabilities can also learn to cooperate by participating in group play, learning to take turns, sharing, and helping other children. Mehlman (1953) and Leland, Walker, and Taboada (1959) related play to increases in personality adjustment, social behavior, and intelligence in children with mild retardation. These increases were small, however, and a cause-effect relationship was not established.

Different types of toys have different influences on the children's behavior. Hendrickson, Tremblay, Strain, and Shores (1981) have recommended specific socially oriented toys to increase the frequency of interactions between preschool children with and without disabilities during free play. Beckman and Kohl (1984) also examined the effects of social and isolate toys on the interactions and play of integrated and nonintegrated preschoolers. The greatest number of interactions were observed when social toys were available. Differences between integrated and nonintegrated groups were mainly a result of substantial differences in the social play condition.

McCormick (1987) compared the effects of different peer combinations on social play in toy play and in a computer activity. The ability to stimulate vocalization

and social play in dyads composed of one preschooler with developmental delays and one nondelayed preschooler was examined. The results showed that the computer activity was at least as effective as the toy play in stimulating vocalizations by the two preschoolers with social and language deficits. Comparisons were made of the vocalizations and social play of the normally developing preschoolers when interacting with one another and those of the normally developing preschoolers when paired with peers with developmental delays. There were more frequent and complex exchanges for the nondelayed dyads than for the mixed dyads.

The classroom environment can be designed to support children's socialization through play. Teachers also can help young children by providing appropriate language and social models to influence their play. The play of children with disabilities develops through the same basic sequence as that of children without disabilities, through sensorimotor (exploratory) and symbolic (dramatic) play. Although the sequence is the same, the kinds of disabilities the children have influence their play. The more severe the disability, the greater the effects (Rogers, 1988). Sherburn, Utley, McConnell, and Gannon (1988) compared two procedures for reducing the violent or aggressive theme play of preschoolers with behavior disorders. Their study suggests that violent or aggressive theme play may be harmful for these children. However, further research must be conducted to explore the long-term effect of this play. It should be noted, however, that aggressive play is different from the rough-and-tumble play exhibited by boys in the early primary grades. With popular boys this type of play becomes games with rules, that is, from chasing games to tag (Pellegrini & Boyd, 1993).

Play also can have a positive influence on the development of the fine-motor, language, and personal-social skills of children with disabilities (Morrison & Newcomer, 1975). Cooperative play teaches children acceptable modes of social interaction—such as sharing, taking turns, accepting responsibility—that young children with disabilities often lack. These children often play independently for long periods of time and may not cooperate with their peers unless they receive verbal encouragement or physical guidance (Whitman, Mercurio, & Caponigri, 1970). In addition, children who become involved in spontaneous play rarely display aggressive behavior. The stereotypical rocking behavior and bizarre vocal sounds of children with severe disabilities also may be reduced or eliminated during play (Wehman, 1978).

Hill and McCune-Nicolich (1981) found an orderly progression of various hierarchial stages of symbolic play in children with Down syndrome. These correlated closely with the children's mental age. They also found a relationship between symbolic development and affective/interpersonal development. Motti, Cicchetti, and Stroufe's research (1983) supports these results. Their study showed striking relationships between the children's symbolic play skills at age 3 to 5, their affective responses at 10 months, and their developmental levels at 24 months of age. Their study demonstrates a coherent pattern of cognitive development that children with Down syndrome display over time.

Children suffering from autism display serious deficits in symbolic play. Early levels for symbolic play skills and multischeme sequences in autistic children relate to their skills in receptive language and nonverbal communication skills. These children engage in less doll-directed play than do other children. They also spend a larger portion of their time in immature forms of play than do children without disabilities or those with mental retardation (Mundy, Sigman, Sherman, & Ungerer, 1984). The range of play skills of children with autism varies based on the severity of their disability. The effectiveness of treatment programs is determined by the improvement in the children's play skills (Rogers, Herbison, Lewis, Pantone, & Reis, 1986).

Research on the symbolic play of children with language disorders indicates that the performance of these children is poorer than that of comparable children without disabilities. However, children with language impairments show superior symbolic play skills to that of younger children in a variety of play situations. This supports the partial independence of language and symbolic play (Terrel, Schwarts, Prelock, & Messick, 1984). Children with language impairments had agent-action-object relations in play that they were not able to produce with speech (i.e., children could not produce word combinations expressively). Weis (1981) developed a language therapy program for these children aimed at adding words and concepts to familiar play relationships. Lombardino and Sproul (1984) studied both structural correspondences and noncorrespondences between play and language of children with language delays. They found that the pattern of noncorrespondence was similar for children with language delays in that they were playing at a level consistent with their receptive language ages, although they produced little or no expressive language. McCune-Nicolich (1982) suggested that when children's cognitive attainments significantly exceed their linguistic abilities, the teacher should examine biological and environmental influences that may relate to the children's language delay.

Abnormalities in the development of symbolic play relate to severe disabilities in language and vision. Children who are visually impaired and children who are autistic are the ones whose play skills are most severely affected; they develop abnormally in both their sensorimotor and their symbolic play. Symbolic play and language functioning are not inextricably bound. Some independence exists between the two. It is possible that children with language impairments may show superior symbolic play performance over their language performance or that children with visual impairments may be slower in symbolic play yet develop language skills well (Rogers, 1988).

Young children with disabilities show a greater combination of immature and mature play patterns than do their nondisabled counterparts, who seem to develop a higher proportion of mature play schemes in free play. These children can benefit from play models and materials that stimulate more mature play levels. Materials and social grouping must be carefully selected to help children with disabilities develop higher levels of play, providing more new information and less redundancy. Capone, Smith, and Schloss (1988) found that blocks, vehicles, books, dolls, rolling objects, and puzzles are the toys that nondisabled children play with most during free play.

When children have difficulty using a particular toy, teachers can construct a task analysis for that toy. They can first introduce toys that require similar skills and later provide toys that require different skills. For example, a truck, a set of blocks, and a ball require the child with a disability to use similar skills. Children with disabilities will then (1) establish eye contact with each toy; (2) grasp it or pick it up; (3) position it for appropriate play (e.g., turn the truck around before rolling it to a partner, position the block above a tower or building, or place the ball so that a push would send it off to a playmate); and (4) release it (e.g., push the truck toward a playmate, place a block on top of a building, or roll the ball toward a play partner).

Teachers should consider the children's disability in organizing the play environment and providing materials. Novelty in play and flexibility of several schema on specific play objects are two elements of play that must be focused for young children with disabilities (Rogers, 1988). Children with visual impairments and children with autism seem to require more play coaching than do other children. To promote these children's play development, sensorimotor schema must be presented, and cause-and-effect sequences must be emphasized and repeated. Most children with disabilities, especially those with autism, are weak in both vocal and motoric imitation. Imitation games should be provided to help children with disabilities improve their observational skills by increasing their tendency to imitate the behavior of adults and peers.

Since children with disabilities may have difficulty in language development, symbolic play activities should be provided for them (Wehman, 1975). Sociodramatic play is symbolic play in which the players stand for individuals other than themselves (e.g., a child takes on an adult role) and in which objects also stand for things other than themselves (e.g., a chair stands for a car). The development of this type of play parallels the development of language, in which sounds stand for objects, actions, or ideas.

Children Who Are at Risk

At-risk children may not have specific disabilities that require that their play environment be modified. However, they do have needs that must be considered in relation to their play.

At-risk children may have been identified in relation to family poverty, alcohol or drug consumption, child abuse, school attendance, educational failure, race, and ethnicity. Evidence shows that a disproportionate number of children who live in conditions of poverty show developmental delays. The deficiency may be result of an organic cause (Ramey, Mills, Campbell, & O'Brien, 1975). Other reasons include the breakdown of the family, the unwillingness or the inability of the government and schools to meet their responsibilities toward children, the permissiveness of society's value system, and the absence of values in the homes or schools (Pellicano, 1987).

At-risk children have often been influenced by an impoverished environment. Parents' social environment affects their child-rearing ability. For example, parental rejection may relate to the social isolation of the parent-child relationship, whereas parental acceptance increases the child's involvement with other adults in the day-to-day parent-child relationship (Gabarino & Sherman, 1980). Ramey et al. (1975) compared the home stimulation of a sample of infants from the general population with a sample of at-risk infants. The results showed that maternal involvement made a difference between these two groups. Teachers should foster this relationship among the families of children in their classes. Mothers, especially those of high-risk children, should be invited to participate in the children's program. Teachers may also have to help these parents improve their relations with their children.

Children Who Are Gifted

Although gifted children's play abilities may be equivalent to those of older children, they still have much in common with typical children their own age. Many gifted children are perceived by their peers as fun to play with. Fiscella and Barnett (1985) studied the play styles of both gifted and nongifted children. They found that gifted children showed higher degrees of physical, social, and cognitive play styles, but the humor and general effect they demonstrated were equivalent to their peers. Boys had more active physical play patterns—teasing and joking—than did girls. On the other hand, girls changed activities more often. The gifted boys' and girls' play styles were more imaginative than those of the typical peers.

Gifted children's intellectual maturity does not shield them from social role expectations. These expectations for boys and girls are reinforced in many subtle or obvious ways, such as the toys and literature selected and the role models portrayed in the entertainment media and at home. Unfortunately, similar patterns may be reinforced in school.

Adults may expect gifted children's social maturity to be the equivalent of their cognitive performance. Such expectations, along with other forms of inordinate pressure, may lead gifted children to assume responsibilities they are not ready for. In the integrated classroom, gifted children should be allowed to interact with same-age peers in areas of possible common interest. The children should participate in areas that challenge and stretch them intellectually. Play activities may include special projects appropriate for them, shared special interest areas, community-based learning activities, or advanced academic work.

Teachers need to accept the gifted children's creative, unusual, and divergent thinking products. They also should stimulate their creative processes. Gifted children need the enrichment of the regular early education environment to meet their needs. Teachers can increase the depth, complexity, or abstractness of these activities when gifted children are involved. Questions and activities designed to elicit fluent, flexible, original, and elaborated thinking can be incorporated into regular activities, such as sharing art, discussions, and story reading (Kitano, 1982).

Teachers' attempts to cater to intellectually gifted young children can create problems in a typical classroom. Most children wish to be like their peers; so do gifted children. Gifted children commonly hide their abilities and act like average children (Whitmore, 1980).

In play, teachers must provide enriched activities for gifted children that are appropriate and reasonable. This may be difficult to provide, but the task is no more difficult than providing appropriate activities for children with disabilities. Kitano (1982) recommended providing activities that enhance creativity and higher cognitive processes, including predicting, planning, and decision making. Activities that promote inquiry, problem solving, and affective development should also be provided. Kitano offered six general recommendations for an enrichment program to consider the gifted children's activities that

1. enhance creativity;
2. enhance higher cognitive processes;

3. enhance executive operations;
4. promote inquiry and problem solving;
5. promote affective development; and
6. incorporate process and content objectives into units.

Safford (1989) suggested that advanced materials be adapted so they can be managed and remain motivating to younger gifted children. These children have normal attention spans despite their more mature interests and more advanced cognitive levels. An activity may be geared to the child's levels in different areas of functioning.

Teachers must provide gifted children with opportunities for working independently and alone, pursuing self-selected activities, organizing self-selected activities, and organizing their own time. They should be helped to develop socially and to interact constructively with peers, sharing responsibilities and following adult direction to conform to necessary (not arbitrary) classroom rules. Schedules must be flexible; when appropriate, children should be able to set their own objectives. The play curriculum should promote group decision making and the development of social skills. According to Cartwright, Cartwright, and Ward (1989), possible types of differentiation include (1) changes in content and method of presentation to be more challenging and (2) some individualization, but also strong group interaction with other gifted children,

Gifted children often struggle to learn who they are and how their differences can be tolerated, managed, and valued. Early childhood experiences can help them cope with differences and can ease the difficulties associated with uneven development (Bagnato, Kontos, & Neisworth, 1987). Gifted children are generally slightly happier, healthier, more popular, and more emotionally stable than are children who are not gifted.

MODIFYING PLAY ACTIVITIES

Play is a spontaneous activity through which children experiment and test life experiences. Through play, children learn to master motor skills, follow directions, laugh, and interact with other children. Children with disabilities also learn to express pleasure and enjoyment, using smiles and laughter with various expressive movements of the head, arms, and body (Hirst & Shelley, 1989).

Play has at least four major values for children with disabilities: (1) to develop gross or fine motor skills, language, and a higher level of social behavior; (2) to involve activities that achieve educational goals; (3) to reduce socially unacceptable behaviors; and (4) to provide enjoyment (Wehman, 1978). As teachers include play in the curriculum, they must carefully select activities and materials for their learning and behavior outcomes and the degree to which they need to be changed for a particular child's limitation (Saracho & Spodek, 1987).

Children with Mental Retardation

Children who are mentally retarded lack spontaneity in play (Paloutzian, Hasazi, Streifel, & Edgar, 1971). Toys and play materials should be selected to promote and stimulate their play behavior. The following criteria can be used in selecting appropriate toys and materials:

1. *Toys and materials should be durable enough to hold up for a long period of time.*
2. *Toys should promote concrete experiences.* Young children who are mentally retarded are usually not at the symbolic or abstract level. They may ignore houses or dolls or transportation vehicles that promote symbolic and imaginative play since they do not know how to use them.
3. *Toys should provide a positive psychological effect.* Some children who are mentally retarded may have a young mental age. Toys should be appropriate for their mental age.

Children who are mentally retarded are not very different from children who are not retarded in their play needs and interests. They need to be part of a social group though they often play in isolation and may encounter problems in groups. These children want social approval, and social success encourages them to continue to participate socially. Since competition is difficult for them to deal with and they may become aggressive when they lose, the cooperative aspects of play should be emphasized (Wehman, 1977).

Children with Behavior Disorders

Play can help children with behavior disorders control their behaviors. As they become aware that they can control materials, they will realize they can control themselves and their interactions with others (Bernhardt & Mackler, 1975).

Group play experiences can provide these children with a common bond for continuous interaction with others during the day. Group play improves these children's relationships with peers, thus increasing their social acceptance. Those who have a restricted repertoire of experiences may be deficient in their social skills, and the deficiency may become evident in their socialization.

Play can release or curb the feelings of children with behavior disorders and reduce their inhibited hostility and anger. Play also allows them to express themselves through their actions, providing emotional gratification.

Children with Hearing Impairments

Play interactions are an essential part of normal child development (Higginbotham & Baker, 1981). Preschoolers who are hearing-impaired follow normal patterns in the development of play skills, but their rate of development may be influenced by socioeconomic status, which might limit their acquiring hearing aids at an early age or their receiving early training or therapy (Darbyshire, 1977; Mogford, 1977). Darbyshire reported deficits in both object substitution and dramatic play among these children. Socioeconomic status and the amount of language experience seem to be critical factors. Given the findings on the relationships between language development and symbolic play, these findings further underline this relationship.

Children with hearing impairments seem to participate in less complex and less social play than do children who hear normally (Mann, 1984). Esposito and Koorland (1989) examined several categories of play behavior of young children with hearing impairments in integrated and segregated settings. The children engaged in more socially advanced play in integrated settings.

The communication deficits of young children with hearing impairments may interfere with their play development (Higginbotham, Baker, & Neil, 1980). Delayed verbal language ability may limit the emergence of cooperative make-believe play involving the symbolic use of objects and sophisticated peer interaction since verbal exchange is essential to maintain such play (Higginbotham & Baker, 1981).

Several studies have examined the symbolic play of children with language disorders. When children with language impairments are compared with similar children who are not impaired, they demonstrate poorer performance in both unstructured and structure play situations than children without disabilities. However, when children with language impairments are compared with younger children without impairments who have the same language level, the children with language impairments show superior symbolic play skills in a variety of play situations. This reflects the partial independence of language and symbolic play (Terrel et al., 1984). Contrary to some views, children with language impairments demonstrated agent-action-object relations in play that they could not produce with speech (i.e., none of the children produced word combinations expressively), suggesting a language therapy approach aimed at adding words and concepts to play relationships that the child could already produce. One therapy technique—INREAL—has already been developed by Weis (1981).

Spontaneous play experiences can help children with hearing impairments develop normal movement potential. Obstacles that restrict their freedom of movement become social rather than physical restraints. Social play provides them with the greatest opportunities for social development.

Play can also promote the speech of children with hearing impairments. They want to communicate their interests, and play words become action words. Although speech is often secondary to action during play in early childhood classrooms, play can extend vocabulary.

Children with hearing impairments tend to have play interests that are similar to those of younger children. Usually these immature interests indicate a deficiency in psychosocial maturation. These children generally have a restricted repertoire of experiences that make them seem more socially deficient than they actually are (Hunt, 1955).

Children with Visual Impairments

Children with visual impairments are significantly delayed in the development of symbolic play. Infants (ages 4 months and up) with severe visual impairments have difficulty coordinating their eyes, hands, and mouths, in contrast to the world of object exploration that opens up to infants who are sighted. However, substantial delays in the development and elaboration of sensorimotor play have been found. Although infants who are blind repetitively and stereotypically play with their own bodies, the development of play with objects is delayed to a great extent. This is congruent with clinical experiences with infants who are visually impaired (Fraiberg, 1977). Fraiberg reported consistent delays in the doll play of four young children who were blind. Other tasks requiring representative thought in the symbolic play of such children also seem to be delayed (Mogford, 1977).

A study of the symbolic play of 16 children aged 18 to 38 months who were visually impaired indicated symbolic acts in half of the children at a mean age of 25.9 months (Rogers & Puchalski, 1984), which is considerably earlier than previous literature had suggested. The performance was also considerably below that of nonimpaired 20-month-olds. However, in this study, symbolic acts were recorded with the frequency of the use of the word *no* and with general sensorimotor skills.

Erikson (1972) has focused on the importance that vision assumes in the young infant's developing play. Children with visual impairments have the same play needs and interests as their sighted peers. They may be afraid to move freely, although they have the necessary movement skills. They need to develop self-reliance and acquire courage to offset their physical insecurity.

Children who are visually impaired can succeed in play when they can use their other senses. Like children with full vision, these children enjoy tactile games with blocks, toys, and materials made of different textures and forms. Most children with visual impairments select play objects that have a definite shape and are easily identified through touch. Complicated forms and soft, somewhat diffuse objects, such as those made of fur or cotton, are difficult for them to understand and may be disliked. Games can be used to develop kinesthetic sense and provide opportunities to move flexibly—by changing directions, stopping, and starting. Games and other physical activities are generally better for developing movement skills in children with visual impairments than are gymnastics and apparatus work. Some of these children encounter problems with balance activities, but they are usually able to climb ropes or play with push toys, swings, seesaws, parallel bars, rings, and other equipment that primarily use the sense of touch (Wehman, 1977). Drama, mime, art, and dance can be used to promote their creativity through body and facial expressions.

Children with visual impairments enjoy socializing with other children, often developing close relationships with small groups within larger groups. This can slow their development of social skills. They must extend their social contact to larger groups of children to be able to play successfully with their peers. They need the security of knowing that they are socially accepted and that their impairment does not restrict their enjoyment of play. They need to have personally satisfying play activities that they enjoy both with others and by themselves.

Children with Orthopedic Impairments

It is important that the play experiences of children who are orthopedically impaired be well planned and organized so that they all participate. They may not be able to engage in self-selected activities, but the opportunities to make choices should be built into their activities. Pictures of various activities can be placed a few inches apart on a piece of heavy cardboard and laminated for protection. A child can select an activity by placing a fist on the appropriate picture (Hirst & Shelley, 1989).

Several researchers (e.g., Brooks-Gunn & Lewis, 1982, 1984; Hanzlik & Stevenson, 1986) have investigated the play of children with orthopedic impairments. They found that children with cerebral palsy need more visual exploration and less tactile exploration with toys than do developmentally matched children without physical problems. They showed a narrower range and lower frequency of play behaviors, and a higher frequency of social behaviors among other groups of children with disabilities.

Some play needs of children with orthopedic problems are difficult to satisfy and may be exaggerated by the large number of hours spent in treatment or in the resource room. Children with serious orthopedic disabilities are limited in their involvement in active games because they cannot stand without support, walk or run with ease, or coordinate their hands and arms easily. Since children who are orthopedically impaired cannot produce movements easily, tensions may be higher for them. Those children who can move and enjoy active play can usually reduce their tensions. Many refuse to play in groups because they feel inferior, become self-conscious, and are afraid of competition or self-testing.

EDUCATIONAL PLAY

There are four major types of educational play: manipulative play, physical play, dramatic play, and games. Each needs to be included in the program of an integrated class.

Manipulative Play

In manipulative play, children play with small pieces of equipment such as puzzles, cuisenaire rods, or pegs and pegboards. Most of the actions are self-contained and there seldom is a dramatic quality to the play activity. Montessori materials are a good example of educational manipulative play. Children may play with a set of wooden cylinders, comparing their lengths or diameters and fitting them into a specially designed case. This activity teaches children to compare sizes and to arrange the materials in a series.

Manipulative materials can teach self-care skills. Young children with disabilities might experience difficulty in dressing. Children can use dolls and dressing frames to practice dressing skills as preparation to dressing themselves. Typical commercial doll clothes tend to be too small and their fastenings can be fragile. A large, 2-foot-tall stuffed doll can be provided with a wardrobe that requires snapping, buttoning, zippering, buckling, hooking, and lacing. Clothes can be made with large heavy-duty fasteners, large hooks and snaps (such as those found on pants), large flat buttons about one inch in diameter, and heavy zippers with a pull ring. A teacher could create an octopus for the children that has a different type of fastener or part of a fastener at the end of each tentacle (see Figure 9.1). Various fasteners can also be sewn to pieces of materials and attached to frames or incorporated in pillows and other articles.

Boards with shoelaces attached that required lacing and knot-tying can take the children through part of the process of putting on shoes. The children learn to put the string through the holes, crossing the middle in proper sequence and lacing the strings alternatively into the next holes. In tying knots, children learn to cross the midline and make an X with the strings. Clues on how to perform the task can be presented to the children. Other kinds of dressing frames can also be made, as shown in Figure 9.2. Different types of manipulative play might be needed by children with different types of disabilities. Boxes can be used in place of boards or frames, as shown in Figure 9.3.

Children with Mental Retardation.   Children with mental retardation often engage in repetitive manual manipulations and physical contacts. They may also pound, push, pull, or throw the materials, much like children at a less mature stage of development. Sensory feedback gained from using manipulative material helps such children move on to the next stage.

FIGURE 9.1

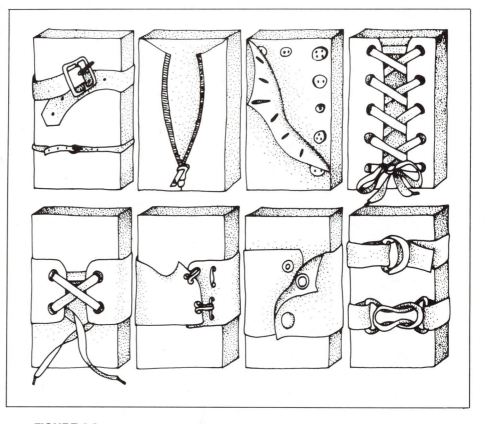

FIGURE 9.2

These children may explore manipulative materials by pushing, pulling, or throwing them. They may put a puzzle together or put the pieces of the puzzles into their mouth. As their play behavior becomes more organized, the children slowly gain manipulative skills with materials—spinning the wheels of a truck, turning a nut on a bolt, placing pegs into a pegboard. Once the children can manipulate these, they can learn to classify different materials, eventually combining the various uses of the materials. For example, children can disconnect cars from a train, undress a doll, or untie a knot. Later, they can dress the doll and use blocks to make different objects (Goetz & Baer, 1973), or include toy cars and buses in their block play (Wehman, 1977).

Manipulative materials can be used to teach number concepts and a variety of academic tasks to mentally retarded children. The Pacemaker Games Program, for example, teaches mentally retarded children about shape and color while promoting socialization (Ross, 1969). The program consists of five simple games using cards, dice, dominoes, shape and color counters, puzzles, checkers, and other table games.

Children with Visual Impairments.   Children with visual impairments need manipulative materials to help them understand their environment and to promote

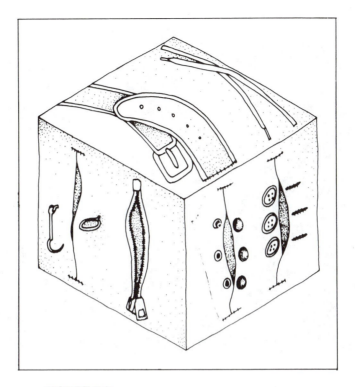

FIGURE 9.3

cognitive concepts similar to those of their sighted peers (Guthrie, 1979). Manipulative materials should offer these children basic concrete experiences. Their shapes should easily be identified and have a variety of textures, and, if possible, provide auditory stimulation. Smell is also important.

Children who have some residual vision should be provided with colorful materials. Children with visual impairments should be helped to notice the sensory qualities of manipulative materials, either visually or by holding, tasting, smelling, shaking, and perhaps dropping or throwing them. The materials should stimulate sensory awareness as well as promote developing concepts and skills. Many of these materials can be used for more than one purpose. A set of pliable rubber squeaky toy creatures, for example, can be squeaked with a light touch to encourage repetitive hand activities such as tapping, squeezing, and touching. If toys have several textures and bright colors, the surface can be explored. This can help children develop their pincer grasp reflex. The toys' other attributes and parts should be identifiable by touch (Guthrie, 1979).

The teacher can place a variety of objects in a box, then have the children put their hands in to identify the objects by touch. Common objects that are familiar to the child should be used at first.

A similar activity can require children with visual impairments to match pieces of material by texture (Saracho & Spodek, 1988). Two different sets of cardboards

covered with material of various textures (e.g., rough, smooth) can be provided. A texture book with each page made of a different textured material is also helpful.

Teachers can collect different sized boxes, nesting boxes within boxes. A noisemaker or flashlight (if the child has light perception) can be placed inside the center box and the children can manipulate the boxes to find the object. The degree of difficulty planned for these activities should be based on the children's ability levels. Manipulative materials that permit the visually impaired to judge weight are also valuable. Children can be asked to judge the weight of materials placed in small containers and arranged in order from lightest to heaviest. Teachers can help children with visual impairments discriminate using clues from their environment. They can learn to use their hearing by using materials such as Montessori sound boxes (Taite, 1974).

Children with Orthopedic Impairments.   Manipulative play may need to be adapted for children with orthopedic impairments. Those who cannot sit well, even with adapted furniture, can lie down on the carpet to achieve the advantages of eye-hand positioning. Children with poor muscular control throughout their bodies can have a foam rubber roll put under their chests while sitting at a table or lying on the floor (see Figure 9.4). The foam roll lifts their body weight from the floor, lets them get their hands out in front of them, and positions their heads so that they can view their hands and the objects in front of them. This position also helps them control their head and shoulders. The roll can be made firmer by rolling corrugated cardboard within the foam rubber. Larger rolls can be made by taping or tying several

additional layers of cardboard together or by using a hollow plastic pipe. The rolls must be firm and strong enough to bear the child's weight. Canvas bags used to cover the rolls can be removed to be washed as often as required (Fallen, 1978).

If tables are high enough for a wheelchair, wooden or rubber stops can be used to stabilize the wheelchair without locks so the child can use his or her arms in manipulative play. Tables also can be built with recesses and supplied with strap harnesses for children who cannot stand or sit without support. Wooden or metal poles can be strapped to the child's body to free the hands, allowing the child to become involved in manipulative play (Hunt, 1955). Battery-operated toys must be wired to a switch to help the child control them and choose among them (Hirst & Shelley, 1989).

There are some commercially available toys that children with cerebral palsy can

FIGURE 9.4

use independently. These toys do not require the child to use skilled fine movements or to manipulate small parts. The most effective adaptations in enhancing active and independent play include stabilizing the toy, restricting the movement of movable toys, and providing grasping aids, manipulation aids, or switches. Modifying toys can compensate for some deficits in hand functioning. A toy can be stabilized by attaching it to a surface with masking tape. Toys with a base can be clamped to a table. Placing pushtoys on top of a cardboard box or tray with edges can create a restricted area. Pulltoys can be placed on a track, and items requiring a banging motion (e.g., tambourine) can be held in a wood frame with springs. Grasping aids can include a universal cuff or quip cuff to help hold stick-like objects such as crayons. Cylindrical foam or tape and foam wrapped around the item will increase the width of an object that the child with cerebral palsy needs to hold (Schaeffler, 1988).

Physical Play

Physical play includes outdoor and indoor play as well as block play. During physical play, children engage in large motor actions such as running, jumping, or riding a tricycle, helping children develop physical skills and use them in new ways.

Children with Mental Retardation.   Some children who are mentally retarded are more limited in their physical skills than are normal individuals, though they may appear more normal in physical ability than in intellectual ability. Hopping, skipping, and galloping are learned by some much later than is normal; others never learn these skills. They may catch a ball with their wrists and arms instead of using their hands. Some of these children require larger, softer balls as well as extra opportunities for catching practice. Most mentally retarded children can perform primary reflex motor activities such as jumping, running, throwing, and climbing.

Children with mental retardation may have low stamina, tiring easily. During physical play, teachers need to watch and help children who show signs of fatigue. They might be encouraged to rest or to play with toys of interest to them. Mentally retarded children are interested in concrete items they handle. They can manipulate toys without engaging in make-believe. For example, they will explore the attributes of a new ball instead of its use. They may become frustrated if they cannot play with it immediately (Hunt, 1955).

Children with Behavior Disorders.   Physical play helps children with behavior disorders function as they become stimulated, relaxed, and emotionally satisfied.

In some cases, however, fear of failure may prevent a child from participating in an activity. Teachers may need to develop strategies to promote participation that will ensure success. Hyperactive children may respond positively to large motor activities (Hunt, 1955).

Children with Visual Impairments. Physical play activities for children who are visually impaired should be as broad as those for their normally sighted peers. These children, however, may not be able to engage in all children's activities. Children who are visually impaired may sometimes refuse to participate in an activity because they are afraid to fail. Physical activities that demand a great deal of skill may be of little value to them and may need to be adapted to be fun.

Children who are visually impaired can feel the different shapes of blocks and can build with them. They may need to develop a sense of balance as they build so their structures do not collapse. Water play, which teaches children to pour from one container to another, is a good physical activity for these children. The ability to pour is related to practical life skills, such as serving juice or milk. Auditory discrimination exercises, such as listening to the sound of liquid pouring into a container, and concepts of *full* and *half-full* are important for them. They need to learn to judge the depth of the liquid by sound to avoid spilling. This type of activity can be varied. Children can pour sand instead of water and learn that all of the sand in a small jar can be poured into a large jar. If all the sand in a large jar is poured into a smaller one, though, some will spill (Taite, 1974).

Children with visual impairments may enjoy outdoor play since the trees, wind, rain, and other natural features are exciting. They also may enjoy seasonal activities such as kite flying and snow games and may want to learn about the seasonal changes in nature. They can use swings, slides, ropes, rings, and seesaws outdoors. Other physical skills that these children can learn include bouncing a ball, skipping, and hopping. They also can learn to roller skate by using one skate first and then two.

Children with Orthopedic Impairments. Safety should not be taken for granted in activities for children with orthopedic impairments. The extent of the disability and the different areas of the body involved must be considered when planning physical play. Play experiences, however, should be restricted only by limitations of the child's physical abilities.

The play of children with orthopedic impairments is usually restricted in time and space since their play depends on the help of others. Their play is controlled by another individual. In spite of this limitation, their play can have a purpose beyond itself, including developing basic motor and social skills. Children need to have wheelchair leaders to engage in some physical activities. Teacher's aides, volunteer adults, high school students, teenagers with mild retardation, or older children of normal intelligence can serve as wheelchair leaders. These leaders must know how to safely manage a wheelchair and the rules and the purpose of the physical activity. They also must know how to talk to the children and know how to touch them when the activity requires physical manipulation for success. The leaders may need to have several practice sessions to ensure the greatest value in the physical activity.

Success in physical activities relies on leaders' willingness to engage themselves and the children with disabilities in the activities. Both the leader and the children with disabilities benefit when they engage in a favorite game. For example, musical wheelchairs can be a game children can enjoy. Each child in a wheelchair starts on a floor spot marker. When the music is played, the wheelchair leaders push the children around the room staying close to the spots. As the music stops, the leaders push the children to stop on a spot. The music plays long enough to allow everyone to get on a spot before the first spot is removed. After each child is dropped from the game, the leader for that child should move the child to the beat of the music or the children can swing their arms and heads to the rhythm or march around the circle in the opposite direction. This way the activity continues as an active experience rather than a passive one (Hirst & Shelley, 1989).

Individuals with orthopedic disabilities tend to have difficulty running fast, yet running should be a part of their program, possibly running slowly. They can wear small football helmets or felt headbands to protect them from falls during active play. Some difficulties can be alleviated if players are paired so each child completes a part of a task but both can achieve the entire act together (Hunt, 1955).

Depending on the level of children's disability, the physical features of the classroom, the outdoor play area, and the school may need to be modified for children who are orthopedically impaired.

1. Buildings may need more entrances and exits.
2. Doors and halls must be wider and without thresholds to allow for more expansive movements and for wheelchairs to pass through.
3. Restrooms may need to include beds and reclining chairs.
4. Toilet facilities must be close to classrooms and playing space.
5. Ramps must be substituted for stairs.
6. Chairs should be sturdy with rubber crutch tips under the legs to avoid slipping. Sand pits instead of dirt or asphalt should be provided under playground equipment. The playground should be surfaced with a combination of grass, asphalt, and dirt. Although asphalt provides the best traction, it is hazardous in a fall. Grass is safest for falling, but is slippery. Hard dirt is excellent for bouncing games and for sliding equipment. It can provide good traction for running, jumping, and supporting crutches (Hunt, 1955).

Children in wheelchairs who cannot build with blocks on the floor can use a scooter (belly board or crawler) in various ways (Fallen, 1978). The scooter board is a rectangular board of $\frac{3}{4}$-inch plywood with heavy-duty casters attached to each corner. The board can be padded with a layer of foam or some other type of cushion and covered with vinyl. Orthopedically impaired children can lie on their stomachs on top of scooter boards while raising their heads, and can propel themselves using their hands or elbows, reach around themselves, and use blocks or manipulative toys.

Children with orthopedic impairments who can partially maintain a sitting position can be helped to sit close to the floor for block building. A large cardboard box, plastic trashcan, or laundry basket can be cut on one side. The other side is left intact, providing minimal support (Fallen, 1978). A strap can be buckled under the arms to help the child sit up. Casters attached under the can, box, or basket help the child move by pushing off with the hands (see Figure 9.5).

Dramatic Play

In dramatic play, children act out roles generally in relationship to their classmates who are playing other roles. These informal dramatic situations often represent the children's life experiences. Dramatic play permits children to develop a sense of self-regard and self-confidence as they interact with their environment. Dramatic play helps them familiarize themselves with their motor, sensory, and intellectual apparatus as they become involved in self-stimulatory activities. Such play helps children create their own world while representing different themes such as hairdresser, post office, restaurant, or grocery store. In block building, children participate in miniature dramatizations. Block accessories help their play evolve beyond building. Sometimes children assume roles in dramatic play situations through puppets.

Children with Mental Retardation.   Children who are mentally retarded have difficulty maintaining an interest in dramatic play over a long period. Their imagination usually leans toward simple make-believe activities such as cowboys and Indians,

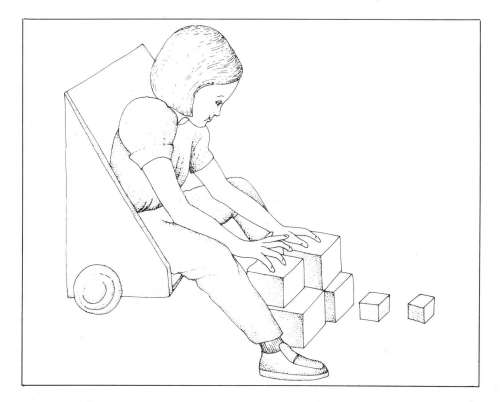

FIGURE 9.5

cops and robbers, playing house and dolls. They chase and capture, shoot and escape—avoiding any complications of right and wrong, trials, or ceremonies. They love playing with dolls, manipulating dishes, and maneuvering furniture. Their make-believe roles are simple, nonverbal, and related to their experiences. These children enjoy repeating these roles daily. Dramatic play can be made more imaginative by furnishing the environment with suggestive equipment. The children can also be stimulated with stories, pictures, and interesting excursions (Hunt, 1955).

Some experts (e.g., Paloutzian et al., 1971; Wehman, 1977) feel that children who are mentally retarded have limited imitation skills and need training in this area. Strategies for imitation training include:

1. Using an adult to train a mentally retarded child in different play situations.
2. Pairing a child who is mentally retarded in dramatic play with a higher functioning child.
3. Grouping two equivalently mentally retarded children with one or more adults.
4. Integrating children who are mentally retarded within a group of children who are not retarded.
5. Using reinforcement such a points, edibles, or praise.
6. Modifying the environment before the onset of play through toy selection, room size or background, and music.

Children with Behavior Disorders.   Play therapists create dramatic play situations, often in miniature, to allow children with behavior disorders to act out conflicting situations. Such play allows children to rid themselves of feelings with which they cannot cope. More often the play communicates to the therapist the nature of the conflicts with which the child is struggling. Because the communication may be in idiosyncratic symbolic form, it often is difficult for nontherapists to interpret. In addition, children should be allowed to expose feelings only to the extent that they can manage them.

Teachers are not child psychotherapists, but they can learn a great deal by observing children's play. They can also provide play activities that will allow children to work through problems on their own.

The value of dramatic play for these children depends on their peers' enjoyment, their expressive ability, and the meanings derived from the play. Psychiatrists affirm that a person can change behavior by assuming the role of another person who has different attributes. Such role taking is used in play therapy (Axline, 1974). The projective and creative elements of dramatic play can be promoted through puppets, pantomimes, and charades and through excursions to places of interest, such as exhibits, museums, and libraries.

Children with Visual Impairments.   Children with visual impairments tend to spend most of their dramatic play time in a world of fantasy. As they act out roles in dramatic experiences, their imagination is enhanced and they gain enjoyment. They also lose their self-consciousness and their understanding is increased. These children need to be encouraged to project themselves into different roles. They can pretend to be the wind, a growing flower, or a lively kitten as authentically as their seeing peers (Hunt, 1955). They also can act out live situations, such as setting the table or baking a cake, though they may have difficulty assuming roles dealing with everyday subjects or imaginative circumstances. Teachers need to plan such activities carefully so all children can participate (Taite, 1974).

At-Risk Children.   Teachers can invite mothers to engage with the children in the classroom during their play. Children may be allowed to play roles with other children's mothers or with their own in the dramatic play area. They can identify with and act out a variety of roles. Children at risk can use play as a catharsis to feelings they have difficulty dealing with. They can use play to communicate the type of feelings they are encountering. Teachers can then help them deal with these feelings through play or some other type of activity. In dramatic play, at-risk children need to enjoy the experiences, express their feelings, and acquire meanings from the activities. Puppets, pantomimes, and a variety of props can help them to assume roles of other persons.

Children need to be provided with an imaginative environment to act out family roles. Stories, pictures, and interesting field trips can help them to become motivated and assume a variety of roles. This becomes important for at-risk children because many (e.g., Ramey et al., 1975) have speculated on the influence of the quality of the home environment on a child's development. Children from different socioeconomic strata can act out their home situations or a situation they may desire to occur at home. Gabarino and Sherman (1980) found that low-risk children had a network that consisted of relatives and friends. When these children met a situation that required a social readjustment and help to relieve their stress, they reverted to resources consisting of family and professionals. This means the teacher must help families build networks that can expand the children's play.

Children at risk can use play to communicate the conflicts they encounter. Play serves as a catharsis as well as a problem-solving situation. It can help the child learn to cope with feelings in a positive way rather than act them out in a hostile manner.

Games

Games are structured activities with specific rules to follow. Simple games or musical game-like activities can be used with young children. Children need to learn the techniques for game playing. Teachers may have to guide the game to help children understand and follow the rules.

Games can be used to practice newly acquired skills, maintain mastered skills, and reinforce task completion. Teachers can make or buy board games for skill practice and development. Only those that do not violate the principles of effective instruction should be used. Games that have effective instructional techniques have several common features.

1. Many responses should be elicited from students. Games that require students to spend too much time "thinking" before responding or waiting for an opportunity to participate should be avoided.
2. The more students participate, the better the game is. Waiting too long to take turns decreases the students' interest.
3. Content must be geared toward each student's level. Students will lose interest if they are frustrated.

These characteristics and appropriate modifications related to the child's disability must be considered in selecting a game (Wesson, Wilson, & Mandlebaum, 1988).

The traditional game of bingo can be used for spelling, social studies or mathematics. War is a card game that can be adapted by dividing children into pairs. The teacher can make War-type card games for any topic that deals with comparable amounts (such as facts, fractions, money, and measurement) or relative positions (such as alphabetically or geographic locations).

Scrabble and similar word games also can be used. Each player has a set of letters and a board. Children change boards every 5 minutes. Players gain points for the words they create and for those words they make by attaching letters to those made by their opponent. The game is played cooperatively rather than competitively.

Boggle is another game that can be adapted. It is played with a set of dice with letters on each side. The dice are rolled, and players create as many words as possible from the letters that fall face up, using only the letters that are adjacent to each other.

Children with Mental Retardation.   Games help children with mental retardation to gain and retain knowledge. A mentally retarded child may be able to perform simple addition as part of the game he or she enjoys, such as keeping score at a baseball

game. Children enhance their sensory awareness by singing, playing games, telling stories, pantomiming, and taking field trips and field walks. The play equipment required for games also stimulates their senses through brightness of color, texture, and shape (Hunt, 1955).

Games for children who are mentally retarded should have few simple directions, require little remembering, have attractive names, and use interesting equipment. Some of these children might have difficulty understanding a game at first. They often can perform parts of the game, though, such as ball throwing, running, and tagging. These parts eventually can be combined. Movements such as running, climbing, turning, and jumping are fun and make it possible for them to learn games and stunts. Games that include singing, dancing, and storytelling—which promote reasoning and memory in children—should be scheduled early in the day and where distractions can be avoided (Hunt, 1955).

Children with Behavior Disorders.   Although games with rules enhance competitive and cooperative play skills, they may be difficult for children with behavior disorders. Special educators often recommend structured learning in teaching games to these children (Wehman, 1977). Simple games are useful because of these children's short interest span. Games that are intellectual or competitive or that require separate scorekeeping may be too stressful for some children. Those that require physical contact between players also should be avoided.

Children with Hearing Impairments.   Children who are hearing-impaired can play active games with other children, although imaginative language games present some difficulty. As they encounter problems learning new games, these children may cling to the old ones, preferring not to change or modify games or make up new ones.

Children with hearing impairments should be encouraged to experiment with different types of games (Hunt, 1955). Often these children prefer contact and aggressive games. Games like tug-of-war and relay races give them the opportunity to learn about sportsmanship, to develop social skills, and to compete successfully. Although some speech is required to play such games, speech is often a secondary requirement.

Children who are hearing-impaired need to understand the instructions given in a game. The teacher must provide instructions at the onset of play because these children do not readily learn them from other children. Once learned, they will not forget a game, skill, or dance, if the teaching method used is thorough.

Since these children appear normal, their hearing peers may not tolerate mistakes they would excuse in other children with disabilities. Teachers may need to help normal children understand the difficulties incurred by children who are hearing-impaired. However, singling these children out for special consideration can be demeaning and embarrassing to them.

Children with Visual Impairments.   Games for children who are visually impaired should be neither so difficult as to cause frustration nor so simple as to cause resentment. These children need encouragement, a permissive approach, and stimulation of their imagination. They do not need to be pampered. The fun of the game is lost when there is no challenge (Hunt, 1955). Their interest in game activities generally develops at a later age than in their sighted peers.

Since children who are visually impaired often need to memorize games and their surroundings, games should be simple when first introduced. Complexities can be added to a game later. Play groups for these children should be small so the teacher can help children individually. As soon as these children thoroughly learn a game, they should have the opportunity to enjoy their new skills with sighted peers.

Children who are visually impaired need to be aware of the size, shape, and composition of the play area to feel secure. However, games should be presented in more than one place. Tours and contest games can orient the visually impaired to an unfamiliar place by helping them explore it themselves as well as having teachers describe it. Playing a game frequently in the same place helps children who are visually impaired to feel secure (Saracho & Spodek, 1988). Since these children must memorize everything in a play space, including equipment and movable facilities, nothing should be changed without informing the child.

The child who is visually impaired needs to know exactly where the teacher and other players are as well as what is happening during a game. Children with full vision and the teacher should talk to each other and to the child with visual disabilities and identify themselves and their location. In this way the child knows exactly where everyone is and what they are doing (Saracho & Spodek, 1988). Since children who are visually impaired are unable to read the nonverbal messages (such as glances and facial expressions) players send to one another during a game, there must be increased reliance on verbal, auditory, and tactile clues.

Children with Orthopedic Impairments.   Children with orthopedic impairments can play basic childhood games through vigorous, skillful movements of their arms and by moving objects through space. They need easy-to-handle game equipment with projectiles that automatically return to the players, either by tilting the playing surfaces or by providing a string or elastic attached to the projectile. Many such children must depend on their teachers for guidance. Like children who are visually impaired, those who are orthopedically impaired prefer not playing new games or modifications of old ones. They need to avoid strong competition but can be involved in controlled competition in group games.

Children who are orthopedically impaired may need larger and lighter balls (such as a 17-inch softball) or other things to throw (such as beanbags, balloons, and cloth bags stuffed with paper). The play space for these children is usually smaller and the equipment is lighter to restrict the area of movement. Crutch and wheelchair users can enjoy playing circle toss or volleyball games with a rubber balloon, because the balloon travels and falls slowly. A light tap is enough to keep the balloon in the air, yet a forceful hit will not knock it out of bounds (Hunt, 1955).

At-Risk Children.   Games that are attractive, especially with bright colors, texture, and shape, are of interest to children at risk. Games that include singing, pantomiming, and stories are appealing to them.

SUMMARY

Various theories have been developed over the years to explain play. Each of these can illuminate the way in which play serves basic human needs and can help teachers develop guidelines for modifying play to make it serve educational purposes.

In creating a play environment, teachers can set up various play centers to support the play of children with and without disabilities. A play environment needs to be safe for all children. Some situations that are not hazardous to normal children, however, may be hazardous to a child with a disability. Concern for the safety of play materials and settings must be as important as a concern for their developmental appropriateness.

Boundaries must be clearly indicated and rules need to be established for what can go on within the play centers. Dramatic play centers should be provided with props for play, including dress-up clothing and various artifacts related to other play themes.

Manipulative play centers need to have tables and chairs that accommodate children with and without disabilities. Manipulative materials should be provided in ways that promote easy access for children and easy return of materials for storage and cleanup. Physical play, either indoors or outdoors, requires enough space and appropriate equipment. There also needs to be a concern for child safety. Games can be provided in various settings, depending on the nature of the game. Each child's capacity must be considered as the teacher creates a play environment and adapts active play activities in an integrated setting.

REFERENCES

Axline, V. M. (1947). *Play therapy.* New York: Ballantine Books.

Bagnato, S. J., Kontos, S., & Neisworth, J. T. (1987). Integrated day care as special education: Profiles of programs and children. *Topics in Early Childhood Special Education, 7,* 28–47.

Beckman, P. J., & Kohl, F. L. (1984). The effects of social toys on the interactions and play of integrated and nonintegrated groups of preschoolers. *Education and Training of the Mentally Retarded, 19*(3), 169–174.

Bernhardt, M., & Mackler, B. (1975). The use of play therapy with the mentally retarded. *Journal of Special Education, 9,* 409–414.

Brooks-Gunn, J., & Lewis, M. (1982). Development of play behavior in handicapped and normal infants. *Topics in Early Childhood Special Education, 2*(3), 14–27.

Brooks-Gunn, J., & Lewis, M. (1984). Maternal responsivity in interactions with handicapped infants. *Child Development, 55,* 782–793.

Capone, A. M., Smith, M. A., & Schloss, P. J. (1988). Prompting play skills. *Teaching Exceptional Children, 21*(1), 54–56.

Cartwright, G. P., Cartwright, C. A., & Ward, M. E. (1989). *Educating special learners.* Belmont, CA: Wadsworth.

Darbyshire, J. O. (1977). Play patterns in young children with impaired hearing. *Volta Review, 79*(1), 19–26.

Ellis, M. J. (1973). *Why people play.* Englewood Cliffs, NJ: Prentice-Hall.

Erikson, E. (1972). Play and actuality. In M. W. Piers (Ed.), *Play and development* (pp. 127–167). New York: Norton.

Esposito, B. G., & Koorland, M. A. (1989). Play behavior of hearing impaired children: Integrated and segregated settings. *Exceptional Children, 55*(5), 412–419.

Fallen, N. H. (1978). Motor skills. In N. H. Fallen & J. E. McGovern (Eds.), *Young children with special needs* (pp. 121–157). Columbus, OH: Merrill.

Fein, G. G., & Schwartz, P. M. (1982). Developmental theories in early education. In B. Spodek (Ed.), *Handbook of research in early childhood education* (pp. 82–104). New York: Free Press.

Fiscella, J., & Barnett, L. A. (1985). A child by any other name . . . A comparison of the play behaviors of gifted and non-gifted children. *Gifted Child Quarterly, 29,* 61–66.

Fraiberg, S. (1977). *Insights from the blind.* New York: Basic Books.

Gabarino, J., & Sherman, D. (1980). High-risk neighborhoods and high-risk families. The human ecology of child maltreatment. *Child Development, 51,* 188–198.

Goetz, E. M., & Baer, D. M. (1973). Social control of form diversity and the emergence of new forms in children's blockbuilding. *Journal of Applied Behavior Analysis, 6*(2), 209–217.

Guthrie, S. (1979). Criteria for educational toys for pre-school visually impaired children. *Journal of Visual Impairment and Blindness, 73*(4), 144–146.

Hanzlik, J. R., & Stevenson, M. B. (1986). Interactions of mothers with their infants who are mentally retarded, retarded with cerebral palsy, or nonretarded. *American Journal of Mental Deficiency, 90,* 513–520.

Hendrickson, J. M., Gable, R. A., Hester, P., & Strain, P. S. (1985). Teaching social reciprocity: Social exchanges between young severely handicapped and nonhandicapped children. *The Pointer, 29*(4), 17–21.

Hendrickson, J. M., Tremblay, A., Strain, P. S., & Shores, R. E. (1981). Relationship between toy and material use and the occurrence of social interactive behaviors by normally developing preschool children. *Psychology in the Schools, 18,* 500–504.

Higginbotham, D. J., & Baker, B. M. (1981). Social participation and cognitive play differences in hearing-impaired and normally hearing preschoolers. *The Volta Review, 83,* 135–149.

Higginbotham, D. J., Baker, B. M., & Neil, R. D. (1980). Assessing the social participation and cognitive play abilities of hearing-impaired preschoolers. *The Volta Review, 82*, 261–270.

Hill, P., & McCune-Nicolich, L. (1981). Pretend play and patterns of cognition in Down syndrome children. *Child Development, 52*, 611–617.

Hirst, C. C., & Shelley, E. Y. (1989). They too should play. *Teaching Exceptional Children, 21*(4), 26–28.

Hunt, V. V. (1955). *Recreation for the handicapped.* New York: Prentice-Hall.

Kitano, M. (1982). Young gifted children: Strategies for preschool teachers. *Young Children, 38*, 14–24.

Leland, H., Walker, J., & Taboada, A. (1959). Group play therapy with a group of post-nursery male retardates. *American Journal of Mental Deficiency, 63*(5), 848–851.

Lombardino, L. J., & Sproul, C. J. (1984). Patterns of correspondence and non-correspondence between play and language in developmentally delayed preschoolers. *Education and Training of the Mentally Retarded, 19*(1), 5–14.

McCormick, L. (1987). Comparison of the effects of a microcomputer activity and a toy play on social and communication behaviors of young children. *Journal of the Division for Early Childhood, 11*(3), 195–205.

McCune-Nicolich (1982). Play as prelinguistic behavior: Theory, evidence and applications. In D. McClowry, A. Guildford, & S. Richardson (Eds.), *Infant communication: Development, assessment and intervention* (pp. 55–81). New York: Grune & Stratton.

Mann, L. F. (1984). Play behaviors of deaf and hearing children. In D. S. Martin (Ed.), *International symposium on cognition, education, and deafness*, Washington, DC.

Mehlman, B. (1953). Group play therapy with mentally retarded children. *Journal of Abnormal and Social Psychology, 48*(1), 53–60.

Mogford, K. (1977). The play of handicapped children. In B. Tizard & D. Harvey (Eds.), *Biology of play*. Philadelphia: Lippincott.

Morrison, T., & Newcomer, B. (1975). Effects of directive versus nondirective play therapy with institutionalized retarded children. *American Journal of Mental Deficiency, 79*, 666–669.

Motti, F., Cicchetti, D., & Stroufe, L. A. (1983). From infant affect expression to symbolic play: The coherence of development in Down syndrome children. *Child Development, 54*, 1168–1175.

Mundy, P., Sigman, M., Sherman, T., & Ungerer, J. (1984). Representational ability, nonverbal communication skills and early language development in autistic children. Paper presented at the Fourth International Conference on Infant Studies, New York.

Paloutzian, R. F., Hasazi, J., Streifel, J., & Edgar, C. (1971). Promotion of positive social interaction in severely retarded young children. *American Journal of Mental Deficiency, 75*, 519–524.

Pellegrini, A. D., & Boyd, B. (1993). The role of play in early childhood development and education: Issues in definition and function. In B. Spodek (Ed.), *Handbook of research on the education of young children* (pp. 105–121). New York: Macmillan.

Pellicano, R. R. (1987). At risk: A view of "social advantage." *Educational Leadership, 44*, 47–79.

Piaget, J. (1962). *Play, dreams and imitation in childhood.* New York: Norton.

Ramey, C. T., Mills, P., Campbell, F. A., & O'Brien, C. (1975). Infants' home environments: A comparison of high-risk families and families from the general population. *American Journal of Mental Deficiency, 80*, 40–42.

Rogers, S. J. (1988). Cognitive characteristics of handicapped children's play: A review. *Journal of the Division for Early Childhood, 12*(2), 161–168.

Rogers, S. J., Herbison, J. M., Lewis, H. C., Pantone, J., & Reis, K. (1986). An approach for enhancing the symbolic, communicative, and interpersonal functioning of young children with autism and severe emotional handicaps. *Journal of the Division for Early Childhood, 10*(2), 135–148.

Rogers, S. J., & Puchalski, C. B. (1984). Development of symbolic play in visually impaired infants. *Topics in Early Childhood Special Education, 3*(4), 57–64.

Ross, D. (1970). Incidental learning of number concepts in small group games. *American Journal of Mental Deficiency, 74*(6), 718–725.

Safford, P. L. (1989). *Integrated teaching in early childhood.* White Plains, NY: Longman.

Saracho, O. N. (1985). Young children's play behaviors and cognitive styles. *Early Child Development and Care, 21*(4), 1–18.

Saracho, O. N., & Spodek, B. (1987). Play for young handicapped children in an integrated setting. Working with mentally retarded and emotionally disturbed. *Day Care and Early Education, 15,* 32–35.

Saracho, O. N., & Spodek, B. (1988). Play for young handicapped children in an integrated setting: Working with hearing impaired, visually impaired and orthopedically handicapped. *Day Care and Early Education, 16,* 31–33.

Schaeffler, C. (1988). Making toys accessible for children with cerebral palsy. *Teaching Exceptional Children, 20*(3), 26–29.

Sherburn, S., Utley, B., McConnell, S., & Gannon, J. (1988). Decreasing violent or aggressive theme play among preschool children with behavior disorders. *Exceptional Children, 55*(2), 166–172.

Spodek, B., & Saracho, O. N. (1988). The challenge of educational play. In D. Bergen (Ed.), *Play as a medium for learning and development: A handbook of theory and practice* (pp. 9–22). Portsmouth, NH: Heinemann.

Spodek, B., Saracho, O. N., & Davis, M. D. (1991). *Foundations of early childhood education: Teaching three-, four-, and five-year-old children.* Englewood Cliffs, NJ: Prentice-Hall.

Strain, P. S., Cooke, T. P., & Apolloni, T. (1976). *Teaching exceptional children: Assessing and modifying social behavior.* New York: Academic Press.

Strain, P., & Fox, J. (1981). Peer social initiations and the modification of social withdrawal: A review of future perspective. *Journal of Pediatric Psychology, 6,* 417–433.

Taite, P. C. (1974). Believing without seeing. Teaching the blind child in a "regular" kindergarten. *Childhood Education, 50*(5), 285–291.

Terrel, B. Y., Schwarts, R. G., Prelock, M. A., & Messick, C. K. (1984). Symbolic play in normal and language-impaired children. *Journal of Speech and Hearing Research, 27,* 424–429.

Tremblay, A., Strain, P., Hendrickson, J., & Shores, R. (1981). Social interactions of normal preschool children: Using normative data for subject and target behavior selection. *Behavior Modification, 5,* 237–253.

Vygotsky, L. S. (1962). *Thought and language.* Cambridge, MA: MIT Press.

Vygotsky, L. S. (1978). *Mind in society.* Cambridge, MA: Harvard University Press.

Wehman, P. (1975). Establishing play behaviors in mentally retarded youth. *Rehabilitation Literature, 36*(8), 238–246.

Wehman, P. (1977). *Helping the mentally retarded acquire play skills: A behavioral approach.* Springfield, IL: Charles C. Thomas.

Wehman, P. (1978). Play skill development. In N. H. Fallen (Ed.), *Young children with special needs* (pp. 277–303). Columbus, OH: Merrill.

Wehman, P., & Abramson, M. (1976). Three theoretical approaches to play. *The American Journal of Occupational Therapy, 30*(9), 551–559.

Weis, R. (1981). INREAL. Intervention for language handicapped and bilingual children. *Journal of the Division for Early Childhood Special Education, 4,* 24–27.

Wesson, C., Wilson, R., & Mandlebaum, L. H. (1988, Winter). Learning games for active student responding. *Teaching Exceptional Children*, 12–14.

Whitman, T. L., Mercurio, J. R., & Caponigri, V. (1970). Development of social responses in two severely retarded children. *Journal of Applied Behavior Analysis, 3*, 133–138.

Whitmore, J. R. (1980). *Giftedness, conflict, and underachievement.* Boston: Allyn & Bacon.

CHAPTER 10

Fostering Creative Expression

CHAPTER OVERVIEW

This chapter describes:

1. The functions of the creative arts in early childhood education.
2. The goals of movement education.
3. Activities in movement education for diverse children.
4. The goals of music education, including singing, using musical instruments, listening to music, and rhythms.
5. Activities in music education for diverse children.
6. The goals of art education.
7. Activities in art education for diverse children.

The creative arts, long a part of early education for young children, should also be part of educational programs for children with disabilities. Movement, music, and art offer young children opportunities to create and appreciate unique products. Creative experiences also promote children's new perceptions of and responses to the world. Through various art media, children explore ways to express themselves better and develop self-discipline. For example, a child with a language disability may learn to use art media to express ideas that cannot be put into words.

For children who are gifted, art materials must be adapted to an advanced level that can be managed and remain motivating to them. These children have age-appropriate attention spans, but more mature interests and more advanced cognitive levels. Most creative activities may be adapted to the child's levels of performance in different areas of functioning, some of which may be expected based on chronological age, others more or less advanced (Safford, 1989).

Creativity often is associated with giftedness. The dimensions of creativity are so diverse that one theorist postulates that creativity and intelligence are not unitary phenomena but together consist of as many as 120 factors. Other theorists agree that creativity and intelligence may consist of a variety of attributes such as sensitivity, fluency, flexibility, complexity, and the abilities to synthesize, analyze, reorganize, and evaluate. Giftedness extends beyond IQ and creativity to more expanded definitions that encompass a variety of abilities and talents (Cartwright, Cartwright, & Ward, 1989).

Originality and divergent thinking are to be valued in the arts. Teachers should value creative thinking and be flexible in their instruction. Good teachers of the gifted are comfortable with different ways of doing things (Safford, 1989). In promoting creative expressions, teachers must avoid pressuring students to conform and produce typical work.

This chapter explores movement, music, and art—the three most widely used expressive media in early childhood education.

MOVEMENT EDUCATION

Individuals vary in the speed, balance, precision, and efficiency of their own movement. Most individuals enjoy moving themselves and watching others move. Precision and grace are qualities people view as beautiful in activities such as dancing, skating, diving, or gymnastics. The essence of these activities is in the aesthetic quality of the movement itself.

Children use movement to make sense of their world, creating ideas through their actions. For example, a child who touches a hot iron will pull away quickly and will be more cautious the next time. The child will recall both the burning sensation and the body movement related to it.

Rudolph Laban (1988), more than anyone else, has influenced movement education. Laban proposed having children explore body movement rather than having them respond to specific directions. Open-ended problems of movement exploration with no right or wrong answers are presented for solution. Follow-up questions encourage children to explore additional alternatives. An understanding of the structure and process of movement education provides the foundation for physical education. Games, gymnastics, and dance promote children's physical and emotional development through movement concepts such as body awareness, space, qualities, and relationships. The parts of the body vary in relation to each other and to objects (e.g., near, far, on, around, under), in the number and variation of actions (e.g., straight, curved, zigzag), and in a wide range of motions (from small to large). Speed and rhythm also affect movement. Their force fluctuates in a continuum from strong to weak and in quality from sudden to sustained, and the flow varies in the degree of its freedom (Copple, Sigel, & Saunders, 1979). These movement elements are the basis of Laban's framework for movement education.

Enjoyment and satisfaction should be a part of the children's movement program as they achieve a higher level of physical skills through games, dances, and gymnastics

activities. Students can acquire confident, positive attitudes and enthusiasm toward physical activity out of and in school.

Goals and Objectives

According to Kirchner, Cunningham, and Warrell (1978), the goals of movement education include the following:

1. Physical fitness and skills in a variety of areas.
2. An understanding of the principles of movement.
3. An awareness of what the body is able to do.
4. Increased self-discipline and self-reliance.
5. Modes of self-expression and creativity.
6. Increased confidence in meeting physical challenges.
7. Greater cooperation and sensitivity toward others.

A number of goals can be achieved by centering on a variety of activities related to a theme. In the theme "moving at different speeds," knowledge objectives can include an understanding that movements differ in speed from very slow to very fast; movement can be modified according to the amount of time it takes to perform the movement. Skill objectives can relate to ways of modifying the speed of movements, accelerating and decelerating slowly and quickly and consciously controlling the speed of body movement. To develop a positive attitude toward movement, children must want to listen, think, and solve problems as well as wish to search for skillful, thoughtful, and original modes of movement exploration. Movement education can also teach appreciation of individual differences, task persistence, self-motivation, self-esteem, and enjoyment.

Activities in Movement Education

Activities in movement education at the early childhood level can be provided through games, gymnastics, and dance and should include movement experiences and body mechanics (which are locomotor, nonlocomotor, and manipulative), apparatus, stunts and tumbling, simple games, and sports skills and activities.

Games.   The main purpose of games is to challenge oneself or (for older children) an opponent. Competition is the essence of games, although it is only enjoyed when students have mastered the skills involved. Formal games are generally introduced in the kindergarten and primary grades. Skills, developed in the early years and fundamental to games, include visual perception (spatial body awareness, spatial relations, form constancy, figure–ground relationships), auditory discrimination (sound localization, rhythm discrimination, figure-ground selection), tactile-touch, kinesthetic, sensory integration (balance, exploration, eye–hand coordination), strength, endurance, flexibility, and motor ability (balance, power, coordination, speed, agility, rhythm). Specific movements include balancing, bouncing, catching, hopping, jumping, pushing, running, tagging, and twisting (Eason & Smith, 1976). Children can improve these skills by practicing them through play.

Individual and partner games can be used in the primary grades to develop individual skills and encourage cooperation. In partner games, the teacher should equalize the competition so that children have the greatest opportunity to develop their skills and experience both success and failure. Continuous failure lowers self-esteem, whereas continuous success creates a false sense of superiority and conceit—feelings children do not need to acquire.

Gymnastics.   Gymnastics can help children learn to control their movements and work safely and aesthetically within their own restrictions. Gymnastics can be offered even in the preschool. Movement tasks and problems are individualized, and a concern for winning or losing becomes irrelevant. Individuals can be expected to work at near-maximum capacity with high levels of effort and concentration.

Dance.   Dance is the most creative of the movement areas. It can be presented informally in the preschool and more formally in later grades. Although not competitive, dance requires a high degree of individual effort and concentration. Through dance, children experience, understand, and create the expressive aspects of movement—analyzing, selecting, and interpreting their movements. A movement idea can be explored through music, rhythm, and words. Children need to have the opportunity to enjoy all three. Music, provided through instruments or records, supports dance activities and should be available.

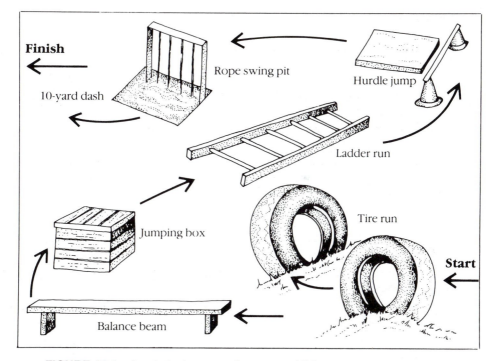

FIGURE 10.1   An obstacle course for young children

Preschool teachers can offer dance experiences in an imaginative, childlike, and appropriate way, promoting the child's physical, intellectual, and emotional needs. Since preschool children learn through play, dance materials should be presented in play form: The teacher introduces an idea but the child "play-dances" based on his or her ability, ingenuity, and inventiveness. Thus, preschool children should learn by trial and error, through exploration and discovery (Fauman, 1983).

Using a balance of games, gymnastics, and dance, movement activities may be developed around themes designed to teach specific concepts and skills. For example, flying may be the theme for a series of activities focusing on jumping and landing in which children explore basic jumps such as jumping from one foot to another or jumping on the same foot. The theme provides a focus to clarify relationships between children and space and to identify similarities and differences in types of movement.

An obstacle course provides a good example of a series of activities used in a movement theme. A series of obstacles can be created that require children to crawl under, jump over, climb through, or walk around them. Objects should be sufficiently spaced so that several children can work on them separately but sequentially. In the obstacle course illustrated in Figure 10.1, a child can move in various ways between the tractor tires on the ground—jumping on one foot, jumping on two feet, or turning in the air while jumping. Another child can balance on the balance beam, assuming different body positions, while a third child climbs or runs through the ladder. Thus, several children can use the different pieces of equipment simultaneously, without waiting for or interfering with each other.

MOVEMENT EDUCATION FOR DIVERSE CHILDREN

An early childhood program should balance a high degree of individualization with many opportunities for group interaction. The development of both large and small motor skills should be emphasized. Children differ from one another, genetically and developmentally. Teachers must develop appropriate activities based on these individual differences. Extreme physical restrictions in some children will broaden the range of the children's capabilities in a classroom. Teachers must make special arrangements for children with disabilities. This requires that they spend more time to plan and think creatively about how to meet their needs (Miller & Schaumberg, 1988). Carefully planned movement programs offer children with disabilities opportunities for new experiences, enabling them to extend their horizons and to become a part of the class, school, and community. Children who have low opinions of themselves can be helped to develop self-confidence through physical activity. Every child, regardless of skill or ability, should have the opportunity to succeed.

Children with disabilities—who may have a poor conception of time, of space, of body image, and of many other perceptual concepts—can benefit from a comprehensive movement education program that includes activities using balance boards, balance beams, obstacle courses, tumbling, and swimming. The following are realistic and attainable goals for children with disabilities, according to Bucher and Thaxton (1979):

1. To understand, appreciate, and enjoy movement experiences.
2. To experience a series of movement experiences.
3. To develop body awareness.
4. To improve physical skills.
5. To understand an appreciate one's physical capacities and restrictions.
6. To cultivate one's physical fitness within one's capacities.
7. To promote a positive self-image.
8. To foster effective interpersonal relationships.
9. To become aware of safety precautions.
10. To learn to protect oneself from injuries that can occur through engagement in physical activities.

Since children with disabilities have a variety of abilities and restrictions, the movement program should be modified to meet their individual needs. Bucher and Thaxton suggest these guidelines for a movement education program for such children:

1. The school should cooperate with health service personnel (physicians and nurses) in planning each child's program.
2. The child's motor skill, ability, and physical fitness levels should be evaluated to develop a program that meets his or her needs.
3. The program needs to be constantly assessed and careful records kept including test scores, activities engaged in, and progress reports. This

process keeps the parents, physicians, and other involved persons up to date concerning the child's progress.

4. Challenges that are within the student's capabilities and limitations and that offer opportunities for success should be provided.
5. Instruction should be individualized and extra assistance made available.
6. Appropriate activities should be selected based on the individual fitness level of each student as well as the student's interests, ability, needs, sex, and age.
7. Activities should be modified for the student based on the child's disabilities, capabilities, and restrictions.
8. Facilities and equipment need to be carefully checked for safety.

The teacher needs to select the exercises and develop a checklist for the student's daily use.

Establishing learning centers in the gymnasium, playground, multipurpose room, or self-contained room is one way to individualize instruction. Table 10.1 and Figure 10.2 illustrate how learning centers can be set up, along with skills to be learned and activities to develop those skills. Learning centers can be established in four general areas of activity with signs in each identifying the skill areas and tasks. Skill sheets

TABLE 10.1 Learning center activities

Skill:	*Skill:*
balance	space relations
Activities:	*Activities:*
balance beam	obstacle course
balance beam benches	gym scooters
balance boards	cargo net
balance block	mini-gym
balance stunts	stepping stones
tumbling activities	bounding boards
balance activities on tumbling mats	wands
balance touch	horizontal ladder
carpet squares	exercise bar
bango boards	jumping box
	jumpropes
Skill:	*Skill:*
eye–hand coordination	body image
Activities:	*Activities:*
bean bags	locomotor patterns
hoops	Simon Says (song)
appropriate balls	rhythm
targets	rope climbing
tennis paddle and sponge balls	jumping boxes
bowling pins and ball	magic rope activities
scoops for catching	dances
flying saucers (frisbees)	horizontal ladder
parachute play	axial movements (bend, turn, twist,
geometric shapes	fly stunts)

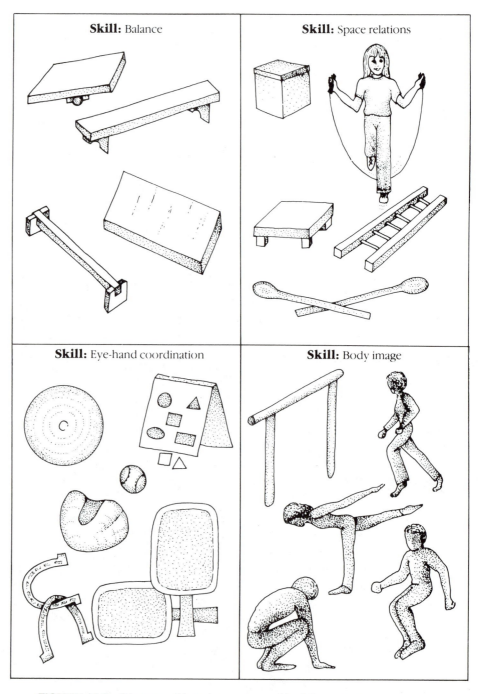

FIGURE 10.2 Diagram of learning centers with skills and activities

related to the activity in the designated area can be provided as guidance for the children. Students can be allowed to move from one area to another before mastering all levels of a skill, so that a series of movement skills is taught and developed simultaneously. Several learning alternatives are provided for each skill, and activities within each area can be varied in complexity to help individuals progress at their own rate. For children who cannot read, instructions for developing a skill may consist of a series of pictures illustrating how a specific skill can be mastered and the types of activities that develop that skill.

Learning centers allow teachers to work with children on a one-to-one basis without taking time from the class. Burton (1977) has identified several ways of implementing learning centers:

1. The teacher presents different types of learning experiences.
2. Children can select the skill(s) they wish to pursue.
3. The teacher discusses the process and performance objectives with each child.
4. The teacher provides instructions on how tasks can be completed, where equipment and supplies are located, and the time limit.
5. The teacher offers enrichment materials, such as pictures, posters, charts, records, films, and books.

In individualized instruction, children progress at their own pace while learning psychomotor skills and developing helping, caring behavior. The teacher circulates around the room helping and testing while children work on their programs. Skills that have been mastered are checked off on the skill sheet and filed in a folder. Children can get help from a teacher or a peer, or can review the large wall charts provided for the specific skill.

Children with Physical Disabilities

Even children with physical disabilities are able to participate in a rigorous physical education program safely and successfully. Children with mild and moderate physical disabilities can attend regular classes and participate in the regular physical education program with some minor modifications for certain activities. Most children with physical disabilities need specific exercises to stretch or strengthen parts of their bodies, improve gait or posture, improve or maintain a range of motion, inhibit unwanted reflexes, increase muscle tone, and the like. These students may have orthopedic problems due to cerebral palsy, spina bifida, scoliosis, strokes, birth defects, or trauma (Smoot, 1985). Physical education activities must be adapted for those children who cannot participate in a regular physical education program (Miller & Schaumberg, 1988).

Children with physical impairments have the same drives, feelings, and needs for regular physical activity as other children and should receive adequate opportunities to participate in well-rounded movement education programs and movement activities. In planning a program for these students, teachers must be sure that activities designed for a particular child are not counterproductive to the goals of physical therapy. The physical therapist can work with the teacher to determine the appropriate physical educational activities to prevent the child from reverting to primitive reflexes (Miller & Schaumberg, 1988; Sherrill, 1986).

Teachers should analyze the skills involved and select the components needed to successfully develop a specific skill. Miller and Schaumberg suggest that teachers raise questions such as the following:

1. What does the body do during a kicking, throwing, or striking motion?
2. How much speed is involved in the activity?
3. How much space and what types of equipment are needed?
4. What criteria for success will be applied? (p. 9)

The answers to such questions can help teachers to adapt physical education to the child with a physical disability. The following primary movements can be used with young children with physical disabilities:

- *Body awareness.* Move head, neck, shoulders, arms, hands, trunk, legs, and feet.
- *Spatial relationship.* Use parts of the body in relation to objects in space; develop laterality and directionality.
- *Balance.* Move in various directions and in different ways to develop dynamic and static balance; use activities that require balancing of objects.
- *Axial movement.* Lie on the stomach and raise the head; raise the arms and other parts of the body that can be raised.
- *Swing and sway.* Sit down and swing (or sway) as many parts of the body as possible; swing arms in many directions—in circles, squares, triangles, rectangles, letter shapes, and number formations.
- *Pushing and pulling.* Sit or lie down and use hands, elbows, arms, or trunk to push some object in as many directions as possible; pull it; pull or push in an upward or downward or sideways direction.
- *Bending and stretching.* Bend various parts of the body while sitting or lying down; bend or stretch parts of the body in as many directions as possible.
- *Twisting, turning, and whirling.* Sit or lie down and twist, turn, or whirl as many parts of the body as possible; twist the body in one direction, then the other direction—to the right, to the left, and other ways.
- *Shaking and beating.* Sit, lie down, or stand and shake as many parts of the body as possible; shake the right (left) side of the body and beat a rhythm with the left (right). (Christensen, 1970)

Basic body movements for young children with physical impairments are first initiated on tumbling mats. The first movements are begun by placing the children in a lying position and having them pull themselves toward the teacher. At the beginning the arms do most of the work, but gradually the teacher should encourage use of the feet. These movements can be done from prone, supine, side, or sitting positions. Although a child in a wheelchair may be unable to perform on balance beams, balance boards, jump boards, sawhorses, stairs, stilts, tables, and tires, the child with a physical disability can be successful with other pieces of apparatus.

The following equipment can be used with such children:

- *Balls.* Throw the ball up and catch it; let it bounce before catching it; throw the ball in many different ways to a partner.
- *Beanbags.* Experiment with the beanbag; throw it up high and catch it; close your eyes and throw (toss) it, alternating from hand to hand.
- *Deck tennis rings.* Throw a ring up in the air and catch it with one or two hands; clap hands before catching it; catch the ring in such a way that it slides over one arm or both arms.

Four-Pin Stretch and *Tetherball* are suitable activities for a spastic cerebral palsied child (Miller & Schaumberg, 1988).

Four-Pin Stretch.   The cerebral palsied child lies prone on the elbows in the center of a rectangular mat. Four plastic bowling pins are placed near each corner. The teacher gives a signal and the child uses his or her feet and hands to attempt to knock each pin down. The child is allowed to move around the mat in the prone-on-elbows

position or in a side-lying position. The child remains on the mat and does not touch any part of the floor. Based on the child's level of skill, the teacher can provide the following adaptations:

1. Increase or decrease the size of the mat or the distance of the pins from the corners.
2. Require a "controlled" knockdown so that the club will not roll off the mat and touch the floor.
3. Allow the child to use only hands or legs.
4. Require the child to grasp or hold the pin in the air with a straight arm, which can be an alternative to knocking down the pins.
5. Provide assistance to allow success, such as helping if the child is "stuck." An assistant can help the child change positions.

Tetherball. The child with cerebral palsy is placed in a good sitting position (i.e., on a bench, straight chair, or wheelchair) in order to use a plastic baseball bat to strike a suspended ball. (An empty milk jug or plastic container can be used instead of a ball, and a stick or old racket can be used instead of a baseball bat). Both hands should be used whenever possible, although if the severity of spasticity does not allow the use of both hands, one hand may be used. When necessary, an ace bandage may be used to tape the bat into the child's hand. This activity develops trunk rotation and attention to controlled batting technique.

Christensen (1970) describes Mickey, a kindergarten boy with cerebral palsy. In his wheelchair, Mickey could use his arms, chest, shoulders, trunk, neck, and head. During Mickey's primary years, his movement education program was adapted to his disability. In self-testing activities, Mickey was able to conduct a leg roll, seal walk, and wheelbarrow (Mickey is the barrow); to grasp the horizontal bar; to travel on the horizontal ladder; and to perform some balancing activities with a wand. Rhythms allowed Mickey to perform modified imitations and any rhythmic activity using hand, shoulder, head, arm, and trunk movements and to play rhythm sticks or other instruments. During softball, Mickey practiced throwing, catching, fielding, and batting.

Children with Health Impairments

Sound physical activity can make a real difference in the lives of children who suffer from different kinds of chronic asthma, although no exercise should be introduced to severely asthmatic children without their physician's written permission (Karper, 1986). For example, asthmatic attacks can be controlled through relaxation training. Exercise may improve overall movement tolerance, contributing to better total body cooperation and improved movement efficiency (Karper, 1986). Nickerson, Bautista, Namey, Richards, and Keens (1983) found that asthmatic children who jogged four mornings per week for 6 weeks significantly increased their 12-minute walk–run distance. Orenstein, Reed, Grogan, and Crawford (1985) exercised children with asthma for an hour three times a week for a period of 4 months. At the end of their program, children participated in walking–jogging–walking endurance activities and recreational games for each session. They significantly improved in walking capability, decreased their submaximal working heart rate, and increased oxygen consumption. Exercise appeared to actually help the children reduce their fear of physical activities. A movement education program can be established using the following guidelines (Karper, 1986):

1. The teacher must have information for each asthmatic student regarding:
   a. number and severity of asthma attacks;
   b. precipitating causes surrounding attacks;
   c. name and amount of medication to be administered;
   d. medication schedule;
   e. side effects from medication;
   f. ways of taking different medications; and
   g. directions to carry if the child has an attack during or immediately after exercising.

2. Teachers must be concerned with exercised-induced asthma (EIA), or asthmatic attacks induced by exercise during or after the activity. Severe attacks are dangerous. Sometimes, simply letting the child rest and breathe lightly at appropriate times during activity slows the first symptoms of an attack. However, the child needs to be aware when the attack is beginning. It is important that teachers do not pressure children into EIA. The teacher should allow the child to guide how he or she feels and relate that feeling back to any adverse outcomes from activity.

3. Asthmatic children can exercise at least three times per week. Usually programs are individually and systematic progressive (Neijens, 1985) and should include a 5- to 10-minute warm-up period, an activity period, and a 5- to 10-minute cool-down period. Children with severe conditions should have frequent rest periods in their program, for example, intervals of 5 minutes of exercise followed by 5 minutes of rest.

4. Warm-up periods are especially important. Students with moderate to severe asthma appear to uphold muscle-building activity better than longer endurance participation.

5. Teachers should involve children in movement experiences that permit a drop in heart and breathing rate every couple of minutes either through planned rest periods or by integrating selected activities in the natural flow of experiences.

6. Four to six minutes of sustained maximal output will generally generate EIA in most children. Exercising indoors is better for children with asthma, particularly in warm and humid climates (Neijens, 1985). Attacks also can be caused by breathing cold air (Noble, 1986). Children need to be instructed to breath through their noses during inspiration to reduce EIA (Neijens, 1985).

7. To reduce potential allergic reactions, dust and mold should be cleaned from gym mats, lockers, and shower rooms.

8. For outdoor activities, weather conditions must be monitored for rain,

dampness, and barometric pressure. Outdoor activities should be avoided during pollen or airborne mold season (Neijens, 1985).

9. Swimming seems to be of more value than dry-land activities, because it does not create as much EIA. Although research has indicated that children can have low EIA from participating in swimming activities, teachers must be careful if skin, ear, nose, or throat problems develop. Parents' and physicians' consent must be obtained for these types of activities.

Movement experiences for severely asthmatic children should also be related to the performance of daily living activities that are important for the child (such as walking, washing, dressing). At all times, teachers must keep the parents and physicians informed concerning the child's progress.

Obesity.   There has been increasing concern about the consequences of childhood obesity. Pediatricians suggest developing strategies to control eating and increase exercise that children can use for lifetime health-promoting behavior. Conventional physical activity must be the norm for these children, with life focusing on activities rather than meals. Skill training for young children (catching, kicking a ball, jumping) can assist them to continue to be absorbed with their peer group's physical activities (Javernick, 1988).

Early childhood educators recommend that these children engage in any moderate physical activity that they enjoy (Wishon, Bower, & Eller, 1983). It is the teacher's responsibility to attend to the problems of obese children's special needs (Javernick, 1988).

Children with Ambulatory Problems

Movement education activities can be adapted for children in wheelchairs by using inexpensive and versatile ropes. An activity that improves extensor and flexor muscles of the arms and legs uses ropes in conjunction with weights and a pulley. A simple eyelet made in the wall with a wooden pin or weight attached to the rope can give the effect of a weight and a pulley, as the rope is pulled through the eyelet against the weight. Two students in wheelchairs, each holding one end of the rope, can face each other with the brakes on one chair to hold it still. The student in the other wheelchair pulls himself or herself toward the student in the stationary wheelchair. The student in the moving wheelchair encounters tension. This activity can be facilitated by tying knots 1 to 2 inches apart in the rope (Frederick, 1971).

Devices added to ropes provide mobility in learning activities. The teacher can tie a rope tightly on one side of the room and give the other end of the rope to a child in a wheelchair at the other side of the room. The child then uses the rope to pull the wheelchair across the room. This activity can be varied by tying the rope to different stationary objects in the room such as doorknobs, other wheelchairs, or windows. Mobility activities can develop other learnings as various numbers, colors, shapes, forms, or pictures are placed at different points in the classroom. An obstacle course can be created with barriers for students in wheelchairs to cross by going around, over, or through them.

Ropes can also be used in conjunction with balls. The teacher can tie a rope to a whiffle ball or to a rubber ball with a hole in it. The other end of the rope is tied to a stationary object or to the student's wheelchair. The student throws or hits the ball with a bat and uses the rope to recover the ball. Other movement experiences can also be adjusted for children with physical disabilities in regular classes, permitting the children to use and explore different movements at their own developmental level without any pressures from their peers or inappropriate performance standards.

This type of program may seem difficult for teachers to manage. However, the benefits to children with physical disabilities far outweigh the effort. Children can make significant progress through their daily efforts. Their self-concepts will improve and they will become more realistic and optimistic about their lives. Parents will also appreciate and support the results. The regular classroom teacher can gain satisfaction by making a significant contribution to these children's quality of life (Smoot, 1985).

Children with Visual Impairments

Children who are visually impaired need higher levels of physical fitness than do persons with normal vision. They use more energy to function at their sighted peers' level. In addition to increasing physical fitness, group physical activities teach responsibility, consideration, cooperation, unselfishness, courtesy, and social aware-ness—all of which enhance their interpersonal relationships.

These children can be successfully integrated into regular activities with only minor modifications. Simple procedures can help them use their other senses. A child with a severe impairment can work together with a classmate who can see normally. Both can run together, with the visually impaired student grasping the normally sighted student's arm just above the elbow. This places the child approximately one-half step behind and one-half step to the side of the sighted student. In this position the visually impaired student can anticipate the sighted student's movements better than through joined hands (Buell, 1970).

Children with visual impairments can take short runs using some type of device to direct them. A good guide is a piece of cord stretched from the start to the finish line and marked at the beginning and at the end with knots. Children can run holding the cord until they feel the knots (Buell, 1970). A ring that slides along the line will allow children to grasp the line but not be slowed down by the friction of a hand on the rope. They can also touch another person as that person goes through movement activities. Success in this activity will encourage them to attempt other types of activities such as tumbling, jumping rope, playing games, and climbing. Then the teacher guides the visually impaired children through the same motions while they touch themselves to feel the movement and to recognize when and where emphasis needs to be placed on speed or strength.

Tumbling is a good activity for visually impaired students. It helps them develop equilibrium, poise, and trust in themselves when their feet leave the ground. Tumbling requires the ability to relocate in the environment, especially after a series of forward rolls. Children with visual impairments must learn to fall safely to prevent serious injuries.

Jumping rope fosters coordination, muscular strength, and cardiorespiratory endurance, as well as a sense of timing and adeptness of performance. Children who are visually impaired can learn to jump rope by first learning to jump high and low without a rope, distinguishing the different jumps, and feeling the jump required. A normally sighted peer can jump in tandem to give the child with a severe visual impairment the feel of jump rhythm. By placing his or her hands on the partner's shoulder, the visually impaired child can gain a sense of the jump rhythm. Once jump skills have been mastered, two turners can swing a long rope back and forth to give the child the feeling of jumping over a rope. When the child is ready, the turners swing the rope in a complete arc and when the rope is over the child's head, they say, "Jump!" The next skill to learn is to run into the long rope and jump. When the rope hits the floor, the turners say, "Run!" The child who has mastered jump skills with the long rope can learn to jump on individual ropes.

Games help children with visual impairments develop social and personal qualities such as leadership, ability to follow, courtesy, respect, enthusiasm, cooperativeness, competitiveness, and faith in others. To avoid confusion, directions for games should be simple and concise. Teachers must wait until they have everyone's attention before giving directions. Games should reflect skills the children have mastered. In a game such as dodge ball, children who are visually impaired need partners to help them dodge the ball when it is thrown in their direction, and when it is their turn to throw the ball, the other players should clap their hands, sing, or make some kind of noise to place themselves (Johansen, 1971).

Volleyball can be modified for players with visual impairments by having them serve by throwing or batting the ball or, when the ball goes in the direction of the visually impaired players, requiring it to bounce once before they toss the ball over the net. In softball, the ball can be placed on a tee for the visually impaired child to hit with a bat. When the child who is visually impaired hits the ball, a partner grasps his or her hand and they run together to first base. If a fielder who is visually impaired picks up a moving ball, the running player is out. Kickball requires using an audible ball or, for children who have a partial visual impairment, a light-colored ball, preferably yellow. The kicker who is visually impaired places the ball on home plate, kicks it, and runs as in softball. Players with visual impairments can pitch by rolling the ball to the batter while the catcher claps hands to guide the pitcher.

Children with Mental Retardation

Movement education develops independence in students with mental retardation, helping them improve physical, mental, and social competencies. The teacher must be aware of the children's level of competency and degree of retardation and of any psychological, social, or behavior problems. Stein and Pangle (1966) presented the following basic constructs of psychomotor functions for children with mental retardation:

1. At any specific age, normal children tend to perform higher than mentally retarded children on most measures of motor proficiency.
2. Although children who are mentally retarded have a low achievement level, they are closer to the norm physically than mentally.

3. Planned and systematic programs in movement education can develop physical proficiency in children with mental retardation.
4. Children who are mentally retarded and are enrolled in the public schools have higher physical abilities than those in institutions.
5. Children who are mentally retarded learn better with activities that require simple skills rather than complex neuromuscular skills.
6. The physical development of children who are mentally retarded has no effect on their sociometric status.
7. Children who are educable mentally retarded can achieve significant IQ gains by participating in planned and progressive movement education activities.
8. Children who are mentally retarded exhibit a stronger relationship between physical proficiency and intelligence than do normal pupils.

Children with mental retardation are often more poorly coordinated than those who are normal. Skills can be learned through repetition, using activities these children enjoy—activities that allow them to develop at their own rate. The teacher should provide assistance or support to these children as needed during activities (Oliver, 1966).

Children with Behavior Disorders

Children with behavior disorders are usually not physically retarded; some may have outstanding coordination and physical fitness. Goals for these children are similar to those for all children. Gymnastics, games, and dance experiences offer vehicles whereby children with emotional problems can develop body awareness and become physically fit. These programs should focus specifically on socialization, development of coordination and movement exploration, and positive redirection of energy.

These children may need different strategies in order to achieve the goals in movement education, increase their attention span, and develop self-discipline. Teachers should be aware of each child's pathology and select appropriate techniques. Before making program decisions, teachers should examine each child's psychological records along with staff recommendations and past experiences in similar situations. The children's progress must be challenged, but not to the point they become frustrated and give up. On the other hand, activities that are far too easy insult their abilities.

Many children with behavior disorders have difficulty hitting or catching a ball, jumping high, playing games requiring considerable organization, and following rules (Waggoner, 1973). Some of these children remain passive and have short attention spans. Alternative activities must be planned for times when such a child's attention begins to decline. Such activities should not all be new because learning many new activities can be upsetting. Since children with behavior disorders have difficulty waiting, remaining quiet, or listening to long explanations, teachers should prepare the environment before the children arrive so that activities can be introduced quickly.

Equipment should be colored brightly enough to attract the children's attention, but not be so gaudy that it frightens them. The children's short attention span also requires that equipment be available for their use throughout the period since they may not be able to stand in line and wait their turn. It helps if an aide is available to work on a one-to-one basis with each child.

MUSIC EDUCATION

Children are exposed to a wide range of sounds throughout their lives. From infancy, they hear vacuum cleaners, airplanes, dogs, doorbells, thunder, rain, and human voices. They learn to discriminate differences in volume, rhythm, tempo, and pitch in speech or music. Music is composed of ordered sounds. It provides pleasure and an outlet for expression during the early years. As children mature, knowledge, concepts, and skills in relation to listening, singing, playing, moving, and reading and writing music develop. A music program in the preschool, kindergarten, and primary grades is mainly composed of singing, playing simple instruments, listening, and creative rhythms. Each of these areas is discussed below.

Singing

Almost all children love to sing. They like songs with good melodies, easy words, and possibilities for action play. The melody in the song should be pleasant, the range limited, and the intervals easy to attain.

The first musical experience in school programs is usually singing in a group. Most preschool children know nursery rhymes and will sing them with enthusiasm. Young children integrate movement, speech, and singing to develop chants that correspond to their melodramatic configurations, repetitive character, and rhythmic movement (McDonald, 1979). The teacher can use chants to describe daily situations and facilitate transitions.

Learning to sing requires a combination of words and vocal pitch. Teachers need to initially use songs that are within the children's range and gradually present other songs that extend that range. Primary-age children can be taught concepts about melody through singing. Appropriate teaching techniques include using physical movements of the hand or body that correspond to the direction of movement of a song's melody and presenting visual cues such as dashes or musical notes, which indicate high-low, same, or up-down tones. These visual cues can be augmented with an accompaniment on a guitar, a piano, or other instrument. The children's cultural backgrounds can suggest a variety of sources for songs besides the music textbook. Children can also compose new songs or adapt familiar ones, and the teacher can record them on a chart or a tape recorder.

Learning to understand and use the sounds of language can be developed with sound picture books. The musical component of song picture books provides a unique way through which children are able to receive, process, and produce language. Although language may be the emphasis, the sounds, grammar, and meaning of language, which are integrated, are also indirectly developed (Bromley & Jalongo, 1983).

Musical Instruments

Musical instruments can be played independently by young children or in a group. According to Suzuki, a Japanese music educator, all human beings are born musical and have a remarkable capacity for learning musical instruments in the same way they learn to speak. This is reflected in the following principles:

1. Begin early (listening from birth, playing from $2\frac{1}{2}$ or 3 years of age).
2. Postpone reading music until the child is technically well established.
3. Include parents in home teaching and practice, and provide a favorable learning environment with parent–child–teacher cooperation.
4. Use carefully graded, musically excellent literature with recording to match (recorded to repeat listening).
5. Use individual lessons to provide careful, thorough technical foundations and nurture the abilities of each child, and group lessons for motivation and support.
6. Use repetition and reinforcement effectively through constant review of previously learned music.
7. Minimize competition and maximize self-development as a goal. (Kendall, 1986)

Instruments to be used in the early childhood classroom can include drums, tambourines, gourds, maracas, metal triangles, a variety of bells (jingle bells, dainty table bells, cow bells), xylophones with good musical quality, and cymbals that vibrate when clashed. Durable instruments that produce good sounds can be made by the teacher or by the students. Commercially made instruments should also be provided, since many homemade instruments do not achieve a high quality of tone. Only instruments with good sound attributes should be bought; toy instruments should be avoided. Opportunities to explore instruments will help children discriminate the quality of pitched and nonpitched sounds. Children can use their imagination to produce original tunes, rhythms, and sounds.

Drums can be made out of coffee cans by removing the lid and covering one end with plastic. A more authentic drum can be made by removing both ends of the coffee can and stretching sheet rubber or animal hide across the openings. A flute can be made out of a foot-long piece of garden hose closed at one end with a cork and with holes bored down one side. This can be played much like a recorder.

Experiences with instruments appropriate for young children include experimenting with sounds, joining in a rhythm band, observing older children or adults play instruments, creating original tunes, and spontaneously playing instruments. Children can use instruments to experiment with new ideas in sound as well as to refine the skills they develop.

Listening

Listening to music helps children learn to discriminate between qualities of sound (e.g., pitch, intensity, rhythm, and patterns). Attentive listening is a prerequisite for learning to sing. Children must remember the song and accurately reproduce its pitch and rhythmic pattern. Children also listen to the music when they create movements.

Young children are most interested in active listening. They respond to music with movement or creative dance, or with appropriate instrumental accompaniment. Children need to listen to a wide variety of music including classical, jazz, and popular music; music from diverse cultures; and avant-garde and twentieth-century serious music. The types of music favored by children should be played most often, but children need to be encouraged to listen to other styles of music as well. Since children imitate the teacher's behavior, the teacher should model an interest in listening to all types of music. Teachers can invite parents, older children, or community members to share their musical tastes and talents in making music with the class.

Rhythms

Young children become aware of rhythmic patterns in music as they match movement with music. They gradually learn to keep time with music as they listen to recordings, sing songs, and recite nursery rhymes or chant. Exploratory and imitative experiences with rhythm help children gain a repertoire of both musical and nonmusical rhythmic movements.

When children create informal and spontaneous rhythms, teachers can add a chant, a hand-clapping, or an instrumental accompaniment. Opportunities to move spontaneously to music, speech rhythms, and movements that are synchronized with a beat assist children in controlling their rhythmic responses. An awareness of the beat and the synchronizing of movement with that beat can be developed through playing action songs and games that use instruments, visual devices such as clocks and metronomes, and recordings with a predominant rhythmic character. Older children, who have better motor coordination than younger ones, can test out rhythmic patterns through clapping and chanting word rhythms of poetry, chant, and song. They should be encouraged to improvise, share ideas, and verbalize their rhythmic understandings through basic musical terms such as fast-slow, long-short, and even-uneven.

MUSIC EDUCATION FOR DIVERSE CHILDREN

Teaching music to children requires knowing the learning abilities of the children as well as the nature of music. The basic elements of a music program—singing songs, playing instruments, listening to music, and rhythmic movement—can widen the horizons of children with disabilities. Music can draw shy, withdrawn children into a group; encourage spastic children to control their movements; increase hyperkinetic children's involvement in learning movements such as acting out a character while sitting quietly for long periods of time; and reduce language problems for children through singing. Children with language disabilities who have difficulty discriminating and making speech sounds can learn songs to overcome these problems (McDonald, 1979). Picture books can help these children learn a song by repetitive listening and singing, thus focusing their attention on specific phonological components of each word and phrase. The singing of repetitive refrains can assist them to

develop auditory discrimination and pronunciation skills as well as general listening skills and an awareness of language (Bromley & Jalongo, 1983).

The following resources may be helpful to teachers:

Glazer, T. (1973). *Eye Winker, Tom Tinker, Chin Chopper: Fifty Musical Fingerplays*. Garden City, NY: Doubleday.

Glazer, T. (1980). *Do Your Ears Hang Low?* Garden City, NY: Doubleday.

Martin, B., Jr. (1974). *Sounds of Laughter*. New York: Holt, Rinehart & Winston.

Quackenbush, R. (1973). *She'll Be Comin' Round the Mountain*. Philadelphia: Lippincott. (Film: *An American Songfest*, Weston Woods).

Rubin, R., & Wathen, J. (1980). *The All-Year-Long Songbook*. New York: Scholastic Book Services.

Weimer, T. (1980). *Creative Dance Movement*. Winston-Salem, NC: Kaplan Press.

Musical experiences also help children with disabilities come into closer contact with their peers and support social relationships. Children with physical and mental disabilities can learn to play in a rhythm band. Several pieces of music are particularly effective and easy to adapt to these children's needs including "Shoemaker's Dance," "The Xylophone Dance," "Tambourine Waltz," and "Drums of Parade" (Schattner, 1967). Teachers need to experiment, trying any piece of music or technique that can help the children realize themselves fully. Children can share a joyous and enriched experience performing for others.

The music goals for children with disabilities are similar to those for all children and include participating in all forms of musical activities, appreciating music, and developing musicianship. The extent to which children with disabilities achieve these goals depends on their capabilities and limitations. Ganato (cited in Bayless & Ramsey, 1978) suggested using the following guidelines for musical activities for children:

1. Teach through creativity.
2. Teach through multisensory perception.
3. Teach at the appropriate developmental level and rate.
4. Repeat in a variety of ways.
5. Avoid drastic changes of gears.
6. Exclude distractions.
7. Provide instruction in small steps.
8. Offer success-assured activities.
9. Avoid overstimulation with too loud or rhythmic music.
10. Consider the children's level of social and language development.
11. Consider children's short attention span or other disabilities.
12. Repeat songs until children have learned them before attempting any variations.
13. Expect small successes; be ready for changes; be flexible.
14. Wait until the children have learned a song before accompanying it with instruments.
15. Share ideas with and seek them from others who work with and care for children with disabilities.

Children with disabilities can feel comfortable with music. They can sing songs about familiar persons or objects such as names, family, pets, and others; sing popular songs such as "Happy Birthday," "Good Morning," "I'm Pleased to See You"; sing television jingles, nursery rhymes, and family favorites; participate in action plays, circle games; listen to music that has humor or an element of surprise; and sing songs that use props (e.g., scarves or puppets), songs that repeat words or phrases, and songs that are used to follow directions.

Raschke and Gleissner (1988) suggested an instructional activity for children who cannot recall the titles of songs previously learned or for selecting which songs to sing. A picture depicts the themes of songs on miniature teacher-constructed record discs. For example, the picture of a spider is used on a record disc for the song "Eency Weency Spider." The record disks are spread out on the floor to help children recall their favorite song. Record sets portraying several themes (i.e., holiday songs, rhythm songs, or basic concept songs) can be constructed. This activity is easily made appropriate for children with different disabilities. Young children with language impairments can point to their song preference, or those with hearing impairments can sign their song preference. The teacher can also include the sign for the theme under the picture.

Young children can use this activity to recall songs they have learned and select the songs they want to sing. They can use the record discs during their free-choice time to "play school" with peers or stuffed animals. Young children can imitate the teacher's behaviors with these materials.

Children with Physical Disabilities

Music activities can be modified for children with physical disabilities to allow them to crawl, roll over, clap their hands, or respond in any way they can. These children can also listen to music, learn to sing and hum, and play rhythm instruments. During rhythm periods, they can sway to music, move their arms, and turn their bodies from side to side. For dance periods, they can watch and clap out rhythms as other children learn the steps of a dance. The teacher or a peer can move a child's wheelchair in time to music, beginning with a simple waltz rhythm, humming with the child as the chair is moved—back and forth, to the right and left, and in circles. When able, the children can move their own wheelchairs propelling them in time to the music—back and forth, around in circles, to the right and left, or in several directions. Children in wheelchairs enjoy this experience as a form of dancing since their wheelchairs become extensions of themselves. A wheelchair dance need not be restricted to one child, as shown in the following steps for at least two children:

1. Wheelchairs are placed facing each other.
2. Wheel back for one measure, then forward for one measure. (Repeat four times.)
3. Each wheelchair circles in place.
4. First wheelchair circles the second.
5. Second wheelchair circles the first.
6. Both return to the first position and bow from the chairs. (Schattner, 1967)

A solo wheelchair dance can be largely self-inspired, whereas a wheelchair dance for two may need assistance and structuring.

Children with physical disabilities can observe dance or gymnastic activities as well as use rhythmic activities during their physical therapy sessions. When the music activity requires instruments, the extent of their coordination and their ability to move must be matched with their instruments. Students with primarily gross motor skills can play drums or tambourines. Sand blocks, rhythm sticks, or sleighbells can be tied to a part of the body the child is able to use (Turnbull & Schulz, 1979). Rhythmic experiences usually improve children's muscles as they develop coordination and control. Singing relaxes tight muscles and offers an opportunity to share, participate in, and enjoy music.

Children with Visual Impairments

Children with visual impairments also need modified musical experiences. These children may have a distorted awareness of space and may need to develop spatial boundaries. They often are physically insecure and may have poor coordination and balance in rhythmic movement. Such students need assistance in exploring movement.

Rhythmic activities can foster the mobility skills of children with visual impairments. Music or activities requiring large movements can be used at the beginning of a lesson, then gradually refined. The child listens to the teacher and feels the teacher's movement as directions are provided along with demonstrations. Rhythmic movements can include "rocks rolling," "swings," "swaying," and "walking in the rain." Circle games such as "Skip to My Lou," "Looby Lou," and "London Bridge" can also build the children's feelings of security and help them achieve social recognition.

The rhythmic ability of children who are visually impaired helps them respond well to percussion instruments. They easily acquire and create rhythmic patterns. Sounds made by bells, tambourines, or other, similar instruments allow visually impaired children to become aware of other classmates' positions so they can avoid collision during movement activities.

These children enjoy using several instruments to complement their singing and movement. They can examine and experiment with the instruments to learn how they are played. They will feel and hear the vibrations of the lasting sound of a gong long after it has been struck. Many characters, events, and dramas can be created with a gong, a tinkling bell, or a drum. Children can integrate these sounds into dances as they move to the whistling and flow of the wind over them, as they run to the sound of waves and passing trucks, or as they move to the sounds made by voices, words, and music.

Children with Hearing Impairments

Music can be amplified and played through headphones to allow hearing-impaired children to enjoy the music. These children can play and feel a wide range of musical instruments. Playing instruments develops eye-hand coordination, helps children feel the various sensations created by sounds, and increases muscle strength, joint motion, and coordination. Children who are hearing-impaired can enjoy humming and clapping along with other children. They can use movement to learn rhythms while observing the rhythmic sequence in different meters and reproducing the pattern through clapping or playing instruments. This kinesthetic approach is a valuable technique in teaching rhythms.

Nursery rhymes help children who are hearing-impaired to acquire rhythm. They can also learn rhythm through tactile sensory perceptions, placing their fingers on a drum or another instrument playing the nursery rhymes. Much repetition is essential for them to feel the rhythm. Nursery rhymes can also help their speech rhythm.

Children with peculiar breathing patterns, poorly developed voices, and language problems have difficulty with singing. They can participate in rhythmic activities through movement or instruments. Marching, hopping, skipping, and other strong rhythmic actions develop the speech rhythm and bodily coordination of children who are hearing-impaired. Together, movement experiences and music improve these children's ability, posture, and physical fitness.

Children with Mental Retardation

Music experiences help children who are mentally retarded develop listening skills, increase their attention span, develop coordination through rhythms, and create spontaneous interest. These children can learn to sing simple songs sometime after their fourth birthday. Although they may have pitch problems, they often can listen for short periods to music that interests them (Graham, 1972).

Children who are mentally retarded usually are monotone singers. They have short attention spans, often lack auditory perception, and are sometimes unable to understand what is required of them in music. Singing songs can help reduce these deficiencies. One technique for teaching them songs is to sing simple songs repeatedly to the children using a variety of illustrative materials. Such songs as "A Little Teapot," "Eency Weency Spider," and various nursery rhymes can be introduced with colorful illustrations and movements to facilitate learning and can strengthen these children's memory and concentration. Moving the body to music, clapping, and brisk stepping can be taught to them through action songs like "Row, Row, Row Your Boat." The large muscle movements used in this song provide additional reinforcement for memory.

Musical experiences for children who are mentally retarded should include playing instruments. The following steps can be used for playing musical instruments with these children:

1. The children explore the musical instruments alone.
2. The teacher and a child play instruments together, labeling the sounds (e.g., This is a drum—boom! This is a bell—jingle, jingle!).
3. The teacher asks the children to close their eyes and questions them. ("What's this sound?" or "Is this a drum?")
4. The teacher taps a rhythm and asks the child to play that rhythm with him or her.
5. The teacher plays or sings a simple rhythm and then the child taps the rhythm.
6. The teacher plays increasingly difficult rhythms and asks the child to play them.

Since the rate of development of children who are mentally retarded is often uneven or slow, musical experiences must be repeated in a variety of modes. The musical achievement of children with disabilities is often higher and with more depth than the teacher might expect.

ART EDUCATION

Art serves as a means of nonverbal communication for young children. In the early years children respond more to visual and tactile experiences than to the representational qualities of art. As they mature, they can continue to work with the same art media in more sophisticated ways, making prints, constructing, modeling, painting, stitching, and weaving.

Children's art abilities progress through a series of stages characterized as the preschematic stage (4 to 7 years), the schematic stage (7 to 9 years), and the stage of drawing realism (9 to 11 years) (Lowenfeld & Brittain, 1987). These stages are based on the characteristics of children's art products, including representation of the human figure, space, color, design, motivation, topics, and materials. For example, a child's work in the preschematic stage may be characterized as follows:

1. General characteristic—discovery of relationship between drawing, thinking, and environment.
2. Presentation of human figure—circular motion for head, longitudinal for legs and arms.
3. Use of space—self as center with no orderly arrangement of objects in space.
4. Use of color—no conscious approach.
5. Motivation topics—activation of passive knowledge related mainly to self-body parts.
6. Use of materials—crayons, clay, tempera paints; large thick bristle brushes; large sheets of absorbent paper.

Lowenfeld's stages of art expression parallel Piaget's stages of intellectual development. They provide an index teachers can use to evaluate children's art abilities. For example, during a cutting activity the teacher can record which children hold scissors properly, are left- or right-handed, cut in an upward rather than downward direction, and are able to state what form they wish to complete before cutting. Clay modeling, Playdoh modeling, paper tearing, and different forms of painting can all be evaluated this way. Having a sense of the children's stages allows teachers to appropriately direct and plan classroom activities in the motor, affective, perceptual, cognitive, and aesthetic domains.

Children's drawings also indicate their style of thinking. Children who draw details usually perceive objects as separate from the field, can abstract an item from the surrounding field, and are analytic individuals. Those who admit details tend to rely on the surrounding perceptual field, experience their environments in a relatively global fashion by conforming to the effects of the prevailing field or context, and are social individuals.

ART EDUCATION FOR CHILDREN WITH SPECIAL NEEDS

Art benefits all children. However, children with special needs benefit more than the other children. Some children with disabilities may not be able to verbally express their feelings, but they may be able to express themselves with a brush. Teachers need to motivate, provide media, offer freedom, and give guidance to learning-disabled students (Hull & Walker, 1984).

Teachers can use art to help children with disabilities develop an awareness of their surroundings, building bridges for communication and motivating them to relate to others. Children can use art to express anger without fear of retaliation. Children who are self-destructive can find something in their art products that is worthwhile. Children with delayed speech development can gradually explore complex nonlinguistic symbolic forms. Art experiences also benefit children who are physically disabled, visually impaired, or neurologically damaged.

The art curriculum for children with disabilities must be modified in content, methods, materials, timing, and sequence and must be presented in a climate of acceptance, openness, and empathy. Challenging experiences can help these children explore ideas, resolve intense feelings, and become less dependent. Some of these children easily become disoriented and upset; some lack self-motivation; some have learned to expect failure; some have limited receptive and expressive abilities; and some have short attention spans. Some children with disabilities also lack self-confidence, have a poor self- image, and expect to fail in their endeavors. These students need successful experiences that make them comfortable with the materials and allow them to express their thoughts and feelings.

Children who lack self-direction need an enthusiastic presentation to help them become interested and involved in art activities. Visual aids such as films, slide presentations and pictures capture their attention and provide stimulation.

Easily understood instructions must be provided to children with limited receptive abilities. These should be supplemented by demonstrations so those who cannot fully understand the teacher's words will be able to follow their actions. Teachers may also stand behind the children and move their hands in the same direction as the children's hands (Hollander, 1971). Encouraging questions allows children to indicate any confusion they might have.

Children with Physical Disabilities

Children with physical disabilities may have learning problems because of their orthopedic or central nervous system. Their physical dysfunctions require that they use aides to assist them around their classes. However, these physical restrictions should not stop these students from working independently to encourage self-reliance. Standard practice with these students suggests that materials be adapted to their specific needs such as attaching materials to the wheelchairs or taping boards to desk for assembling collages (Rodriguez, 1985).

Simple devices that are easily produced or purchased can aid children with physical disabilities. Students who are not able to hold a brush because of limited manual dexterity can use a foam hair curler. The curler slides right over the brush handle or pencil. Foam bought in fabric stores can make the tool thicker. Dowels can be drilled out to fit over a drawing tool or brush. Velcro strips can be glued to drawing tools to connect to a Velcro band slipped on a student's hand. This keeps the brush from slipping out of the hands of a child with a physical disability, who may have a weak grasp (Rodriguez, 1985).

Additional adaptive devices consist of everyday items. Roll-on deodorant applicators and squeeze bottles can become fun tools for brushless painting that these children can use as they support good upper-body movement. Such art activities appear attractive to them (Rodriguez, 1985).

Children with physical disabilities who can move only their arms, hands, and fingers can still participate in the art program. Those with limited fine motor skills may need help holding pencils, crayons, or paint brushes. A ball of clay or a foam rubber sponge wrapped around a pencil, crayon, or brush can help. Students with jerky or uncoordinated movements may knock the paper from the easel or table, spill paint, or knock other supplies to the floor. These children may need a separate work area with sturdy holders in which to snugly insert paint jars. Their papers can be taped to easels or to the surfaces on which they are working. Students who cannot manipulate small objects may have to use large objects for their artwork. If they cannot use paint, they might work with crayons or collage. Felt-tipped pens, soft-lead pencils, and ballpoint pens are good drawing tools that require little pressure and do not have to be refilled.

Children with Visual Impairments

Often children with visual impairments are not included in an art program. These children appreciate art tactually and enjoy a variety of textures and forms. They need opportunities to actively participate in the creative process and discover their own place in the world of art. Art activities appropriate for the visually impaired depend on the degree of their disability, their perceptual experiences, and their age. These children need to be encouraged to become involved, but they should not be too overwhelmed.

Children whose sight losses range from mild to severe depend on their sense of touch for information. They must learn to discriminate among the different materials by identifying their characteristic qualities. This may be achieved by asking them to describe the medium they are working with (Rodriguez, 1985).

Students who are visually impaired learn through multisensory instruction, combining auditory, tactile, and kinesthetic experiences. Teachers can provide verbal instructions while allowing the students to feel the texture of the material. For example, in tying a knot, the teacher guides the student's fingers and hands through the sequence of steps while giving directions verbally. A variety of materials including boxes, balls, cups, different types of paper, wood, textiles, sand, yarn, pipe cleaners, wires, rubber, and plastic can be provided. The children will begin to work with just a few materials and gradually extend their repertoires.

These children enjoy modelling with clay, making prints, pasting collages, and fingerpainting. They can explore a wide range of textures and refine their tactile sense. Playdough can be made in different colors; adding a dash of food coloring mixed with flavor extracts gives it color, flavor, and taste. Orange coloring along with orange extract makes the Playdoh smell like orange, or yellow with lemon extract, or green with mint, and so on. Food extracts can be matched to color in poster paints to strengthen the visually impaired students' understanding of the relationship between colors and natural flavors (Rodriguez, 1985).

Children who are visually impaired need to know the boundaries of the paper they use. Teachers can guide their hands along the edges. Teachers may also want to tape their paper to the table surface. If they are working with paste, teachers need to place the glue side up (Rodriguez, 1985).

Children with Hearing Impairments

A hearing loss alters a child's communication, speech, and language. With art activities, just like any other activities, it is essential that the child understand all directions and requirements of the activity. Teachers may need to write the directions on the chalkboard, chart tablet, or any place the students are able to see it.

Children who are hearing-impaired are keen observers, which can help them excel in art (Krone, 1978). Although art can do little for the children's hearing loss, it can help them resolve their emotional detachment caused by a lack of environmental awareness and interaction. The teacher should offer art experiences that allow the children to symbolize their feelings through art; three-dimensional art such as modeling or carving is helpful.

Since these children's experiences are diminished and distorted by their disability, they need many experiences to help them develop greater environmental and body awareness. They need a variety of sensory experiences in order to acquire knowledge about themselves and the surrounding world and to substitute for information they are unable to hear. Art experiences can help them identify and interact with the world of space and motion.

Children with Mental Retardation

Educators often disregard the value of art for children who are mentally retarded, considering it a frill or a fill-in. However, art experiences are educationally valuable as well as personally satisfying for these children. Children with mental retardation often

have normal patterns of growth in art expression, although they may develop at a slower rate. The artistic abilities of these children are characterized as follows (Uhlin, 1979):

1. Slow rate but a normal pattern of growth.
2. Simple or primitive forms but good motor coordination.
3. Lack of experiences expressed in preservation of form and subject.
4. Poor spatial Gestalt features indicating a lack of energy expended for association in the perceptual task.
5. Haptic-type, or tactile experiences expressed in:
    a. a body-self centering of viewpoint concerning the space of the drawing or painting
    b. piece-method approach to modeling
    c. lack of spatial depth in drawing or painting
    d. bold, continuous-line character in drawing
    e. emotional exaggeration, deletion, or distortion of form when motivated with a particular experience
    f. emotional employment of color
    g. expression of tactual kinesthetic awareness.

Children who are mentally retarded need to develop a sensitivity to form and space, increased intellectual flexibility, greater emotional sensitivity, an enriched conceptual repertoire, and more social confidence. In view of these needs, teachers should (1) design structured activities, starting with shape; (2) select activities that have display possibilities; (3) direct children to discovery of new forms; (4) use activities that the children may have engaged in at home such as cutting, pasting, or assembling; (5) demonstrate art projects clearly in a step-by-step progression; (6) select materials a size larger than the hand; and (7) include many three-dimensional activities (Lavano-Kerr & Savage, 1972).

Children with mental retardation are able to express themselves and are capable of learning restricted art concepts through systematic teaching and through the use of specific instructional materials. Drawing with a heavy crayon helps develop kinesthetic skills and provides the teacher with an indication of progress. Making simple puppets is also a good activity. Puppetry helps these children identify roles and respond to them as they create conversations among their puppets. Young children can make jewelry by rolling a salt–flour dough mixture into beads, puncturing them with toothpicks, and laying them out to dry. After the beads are dried, they can be painted, varnished, and strung to wear as a necklace.

These children also respond well to bright, shiny materials which captivate their interest. Like children who are visually impaired, children who are mentally retarded also benefit from textural and tactile experiences such as fabric and clay activities (Rodriguez, 1985).

Children with Behavior Disorders

Children with behavior disorders exhibit aggressive or withdrawn behaviors that disrupt their learning. Their self-esteem is low; therefore, art activities should concentrate on the students' sense of self such as self-portrait. The "Brown Bag" can be used with children with emotional problems. Items to place in the bag should be those that are meaningful to individual students such as birthday cards, ticket stubs, photographs, letters, postcards. These items can also be gathered to make a collage. Designs can include the students' names, or students can draw images to communicate their ideas (Rodriguez, 1985).

Art activities can allow children with behavior disorder to express what they really feel. Their moods (e.g., happy or sad, calm or tense, frightened, worried or confident) can be illustrated through color and form (Miller, 1986). Art activities, much like play activities, have long been used as a form of therapy for young children (see, for example, Kramer, 1972; Naumberg, 1973). Art allows children to express ideas and feelings in nondiscursive ways. The graphic symbols of art may represent unconscious and often repressed elements of a child's personality and may communicate elements of that child's feelings, mood, and private fantasies (Kramer, 1972).

The teacher, although not an art therapist, can use elements of the art program to reach these children and help them deal with themselves in the context of the school setting. Often the opportunity to express a feeling can provide enough of a catharsis so that the young child will not be troubled by disturbing feelings. The expression of feeling is also a step in the development of ways of understanding and coping with feelings. Sometimes, however, art can be used to hide feelings, providing a defense against apparent exposure through stereotyped products.

Care must be taken that art materials provided for children with behavior disorders are appropriate. Materials that are easily controlled, such as crayon and chalk, are best for some children, since they may have difficulty coping with freedom of other materials. Malleable materials such as clay may be best for others. Some children will be fearful of new and unfamiliar material. Others will take pleasure from the tactile and kinesthetic sensations derived from a range of material. It is helpful for the teacher to approach art with these children tentatively, offering a choice of materials and taking cues from their responses rather than prescribing the same art experiences for these children as for others.

The teacher must be careful in interpreting the art products of children. Often meanings that are expressed in children's artwork are symbolized in strange ways. The children themselves may not be aware of the meanings expressed and may be unsure as to the nature of the representation. Their level of development will also place limits on their artistic productions, which can further complicate interpretation. From the classroom teacher's point of view, art experiences for these children, as for all children, should be concerned with providing pleasure and satisfaction along with increased skill in using the material.

Children with behavior disorders also need to feel valued. Creative expression through art can help them develop a positive self-concept, value as a person, and self-confidence in their ability to perform. Creative expression does not have a correct or incorrect way, but the successful completion of art projects can contribute to the positive feelings they can develop about themselves. Empathy, respect, pride, and confidence can be transmitted through art (Miller, 1986).

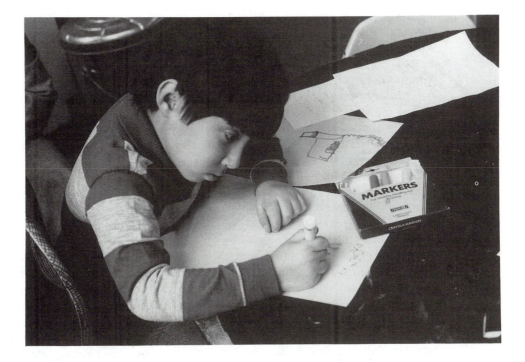

Children with Learning Disabilities

Children with learning disabilities are not deficient in intelligence. They have difficulty processing information, which has an impact on their academic skills such as reading (Rodriguez, 1985). These children are often immature. Although they appear average, they do not learn like average students. Their disability often is hidden. These children do not know how to organize themselves, to start something, to continue it, and to stop it. Their attention is unfocused and dispersed, and they lack the organization to cope efficiently with the freedom that is usually associated with expressive arts. During art, the teacher must become the child's focusing mechanism.

Children with learning disabilities need boundaries to be able to learn effectively and to create fully. Teachers must restrict the students' space, time, choices, amount of materials to use, amount of work to be completed, directions, and discussion. This type of restriction does not limit the ability of children with learning disabilities to express themselves. It provides them with parameters and borders to permit them to organize their expression. Although these children need adult support for a longer period of time than do other children, they also need to be continuously assisted to become independent. They can learn sophisticated material if the teacher breaks it down into simple parts to teach it step by step (Smith, 1988).

These children are often unable to sequence events. Initial art products can include two-step situations, integrating the children's personal experiences. For instance, the children might draw a story in two parts: The first picture indicates that a girl was given a piece of candy, and the second picture indicates what she did with the candy (ate it, gave it to someone else, lost it). The children can gradually work with more complicated stories until they are able to sequence a story with many parts. Sequencing is also important in other art experiences (such as sculpture and printmaking) that require that a large number of directions to be followed in order.

Children with learning disabilities may become upset when they think they have made a mistake on a project. They can be provided with projects using material that can be reshaped or changed often. For example, children who draw on the blackboard or use fingerpaint can easily erase and start a new drawing. Clay can be molded and remolded into many different shapes, allowing children to work over a clay project until they are satisfied. More advanced children can weave, creating a more structured product that also can be easily modified. After experience with these materials, children will realize that it is possible to alter one's plans and that it is not necessary to develop the object exactly the way they wished the first time (Krone, 1978).

Children with learning disabilities can benefit from the art experiences. Through them, they can be helped to modify their behavior characteristics such as having a short attention span, having difficulty in completing a task, being hyperactive, and having problems with remembering information. Children who have problems completing a task can engage in art activities that are of interest to them long enough to help them complete a simple art project such as painting a picture about something they have recently seen or creating a print with a leaf, twig, or piece of rock they have found in the schoolyard. Tactile kinesthetic activities can be integrated in the art process to help them retain information while at the same time challenging them and motivating them to create a product and facilitate their attending skills (Miller, 1986).

Children with Language Disabilities

Art is an important means of communication for children who have difficulty expressing themselves in language. Children with language problems usually have receptive and expressive communication gaps. They often have an impaired sensory system. Children with communication disorders may hear or see words but not derive meaning from them. Art reinforces their language concepts and develops visual symbolism. For example, children may draw a kite after seeing one, naming and describing the qualities of the kite (shape, color, texture, weight) and identifying these quality words as they reproduce the kite. Pictures or slides of a variety of kites can be shown and discussed as their similarities and differences are compared. Then the children can fly the kite they used as a model or watch others fly it, observing and describing the manner in which the kite flies, the importance of the wind (cause and effect), the sound of the wind as it blows the kite, the way the kite moves, and the importance of the string. Children can recapture this experience as they draw or paint. This procedure encourages children to use their sensory capacities to better understand and express themselves verbally and artistically (Krone, 1978).

Art activities can introduce children with language disabilities to their fantasy world by encouraging them to talk about their artistic projects. Nonthreatening questions about the projects can help these children bring about verbal responses similar to free association. They can gain insight into their personality and problems and the process can help them to expand their self-awareness (Miller, 1986).

Teachers and parents are often unsure how to respond to children's art. Complimentary, judgmental, valuing, questioning, probing, and corrective are six traditional approaches to viewing children's art and to analyze the impact each one has on the child as an artist (Schirrmacher, 1986). These are presented in the list below.

Traditional Approaches to Children's Art

1. *Complimentary approach* is achieved by complimenting the children's work.

   Example: "That's a beautiful painting" or "Oh, how lovely" or "Yes, very nice" are typical of the complimentary approach.

2. *Judgmental approach* is achieved by simply telling all children that any and all of their art is good rather than ranking it as good, better, or best. Teachers need to be sure that they do not overuse it; otherwise, they will lose their credibility with the children and their statements may become empty judgments communicating a rubber-stamp production line attitude.

   Example: Adults can tell children, "That's great work, Susan!"

3. *Valuing approach* is when teachers tell children how they value their work. Children draw to communicate themselves, not to please adults. Teachers must show children they appreciate the time and effort they spent creating their art, but they should not reward and encourage the process.

   Example: "I like that a lot" or "Oh, I just love it!"

4. *Questioning approach* refers to when the adult directly and bluntly asks, "What is it?" or "What is that supposed to be?" Most children are not able to verbalize their art representations. When teachers demand to know what something is, children may shrug their shoulders, shade their eyes down and say, "I don't know," or walk away. The teacher's persistence may leave no recourse for the child but to give any response to verbally play along with the teacher and end the interrogation. This may lead to a negative attitude toward their creation.

5. *Probing approach* refers to the teacher's attempt to draw from children some hint, title, or verbal statement regarding their artwork.

   Example: "Please tell me about it" or "What would you like to say about this?"

Probing is less presumptuous and abrasive than questioning, and it supports an integrated approach to curriculum development where art is integrated with other areas. Its major value may be in that it may encourage children to talk about their art and may not place as much value on the product than the process, or on the adult's judgment instead of the child's.

6. *Corrective approach* is when teachers make remarks about the children's work in comparison to the real world.

> *Example*: A child draws a tiger. "Very good, but next time remember to draw stripes on your tiger. Tigers have stripes."

Such well-intentioned remarks may suggest that children will be able to improve their art by comparing and making it closer to reality. However, children may choose to be free and add or exclude details. Adult corrections or criticisms only suppress children's motivation to express themselves and fail to foster artistic growth.

The approaches noted are commonly used by teachers. Alternatively:

- Teachers should permit children to explore their artistic discoveries without comparing, correcting, or projecting their standards and values.
- Teachers should deviate from probing for representation in children's art to emphasize the abstract, design qualities, or "syntax" (such as shape and form) (Eisner, 1982) to motivate their aesthetic awareness (Wachowiak, 1985).

An integration of these strategies may be more effective. Children's ideas are fresh and their interests in sharing their art is high right after they have completed their artwork. This may be the best time for teachers to discuss the artwork with the children (Smith, 1983).

Children Who Are Gifted

Children who are gifted function above the normal expectancy level of their age, which makes them exceptional and have unique educational needs. Although they have an outstanding capability, they may not be interested in predictable activities. Their problem-solving preferences might encourage them to collect items for a "Theme Collage Kit" when they are working on a collage. Items for this activity should denote a definite topic, such as seasons. For example, winter can include pinecones, mistletoe, and a glove. The themes "Tools of the Trade" can involve a carpenter collage with such items as nails, sandpaper, ruler, and screws. These collages encourage class discussions, which are meaningful to students (Rodriguez, 1985).

SUMMARY

Children express their thoughts and feelings in many ways. Although language is the predominant mode of expression for most people, movement, music and art are also important, especially during childhood. Education in these forms of expression should be offered to all children, including those with disabilities, for they extend the child's way of understanding the world as well as allow for the creation of unique creative communications. Personal ways of knowing related to art, music, and movement are highly satisfying to young children and may be especially important to children who are less successful in using conventional forms of expression.

Early childhood teachers working with children with disabilities need to know the basic elements of each expressive mode as well as how children develop in their ability to use each mode. They need to be aware of the skills and competencies of each child in relation to his or her expressive abilities. By meshing the knowledge of the child with the knowledge of the media of art, movement, and music, teachers can develop activities that are satisfying to children and also allow them to extend their abilities beyond stereotyped forms into true forms of personal expression. These activities need to be designed so that they are free from hazards and are safe for children. Teachers must be especially cautious when children with disabilities are involved.

REFERENCES

Bayless, K. M., & Ramsey, M. E. (1978). *Music: A way of life for the young child*. St. Louis: Mosby.

Bromley, K. D., & Jalongo, M. R. (1983). Song picture books and the language disabled child. *Teaching Exceptional Children, 16*(2), 115–118.

Bucher, C. A., & Thaxton, N. A. (1979). *Physical education for children: Movement foundations and experiences*. New York: Macmillan.

Buell, C. (1970). The school's responsibility for providing physical activities for blind students. *Journal of Health, Physical Education and Recreation, 41*(6), 41–42.

Burton, E. C. (1977). *The new physical education for elementary school children*. Boston: Houghton Mifflin.

Cartwright, G. P., Cartwright, C. A., & Ward, M. E. (1989). *Educating special learners*. Belmont, CA: Wadsworth.

Christensen, D. (1970). Creativity in teaching physical education to the physically handicapped child. *Journal of Health, Physical Education and Recreation, 41*(3), 73–74.

Copple, C., Sigel, I., & Saunders, R. (1979). *Educating the young thinker*. New York: Van Nostrand.

Eason, R. L., & Smith, T. L. (1976). A perceptual motor program model for learning disabled children. *Physical Education Research Journal, 33*(1), 4.

Eisner, E. W. (1982). *Cognition and curriculum—A basis for deciding what to teach*. New York: Longman.

Fauman, L. S. (1983). Dance for preschool children. *Journal of Physical Education, Recreation and Dance, 54*(6), 56–58.

Frederick, J. (1971). Ropes for wheelchairs. *Journal of Health, Physical Education and Recreation, 42*(3), 50.

Graham, R. M. (1972). Seven million plus need special attention. Who are they? *Music Educators' Journal, 50*(8), 22–25.

Hollander, H. C. (1971). *Creative opportunities for the retarded child at home and in school*. New York: Doubleday.

Hull, H., & Walker, R. (1984). Art in special education: A conversation with a classroom teacher. *Pointer, 29*(1), 46–48.

Javernick, E. (1988). Johnny's not jumping: Can we help obese children? *Young Children,* *43*(2), 18–23.

Johansen, G. (1971). Integrating visually handicapped children into a public school physical education program. *Journal of Health, Physical Education and Recreation, 42*(4), 61–62.

Karper, W. B. (1986). Childhood asthma and physical education. *Physical Educator, 44,* 250–254.

Kendall, J. (1986). Suzuki's mother tongue method. *Music Educators' Journal, 6,* 47–50.

Kirchner, G., Cunningham, J., & Warrell, E. (1978). *Introduction to movement education.* Dubuque, IA: Brown.

Kramer, E. (1972). *Art as therapy with children.* New York: Schocken.

Krone, A. (1978). *Art instruction for handicapped children.* Denver: Love.

Laban, R. (1988). *The mastery of movement* (4th ed.). London: Macdonald & Evans.

Lavano-Kerr, J., & Savage, S. (1972). Incremental art curriculum for the mentally retarded. *Exceptional Children, 39*(3), 193–199.

Lowenfeld, V., & Brittain, W. L. (1987). *Creative and mental growth* (5th ed). New York: Macmillan.

McDonald, D. T. (1979). *Music in our lives: The early years.* Washington, DC: National Association for the Education of Young Children.

Miller, M. A. (1986). Art—A creative teaching tool. *Academic Therapy, 22*(1), 53–56.

Miller, S. E., & Schaumberg, K. (1988). Physical education activities for children with severe cerebral palsy. *Teaching Exceptional Children, 20*(2), 9–11.

Naumberg, M. (1973). *An introduction to art therapy.* New York: Teachers College Press.

Neijens, H. J. (1985). Children with lung disease and exercise. In R. A. Binkhorst, H. C. J. Kemper, & W. H. M. Saris (Eds.), *Children and exercise XI.* Champaign, IL: Human Kinetics.

Nickerson, B. G., Bautista, D. B., Namey, M. A., Richards, W., & Keens, T. G. (1983). Distance running improves fitness in asthmatic children without pulmonary complications or changes in exercise-induced bronchospasm. *Pediatrics, 71,* 147–152.

Noble, B. (1986). *Physiology of exercise and sport.* St. Louis: Mosby.

Oliver, J. N. (1966). Add challenge with variety in activities. *Journal of Health, Physical Education and Recreation, 37*(4), 37–39.

Orenstein, D. M., Reed, M. E., Grogan, F. T., Jr., & Crawford, L. V. (1985). Exercise conditioning in children with asthma. *The Journal of Pediatrics, 106,* 556–560.

Raschke, D., & Gleissner, L. (1988). Top ten hit parade. *Teaching Exceptional Children, 20*(3), 58–59.

Rodriguez, S. (1985). Art for special needs . . . It's exceptional. *Arts and Activities, 98*(4), 44–46.

Safford, P. L. (1989). *Integrated teaching in early childhood: Starting in the mainstream.* White Plains, NY: Longman.

Schattner, R. (1967). *Creative dramatics for handicapped children.* New York: John Day Company.

Schirrmacher, R. (1986). Talking with young children about their art. *Young Children, 41*(5), 3–7.

Sherrill, C. (1986). *Adapted physical education and recreation* (3rd ed.). Dubuque, IA: Wm. C. Brown.

Smith, N. R. (1983). *Experience and art: Teaching children to paint.* New York: Teachers College Press.

Smith, S. L. (1988). The role of the arts in the education of learning-disabled children. *The Pointer, 32*(3), 11–16.

Smoot, S. L. (1985). Exercise programs for mainstreamed handicapped students. *Teaching Exceptional Children, 17*(4), 262–266.

Stein, J. U., & Pangle, R. (1966). What research says about psychomotor function of retarded. *Journal of Health, Physical Education and Recreation, 37*(4), 40–46.

Turnbull, A. P., & Schulz, J. B. (1979). *Mainstreaming handicapped students: A guide for the classroom teacher*. Boston: Allyn & Bacon.

Uhlin, D.M. (1979). *Art for exceptional children*. Dubuque, IA: Wm. C. Brown.

Wachowiak, F. (1985). *Emphasis art*. New York: Harper & Row.

Waggoner, E. (1973). Motivation in physical education and recreation for emotionally handicapped children. *Journal of Health, Physical Education and Recreation, 44*(3), 73–77.

Wishon, P., Bower, R., & Eller, B. (1983). Childhood obesity. *Young Children, 39*(1), 21–27.

CHAPTER 11

Teaching the Language Arts

CHAPTER OVERVIEW

This chapter discusses:

1. The goals of a language arts program for young children with diverse needs.
2. Expressive and receptive communication skills for young children.
3. Expressive and receptive language experiences for young children with diverse needs.
4. A literature program for young children with diverse needs.
5. Criteria for selecting books that are appropriate for young children with diverse needs.
6. A variety of ways to present poetry to young children with diverse needs.
7. Ways to prepare storytelling, puppetry, and creative dramatics for young children with diverse needs.
8. The development of young children's written language.

Children come to school having learned a great deal about their native language and how to use it. They have developed an extensive vocabulary and have learned most of the important grammatical rules. They have also learned to use language for many purposes in a number of settings. Young children generally reach a high degree of language competence before the onset of formal instruction.

An early childhood language program needs to build on what children have already learned about language in their early years. It should extend that knowledge in a systematic way and fill in gaps that exist in language learning. This chapter addresses both the expressive and receptive language arts. Reading is specifically covered in the next chapter. It discusses ways of modifying regular classroom programs to meet the needs of children with diverse needs.

The goals of an early childhood education language arts programs include:

1. *Developing basic oral language skills*—learning to speak in sentences, express ideas in logical sequence, enunciate clearly, and pronounce words correctly.
2. *Developing listening skills*—learning to attend, increase attention span, and understand what is said.
3. *Building a meaningful vocabulary*—developing a vocabulary to use in a variety of contexts.
4. *Developing writing skills*—learning to express thoughts in writing as well as in speech.

The goals of a language arts program for children of diverse needs should be no different from that for average children. The degree to which these goals can be achieved may vary, however. Most children develop language skills and usage early in life without direct or deliberate teaching. At times, however, most children will exhibit some problems in language development. They may not respond to queries unless the verbalizations are accompanied by gestures. Their verbal responses may not make sense. The words they use may be inappropriate or their syntax wrong. Or they may seem to have difficulty understanding when others are communicating to them.

A number of disabilities are associated with problems in children's language development. Children who are developmentally delayed, for example, often are delayed in speech and language development. Such delays may also be associated with mental retardation. Blind children, especially in the preschool years, may have a different pattern of language development than do sighted children. These differences usually fade as the children mature. Children with speech and hearing problems also will have problems in achieving the goals of a language arts program to the extent that normal children might.

A teacher who senses that a child is having a language problem and who suspects that other problems might exist should arrange a hearing examination using an audiometer for the child. Deafness and hearing losses account for many learning disorders and, if not diagnosed during the early years, can lead to later difficulties in academic skill acquisition (Hare & Hare, 1979). If no problem is identified, further assessment should be done. It should be determined whether the child hears different speech sounds; has delayed motor control of the tongue, jaws, and palate (which can affect articulation); or has a neurological problem. An assessment of the problem will suggest appropriate treatment as well as appropriate instruction. A speech and language specialist should be consulted in such cases.

On the other hand, young children who are gifted need alternative and expanded opportunities for language learning. The materials they can enjoy, the books they like to read and have read to them, and the conversations they hold must be appropriate to their developmental level. These children may be particularly sensitive to the feelings

of adults and can become skillful manipulators. Teachers need to help them use and not abuse their special gifts (Cook, Tessier, & Armbruster, 1992).

Several options are available in designing language programs for gifted students. In preparing a language curriculum, the teacher must learn to identify and plan appropriate activities for these children. The teacher must know the nature of their giftedness—their intelligence, their characteristics, and their special educational needs. He or she needs to individualize a program to meet those needs. Teachers must also be aware of appropriate curriculum models and individualized teaching techniques (Rogers, 1989).

THE LANGUAGE ARTS PROGRAM

The language arts include the receptive activities of listening and reading as well as the expressive activities of speaking and writing. In preschool and kindergarten, the focus is on oral language activities. These activities interrelate with one another as children observe the world around them, generate and express ideas, and gain ideas from others. Gradually children become aware of the relationship between spoken and printed language. They learn to receive ideas and impressions through both listening and reading; they learn to share their own ideas, impressions, and feelings through speaking and writing. Many experiences can be offered to young children to enhance skills in listening, speaking, reading, and writing and to make them aware of the beauty and function of language. This can be done through such activities as children's literature, choral speaking, puppetry, creative dramatics, and discussions in which children describe sensory experiences and interpret pictures. As children move through the primary grades, there is increased emphasis on written language skills. The mechanics of handwriting, spelling, and grammar are taught with an emphasis on writing as another form of language communication.

Whole Language

Recently language arts specialist have been advocating an approach to teaching language and literacy called *whole language*. There are many definitions of whole language, but all share a set of common beliefs. Ganopole (1988) summarized the characteristics of whole language:

1. A view of learning as an active constructive process in which prior knowledge, interests, and self-motivated purposes play a major role.
2. A view of language as central to learning.
3. An acknowledgment of the important role social interaction plays in the learning process.
4. A functional view of language learning that suggests that language is learned through actual use in efforts to accomplish relevant purposes.
5. A view of reading as a meaning-making process in which meaning is constructed by building associations between the text and what is already known and believed.
6. A view of writing as a meaning-making process in which writers make their own connections and construct their own meanings. (p. 88)

Language is viewed as an indivisible whole instead of segregated elements of speaking, writing, listening, and reading. Reading instruction does not begin when a child is judged "ready to read." Rather, reading, like the other language arts, develops as the child gains increasing linguistic competence through the early childhood period. Students' needs and interests become the core of instruction.

Elements of a whole language programs can serve for all children. However, some children need explicit instruction in various elements of the language arts. The key, it seems, is that language and literacy be seen as a unified whole, that teaching in these areas be integrated, and that the skills that children develop in language and literacy be used by the children in a range of situations.

Children's Literature

Literature provides children with joy and excitement. When they read something that is interesting to them, they are motivated to complete the task successfully and can feel a sense of competency. Good literature is written in a natural way and with little overt attempt to control vocabulary, syntax, and concepts. The best literature employs language and experiences that are familiar to children, who bring their knowledge about language and the world to literature. They use the text, context, syntax, and letters to construct meaning. They can bring their personal background to the reading situation and predict what will happen next in relation to meaning. However, children with learning disabilities need less complex books that are not overwhelming to them. McClure (1985) suggested accommodating the needs of the children with learning disabilities for predictability and regularity within a literature-based reading program.

Many beautifully illustrated and well-written books are available for young children. The following guidelines by Jacobs (1972) can be used in selecting literary materials for children:

1. *Provide a balance of contemporary and classic literature.* Contemporary literature considers the minds of modern children, the tempo of their world, their delights and enthusiasms, and the language patterns appropriate for their developmental level. The classics reflect cultural continuity.
2. *Provide a balance of realistic and fanciful literature.* Realistic literature refers to possible events, projecting children into time and place settings with seemingly real people. Incidents and events invented by the author seem actual. "Make-believe" stories about fanciful events also should be included.
3. *Provide a balance of fictional and informational reading matter.* Fiction and informational reading present children with two modes of knowing about the meanings and promises of life.
4. *Provide a balance of popular and precious materials.* An abundance of popular books as well as books of high-level literature reflecting both teachers' and children's individual preferences should be available.
5. *Provide a balance of expensive and inexpensive books.* Many inexpensive books are written by reputable writers and illustrated by excellent artists. These should be carefully selected and offered in class. However, children need to experience high-quality, well-produced books as well.
6. *Provide a balance of periodical and book reading.* Children need to be presented with the best current children's newspapers and magazines appropriate for their age group, as well as books.
7. *Provide a balance of prose and poetry.* A rich and balanced contact with literature offers a developmental language program through books and stories, storytelling, poetry, dramatizing literature, choral speaking and reading, puppetry, and creative dramatics.

Literature for Gifted Children.   Children who are gifted can benefit from children's literature as much as can normal children or those with disabilities. Children who are gifted enjoy stories that lend themselves to exploration and correct utilization of a large vocabulary, an intense curiosity, a heightened sensitivity to self and others, and an appreciation of beauty and a sense of humor (Baker & Bender, 1981). The intellectual capacity of these children allows them to learn greater quantities of material at a rapid rate, develops in them a desire to learn, and provides them with a breadth and depth of knowledge and a tendency for creative thinking and production. Barbe and Renzulli (1981) believed that children who are gifted differ from normal children in timing and pacing, depth and degree of teaching style and materials, and their responses. According to Greenlaw and McIntosh (1986), children's literature for the gifted should consider vocabulary, curiosity, sensitivity, beauty, and humor.

Vocabulary.   Children who are gifted have an accurate use of a large and varied vocabulary, even at an early age. They engage in word play, and the more they are exposed to words in a rich context, the more they absorb and make use of their vocabulary in communicating with others. The following are examples of books that can be used for developing vocabulary:

Hyman, Trina Schart. (1983). *Little Red Riding Hood.* New York: Harper & Row.

Lesser, Rika (reteller). (1974). (illustrator Paul Zelinsky). *Hansel and Gretel.* New York: Dodd.

Loebel, Arnold. (1983). *The Book of Pigericks.* New York: Harper & Row.

Mikolaycak, Charles. (1984). *Babushka.* New York: Holiday House.

Wells, Rosemary. (1979). *Max's First Word.* New York: Dial.

Wells, Rosemary. (1979). *Max's Ride.* New York: Dial.

Curiosity.   Gifted children usually have an insatiable curiosity that requires that they be provided with an abundance of books on a variety of topics. These books should stimulate their curiosity and help them raise questions. The following are examples of books that reflect children's curiosity:

Ahlberg, Janet, & Ahlberg, Allan. (1978). *Each Peach Pear Plum.* New York: Viking.

Fritz, Jean. (1973). *Then What Happened, Paul Revere?* New York: Coward.

Gardner, Beau. (1980). *The Turn About, Think About, Look About Book.* New York: Lothrop.

Hoban, Tana. (1984). *Is It Rough? Is It Smooth? Is It Shiny?* New York: Greenwillow.

Tinkelman, Murray. (1982). *Rodeo.* New York: Greenwillow.

Sensitivity.   The gifted children's sensitivity to self and others is one of their hallmarks (Roedell, Jackson, & Robinson, 1980). Children's literature reflects this sensitivity in a way that is neither saccharin nor maudlin (Greenlaw & McIntosh, 1986). The following are examples of books that can be used to develop sensitivity:

Bulla, Clyde Robert. (1979). *Daniel's Duck.* New York: Harper & Row.

Carrick, Carol. (1980). *The Climb.* New York: Clarion.

Hughes, Shirley. (1983). *Alfie Gives a Hand.* New York: Lothrop.

Isadora, Rachel. (1979). *Ben's Trumpet*. New York: Greenwillow.

McCully, Emily Arnold. (1984). *Picnic*. New York: Harper & Row.

Beauty.   The gifted children's appreciation of beauty is a concomitant to sensitivity. Books on beauty should enhance these children's appreciation of art. Although many of the books identified earlier reflect an appreciation of beauty, the following are examples of other books that do this:

Bierhorst, John. (1984). *Spirit Child*. New York: Morrow.

Locker, Thomas. (1984). *Where the River Begins*. New York: Dial.

Louie, Ar-ling. (1982). *Yen Shen*. New York: Philomel.

Steptoe, John. (1984). *The Story of Jumping Mouse*. New York: Lothrop.

Yolen, Jane. (1979). *The Seeing Stick*. New York: Crowell.

Humor.   The sense of humor of children who are gifted is both quick and sophisticated. Their ability to manipulate language helps them be adept at punning and other word plays. These children enjoy books that play on words and present gentle humor or subtle satire that sometimes goes over the heads of their normal peers (Greenlaw & McIntosh, 1986). Many reading materials reflecting the gifted children's broad interests and abilities in a humorous way should be included in the selection of books. These books are suggested in sources such as Polette's (1981) *Picture Books for Gifted Programs*. The following are examples of humorous books:

Daly, Niki. (1984). *Joseph's Other Red Sock*. New York: Atheneum.

Elwell, Peter. (1984). *King of the Pipers*. New York: Macmillan.

Gage, Wilson. (1984). *Cully. Cully and the Bear*. New York: Greenwillow.

Heine, Helme. (1982). *Friends*. New York: Atheneum.

Stevenson, James. (1982). *We Can't Sleep Now*. New York: Morrow.

Choosing Books for Children.   Good picture–story and story books transmit the mores, attitudes, and values of the culture. They also help children experience other people's emotions. Factual, realistic, and imaginative literature extends and satisfies children's curiosity and nurtures their interests. Books provide children with opportunities to learn the language, free them to explore the meaning of language, and stimulate them to use their higher mental processes. Through books, they think about meanings, see relationships, remember similar feelings and occurrences, and develop concepts, while generalizing and abstracting ideas.

Children with learning disabilities need books that are written in a predictable format. Such literature should be written in a rhythmical, repetitive pattern to help children predict what is on the following page. A good example is Bill Martin, Jr.'s *Brown Bear, Brown Bear, What Do You See?* (Holt, Rinehart & Winston, 1983):

Brown bear, brown bear, what do you see?

I see a red bird looking at me.
Red bird, red bird what do you see?
I see a yellow duck looking at me.
Yellow duck, yellow duck, what do you see?
I see a blue horse looking at me.

Brown Bear is one example of a predictable book, which has repetition. The words, phrases, and themes are repeated, and the pattern is easily discerned after reading a few pages. Other excellent and predictable books use a cumulative pattern where previous ideas are integrated into subsequent ones, such as *I Know a Lady Who Swallowed a Fly* or *The Gingerbread Man*. A third type of predictable book is one that uses familiar sequences such as *The Very Hungry Caterpillar* (Carle, 1979). Predictable books can provide a rewarding experience for learning-disabled children. They are a viable alternative and an excellent supplementary method to reading instruction.

Books for children who are gifted must spark their interest and stimulate them to independently pursue more information in the specified knowledge field. Enrichment activities should reflect the excitement and joy of professionals performing their work; demonstrate the types of work, activities, or projects that professionals in a specific field engage in; and illustrate the variety of career opportunities in a broad field of study. Books in this category include handbooks, biographies, fictional stories, and picture books that provide writing models for young children.

Teachers have to be conscious of the unintended messages in even apparently innocuous nursery rhymes. These may contain sex-role stereotypes (Callahan, 1986). For example, Little Bo Peep sits passively waiting for the sheep to come home. In contrast, Little Jack Horner, even though he has ruined a pie, states "What a good boy am I." Other messages of sexism, ageism, and cultural bias also can be found. Although this does not mean that these revered stories should not be included in an early childhood program, it does require that teachers deal with these messages to avoid teaching bias to young children. The *Anti-Bias Curriculum* (Derman-Sparks & A. B. C. Task Force, 1989) contains many good suggestions for children's books that can be used in an early childhood classroom. The Council on Interracial Books for Children (1980) also has published guidelines for selecting books for young children.

Reading Stories. Reading stories to young children helps to share the joy and wonder of a broadening acquaintance with the world of books. The reader takes the children on a literary journey, stretching their experience and extending their world of words and feelings. This activity develops children's desire for more stories and poems and influences their literary taste.

Storytelling. Telling stories, rather than reading them, provides intimate contact and rapport with children since there is no barrier between the teller and the children. The content of the story can be adapted to the children's needs and interests. The pace of the story can be adjusted to the children's attention and developmental levels. Difficult words or phrases can be explained in context. Stories can be personalized by substituting the children's names for those of characters.

Poetry.   Arnstein (1962) defined poetry as an art that is intended for enjoyment, as are music and painting. Many people, including children, enjoy listening to music, examining paintings, and hearing or reading poetry. Of course, just as some people are not responsive to music or graphic arts, some will not be responsive to poetry.

Poetry can easily be introduced to young children. They enjoy the sound and feel of words and are intrigued with their rhythmic qualities. As children search for harmony in their own lives, their rhythms and rhythmic interpretations become poetic in nature.

Using Puppets.   Another enhancement of children's literature is puppets. Children can manipulate puppets to act out stories. Puppets are a good vehicle to be used in an integrated classroom to help children explore different disabilities.

Puppets can easily hold the children's interest during a presentation designed to make them aware of disabilities. Hand and rod puppets can be used to represent children with different disabilities. Puppets representing children with and without disabilities can interact and ask questions of each other in a presentation. Scripts can be developed to include information on children's disabilities and appliances used to compensate for those disabilities. Puppet presentations help children dispel myths and fears and help them to understand and accept children with disabilities. Scripts must be realistic with a lively dialogue. They should include those parts of the lives of children with disabilities that are similar to those of children without disabilities (such as family situations). The puppet representing the child with a disability might show surprise in discovering that children with disabilities have a lot going for them in their lives. Puppeteers may need to be trained to present disabilities properly (Binkard, 1985). The person who serves as the puppeteer must know about the disability and must know the script to present it well.

Expressive Language Arts

Helping children develop expressive language skills should go hand in hand with developing their receptive language skills. Indeed, one feeds into the other in a number of ways.

Choral Speaking and Reading.   Choral speaking or reading takes place when a group of children read a story or a poetry selection together. Choral reading can help children become more aware of the sounds and cadence of literature. Children can help choose selections they most enjoy, although teacher guidance is necessary. Children can participate in these choral language activities well before they learn to read. Often their favorite stories have been read to them so often, they have actually memorized them and can say them word for word. Teachers must be responsive to what children can do and what they like.

Puppetry.   Puppets have been around for centuries. They provide children with opportunities to enrich and expand their language skills and challenge their imaginations. Children are often less self-conscious with puppets than in a dramatic performance. Children can perform puppet shows for each other. This can lead to asking questions and experimenting with the puppets after the show.

Puppet presentations should be varied, based upon the children's developmental levels. Younger children (ages 3 to 5) may have spontaneous dialogues with puppets, and older young children (ages 6 to 8) may put on a formal puppet play. Simple puppets should be used with the youngest children. These can be made out of a paper bag or a sock.

Creative Dramatics.   Creative dramatics, the act of dramatizing stories read or heard, is a developmental step that grows out of children's dramatic play. In dramatic play, the children create the characters and construct a plot as they play it out. In creative dramatics, the plot and characters are given to the children and they improvise a script based on that plot.

Creative dramatics activities are informal dramatic experiences, including pantomimes, improvised stories and skits, movement and body awareness activities, and dramatic songs and games. Its purpose is more to support children's growth and development than to entertain an audience. Children create plays by improvising action and dialogue rather than by memorizing written scripts. Or they can compose written scripts and record their improvised product. Children may wish to share their creations with an audience, especially if they have spent a great deal of time preparing them. Creative dramatics develops language skills, improves socialization skills, stimulates creative imagination, helps develop an understanding of human behavior, and fosters group work and group problem solving.

Through dramatization, children can bring the printed world created by authors closer to the world they know as they assume the roles of the characters in the story or poem. To achieve this, the teacher reads the story and makes children aware of its dramatic quality, but does not directly prescribe dramatic activities. Children can easily capture the dramatic quality of the literature and make their own dramatic presentations.

Creative dramatics is a powerful vehicle for enriching the learning of children with physical, mental, emotional, and sensory impairments. Creative dramatics activities have to be appropriately planned and adapted to children's specific disabilities. Creative drama helps children become more aware and capable in developing their social skills and in using their senses, voices, bodies, emotions, imaginations, and intelligence (Warger, 1985).

Several studies have been conducted on preschool children's use of drama in relation to language development (Adamson, 1981). Dramatic activities provide language experiences that are concrete and require children to participate firsthand. The visual and physical aspects of drama also enhance language development just like sign language.

Drama requires using the whole body for transmitting information (Brown, 1988b). Brown (1988a) suggested four basic methods in which sign language is integrated into a drama activity:

1. Signs are used together with speech to clarify new vocabulary.
2. Signs are used to create or define a character in the drama activity.

3. Signs are transformed into puppets or objects to be used in the drama activity.

4. Signs are used to illustrate a concept or action within the drama activity.

The teacher and children might sit in a circle. The teacher shows the children a picture of a giraffe and how to make a giraffe with their body. The teacher can ask for the children's help to tell a story about the giraffe. As the teacher continues, the children use their bodies to tell the story using drama. The teacher might say, "The giraffe had big eyes, little ears, a little tail, long legs, a long neck, and spots all over his body. It has a long tongue to eat the leaves off the trees. Can you make your giraffe eat the leaves off trees? Now let's make our whole bodies look like giraffes."

Discussion Sessions.   Discussion sessions are periods during which a child usually speaks to a group or the whole class while the others listen, ask questions, and make responsive comments. Examples of these activities are "show and tell" and "sharing time." An object from home or even an event may be shared during these activities. Discussions can also be less formal, taking place between the teacher and a child or a small group of children.

Topics for discussion sessions can include classifying objects by shape, texture, or sound and then using them in manipulative games. Opportunities to smell, touch, see, taste, and hear are firsthand experiences that need to be described and often provide a good basis for discussion sessions. Describing sensory experiences helps extend children's vocabularies as they search for proper words or seek analogies.

Children also might tell a story illustrated by a single picture, a picture book, or a sequence of pictures during a discussion session. Appropriate pictures can be found in magazines, discarded schoolbooks, or picture dictionaries. Commercially available discussion pictures also can be used.

MODIFYING THE LANGUAGE ARTS PROGRAM FOR CHILDREN WITH DIVERSE NEEDS

Children with disabilities need and can benefit from different types of language activities, depending on their physical, motor, sensory, cognitive, and social abilities. Impairment in one or more of these developmental areas affects a child's language in different ways. Physical disabilities, such as cerebral palsy, affect muscle coordination and can create speech disorders as well as problems in writing. Sensory disabilities that create difficulties in children with hearing and visual impairments affect children's abilities to learn language and limit their developing concepts based upon directly accessible sensory data. These children also may have delayed speech.

The teacher should attend to children with delayed language problems, arranging for assessment to determine what help should be provided. Psychological and hearing tests as well as a physical examination might be arranged. Home visits or parent interviews can provide additional information. Children as young as 3 and 4 years of age can be assessed for language disorders and referred for proper treatment.

The classroom teacher is responsible for notifying the speech specialist of problems identified in class and for requesting specific suggestions on how to work with the child.

Serious language disabilities require the help of professionals. A team may include the teacher, speech specialist, psychologist, social worker, and audiologist. Other professionals (such as a dentist, occupational therapist, physical therapist, and one or more medical specialists) also may be involved as needed. The teacher is responsible for identifying the language problems, communicating with the parents, referring the child to the appropriate specialists, and carrying out the recommendations made by the team. The teacher supports the speech specialist by including class activities that serve as a follow-up of the specialist's lessons.

Supporting language development requires more than helping children with language delays to produce appropriate linguistic utterances. They should be helped to engage in social exchanges, using language that is spontaneous, accurate, and appropriate. Raver (1987) suggested integrating speech and language training into situations that reflect the natural environment. The most powerful linguistic and nonlinguistic methods will not prevent misarticulations or immature syntax. However, appropriate methods can help preschool children with language delays or disorders to increase their rate of spontaneous language and the appropriate content, form, and use of language.

Children who are hearing-impaired are unable to associate the sounds of language with their experiences. They may have a limited vocabulary; become confused with synonyms, prefixes, and suffixes; arrange words in improper order;

omit prepositions and articles from sentences; and create sentences with poor syntax. An intellectual disability can also delay language development. The language of children who are mentally retarded develops at a slower pace than in their normally developing peers. These children's language performance may be only slightly below normal, may appear to be normal, or may show a serious deficit compared to normal children. The inadequate language skills of children with disabilities during early childhood can create two major problems: (1) Their inability to communicate effectively during the formative years may have detrimental effects on social skills and the ability to adjust to life; and (2) their inadequate language skills may limit their later academic success in school. Thus, language arts activities in all four language skills—listening, speaking, writing, and reading—must have a high priority for children with disabilities.

Listening

Listening includes hearing, recognizing, interpreting, and understanding. Listening periods should be scheduled when children are expected to listen. Teachers need to vary their presentation approach to include just listening (as in giving directions), listening paired with visual cues (as in providing stories on a flannel board), and listening while participating (as in playing rhythm instruments or dancing). Strategies should differ for the children based on their need.

Using audiovisual material can also enhance listening skills. Children can listen to record players or cassette tape recorders. The teacher can create listening stations with headsets attached to these machines so listening activities do not disturb others.

Careful selection of materials for listening activities is important. Materials should be of interest to and developmentally appropriate for each child. The teacher can provide opportunities to interpret materials and experiences in an individualized way and simultaneously provide imaginative experiences as the basis for conceptual thinking. A simple framework must be designed for a child to master enough tasks to feel successful.

Burks, Good, Higginbotham, and Hoffman (1967) described Stephen, who was active, had aggressive outbursts, and preferred nonverbal communication. The teacher designed activities to change his attitude toward verbal communication. Formal speech training was postponed and a discrimination program with little direct relation to speech sounds was implemented to acquaint Stephen with the classroom and help him learn to follow verbal directions to which he responded motorically in relation to space discrimination (e.g., "Crawl over the table and between the chairs"). A special audiotape was prepared to allow him to listen to certain sounds in isolation—a telephone ring, an alarm clock, a window closing, and a vacuum cleaner. Once Stephen could distinguish these sounds, he listened to records and stories. Later he was encouraged to respond to the stories until he began to make up and record his own. The teacher worked with Stephen one-half hour a week for a total of eight sessions and used appropriate group activities to reinforce Stephen's learning.

Learning to follow verbal directions should be part of a listening program. Most young children with disabilities who first attend school do not have the necessary direction-following skills. Yet, although teaching direction-following skills requires considerable time and energy, the attainment of such skills by children is essential for smooth classroom management. Scheuerman, Cartwright, York, Lowry, and Brown (1974) developed a three-phase instructional program addressed to this problem. In Phase 1 students learned to follow a one-component local direction (e.g., "Stand up"). In Phase 2 they followed a one-component distant direction (e.g., "Go to the door"), and in Phase 3 they learned to follow a two-component local direction (e.g., "Stand up, then raise your hands"). Brown et al. (cited in Scheuerman et al., 1974) offer the teacher three alternative methods for teaching direction-following skills: (1) Model the specified directions for the students, (2) physically guide the students through the specified directions, or (3) have students perform tasks implicit in the specified directions.

Children with disabilities must be able to understand directions to be successful. Short activities with few distractions should be presented to children who are visually impaired to encourage them to complete their task. Children who are behaviorally disordered also need this type of structure. Teachers must provide more environmental control in large-group activities in which children, for behavioral or emotional reasons, cannot work. For instance, having children remain seated in a circle while two other children greet them is simpler than having students walk around the room randomly and greet people nonverbally. An activity can be used based on the children's topic of interest (e.g., imitating a machine, developing a sound effects story about a car) (Warger, 1985).

Directions for children with mental retardation require more examples and activities at lower conceptual levels. Large-group teacher-directed activities instead of small-group activities, and student-directed activities instead of small-group directed ones, are probably necessary. Based on the group's level of conceptual functioning, a number of imitative activities probably will be needed to reinforce and motivate performance in the activities. Concrete examples are essential. For example, the teacher may need to show the children an object (e.g., vacuum cleaner, fish), show them ways to imitate the object, and allow them to copy the teacher's movement before asking them to create their own (Warger, 1985).

Nursery rhymes can help develop children's listening skills. Nursery rhymes have repetitive rhythms and words as well as obvious beginnings and ends, and provide a structured framework for social interaction between adults and children. Rogow (1982) found that nursery rhyme routines promote interactions between mothers or teachers and young children who are developmentally blind or physically disabled. Daily nursery rhyme sessions increased the frequency of the children's communication behavior. Rogow also found that familiar nursery rhyme routines are useful in teaching language to children with mental retardation. Her results showed that nursery rhymes are important in teaching social interactions and emphasizing word recognition. However, the words in nursery rhymes may need to be simplified. Although nursery rhymes usually have simple repetitive rhythms and a gestural component, they often have difficult words. If the rhythm is kept and the words are simple enough to be relevant to the children's own environment, the rhymes are likely to gain their attention.

Listening builds memory skills and recall. To help children extend their memories, the teacher can read a passage and then ask the children a series of questions about it. Listening activities also can be provided to help children infer, compare, follow directions, and sequence incidents. The teacher can record common sounds to help children discriminate hearing sounds. These sounds can range from simple to complex and from the known to the unknown. The teacher can start with sounds familiar to the child such as those of a car or train, or animal sounds. The teacher then can go to less familiar sounds. A tape with sounds of different musical instruments or various types of music can be included. As the child's listening skills develop, the tapes can become more complex. Using musical instruments helps children discriminate high and low sounds. Sound boxes similar to those developed by Montessori can be used to match sounds that are alike or to seriate sounds from high to low pitch or from loud to soft.

Children with Speech and Language Disorders.   Children with speech and language needs require practice in listening to obtain the necessary language skills. Some of these children have difficulty with articulation because they do not hear accurately or they do not have good speech models.

Children with Hearing Impairments.   Children with hearing impairments have a hearing loss and need to learn to use the residual hearing available to them. Some of these children prefer to learn using their sense of sight or touch rather than their sense of hearing. These children need the opportunity to combine the use of their receptive modalities, using these skills first.

Children who are hearing-impaired need specific auditory training to develop listening skills. Children with mild hearing impairments easily may be neglected in the regular classroom because these children rarely ask to have a direction repeated. Teachers should know each child's listening level. Auditory restrictions primarily affect the commands and group interactions of the hearing-impaired. Conceptual understanding can be facilitated through visual aids whenever possible. Group activities should be implemented in a way that visual cues are used. For instance, lighting a flashlight or waving a large scarf can indicate a change in a group activity. To increase opportunities for interaction, directed movement should be well defined by designating chairs or by using masking tape on the floor or carpets (Warger, 1985). Children with hearing disabilities need to associate sounds with objects, actions, and people. In addition, these children need to become aware of sounds and develop discrimination skills that help them distinguish various sound and speech patterns. Deaf children can learn to attend through their eyes, speech-reading as well as following nonverbal cues or sign language. Since these children depend more heavily on visual cues, directions must be specific and clear. Hearing-impaired children can enjoy literature through carefully selected picture–story books and other materials. Telling stories with the aid of a flannel board or pictures is also helpful.

Conversation with Speech-Reading.   Children with borderline hearing loss may get along in a normal classroom without difficulty by using speech-reading. Some children need hearing aids in addition to speech-reading.

Speech-reading specialists teach speech-reading. Children practice speech-reading in the regular classroom and the teacher should provide practice opportunities. The list below gives several guidelines to facilitate speech-reading.

Guidelines to Facilitate Speech-Reading

1. *Face the hard-of-hearing child.* When speaking, teachers should be in a position so that hearing-impaired children are able to see them speak.

2. *Speak clearly and naturally.* Teachers should use intelligible speech that can be understood by any child in any part of the classroom. They should speak in an easy, relaxed way without exaggerating their speech or speaking at an overly slow rate.

3. *Speak in a position where light is shining on the teacher's face rather than in the eyes of the child attempting to understand what is being said.* Poor lighting may blind the hard-of-hearing child and may create shadows on the speaker's face, distorting normal movements that the hard-of-hearing child identifies through speech-reading.

4. *Repeat an instruction in the same words, but only once.* Instructions should be repeated once using the same words. Instructions can be rephrased on the next repetition. The hard-of-hearing child must be helped to understand instructions or questions. If the teacher calls on someone else, it can be devastating for the child.

5. *Speak expressively by means of appropriate vocal inflections, gestures, bodily movement, and so forth.* The hearing-impaired child can speech-read expressions. However, violent gestures and head and arm movements far away from the body distract the attention of the speech-reader from the face. (Johnson et al., 1967)

Speech-reading is learned through both formal and informal instruction. Speech and language specialists, classroom teachers, or parents can teach simple speech-reading. Sensory perceptions are used to learn and understand language. Speech-reading instruction should occur in natural settings and focus on the visual impressions of speech. Beginning instruction requires that speech-reading be practiced in isolation so the child can focus on the visual stimuli, eliminating auditory stimuli. The teacher must whisper or mouth words. This takes practicing silent speech in front of a mirror until the speech feels and looks normal. Instruction and practice in speech-reading should have a normal amount of lip movement and be at a normal rate of speech. That is what the child will find outside the classroom. The child must learn to read and understand speech at a normal rate.

Speech-reading lessons should be developmentally appropriate and be related to the child's interest. Practicing speech-reading with several speakers who look different and have different speech patterns is effective. After the child can read voiceless speech, let him or her read speech that can be partially heard and seen. Such children will have to follow conversations with both ears and eyes in normal situations.

Instruction in beginning speech-reading is easiest in a context that is familiar to the child. Johnson et al. (1967) give the following suggestions:

1. Use colloquial expressions, such as "Hello," "Good morning," "How are you?" and "Good-bye."

2. Use nursery rhymes, such as "Jack and Jill," "Mary Had a Little Lamb," or "Humpty Dumpty."

3. Use language in familiar categories, such as days of the week, months of the year, the alphabet, numbers.

Once the child with a hearing disability has gained some facility in speech-reading with familiar material, less familiar language can be introduced, possibly through units such as the family or zoo animals. Audiovisual materials and simple directions can make instruction more effective. For example, "Find the boys" or "Tell the story about the cat." The unit should be progressive. The teacher can begin with a simple, familiar picture and move to a complex use of words in sentences and stories.

Telling a story is complex and, as in Wanda Gag's *Millions of Cats* (1928), should involve much repetition. Stories should be selected based on the child's interest and attention span. A simple outline or a set of pictures to show the sequence of events helps children follow the story. Long stories can be condensed or divided into sections to help children keep up with the sequence. The teacher can tell each section separately and emphasize its main points by asking questions. When all sections have been completed, the story is retold in its entirety. It is best to avoid extremely long stories.

Children with Visual Impairments.   Children who are visually impaired depend on others in using auditory cues. Children with visual impairments may miss the nonverbal qualities of attending and eye contact as well as the ability to reflect someone's thoughts and respond to their questions.

Teachers can use their ingenuity to develop materials and activities that extend the listening skills of these children. Experience will guide the teacher to continually provide new listening opportunities. Children with visual impairments rely on listening more heavily than do other children. Although they use their other senses, their safety depends to a great extent on their ability to hear sounds in their environment. Reading and telling them stories are rewarding experiences that promote listening skills. Sharing a good book with the teacher and classmates enlarges the children's literary world and helps them live vicariously through the literary characters in the story. Visually impaired children may react to the story or may wish to write about it on a Braille typewriter.

Beatrix Potter's and A. A. Milne's stories, the Mother Goose stories and other nursery rhymes, and children's favorites such as the *Paddington, Curious George,* and *Madeleine* stories as well as *Charlotte's Web, The Biggest Bear,* and *Winnie-the-Pooh* have all been recorded. If commercial records are not available, the child's own favorite story can be recorded on tape, allowing him or her to listen to it as often as desired.

Children with Physical Impairments.   Children with physical impairments need help in relating sounds to possible sources and in comprehending this relationship. This is especially true with children with health problems. Adults may forget there may be so much attention to other areas of learning that listening is neglected. Even if children listen, they may not understand what they hear.

Children Who Are Gifted.   Children who are gifted and who have already developed basic skills need to be challenged with more advanced auditory and comprehension skills. Children's listening can be improved through experiences with children's literature and discussions. They may be able to help other children attend to descriptions, sensory experiences, and pictures.

Speaking

Theories of language development do not suggest that individuals with disabilities develop language any differently than do children without disabilities. However, children with language impairments develop language at a slower rate, and the developmental sequence of language behavior can be affected by speech disorders. In planning and implementing speaking activities, the teacher needs to assess the nature and degree of children's disorders.

Sign language helps children with language disabilities develop their language effectively. Many studies show that sign language can be learned when integrated into the curriculum (e.g., Carr & Kologinsky, 1983; Daniloff, Noll, Fristoe, & Lloyd, 1982; Konstantareas, 1984). These studies reveal that these children can develop communication through sign language. This visual language often enhances many of the children's oral language (Acosta, 1981). Sign language also allows for communication with persons who are hearing-impaired.

Integrating language and movement helps children who use the kinesthetic and tactile senses for learning. The pairing of language with movement develops the children's vocabulary and language concepts. All movement activities should be fun. The classroom teacher, physical education teacher, and speech and language therapist can work to coordinate the development of an instructional program to integrate language with movement activities. The program should allow all children to participate to the maximum (Hopper, Hanrahan, & Nelson, 1986).

Children with visual impairments need activities that have more auditory and kinesthetic input. Language activities should also include concepts and experiences that can fill up the unknown gap of visual experience. Children can move like fish only if they know the way fish swim. If they are to pretend to be an astronaut in outer space, children must have a sense of the meaning of weightlessness (Warger, 1985).

Children with physical impairments can participate in movement activities that have been adapted for them. These children could show how the president of the United States might eat a bowl of soup or a football player waves to fans instead of having them walk like these people. They could also pretend that just one part of their body, such as their feet, is imitating fish. Dialogue or sound activities can be substituted for physical movements, which might also keep the children from tiring too soon (Warger, 1985).

Many children with hearing impairments are language delayed. These children must learn language within the context of dialogue or communication in order to use it functionally outside the classroom. A combination of different approaches might be necessary since each approach has advantages and disadvantages.

Clarke and Stewart (1986), in reviewing the literature, identified the following approaches to develop language in hearing-impaired students:

The *story-and-drill approach* is considered one of the first instructional methods to be used with the hearing-impaired, and many educational programs for the hearing-impaired still consider this approach a viable one. Stories are used to develop language. When stories are used, children are required to understand language that has been already selected for them.

The *Fitzgerald Key* was developed in 1929 by Fitzgerald to guide correct sentence patterns and to help children visualize language from a syntactic point of view.

The *natural approach* was used to counteract the syntactic device found in the Fitzgerald Key. A predetermined word list developed in 1950 by the Central Institute for the Deaf includes a set of language drills by Croker, Jones, and Pratt. The following principles are included in the natural approach:

1. Language and vocabulary are provided based on the child's needs.
2. Language is learned through a meaningful communication environment instead of through meaningless drills and textbook exercises.
3. Language usage is learned through conversation, discussion, and written composition as well as using the academic skill curriculum areas.
4. Language principles are introduced incidentally using natural language-learning situations and are explained in real situations and practices in conversations, stories, and games.

Using the natural approach does not mean that language is learned haphazardly. Linguistic principles are acquired incidentally, according to the child's intellectual and cognitive status. The success of the method depends on the means of communications that can develop academic social skills.

The *patterning approach* was developed by St. Joseph's School for the Deaf in St. Louis. It is based on a structural form of language learning. The language lessons are supplemented with natural experiences including conversational formats with an emphasis on commands, requests and questions. This approach is difficult to relate to the fluency of language performance at all levels to the meaning and understanding of utterances.

Programmed instruction, developed in the 1960s, uses teaching machines with the hearing-impaired to drill and practice language skills. A drawback of this approach is the lack of real-life experiences in programmed instruction, which decreases the method's instructional effectiveness. Recently the inclusion of computers and video-tapes into this approach has seemed promising.

Behavior modification relies mainly on specific and restricted imitations to shape behavior. Children with hearing impairments (who may also be severely retarded or multiply disabled) have been the focus of operant-conditioning programs. Behavior modification does not consider developmental language patterns. This approach depends on the use of functional language patterns developed for the program, disregarding their relationship to the individual child's present level of language development. This technique sometimes is effective, but it must be used appropriately and with caution.

Linguistically based approaches were developed for hearing-impaired children. These include the McCar Lessons Syntax and Peck's Patterned Language, which are based on informational grammar. The Rhode Island Curriculum is considered the most popular and influential of these programs. The goals of this curriculum are to develop basic underlying knowledge and to integrate language into the curriculum using events, stories, and experiences expressed in simple sentence patterns. This procedure is only applied to sentences that are meaningful to children so they can memorize the syntax and internalize the simple relationships in the sentences.

Developmentally-based language instruction programs consist of developmental structures that guide teachers to plan language experiences, which are related to development syntactic categories. The emphasis of the developmental communication components of the language program is on dialogue or communication together with modeling or expansion techniques. Communication exchanges help children to induce rules as well as the spontaneous delayed interactions pertinent to language acquisition. From their review of the approaches in language instruction for the hearing-impaired, Clarke and Stewart (1986) suggested that instruction should (1) be guided by characteristics associated with the normal process in language acquisition, (2) emphasize conversations or interactive communication, and (3) ensure that authentic language is used in a natural way.

Many educators advocate a naturalistic approach to remediate children's language deficits. Warren and Kaiser (1986) suggested incidental teaching as a way to provide language training. Incidental teaching includes interactions between adults and children that arise naturally in unstructured situations, such as free play. The adults systematically transmit new information or provide the children with practice to help them develop their communication skills. However, the children control the teaching situation by showing interest in the environment.

Children usually request the adult's help to initiate an interaction. A child might request a ball by pointing to it on a high shelf and saying, "Ball." The children can also comment and provide directions to initiate an incidental teaching episode. Children can orally or nonvocally indicate their preponderant interest to them. When a child offers the topic (e.g., ball) and the opportunity, the adult takes advantage of that opportunity to teach new language forms.

Incidental language teaching can be used by (1) arranging the setting in a way that encourages children to initiate incidental teaching opportunities, (2) providing environmental language targets that are at the child's skill (Bleck & Nagel, 1982) level and interest, (3) eliciting elaborated language from the child's initiations to the targeted forms, and (4) reinforcing the child's attempts to communicate specifically with emphasis and access to the objects in which the child has expressed an interest. Incidental teaching episodes should be brief, positive, and oriented toward communication instead of language teaching per se.

Children can have a speech disorder or a language disorder, or a combination of both (Heward & Orlansky, 1980). Speech is considered impaired if it attracts unfavorable attention to itself or interferes with communication. Children who have a receptive language disorder usually have a restricted vocabulary. Language difficulties often are found in children with learning disabilities (Cratty, 1980) and in children with severe physical disabilities, such as cerebral palsy, muscular dystrophy, and spina bifida (Bleck & Nagel, 1982; Hopper, Hanrahan, & Nelson, 1986).

Language training for nonverbal children requires intensive individual attention. However, many educational settings have too many children and too few staff to provide such training. Guralnick (1972) suggested using nonprofessionals, such as parents or college and high school students, as volunteers. Such volunteers should be provided with a mandatory training program before working with classes.

Writing

Writing, like reading, is based on printed symbols. Handwriting, the most concrete language arts skill, is primarily a motor skill that requires visual ability as well as motor coordination. In writing, children (both with and without disabilities), identify and produce forms, including manuscript and cursive letters, punctuation marks, Arabic numerals, the conventions for arrangement and spacing, and the conventions for margins and headings. Writing develops visual-motor perception and is an important communication skill.

Children begin to develop writing skills long before they enter the primary grades, moving from scribbling to forming letters. Writing manuscript letters entails making vertical, horizontal, and diagonal lines as well as circles and circle segments. Children must learn to hold writing implements and make these forms accurately, combining them into letters. They must also be able to apply enough pressure on the writing instrument to make their marks while holding the paper in place. Early childhood art activities have many elements that prepare the child for writing. Although painting and crayoning offer a freer form than does writing, there are elements common to them all. Thus, children can be helped to experience some aspects of writing early, and those children who are having difficulty learning to write may go back to earlier forms.

Major problem areas in handwriting include visual-perception input, visual–spatial relationships, visual imagery, and visual–motor ability. *Visual-perception input* refers to accurate perception of a configuration. Persons with problems in this area are unable to perceive a shape correctly. They may write twisted letters, inconsistently reverse letters, and slant letters diagonally. Children can learn to recognize similarities and differences among letters. Cardboard letters can be used to help them visually recognize like and unlike shapes. Using cut-out letters and shapes along with parquetry blocks helps children learn to discriminate and group shapes. Children can match shapes to form designs that the teacher constructs or can match the shapes to pictures of designs. They can also work with shapes made of sandpaper, clay, playdough, crayons, or tagboard with the children ultimately forming letters on paper. Remediation requires visual sequencing such as matching manipulative objects with a row of pictures of the same objects and copying items in proper sequence.

Children form *visual–spatial relationships* by relating themselves to the space around them or relating two objects in space to each other. This skill helps children write letters on a line, organize letters on paper, space letters appropriately, and proportion the size of letters. Children with visual-motor difficulties may write very heavily or very lightly. They may hold the pencil with a tense grip that causes them to make holes in the paper or with such a light grip that their letters are barely seen. These children may also erase many times as they try to write proper letter shapes.

Children with *visual imagery* (short-term visual recall) problems are unable to

transfer words from one paper to another or from the chalkboard to a paper. As they copy, they omit letters or entire words or write letters out of sequence. They also have difficulty making motor and spatial judgments. These shortcomings may be the result of poor motor skills, unstable and erratic temperament, faulty visual perception of letters, or difficulty in retaining visual impressions.

Handwriting is a *visual and motor task*. The teacher needs to carefully plan handwriting activities for visually impaired children. Children with severe visual disabilities can learn to use Braille, but they must learn to use other types of communication as well. Special devices are available to help them write letters, spell words, and sign their names. Providing darkly lined paper and large pencils makes writing easier for the visually impaired. Sand and clay writing are good exercises to develop motor skills. The ability to type is also a useful skill. An electric typewriter or a computer with a word-processing program may be helpful for a child with severe motor difficulties. Computers with joysticks also may be used.

Aggravating writing disorders can be avoided if children have a good writing foundation (Lebrun & Van de Craen, 1975). Children must be able to learn directionality, such as left to right and up and down. Spatial orientation and directional sense are essential for young children. Left-handed children need extra help; they must follow different writing directions. Graphomotor skills are enhanced through drawing, painting, or coloring. The development of prerequisite skills with these media will help writing skills. Gross motor and fine motor skills are basic to success in writing. Children need to control their finger and arm movements during writing activity. Movement activities, finger plays, and the use of manipulatives can help children gain body control. Rhythmic activities increase children's awareness of their bodies. Handwriting activities for children should evolve from meaningful experiences and be integrated with other activities that have definite writing purposes and that are individually determined and practical.

Teachers need to help children make letter forms carefully. Templates that allow children to draw prescribed forms may help them gain greater control of their strokes. Such forms are available for Montessori programs. Tracing and copying letter forms also helps. Sometimes writing instruments need to be modified to enable children with motor problems to grasp them adequately. Extra-thick pencils may be easier to hold than those of normal thickness, and even these may need to be wrapped in tape or run through a small ball to allow a greater ease in handling.

The teacher of children with disabilities needs to determine which form of writing to teach. Until the 1960s, special education and learning disabilities specialists recommended teaching cursive writing because words written in cursive were

considered to be more easily perceived as whole units. Cursive writing focuses on left-to-right progression. The flowing motion avoids reversals, spacing and alignment are easier to keep, and a transfer to another kind of alphabet is avoided. More recently, specialists have suggested teaching manuscript writing. It resembles book print, it helps reading instruction, it seems more legible, and the shapes are easier to form.

The authors of DISTAR and the *ita* alphabet favor their own transitional alphabets which provide a more regular relationship between letters and the sounds they represent. They believe that their special alphabets have the advantages of manuscript writing and that the use of additional symbols fosters beginning reading instruction and creative writing. A compromise approach is suggested in which manuscript writing is modified to resemble italic writing like the print used in books (Hanson, 1976). Capital letters are written in the block form familiar to preschool children, and it is a form of writing based on natural hand movements. The teacher needs to make some judgment about which orthography to use. This should be based on a judgment of what would be easiest for the children and most acceptable to others in the school.

LeBlanc, Etzel, and Domash (1978) suggested using cuing procedures that are gradually withdrawn with children who have difficulties in learning to write. A child who cannot write the word *red,* for example, can be given a worksheet on which the letters *r*, *e*, and *d* are presented many times. The first presentation would use a solid line with an X at the point where the child should start to trace each letter. The X would be faded and then eliminated, and the solid line would give way to a dotted line as the whole letter was replaced by a smaller and smaller portion of each letter. As the child traces the form, he or she becomes less dependent on the cues and more independent in reproducing the proper form of each letter. Ultimately the child puts the letters together to create a word. Since developing such a program takes a considerable amount of time and effort, the authors suggest using such procedures only when normal methods do not succeed.

Children who are gifted must be provided with opportunities to explore writing in the early childhood classroom. Writing is an essential precursor to the reading process and later helps to integrate reading and writing skills (Ganopole, 1988). These children can experience a wide range of writing tasks that encourage an interest in writing and develop good writing skills. Since expressive writing can easily be adapted for exploration and discovery, it should be emphasized. The children should engage in activities that reflect the reading-writing connection (Graham & Harris, 1988).

Journal writing is an activity that fulfills many requirements. Personal, dialogue, and reading journals help students explore different writing styles and engage in purposeful reading and writing tasks. A personal journal offers students an opportunity for introspective writing and encourages creative and reflective thinking. Journal entries can be written daily and include both children's personal writing and their drawings. Students can use a conversational format in the dialogue journal and receive personal responses from a peer or the classroom teacher. The reading journal can be a private or a shared activity. Students can also keep reading journals, writing their thoughts or comments about any reading material that they have completed. Classmates may read what has been written, comment on the journal entry, or make new entries into the journal.

Children who are gifted can use computers for reading logs, dialogues, and add-on stories (Wepner, 1988). They can use their reading logs to respond to reading materials. They can discuss, evaluate, and keep a record of what they read. The teacher can review the comments and write messages to the students to reinforce or challenge their thinking. Computer dialogues are similar to written dialogue journals. The difference is that students use a word processor to experience a free flow of ideas without the sometimes troublesome interference of delayed motor skills.

Add-on stories promote gifted students' socialization and provide opportunities to collaborate and share. Add-ons are used before reading (predicting), during reading (comprehension check), and after reading (expansion skills).

Spelling. Many linguists and early childhood educators (e.g., Chomsky, 1981) suggest that teachers should not concern themselves greatly with the correctness of young children's spelling when they begin to write. Children will invent spelling when they first begin to write, writing words in a way that sounds right to their ears and making their own relationship between written letters and spoken sounds. As they mature and gain greater experience with written language, the rules the children originally created will drop out and conventional spelling will fall into place.

Some children will have difficulty with spelling even through the elementary grades, continuing to spell phonetically or making totally inappropriate letter substitutions. Often the errors made result from a lack of visual or auditory skills. Analyzing the errors children make can help the teacher identify the child's specific problems. Prerequisite skills in the auditory or visual area may need to be taught. Teachers can then build a program to help children overcome their spelling problems, which may parallel their reading problems (Hart, 1981).

The mechanics of writing may cause problems for children with disabilities to which teachers must necessarily respond. It is important, however, to be aware that learning to write is not just learning the mechanics of writing. Children with and without disabilities must learn to express meaning through writing (Lebrun & Van de Craen, 1975). When mechanical problems block the achievement of that goal, they must be dealt with before the children can use writing as a form of expression.

THE LANGUAGE LEARNING ENVIRONMENT

In general, all children, including those with disabilities, benefit from a rich language learning environment that immerses them in meaningful language activities throughout the day from the preschool on. Dudley-Marling and Searle (1988) provided the following guidelines for creating a favorable language environment:

- *Physical setting should encourage interaction.* Opportunities for discussion can include activity centers, pet area (such as where gerbils or fish are kept), and so on. Manipulating concrete materials (such as magnets, lenses, or sets of electronic components for creating circuits) allows children to use language as they plan, observe, and report cause-effect relationships.

- *Language opportunities should encourage interaction and learning.* Children usually are eager to discuss and share what they know. Such talking can be integrated into learning activities. A story about bears can encourage children to discuss and share their own personal experiences with bears. For some children this experience is probably restricted to cartoons. Others may have taken trips to the circus or zoo, or have camped where food had to be locked in cars or hung from trees to prevent unwanted intrusions from bears.

- *Language opportunities should be designed for a variety of purposes and audiences.* All classroom activities should have a purpose, such as decision making, problem solving, or predicting. Projecting into the experiences and feelings of their peers can be effective in small groups without the teacher. Computer programs, such as LOGO, or computer simulations can generate a rich variety of language.

- *Teachers' responses should encourage children's discussion.* Language is best learned when children direct the conversation to their own ends. An interested listener is the most efficient stimulant. The teacher can reflect on what the child has said to show interest in the child's initiation. When the child asks, "Boy *have* you seen the neat stuff at the circus?" an open response can invite the child to talk more about the circus. Show and tell is another activity that encourages children to engage in conversation.

SUMMARY

This chapter has focused on the receptive (especially listening) and expressive (speaking and writing) aspects of the language arts, including children's literature. Language learning is an integrated process from the preschool through the primary grades for all children. Modifications are needed in each area of the language arts for dealing with diverse children, especially for children with language-related disabilities.

The language arts should not be isolated from other program areas. Language problems often affect the other curriculum areas. Delayed language development in a young child frequently manifests itself later in marked slowness in learning to read and a lack of ability to express thoughts in writing. This may continue throughout the years. A language environment should foster the children's optimal language learning. The teacher promotes language functioning through encouraging and teaching communication skills, including expression, in a variety of forms. A wide range of alternative approaches must be provided in all aspects of the curriculum.

REFERENCES

Acosta, L. K. (1981). Instructor use of total communication: Effects of preschool Down's syndrome children's vocabulary and attempted verbalizations. Unpublished doctoral dissertation, University of Iowa, Iowa City.

Adamson, D. (1981). Dramatization of children's literature and visual perceptual kinesthetic intervention for disadvantaged beginning readers. Unpublished doctoral dissertation. Northwestern State University of Louisiana, Natchitoches.

Arnstein, F. J. (1962). *Poetry in the elementary classroom.* New York: Appleton-Century-Crofts.

Baker, P. D., & Bender, D. R. (1981). *Library media programs and the special learner.* Hamden, CT: Library Professional Publications.

Barbe, W. B., & Renzulli, J. (1981). *Psychology and education of the gifted* (3rd ed.). New York: Halstead Press.

Binkard, B. (1985). A successful handicap awareness program run by special parents. *Teaching Exceptional Children, 18,* 12–16.

Bleck, E., & Nagel, D. (1982). *Physically handicapped children.* New York: Grune and Stratton.

Brown, V. L. (1988a). Integrating drama and sign language. *Teaching Exceptional Children, 21*(1), 4–8.

Brown, V. L. (1988b). Integrating drama and sign language: A multisensory approach to language acquisition and its effects on disadvantaged preschool children. Unpublished raw data.

Burks, H. L., Good, J. A., Higginbotham, E. S., & Hoffman, C. A. (1967). Treatment of language lags in psychotherapeutic nursery school. *Journal of Special Education, 1*(2), 197–206.

Callahan, C. M. (1986). The special needs of gifted girls. In J. R. Whitmore (Ed.), *Intellectual giftedness in young children: Recognition and development* (pp. 5–15). New York: Haworth Press.

Carle, E. (1979). *The Very Hungry Caterpillar.* Cleveland: Collins, William and World.

Carr, E. G., & Kologinsky, E. (1983). Acquisition of sign language by autistic children II: Spontaneity and generalization effects. *Journal of Applied Behavior Analysis, 16,* 297–314.

Chomsky, C. (1981). Write now, read later. In C. B. Cazden (Ed.), *Language in early childhood education* (rev. ed.) (pp. 141–149). Washington, DC: National Association for the Education of Young Children.

Clarke, B. R., & Stewart, D. A. (1986). Reflections on language programs for the hearing impaired. *Language of Special Education, 20*(1), 153–163.

Cook, R. E., Tessier, A., & Armbruster, V. B. (1992). *Adapting early childhood curricula for children with special needs* (3rd ed.). Columbus, OH: Merrill.

Council on Interracial Books for Children (1980). *Guidelines for bias-free textbooks and storybooks.* New York: Author.

Cratty, B. (1980). *Adapted physical education.* Denver: Love.

Daniloff, J. K., Noll, J. K., Fristoe, M., & Lloyd, L. L. (1982). Gesture recognition in patients with aphasia. *Journal of Speech and Hearing Disorders, 47,* 43–49.

Derman-Sparks, L., & the A. B. C. Task Force (1989). *Anti-bias curriculum: Tools for empowering young children.* Washington, DC: National Association for the Education of Young Children.

Dudley-Marling, C., & Searle, D. (1988). Enriching language learning environments for students with learning disabilities. *Journal of Learning Disabilities, 21*(3), 140–142.

Gag, W. *Millions of Cats.* (1928). New York: Coward, McCann.

Ganopole, S. J. (1988). Reading and writing for the gifted: A whole language perspective. *Roeper Review, 11*(2), 88–92.

Graham, S., & Harris, K. R. (1988). Instructional recommendations for teaching writing to exceptional students. *Exceptional Children, 54,* 506–512.

Greenlaw, M. J., & McIntosh, M. E. (1986). Literature for use with gifted children. *Childhood Education, 62*(4), 281–286.

Guralnick, M. J. (1972). A language development program for severely handicapped children. *Exceptional Children, 39*(3), 45–49.

Hanson, I. W. (1976), Teaching remedial handwriting. *Language Arts, 53,* 428–431ff.

Hare, B.A., & Hare, J.M. (1979). Learning disabilities in young children. In S. G. Harwood (Ed.), *Educating young handicapped children: A developmental approach* (pp. 261–292). Germantown, MD: Aspen.

Hart, V. (1981). *Mainstreaming children with special needs.* New York: Longman.

Heward, W. L., & Orlansky, M. D. (1980). *Exceptional children.* Columbus, OH: Merrill.

Hopper, C., Hanrahan, L., & Nelson, S. (1986). Developing movement and speech/language programs for handicapped children. *Physical Educator, 43,* 192–194.

Jacobs, L. B. (1972). Providing balanced contacts with literature for children. In L. B. Jacobs (Ed.), *Literature for children* (pp. 32–38). Washington, DC: Association for Childhood Education International.

Johnson, W., Brown, S. F., Curtis, J. F., Edney, C. W., & Keaster, J. (1967). *Speech handicapped school children.* New York: Harper & Row.

Konstantareas, M. M. (1984). Sign language as a communication prosthesis with language impaired children. *Journal of Autism and Developmental Disorders, 14,* 9–25.

LeBlanc, J. M., Etzel, B. C., & Domash, M. A. (1978). A functional curriculum for early intervention. In K. E. Allen, V. A. Holm, and R. L. Scheffelbusch (Eds.), *Early intervention: A team approach.* Baltimore, MD: University Park Press.

Lebrun, Y., & Van de Craen, P. (1975). Developmental writing disorders and their prevention. *Journal of Special Education, 2*(2), 201–207.

McClure, A. A. (1985). Predictable books: Another way to teach reading to learning disabled children. *Teaching Exceptional Children, 17,* 267–273.

Polette, N. (1981). *Picture books for gifted programs.* Metuchen, NJ: Scarecrow Press.

Raver, S. A. (1987). Practical procedures for increasing spontaneous language in language-delayed preschoolers. *Journal of the Division for Early Childhood, 2*(2), 226–231.

Roedell, W. C., Jackson, N. E., & Robinson, H. B. (1980). *Gifted young children.* New York: Teachers College Press.

Rogers, K. B. (1989). Training teachers of the gifted: What do they need to know? *Roeper Review, 11*(3), 145–150.

Rogow, S. M. (1982). Rhythms and rhymes: Developing communication in very young blind and multihandicapped children. *Child Care, Health and Development, 8,* 249–260.

Scheuerman, N., Cartwright, S., York, R., Lowry, P., & Brown, L. (1974). Teaching young severely handicapped students to follow verbal directions. *Journal of Special Education, 8*(3), 223–236.

Warger, C. L. (1985). Making creative drama accessible to handicapped children. *Teaching Exceptional Children, 17,* 288–293.

Warren, S. F., & Kaiser, A. P. (1986). Incidental language teaching: A critical review. *Journal of Speech and Hearing Disorders, 51,* 291–299.

Wepner, S. B. (1988). Creating computer environments for gifted learners in primary classrooms. *Reading, Writing, and Learning Disabilities, 4*(3), 155–170.

CHAPTER 12

Teaching Reading

CHAPTER OVERVIEW

This chapter discusses:

1. The goals of reading instruction appropriate for young children with diverse needs.
2. Problems encountered by diverse children who are learning to read.
3. Ways to prepare children to read.
4. Prerequisites children need for learning to read.
5. Suggestions to help children gain these prerequisites.
6. Approaches to word recognition skills for diverse children (e.g., children who are gifted, children who are hearing-impaired, children who are visually impaired).
7. Basal reading programs for diverse children (e.g., children who are mentally retarded, children who are visually impaired, children who are hearing-impaired).
8. Instructional reading materials and resources for diverse children.
9. A management system in reading instruction.
10. Flexible ways of grouping children for reading instruction.

The goal of reading instruction is to teach children the necessary skills to interpret the written code in order to gain meaning from written messages. Comprehension is helped by making available alternative sources of information, including word forms, syntactical structures, and the context of words.

Learning to read is a constructive problem-solving process. Children are given information to interpret. They relate the ideas they gain from the printed page to their knowledge and experience. The reading process and the teaching of reading must focus on children's own thinking processes and on their ways to approach, learn, and remember information in print (Mason, 1986). In contrast to conventional wisdom, children do not begin to learn to read when they enter first grade. The process begins long before that time, when children begin to engage in a range of language activities and are emersed in a print-rich environment. Given the view of beginning reading, called *emergent literacy*, we have come to understand that the preschool teacher, rather than serving to protect young children from reading instruction, should immerse them in a program of *emergent literacy*. Thus that teacher helps to build in children the prerequisites for becoming a competent reader.

Garner (1987) describes several conceptions of reading comprehension that are advocated by experts in reading instruction. Schema theory is the view that is most widely accepted today. *Schema* are repertoires of expectations that are found in the memory system and are used to interpret new information (McNeil, 1984). Incoming information that conforms to the individual's expectations is encoded within existing schema. Information that fails to conform to those expectations may not be encoded or may be distorted until new schema are created. The expectations guiding the encoding of information also guide the retrieval of information (Anderson, 1984).

Schema theory suggests that reading is not simply a matter of developing letter-sound associations; it is more than sounding out individual letters, then stringing them together to form words. Reading is an information-processing activity with existing competencies based upon concepts and strategies that initially are gained early in the process of learning to read. These concepts and strategies are continually being reconstructed as children develop a greater understanding of the written language, which is closely related to their understanding of the spoken language.

For children to become literate, they must have a sense of a literate environment and feel the need to communicate through the written word. Children who lack experience with the reading process may have problems learning to read. If they have not been read to, for example, they may focus more on word calling rather than on the flow of meaning. Having a rich background of experiences, including having been read to and told stories, helps beginning readers associate the reading process with language and thinking processes (Spodek, Saracho, & Lee, 1984).

PROBLEMS THAT CHILDREN WITH DIVERSE NEEDS HAVE IN LEARNING TO READ

Not all children with disabilities are slow learners or have difficulty in learning to read. Children who have physical disabilities may have difficulty in moving from one place to another, but may not have any problems learning to read. Similarly, children with visual and hearing impairments may learn at the same rate as their normal peers. However, they may need to be provided with adaptations to instruction, such as sign language and Braille. Children with visual impairments, learning disabilities, and physical impairments perform better at reading than do those with hearing impairments (Bennett, Ragosta, & Stricker, 1984). Methods that are appropriate for some children with learning disabilities may be inappropriate for others.

Children who are gifted have special talents and almost as many needs as do other children (Clark, 1988). Although these children may be early speakers and readers, some do not develop literacy skills early (Cassidy & Vukelick, 1980; Jackson, 1988). Thus, gifted children are as unique and varied in their abilities as are their "normal" peers.

Teachers who have children with disabilities in their classrooms are bound to meet a variety of challenges. Children with mental retardation must be taught at a very slow pace with much repetition. Children who have reading disorders need special instruction to develop strength in their areas of weakness. Children with behavior disorders need help in controlling behaviors that block their learning. A reading program that integrates children with disabilities must provide the proper range of methods to accommodate these differences.

PREPARING CHILDREN TO READ

Early childhood programs introduce preschool and kindergarten children to literacy-oriented activities. Researchers have become interested in what can help prepare the young child for initial reading instruction (Saracho, 1985b). Not all researchers agree about whether formal reading instruction should be introduced before the first grade,

or how it should be introduced (Raver & Dwyer, 1986). However, there is increasing agreement that literacy-related activity should begin early in the preschool program.

The term *reading readiness* has been replaced by the phrase *emergent literacy* in early childhood programs. Emergent literacy describes the children's early stages in their development toward literacy; it precedes the conventional reading of print (Clay, 1979). Literacy development begins early in life and continues to develop every day in the contexts of the home and community. Children at every age have some degree of literacy skills, which everybody develops into mature reading and writing (Teale, 1986). In emergent literacy, a child's scribble marks on a page, even when no letter is discernible, is considered writing. However, those children who can differentiate between their scribbles and drawing definitely know the difference between writing and pictures. Giving the impression of reading parallels that behavior. Although such behavior cannot be called reading in the conventional sense, the activity is regarded as legitimate literacy behavior.

According to Morrow (1993), (1) reading is acquired through socially interactive and emulative behavior, (2) children acquire the ability to read as a result of life experiences, (3) children acquire reading skills when they see a purpose and a need for the process, and (4) being read to plays a role in the acquisition of reading.

Often children benefit in comprehension skills from their assimilation of and familiarity with vocabulary and syntactic structures in books that have been read to them. Children who have been read to frequently and early tend to read earlier than others and learn to read more easily (Clark, 1984; Durkin, 1966; Hiebert, 1981; Schickedanz, 1978). Furthermore, reading to children at school or at home generally leads them to associate reading with pleasure and provides them with models for reading. In fact, when children begin to read on their own, they often choose books that have been read to them earlier.

Children's comprehension skills are developed as they assimilate familiar vocabulary and syntactic structures in books they have heard. Children who have frequently listened to stories tend to read earlier and more easily than others (Durkin, 1966; Hiebert, 1981; Clark, 1984; Saracho, 1987). In addition, children who have listened to stories at home or at school usually perceive reading as enjoyable and informative, thus developing a positive attitude toward reading (Saracho, 1987).

Literacy requires representation skills for children to learn to read and write. Children acquire these skills beginning in infancy and continue to develop these skills throughout life. Words written on a page require children to identify the meanings of symbols. Through reading, children acquire meaning from the printed word. The goal of reading instruction is to teach children the necessary skills to interpret a written code to gain meaning; therefore, learning experiences that develop children's representation skills must be provided in early childhood classrooms (Saracho, 1985b). The printed visual features allow a reader to interpret meaning through comprehension. Most children who read fluently and understand what they read have good comprehension, which is facilitated through the alternative sources of information such as word forms, syntactical structures, and the context of words. Readers who have problems with immediate comprehension can use mediated comprehension.

Research has shown that reading to children can develop literacy for them in many ways. Reading the same story to children over and over again is an important technique (Morrow, 1986; Sulzby, 1985; Yaden, 1985) because children acquire an understanding of the functions of print, a sense of how print is used, and a realization of what people are doing when they are reading (Smith, 1978). Reading stories to children develops their positive attitudes toward reading (Saracho, 1987). Storybook experiences teach children how to handle a book and its front-to-back progression—the beginning, middle, and end of a story—and the concept of authorship (Clay, 1979; Torvey & Kerber, 1986). Listening to stories helps children become aware of the functions, form, and convention of print, as well as develops their metacognitive knowledge about reading tasks and interaction with teachers and parents (Mason, 1980). *Metacognition* refers to the individual's own awareness of the way learning occurs; therefore, it nurtures a person's own learning.

Readiness to read is the ability to profit from reading instruction. Traditionally, it has referred to the time at which children are able to succeed in beginning reading instruction. It also identifies later stages when they can move from one level of reading achievement to a higher level in a productive and effective way. One approach to reading readiness takes a maturational point of view, which suggests that children who are not capable of benefiting from reading instruction wait until they reach the stage of development to benefit from such instruction. A more proactive approach to reading readiness suggests that the teacher provide these children with activities that will help them build their language competencies so that they become ready. This latter perspective is consistent in many ways with an emergent literacy approach. Kirk, Kliebhan, and Lerner (1978) identified the components of reading readiness as mental maturity, thinking skills, visual abilities, auditory abilities, speech and language development, physical fitness and motor development, social and emotional development, and motivation.

Mental maturity relates to the child's level of intellectual development. It is influenced by both maturation and the experiences the child has had.

Thinking skills are the specific intellectual abilities the child uses to organize and deal intelligently with information. These skills are developed as children continually try to make sense of their world.

Visual abilities are the capacity to perceive, identify, discriminate, and recall visual shapes and forms. These develop through exploration, recognition, and discrimination of objects or forms. Children must discriminate visually between letters to read. Manipulating objects helps develop their visual discrimination skills (Spache & Spache, 1986).

Auditory abilities are children's capacities to perceive likenesses and differences in sounds, including differences in highly similar pairs of words that are presented orally, as well as to recall these likenesses and differences. The best indicators of auditory ability are children's speech and conversation, since auditory problems are often related to speech problems.

Motor development begins when the infant kicks, crawls, walks, runs, and jumps. It is also related to eye-hand coordination. Although the relationship of motor development to reading is vague, the assumption is that motor skills help children to copy work and turn pages. Motor development is especially important to the reading skills of children with visual disabilities.

Working at learning activities in a classroom is a social activity. Children must be able to work with others in a cooperative manner during reading instruction, controlling their behavior and meeting realistic standards. They also must be able to work independently when not under the direct supervision of the teacher. These elements require social and emotional maturity. Learning to read can be frustrating to any child. A sense of failure or of not meeting expectations can lead to emotional problems. Prereading and initial reading instruction are important to exceptional learners.

HELPING CHILDREN PREPARE TO READ

In a real sense, all aspects of a rich early childhood program prepare children to read. Such a program provides a wide range of intellectually stimulating language activities. Science experiences help develop intellectual as well as auditory and visual skills. There is strong social and emotional support as children learn about themselves and others and develop an increased ability to work with others, including adults. Physical activities indoors and outdoors support physical development and social skills. In addition, children in such a program broaden their range of knowledge and learn to communicate that knowledge in a variety of ways. By hearing stories told and read, young children develop a desire to learn to read. These are elements of a strong prereading program. It is generally evident that the language activities in the class, including reading and telling stories and engaging children in discussions, prepare children for reading. Dramatic play, art activities, and all other activities that help children become symbol makers are also important in preparing young readers (Dyson, 1993; Snow & Tabors, 1993).

A prereading program, though informal, should be systematic. All children, including those with disabilities, should participate in all activities. Story reading, discussions, and other opportunities for using expressive and receptive language are examples of these activities.

When a child does not seem to be learning from informal activities, the teacher needs to analyze the nature of the problem. Sometimes a disability does not allow a child to gain what others do from an informal activity. The activity may need to be modified or the teacher might have to use some form of direct instruction. Children with learning disabilities, for example, may not be able to identify similarities and differences in sounds unless these are clearly pointed out to them. After initial training and practice, they may be successful in identifying such similarities and differences in informal situations.

At times, a teacher may have to break up a complex learning activity into its simpler parts. The child can learn these simpler components before putting them into a complex whole. For example, in helping children with auditory discrimination skills, a teacher might first provide a child with a set of Montessori sound boxes, or their equivalent. The child can hear the sound made by shaking the boxes, note the difference in sounds made by each box, then seriate the boxes by the sounds made. The child can then match each box by sound with a comparable box in another set. The discrimination is easier because the child hears the sounds in isolation. Later, children can listen to sounds of other objects in the room as well as in the neighborhood, comparing them to one another. Finally, the teacher can help the child focus on the sounds of words that are alike or different.

Some children are easily distracted. The teacher might need to isolate the learning environment to reduce possible distractions. Secluding a section of the room by using furniture or equipment as a screen can help. Using headphones to listen to records rather than listening through the record player's speaker also might help. Instruction given to these children should be simple, clear, and free from irrelevancies and distractions.

Once the child has gained a skill or a concept, the teacher should provide opportunities for practice. The teacher also should check back regularly to be certain the child retains the skill or concept learned.

Precocious Readers

Not all children who are gifted are precocious readers. Nor is early reading ability necessarily a sign of general ability. A characteristic of precocious readers is their ability to capitalize on their strengths and compensate for their weaknesses. Precocious readers have varied skills and reading styles. As a group, they have above average intelligence, but their individual intelligence test scores may range from below to above average (Jackson, 1988). Preschoolers with the highest IQ scores are not necessarily precocious readers (Jackson & Myers, 1982).

An important factor in precocious readers is their ability to comprehend written text. This is related to their general language and reasoning abilities and their knowledge of the content (Curtis, 1980). Highly specialized children may display remarkable decoding skills but may not comprehend what they have decoded. These children may not be especially intelligent or verbally adept; they may have hyperlexia. *Hyperlexics* are identified as children who are autistic or mentally retarded but have unusual and precocious reading behaviors (Healy, 1982).

Precocious reading depends on an environment that supports children's learning to read and on the individual's learning style (Jackson, 1988). Precocious readers display two types of reading behaviors: conceptual and analytical (Jackson, Donaldson, & Cleland, 1988). *Conceptual* readers can read text with speed, use contextual cues to correct oral reading errors, read words correctly that do not conform to phonological rules, and use context clues to provide missing words in a cloze task. Conceptual readers continuously process meaning and attend to large units of text. *Analytical* readers can apply phonological decoding rules, and show fewer omission and insertion errors (Jackson, 1988). These readers focus on the smaller units of text.

Precocious readers do not use phonetic rules to decode unfamiliar words (Jackson, 1988). These children memorize sight vocabulary and have difficulty decoding unknown words. Such children might benefit from basic phonics instruction.

Reading strategies must be individualized for precocious readers. There is no program that meets the needs of all of them. Each child's strengths and needs should be identified and a reading program designed accordingly. Language activities should be matched to what children can do. If the activities are successful, the children will want to continue them. Such activities also should be related to the children's interests.

In addition to receiving oral language experiences, children can be helped to gain knowledge of the written language and to begin to understand the reading process. Reading to children individually or in small groups can help. As an adult or older child reads, the words that are being read can be pointed out. If the same story is read repeatedly, the children will anticipate words and even point to the correct words in the text. In this way, they will learn to associate the words seen with the words heard. The children also will see that letters are organized into words with spaces between and that these words follow from left to right on the page. They will notice the relation of the sounds read aloud to the written words on the page. Thus, they gain a sense of what occurs in the reading process.

Children also can dictate stories to adults to be read back to them or to the class later. This will help them associate written with spoken words. As the children learn to form letters, they can begin to write their own stories, inventing spelling before they learn to spell properly. The letter–sound associations they create will be fairly regular. If incorrect, they will easily be replaced when the children learn to spell (Chomsky, 1981). Thus, the transition from prereading activities to beginning reading instruction becomes a smooth, natural one.

Before beginning formal reading instruction, the teacher must assess two features of the child's understanding of the spoken language. Children need to be able to listen to and to understand simple stories and the specific words and phrases. The prereading program must focus on these specific factors of language and communication.

Before learning to read, children also must learn that our oral language can be broken into a range of linguistic units. These units include phrases, words, syllables, and distinctive sounds (phonemes). This requires knowing the oral language intuitively and gaining an analytic sense of the way language is arranged. These oral segments are later matched to written segments as children learn to read. Grapheme discrimination, the ability to distinguish among letters of the alphabet and other graphemic symbols, is also important. Although most kindergarteners can distinguish and name most letters of the alphabet, many kindergarten children with disabilities cannot.

The way children perceive the reading process influences how they learn to read. Saracho (1983) investigated the perceptions of reading of 3- to 8-year-old children. She found that their perceptions of reading were closely related to their reading experiences. In a later study, children's reading experiences in school, home and the community were shown to influence their understanding of the reading process (Saracho, 1984). Children assign meaning to print in the context of their environment (Saracho, 1985b), where many opportunities emerge for children to learn about print.

Attitudes toward Reading

An important element in learning to read is children's attitude toward reading. Martin (1984) found that almost one in five gifted students had a negative attitude toward reading. Students reported that reading was too time-consuming or was a low-priority activity. If teachers know their children's attitudes toward reading they can design appropriate reading experiences, adapted to the children's particular interests. Martin suggests the following strategies to improve the reading attitudes of children who are gifted:

1. Reading material should be selected using student input and student interests. Children need to share what they have read.
2. Prereading activities should be used to raise the students' interest in the reading material. A reading assignment can become meaningful and more attractive to gifted learners by relating their prior experiences to new reading information and discussing reasons for reading.
3. Gifted learners must be challenged to make them use higher-order thinking skills. Children who are gifted can easily become bored if the reading tasks are too simple.
4. The attitudes and interests of children who are gifted must be identified to determine the specific instructional strategies to change any negative attitudes toward reading. An interest inventory can provide information in the selection of reading materials. (Martin & Cramond, 1983).

At the beginning of the school year, a reading attitude scale (e.g., PRAS—Saracho, 1986, 1988) could be used to assess young children's attitudes. Changes in these attitudes also can be detected later in the school year.

Teachers should work to create a desire to read in children as early as possible. They need to support children's interest in looking at books and pictures. Eventually reading itself will become satisfying. Children with disabilities may need more help in learning to enjoy reading because of the problems they may have with the learning process.

Young children starting to read have much information about the written language. They know about its graphic features and can distinguish words and letters from nonwriting graphic displays. During their preschool years children learn about the characteristics of words and about the relationship between printed and written words. They also begin to perceive words as combinations of sound segments (Schickedanz, 1982). This knowledge of the reading process can be built upon in beginning reading instruction.

In summary, a prereading program must make sure that:

1. The student has the necessary intellectual, motor, and language competence and an awareness of the way language is used to teach reading.
2. The student can segment the spoken language into words, syllables, and phonemes.
3. The student knows and can discriminate among the letters of the alphabet.
4. The student is interested in learning to read.

TEACHING READING TO CHILDREN

Learning to read is a gradual process. Not all the children in a class will start to learn at the same time or learn at the same rate. A beginning reading program must be individualized and flexible, reflecting the range of abilities in the class. The teacher should provide reading instruction for those who are ready and help others develop their prereading skills. Word recognition skills, phonetic analysis, and contextual analysis skills need to be developed.

Word Recognition Skills

Word recognition skills help children become independent readers by learning to pronounce and understand new words. Children can learn to analyze words through the language experience approach, the whole-word method, phonics, or contextual analysis. Since great variance exists among children, teachers must try different teaching methods. An integration of these methods may be best for any reading situation.

Naturalistic Approaches to Teaching Reading. The Language Experience Approach to reading (LEA) can be used to teach reading in a natural way. The LEA requires that the children's repertoire of experiences and language be used in the teaching of reading (Saracho, 1985b). The two words *language* and *experience* best describe this approach (Stauffer, 1980). Reading is integrated with the other language arts as children listen, speak, write, and read. The children's own ideas and personal experiences are used to produce reading materials, which helps them see the relationship between the written word and spoken language. Since students differ in both language and experiences, the content of such a reading program varies from child to child and from group to group. The child's speech represents the language patterns, and experiences provide the content.

A recent approach to teaching reading and language arts, called *whole language,* is akin to the LEA. It is built upon the integration of all of the language arts, including reading. Children come to see that speaking, writing, listening, and reading are all related processes. Like the LEA, whole language engages children in writing and reading as early as possible so that they construct the materials they will later read (Raines, 1990).

In the language experience approach, children first dictate stories about their experiences to the teacher, who writes them on experience charts. These charts are used for teaching reading. Later, as children learn to write, they produce their own stories rather than dictate them to the teacher. Since the children create the instructional material, there are seldom problems with comprehension. Even difficult material is understood and remembered. Children move from reading their own material to reading the work of other children and reading books.

The language experience approach does not deny the need to learn letter-sound associations. It does suggest that this skill is learned best through organic activities. This process of learning to read more closely parallels learning a native language than learning a second language (Spodek, 1985).

The language experience approach to reading can be used even with children who have sensory impairments. Children with hearing impairments are deprived of some of the feedback normally received from the language of others. However, language experiences amplify their vocabulary. These children may need to have language interpreted during language experiences. As the teacher records children's experiences and goes over charts, the interpreter signs the language. A child who is partially hearing-impaired may gain this experience by sitting near the chart with a classmate close by to help out informally.

Fingerspelling can also be used for this activity. Most deaf children can fingerspell the alphabet by age 5 (Andrews, 1988). Experience stories can be told by children through fingerspelling, then written down by the teacher. The child dictates to the teacher, who reads it back to the child. The child can then fingerspell what is written on the chart.

Teachers can write accounts of children's experiences for discussion. These stories can be collected into a book with the child's name in the title. These books can be sent home periodically for parents to read with them. Later, the children can follow along in their books as the teacher reads the stories, or can write stories from dictation (Maxwell, 1986).

A variety of reading strategies can be used with children who are gifted. A Directed Reading–Thinking Activity (DRTA) (Stauffer, 1975) provides them with opportunities to use critical thinking skills. It also provides them with the opportunity to interact with their classmates. The Inquiry Reading Program (Cassidy, 1981) permits children who are gifted to select their own topics, locate their own resources, and set their own schedules.

Children with visual impairments may not be able to see the writing on the chart. Despite this, they also can participate. A child who is partially sighted, for instance, might be placed in a position to see and hear better. Teachers should use large print on charts and take care that the letters and words are uncluttered. The child can either write experiences in Braille or have the teacher or resource person record them. When Braille is introduced to children in class, they will perceive it as an exciting new tool to help store ideas. The language experience approach cannot simplify learning the Braille code system. But the code will be important to children who need to use it to read their own dictated words. Short stories and words stored in word banks can be recorded in Braille. These can bridge children's access to books.

The language experience approach to reading promotes independence in children with visual impairments. These children can manipulate, add to, and interact with their word banks as they function independently at the learning centers. The ability to manipulate words, to construct sentences, or to label objects gives them a feeling of control over their environment. The child's independence, self-respect, and sense of control motivate continued learning (Curry, 1975).

Reading experience charts help develop a wide range of word recognition skills. Since the chart is based on the children's experience, it is easy to teach the use of context clues. The child's intuitive knowledge of sentence structure and shared experiences recorded on the chart make this approach effective. Individuals and small groups of children who have been writing their own stories and charts can be introduced to simple, short reading charts.

A good foundation builds on each child's language knowledge and stimulates reading. As the child progresses, the reading charts can become longer and more elaborate. Children also can write their own stories on smaller sheets of paper and can start writing and reading books.

Whole-Word Method.   The whole-word method enables a child to look at, think, and say a word, identifying it on sight without any kind of analysis. Functional reading and survival reading programs have emphasized teaching sight words that are necessary to survive in everyday living (Zjawin, Longnecker, Pelow, & Chant, 1981). Whole-word methodology promotes vocabulary and word identification through labeling high-frequency words and identifying words commonly needed for reading comprehension. Whole-word methodology requires three subskills:

1. Visually discriminating letter strings, which demands letter recognition, attention to letter order, and focus on the entire word.
2. Relating and remembering labels for the letter strings.
3. Retrieving and speaking labels as the strings are observed. (Venezky, 1975)

This method does not require the child to analyze words or their parts by their sounds. Since children memorize many specific words and letter patterns, this approach is limited by their memory capability (Williams, 1979). Some children can increase their reading vocabulary with this approach; others with a short memory span cannot. George D. Spache and Evelyn B. Spache (1986) recommended teaching children words as a foundation to vocabulary using (1) firsthand experiences, (2) direct teaching providing many meaningful relationships, and (3) incidental learning from casual contact with words using one or more language media.

Children with strong visual memory abilities but poor auditory analysis skills can use the whole-word approach. However, they may have comprehension problems, recognizing and reading words but not being able to interpret what they read. Learning-disabled children have difficulty in reading, especially in word recognition skills (Reid & Hresko, 1981). They lack the ability to analyze each word they meet and still read fluently. To become effective readers, these children need to become proficient in using whole-word methodology (Simms & Falcon, 1987).

One strategy used in this approach for children with learning disabilities is to reduce information into small, related units of instruction. According to Gillet and Temple (1990), using input organization based on categorization and classification helps children develop strategies for recognizing words in print. When children enter school, they already have some skills in categorizing and classifying. They can apply these skills to the reading process (Simms & Falcon, 1987).

A group of five children can be taught categories in which they can read few or no words. A new category is introduced with an extended discussion. For example:

Today, class, we are going to begin *action words.* Who can give me an example of *action?* . . . The first word is pull. . . . Can someone stand up and show us how to pull something? . . . Can someone use *pull* in a sentence?

As each word in a category is presented, its meaning is discussed, a sentence is generated, and its relationship to the category and to other words in the category is stressed. Each word is written on the board or on a large word card as it is introduced (Simms & Falcon, 1987, p. 31).

Several techniques for sight word instruction can be employed with exceptional children. Individual and group drills can be used with word cards, oral and written sentences, or scrambled word sheets. A single category is the major focus in all the activities and materials. Once children can read every word in a category, they are ready to learn a new category.

Many *children with language and learning disabilities* may have difficulty with word retrieval. They will understand words but be unable to use them in spontaneous communication. During oral reading some of these children may interchange words on the page with different words that have similar meanings, such as *dog* for *puppy*. Others may define the words but not pronounce them. Still others may examine a word such as *inspection* and say, "I know that it means to look over something carefully, but I can't say it." Children may identify letters or sounds correctly, but be unable to retrieve the name or sound. Cuing techniques—such as using multiple-choice questions or presenting the initial sound of the word—can be helpful with these children. In regular reading instruction, these children should receive extra opportunities to recognize and associate responses. Initially, the sight vocabulary should be composed of nouns and verbs to help the children associate objects or pictures with the printed form (Johnson, 1979).

The whole-word method can help *children with sensory impairments* when taught in context and when taught analytically. Time and experience are needed to build concepts, learn sight words, and read selections. Children with hearing impairments need to learn sight words and sound-symbol associations visually within meaningful contexts. Although children with visual disabilities use auditory cues to compensate for limited vision, they also should acquire sight words in meaningful contexts.

Special strategies to teach basic word identification to children with visual impairments involve the principle of multimodal input. These methods are called visual-auditory-kinesthetic-tactile (VAKT). They show the integration of a visual stimulus (the printed word), its verbal analog (the pronunciation), and a kinesthetic-tactile aspect, usually the tracing or writing of the word.

Children with severe visual disabilities can be provided with expendable Braille materials. A wide variety of thermoform Braille materials should be available to them. The teacher can place words from the word bank on top of the children's desks and encourage them to read them in varied order, reading the sentence aloud to their peers. Resource pages with words and objects to cut, label, and sort also can be provided.

An approach to teaching sight words to children with visual impairments is the gestural communication or sign language system. Pairing signs with their visual–verbal representation can help students remember them. Signing can be used in reading instruction. For instance, for the word *house* the sign can be made by drawing the outline of a peak roof with the hands. The tips of the open hands are placed together to represent a roof peak and then moved apart and down, tracing the roof line. The word *fight* can be represented by miming the basic physical action of a fight; both hands make a fist and move in a back-and-forth position.

Words and concepts can be conveyed through gestures or signs combined with facial expressions, body movements, and fingerspellings, while simultaneously forming the words on the lips. The integration of multiple sensory pathways is inherent in gestural communication. Fingerspelling and sign language (the kinesthetic, multimodal, motivating, classical conditioning, and sensory training principles) are the foundations of this learning theory included in high-quality reading and language instruction (Raver & Dwyer, 1986). Carney, Cioffi, and Raymond (1985) demonstrated the feasibility of using sign language to teach basic word acquisition to children with mild disabilities who had problems acquiring sight words through typical approaches.

Children who are mentally retarded can benefit from whole-word methodology. Brown et al. (1974) designed several practical programs to teach trainable retarded students to verbally label sight words, to functionally read nouns and adjective-noun phrases, to spell printed words, to complete sentences that include the verb form *to be* and nine different prepositions, and to show they understand the words by touching the objects to which the words or sentences refer. When used with these children, the whole-word method should contain simple, familiar words.

Reading activities should be playful and fun, while being purposeful. Raver and Dwyer (1986) suggested using training cards to teach sight words to *children with visual impairments, mental retardation, cerebral palsy*, and *severe language delay*. Three-by-ten-inch cards printed with the names of common objects (e.g., ball, puzzle) and the names of children are used. About three word cards are introduced each week. On the third week, the size of the cards is reduced to 2 by 4 inches. Each new card is presented to the group in a similar way:

1. The teacher holds up the new card and says, "This card says [*puzzle*]."
2. The teacher goes to the cabinet where the puzzles are stored, takes one out, and begins to play with it.
3. The teacher continues to play with the object while restating the word *puzzle* and pointing to the word card that has the word *puzzle* printed on it.
4. After the demonstration, the teacher invites the children to play with the object.
5. Each child has a set of word cards in the paper pocket on the back of his or her chair. Children select the correct word card from their paper pocket and show it to the teacher before they can get permission to remove the object from the shelf.
6. When the individual children use a word card, a verbal requested is provided.

Sentence building usually occurs around the fifth week. Children place the card for their name on a language board. Beside this card is the word card of the object the children want to manipulate. The sentence may read, "Cliff book. Cliff wants a book, please." Children must use a full sentence when showing a card. For example, when showing the *ball* word card, children can request the object by saying, "I want a ball, please." Initially, the teacher models all language responses and the children imitate the phrase. Gradually, the teacher offers fewer prompts until the children respond spontaneously.

The teacher corrects incorrect choices, permitting the children to learn to read each card correctly by trial and error. Word cards have a communication power and spontaneous extensions toward reading instruction. Children begin to identify and sound beginning consonants on some word cards spontaneously. In Raver and Dwyer's study, the children initially used the cards before they actually read them. They learned to read the cards by observing which object or action a card allowed them to use or engage in.

Phonics. Phonics uses letter-sound relationships to help children sound out written words. Most children who have trouble developing beginning decoding skills have problems with phonological aspects of language (Perfetti, 1985). According to Liberman and Shankweiler (1985), the grasping words that have parts (phonemes, syllables, morphemes) represent the most basic phonological problem of poor readers. This basic awareness deficit relates to two other phonological processes involved in the acquisition of early decoding skills: (1) Students do not have access to the phonological representations of the names of objects, and (2) students do not have the knowledge of phonetic properties as a base for short-term memory operations that underlie the processing of connected oral or written language.

Much of the poor reader's basic problem relates to phonology rather than to syntax or semantics (Snider & Tarver, 1987). The five subskills for decoding with phonics are letter differentiation, association of sounds and letters, blending sounds, identification of sounds within a word, and sound matching within words (Venezky, 1975).

Children who experience severe problems with the phonological aspects of prereading skills need to learn to sequence and blend sounds to identify words (Fox & Rought, 1980). Language-disordered children are not likely to learn this on their own. Phonics can help improve most children's reading. Some educators believe that the phonics method, or part-word approach, is the only way to teach reading. Other educators caution against its overuse.

In fact, phonics helps beginning readers to pronounce and recognize only words for which auditory memories are already stored. Phonics helps as decoding words produces a pronunciation of that word that is helpful in its recognition. If the pronunciation is similar to a spoken word and if some meaningful association to that word has already been stored in the reader's memory, without previous knowledge of the word, decoding creates only a meaningless group of sounds (Spache & Spache, 1986). Guszak (1985) found that some children fail to use context clues in reading, neglecting to attend to the meaning of the passage and placing too much attention on the analysis of individual words. Goodman (1968) suggested that an overemphasis on phonics in reading instruction leads children to believe that word analysis is an end in itself rather than an aid to gaining meaning.

The phonics approach isolates every sound of the English language and relates it to its written symbol. The teacher presents these symbols and isolated sounds to the children. Teachers without specialized speech training may have difficulty giving each sound its accurate pronunciation. They may not, for example, place their tongues in the exact proper position when saying isolated sounds. It is difficult to pronounce the *p* without adding a vowel utterance to it. Thus, teacher mispronunciations may provide the wrong examples to their students. In addition, teaching a sound in isolation may cause children to have difficulty identifying the same sound in context.

Phonological awareness can be developed by modeling and by encouraging and reinforcing play with language that emphasizes the sounds of language. Teachers should include language-disordered children in sound play, making up nonsense words, adding endings to words, using alliteration, rhyming, and practicing the pronunciation of words. Teachers can prompt phonological corrections—another manifestation of early phonological awareness—focusing the children's attention to specific and appropriate features of words. For instance, if a child has difficulty saying a word, the teacher might say, "That's a hard word for you to say." Or when reading a story to the class, teachers might point out and comment on the length of a word such as, "Hippopotamus—that's a long word!" (Schuele & van Kleeck, 1984).

Most preschool language-disordered children are not ready for complex structured tasks designed to teach these skills. However, some children may succeed with very simple structured tasks such as segmenting initial sounds. (A discussion of levels of difficulty on the different tasks of phonemic segmentation is found in Lewkowics, 1980.)

Repeating the initial sound or telling the child to "say just a little bit" can help simplify that use in beginning reading. Older preschool children with language disorders may succeed with the beginning stages of structure (Schuele & van Kleeck, 1987). In addition, auditory discrimination can teach children about the sound structure of oral and written language.

The phonics approach is inappropriate for hearing-impaired children, who may be unable to distinguish speech sounds and who may produce inaccurate sounds in their own speech. They will probably fail to clearly hear structure words such as *and* or morphological endings such as *ed* and *ing*, because these are usually unaccented. These children can become confused and have trouble with words that have minimal sound differences and words having multiple meanings. Colloquial expressions or unclear input from the language of others can compound the problem.

Friedman and Gillooley (1977) suggested using artificial orthographies—that is, special alphabets that simplify letter-sound associations such as *ita* (the initial teaching alphabet)—with hearing-impaired and deaf students. These orthographic approaches help beginning readers gain a rapid mastery of sound-symbol correspondence by using sets of symbols that may bear little resemblance to the familiar letters of the alphabet. Friedman and Gillooley found that the influence of orthographic structure begins at the earliest stages of learning to read (first- and second-grade levels) and continues throughout a more advanced stage (fourth-grade level). Deaf children learned the rules of orthography as well as hearing children with whom they were compared. They also developed a compensatory skill that allowed them to have a superior perception of unstructured items.

Children who were deaf before acquiring language are generally far behind their age-matched counterparts in reading achievement. Since they lack experience with the sound elements of language, they presumably must decode written materials to meaning directly, without the mediation of acoustic cues—"hearing the word in their head"—so essential in developing phonic skills in young hearing readers.

Contextual Analysis.   Contextual analysis allows the reader to determine word meaning by the position or function of a word in a familiar sentence pattern (Spache & Spache, 1986). Context clues help identify unfamiliar words through syntactic, semantic, pictorial, typographic, and stylistic prompts. Materials used in teaching contextual analysis should be familiar and brief and should include simple words from the children's sight vocabulary. Teachers should place words in their meaningful context after they have been decoded, using the word in a phrase or identifying the word as a nonsense word (Williams, 1979).

Children who are educable mentally retarded (EMR) do not perform as well as comparable children who are not retarded on tasks requiring short-term memory. However, these children can learn to use context analysis (Estes, 1970; Spitz, 1973). They will need additional instruction that teaches the same words in varied contexts (Ramanauskas, 1972). Using activities that emphasize context utilization skills can be more effective than teaching the use of context directly.

Milgram (1973) found that children who are mentally retarded have difficulty with verbal problem-solving tasks and with learning tasks involving verbal mediation. These children were unable to use relevant cues and employ information-processing strategies. Thus, they will probably have difficulty discovering rules for analyzing context, selecting relevant information, and maintaining attention. This may lead to problems in reading, causing the children to perform below their potential. To benefit from contextual redundancy, the child must discover relevant cues. Because children with mental retardation fail to find the relevant dimension of a task, they do not have this ability to learn by discovery.

The printed language is the main form of communication that is held in common by persons with speech and hearing impairments. Reading stimulates these children intellectually, but learning to read may be difficult for them. Reading is based on the spoken language; symbols that make up reading are based on language patterns. Children with hearing impairments cannot hear these language patterns and thus cannot easily convert written symbols into oral symbols. They lack the oral referents to many written words. Hearing-impaired children can learn to use contextual analysis if they have language and concepts to help them meaningfully recognize printed symbols. The experiences are provided through school events and activities. The children learn the concrete words that name objects and visible elements in their environment in their formal reading programs.

Using context in reading provides an effective way to gain meaning. The child internalizes the rules of language structure and the necessary conceptual background to respond to the meaning of the context. Children's ability to predict from context using syntactic cues is less well developed than their ability to use semantic cues.

Basal Reader Programs

The basal reader approach continues to be used extensively in schools, although its appropriateness has been questioned through the years. The basal reading program is probably the most common way reading is taught in the kindergarten and primary grades. Traditionally, such an approach is based on a program that includes a series of reading texts and related supportive materials designed to help children learn to read. The child learns to read single words in isolation and then to read with greater meaning and speed by grouping words. In addition to providing word recognition techniques, basal readers offer children opportunities to develop comprehension skills, including reading for information, reading to organize, reading to evaluate, reflective reading, and reading for appreciation. Newer basal reading series have moved away from the "whole-to-part" approach to learning to read. Some have become more literature-based and have related other language arts activities to learning to read.

In determining the characteristics of reading programs for the gifted, Mangieri and Madigan (1984) sent a questionnaire to 150 school districts in the United States. Their findings revealed that many districts use enrichment as a major part of their program, the use of a basal reading series (sometimes at an accelerated speed) is very popular, and the regular classroom teacher is responsible for most of the reading instruction for children who are gifted.

Basal readers are written for children who are sighted. Transcribing them into

Braille does not help children who are visually disabled since the language content of basal readers is heavily dependent upon illustrations. These cannot be seen clearly by the child with a visual impairment. The stories in these readers are senseless without these pictures. Comprehension cues and interest-arousing aspects are lost and the stories lose their appeal. In addition, basal readers have a sense of verbal unreality for children who are visually impaired because most of their language refers to objects and concepts that these children may not have experienced. These convey no meaning to them (Cutsforth, 1951). For example, the visually impaired child has no referent for green grass or a blue lake and may be compelled to memorize such terms. These abstract descriptors are difficult for such children to understand and can cause them to lose interest in reading (Curry, 1975).

There is no specific reading program designed for children with hearing impairments, though a basal reading series, "Reading Milestones," was specifically developed with such children in mind. LaSasso (1987) found more than 20 basal reading series used with hearing-impaired students. These include "Reading Milestones" (Dormac), "Ginn 360" and "Ginn 720" (an updated version) (Ginn and Company), "Houghton Mifflin Readers" (Houghton-Mifflin), and "Reading Systems Unlimited" (Scott Foresman). LaSasso's study identified the strengths in these readers for hearing-impaired students at the primary level (see Table 12.1).

Apparently the most appropriate basal reader series for children with these characteristics is "Reading Milestones." This series has appropriate syntax and figurative language, repetition of vocabulary, phonics emphasis, conceptual load, and supplementary materials.

Most basal readers are geared to children with reading levels equivalent to their grade levels. Children with mental retardation, who usually read below their grade level, may find the content of these readers inappropriate, uninteresting, and even humiliating. Hillerich (1974) suggested evaluating reading programs and textbook series. Some readers, such as the "Functional Basic Reading Series" (1963, 1964, 1965), written specifically for retarded children, or the "Bank Street Readers" (1965) may be more appropriate for retarded readers and may better help them learn though they are somewhat dated.

All books for young children—whether part of the literature program, information books, or reading textbooks—need to be assessed for how they treat their human characters. Teachers need to be aware of racism, sexism, ageism, and classism as well as stereotyped treatments of people with disabilities. A guide in selecting appropriate books for children is *Guidelines for Bias-free Textbooks and Storybooks* published by the Council on Interracial Books for Children (1841 Broadway, New York, NY 10023). If books that reflect stereotypes are used in the class, the teacher needs to talk with the children about them, possibly explaining why such stereotypes exist and helping children understand that such stereotypes do not reflect reality.

Appropriate basal readers can help socialize children by describing experiences that prepare them for their roles in society while teaching reading. The content of basal readers also can help children solve problems. Since the children can learn to deal with difficulties by reading about them, basal readers can nurture independent behavior.

The characters in the basal readers can become role models for children.

TABLE 12.1   Strengths of Basal Reading Series for children with hearing impairments

Basal Reading Series	Strength
"Reading Milestones"	1. Vocabulary appropriate in terms of difficulty 2. Sufficient repetition of vocabulary 3. Syntax appropriate in terms of difficulty 4. Appropriate idiomatic or figurative expression load 5. Appropriate interest level 6. Phonics emphasis not too heavy 7. Appropriate conceptual load 8. Helpful supplementary materials 9. Usefulness not limited to children who are linguistically competent 10. Can be used with some modification with most hearing-impaired children at this level
"Ginn 360/720"	1. Appropriate interest level 2. Appropriate conceptual load 3. Helpful supplementary materials 4. Useful information from diagnostic tests 5. Can be used with some modification with most hearing-impaired children at this level
"Houghton Mifflin Readers"	1. Appropriate interest level 2. Helpful supplementary materials 3. Useful information from diagnostic tests 4. Can be used with some modification with most hearing-impaired children at this level
"Systems Unlimited"	1. Appropriate conceptual load 2. Helpful supplementary materials 3. Can be used with some modification with most hearing-impaired children at this level

However, achievement themes for males are found in the basal readers with greater frequency than for females. Achievement imagery in basal readers needs to be equalized for both sexes (McCloud, Mitchell, & Ragland, 1976). Without this change, other role-modeling materials must be provided for the girls in the class.

Increasingly, basal readers are incorporating literature in their texts. This has the advantage of providing more interesting and better written stories. The language of the readers has also become more realistic with the inclusion of these materials. Supplemental reading materials, including easy-to-read story books used in classes, also extend the reading opportunities provided to young children.

Instructional Materials

Reading instruction is concerned with materials, approaches, and testing procedures. Stimulating instructional reading materials, including books, worksheets, and audio-visual materials, can improve children's reading. Materials should be evaluated in relation to reading difficulty, interest, relevance, and their potential for helping to achieve reading goals.

The Federal Act on the Education of the Blind, as amended by Public Law 91-230 (1970), provides blind students who are enrolled in educational programs below college level with textbooks and educational aids through the American Printing House for the Blind. These materials are dispensed to the various educational programs through quota allocations, determined by the total number of blind pupils registered in a school.

The teacher can use the services of the American Printing House for the Blind to select the best types of educational materials, including textbooks and recordings. It is helpful to determine the type of school program that students with visual disabilities are attending, the degree of vision they have, and the reading materials they are using. For example, children who are partially sighted employ more of their residual vision by using regular ink and large-type readers and decreasing the use of Braille.

Instructional materials that help children organize groups of objects, explore patterns in a systematic fashion, and schematize figures and patterns help develop the children's visual perception. Students with visual impairments may need to use their fingers to follow reading words to foster their perceptual skills.

Braillers. Braillers—machines that produce Braille characters on paper—can be stored in the classroom on shelves within children's reach. Ideally, there should be a Brailler at the desk of each primary-grade child who is visually impaired and who needs to use one, just as sighted children have pencils and paper available. The opportunity to experiment and practice with the Brailler is essential to the child who is visually impaired in order to learn to read and write and to learn the keys of the Brailler. The Brailler can be used to write stories, copy words for the word bank, or write sentences.

Some educators have reservations about instruction in reading and writing Braille for children who are visually impaired. Braille is difficult, but it is possible to learn to read it visually. Children with unimpaired vision are curious about it and think using it is fun. Teachers and sighted children decode Braille visually by using the Braille chart. Specialists should be responsible for teaching Braille reading and writing as well as providing appropriate books and reference materials.

The child who is blind will need other supplies also. The Braille alphabet is important for the severely visually impaired. Each child should have a copy of this alphabet, and his or her Braille name should be taped to the desk for reference. An abundant supply of Braille paper (heavy bond paper) should be available in the classroom. These children must have a supply at their desks and know where to get more when they need it. They should have their own binders for the paper, along with a hole puncher to allow them to file their papers and have them at their disposal.

Braille words are small and are easily kept in envelopes or deposited in a file box that becomes their word bank. Each school with children who are severely visually impaired should own a thermoform machine that uses a heat process to make copies of Braille pages, and teachers can copy dictated stories or instructional materials for the blind children on these machines (Curry, 1975). The state Commission for the Blind or the Department of Social Services may pay the special reading teacher to help children with visual disabilities and may provide instructional material.

Tape Recorders. Cassette tape recorders allow children who are visually impaired to listen to taped stories in the classroom while reading along in Braille. Children can make recordings for others to listen to and to follow along with thermoform copies. Recorders also can be placed in different learning centers to provide more elaborate instructions for these children, similar to those provided on assignment cards for sighted children. These recorders should be accessible to children with and without disabilities. The children's personal recordings can be used to record lessons as well as to help the teacher assess their work. The teacher may use the same content and concepts in these recordings as in a textbook. The material should be revised so concepts are presented in simple language and at the child's level.

Several other pieces of equipment can be used to strengthen concepts. Audio-tutorial lessons, for example, allow students to learn at their own pace. Such lessons may include an audiotape accompanied by a workbook, a filmstrip, a set of slides, or videotape. Pacing machines for reading, electronic readers, and computers also can be used with children with disabilities.

Ross and Wright (1987) suggested several guidelines for the classroom environment of a reader who is gifted.

1. Provide instruction in basic reading skills (when necessary).
2. Provide instructions in critical and creative comprehension skills.
3. Offer reading materials that are creative and challenging.
4. Provide long-term, thought-provoking opportunities for gifted readers to share their products.

Reading occurs in all areas of the curriculum. A strong writing-reading connection in the classroom can help integrate learning (Ganopole, 1988). Writing tasks can easily be adapted to meet the gifted readers' exceptional needs.

TEACHERS' MANAGEMENT SYSTEMS

Once teachers have assessed their students, developed appropriate instructional methods, and selected materials, they need to design a workable management system for the classroom. Individuals must work together to meet all their needs in a class. Careful planning can provide the basis for effective reading instruction for children with disabilities within the regular classroom. Children's special services in reading should be scheduled during the reading period so they will be taken out of the classroom when they usually experience failure, rather than during activities when they experience success. The classroom teacher should work closely with the special reading teacher to coordinate these children's programs.

Assisting the Teacher

Additional adults—reading specialists, parent volunteers, college students, or teacher's aides—might serve as resources in a class. Children also can serve as tutors. Tutoring gives the child a feeling of importance and can increase self-esteem. It also provides a review of reading material in which that child is working. In the process, the reader will encounter tasks that require some skills that need to be developed. These tasks may challenge, excite, and stimulate the child to be degree that he or she starts a learning plan and seeks help.

Another successful approach is the "buddy system," using teams of two members each. The younger team member may be in grades 1 to 3, and the older team member is usually of middle school age. During their meetings, the older buddies help the children select books, listen to them read, help them with difficult words, and read aloud to them. The buddy is also a friend (Himmelsteib, 1979). The reading teacher and the classroom teacher serve as consultants for these volunteers, recommending suitable activities and games and providing in-service workshops for them.

Grouping

Grouping is one way of individualizing instruction. Many students may have common needs; it is more effective to teach them in a group than individually. For instance, children who need to learn to use initial consonant substitution may be grouped together for that topic. In addition, some children usually learn better in a group than individually, learning from one another's responses. Many children seem less pressured and more relaxed in a group setting.

Children can be grouped for reading instruction within a classroom or by interclass grouping arrangements, by achievement level, age, or interest. According to Wilson and Ribovich (1973), the most common ways that teachers group children include

1. *Heterogeneous grouping*, where children are instructed in the same grade disregarding ability of achievement.
2. *Homogeneous grouping*, where children are divided based on academic ability.
3. *Special grouping arrangement*, where children are grouped across grades based on reading or other achievement levels regardless of age.
4. *Team teaching arrangement*, where children are grouped based on the strengths of individual teachers and where a team of teachers plan together for the instruction of children assigned to them.

Wilson and Ribovich have suggested using alternative grouping patterns, including open grouping, flexible skill grouping, and paired grouping. In *open grouping,* children can select their own groups. Children may decide to join a reading group because they want to be challenged or because they are interested in the story being read. This type of grouping requires that the activities and stories be announced ahead of time so the children can plan their selections. Before the group meeting, the teacher can have the story read to visiting children who may have difficulty reading it themselves. Thus, visiting children will be able to discuss what they already know about the story.

In *flexible skill grouping*, children are grouped temporarily according to their similar skill strengths or skill needs. Children in a group are similar in one skill area, though not necessarily similar in all skill areas. Children's status in relation to a particular skill changes, and therefore the groupings change. Flexibility is employed when children's differences are perceived as considerable and dynamic.

A third alternative is *paired grouping* in which children are divided flexibly and temporarily in pairs. One child may teach the other and they both learn together. Paired grouping, like skill grouping, assumes that strengths and needs are often independent of general ability level or reading level. An individual's strengths can be demonstrated and internalized by teaching someone else, yet each child's needs are met by receiving help. All children can teach and be taught. For instance, Michael may help Janie with sounds and may receive help from Dahlia on syllabication. Pairing can cross ages, with students at one level helping younger children at another level.

Multi-age grouping, also called family grouping, offers an enriched intellectual community for children and permits cross-age tutoring (Spodek, 1985). Children help and instruct one another, the pressures of age expectations are alleviated, and the individual's own abilities are the basis for judgments about programs. There has been increased interest in multi-age grouping in recent years (Katz, Evangelou, & Hartman, 1990). Such a grouping can provide additional flexibility in integrating children with disabilities into a class.

Another way to provide for individualization is by creating a wide range of learning alternatives for children to select. Independent and group learning are encouraged through an environment in which children are permitted to behave freely and reasonably. A classroom organized into interest centers encourages children by supporting activities in which they participate. Experimentation and continuous modification of the physical setting can support a dynamic learning situation.

Reading through Discovery and Investigation

Children can learn to read through discovery and investigation. Teachers can plan reading lessons related to their instructional goals. Reading becomes personalized by having children experience and internalize reading materials.

A group of first-graders may be fascinated with the story of the Gingerbread Man. The teacher will provide a series of activities related to the story. Such activities can include reading, telling, and listening to the story; viewing a film of the Gingerbread Man; learning a song; and dramatizing the story. This can be done by first having the children discuss the Gingerbread Man and asking the children questions such as "What type of character is the Gingerbread Man?" "How does he run?" "How does he walk?" They can imitate the Gingerbread Man and develop their own dialogues based on the familiar story. They can then write stories about or draw pictures of the Gingerbread Man.

One morning they can bake a Gingerbread Man, then go for a walk. When they return to their classroom, they will find their Gingerbread Man gone. In his place they find a note that might say, "I went to the principal's office." The class can go to several places, each time finding a note. The final note will send them back to their room, where they find the Gingerbread Man. Each note should reflect their reading vocabulary. When they arrive at their classroom, they can discuss the experience and eat the Gingerbread Man.

Follow-up activities can include reading more about baking. Other stories and other interests about the Gingerbread Man may develop. The teacher can construct a chart for children to plot their working location, plan their activities, and record their progress. For example, John and Joe may conduct research in the library, Frances may discuss the Gingerbread Man with a group of other children, and Pablo may write a book on the Gingerbread Man with another group of children (Spodek, Saracho, & Lee, 1984). Using the children's interests can promote reading skills because the reading material will be relevant and interesting. Teachers need to be careful that topics are changed once children lose interest.

SUMMARY

Reading—the process of abstracting meaning from the written language—is one of the most important academic skills. Anyone who expects to function independently in our society must acquire this skill. Before children begin to learn to read, they must gain basic knowledge of the language and develop auditory discrimination skills, visual discrimination skills, and motor skills.

There are many approaches to teaching reading to children, including the whole-word approach, the phonics approach, the language experience approach, and the basal reader approach. No one approach is best for all children with all types of learning characteristics in all situations. Most teachers use a combination of approaches.

In integrated classes, teachers must be aware of the advantages and disadvantages of each approach for teaching reading. They must assess their children's abilities and tailor programs so each child's program includes elements of each approach. Careful preparation of the learning environment and thoughtful selection of teaching material are vital. Most important, the reading program should be carefully coordinated with the total language arts program in the classroom, a topic that is addressed in chapter 11.

REFERENCES

Anderson, R. C. (1984). Some reflection on the acquisition of knowledge. *Educational Researcher, 13*, 5–10.

Andrews, J. F. (1988). Deaf children's acquisition of prereading skills: The reciprocal teaching procedure. *Exceptional Children, 54*, 349–355.

Bennett, R., Ragosta, M., & Stricker, L. (1984). *The test performance of handicapped people* (Report No. 2: Studies of Admission Testing and Handicapped People). Princeton, NJ: Educational Testing Service.

Brown, L., Huppler, B., Pierce, L., York, B., & Sontag, E. (1974). Teaching trainable–level students to read unconjugated action verbs. *Journal of Special Education, 8*(1), 51–56.

Carney, J. J., Cioffi, G., & Raymond, M. W. (1985). Using sign language for teaching sight words. *Teaching Exceptional Children, 17*, 214–217.

Cassidy, J. (1981). Inquiry reading for the gifted. *The Reading Teacher, 35*(10), 17–21.

Cassidy, J., & Vukelick, C. (1980). Do the gifted read early? *The Reading Teacher, 33*, 578–582.

Chomsky, C. (1981). Write now, read later. In C. Cazden (Ed.), *Language in early childhood education* (pp. 141–145). Washington, DC: National Association for the Education of Young Children.

Clark, B. (1988). *Growing up gifted* (3rd ed.). Columbus, OH: Merrill.

Clark, M. M. (1984). Literacy at home and at school: Insights from a study of young fluent readers. In H. Goelman, A. Oberg, & F. Smith (Eds.), *Awakening to literacy.* Exeter, NH: Heinemann.

Clay, M. M. (1979). *Reading: The patterning of complex behavior.* Exeter, NH: Heinemann.

Council on Interracial Books for Children (1980). *Guidelines for selecting bias-free textbooks and storybooks.* New York: The Council.

Curry, R. G. (1975). Using LEA to teach blind children to read. *The Reading Teacher, 29,* 272–279.

Curtis, M. E. (1980). Development of components of reading skill. *Journal of Educational Psychology, 72,* 656–669.

Cutsforth, T. D. (1951). *The blind in school and society.* New York: American Foundation for the Blind.

Durkin, D. (1966). *Children who read early.* New York: Teachers College Press.

Durr, W. K., Hillerich, R., & Johnson, T. G. (1983). *Getting ready to read.* Boston: Houghton Mifflin.

Dyson, A. H. (1993). From prop to mediator: The changing role of written language in children's symbolic repertoires. In B. Spodek & O. N. Saracho (Eds.), *Language and literacy in early childhood education: Yearbook in early childhood education* (Vol. 4). New York: Teachers College Press.

Estes, W. K. (1970). *Learning theory and mental development.* New York: Academic Press.

Fox, B., & Rought, D. K. (1980). Phonemic analysis and severe reading disability. *Journal of Psycholinguistic Research, 9,* 115–119.

Friedman, J. B., & Gillooley, W. B. (1977). Perceptual development in the profoundly deaf as related to early reading. *Journal of Special Education, 11,* 347–354.

Functional Basic Reading Series. (1963, 1964, 1965). Pittsburgh: Stanwix House.

Ganopole, S. J. (1988). Reading and writing for the gifted: A whole language perspective. *Roeper Review, 11*(2), 88–92.

Garner, R. (1987). *Metacognition and reading comprehension.* Norwood, NJ: Ablex.

Gillet, J. W., & Temple, C. (1990). *Understanding reading problems: Assessment and Instruction* (3rd ed.). Boston: Little, Brown & Co.

Goodman, K. S. (1968). *The psycholinguist nature of the reading process.* Detroit: Wayne State University Press.

Guszak, F. J. (1985). *Diagnostic reading instruction in the elementary school* (3rd ed). New York: Harper & Row.

Healy, J. M. (1982). The enigma of hyperlexia. *Reading Research Quarterly, 17,* 319–338.

Hiebert, E. H. (1981). Developmental patterns and interrelationships of preschool children's print awareness. *Reading Research Quarterly, 16,* 236–260.

Hillerich, R. L. (1974). So you're evaluating reading programs. *Elementary School Journal, 75,* 172–182.

Himmelsteib, C. (1979). Buddies read in a library program. *Reading Teacher, 29*(1), 32–38.

Jackson, N. E. (1988). *Teaching gifted children through motor learning.* Springfield, IL: Charles C. Thomas.

Jackson, N. E., Donaldson, G. W., & Cleland, L. N. (1988). The structure of precocious reading ability. *Journal of Educational Psychology, 80,* 234–243.

Jackson, N. E., & Myers, M. G. (1982). Letter naming, time, digit span, and precocious reading achievement. *Intelligence, 6,* 311–329.

Johnson, D. J. (1979). Process deficits in learning disabled children and implications for reading. In L. B. Resnick and P. A. Weaver (Eds.), *Theory and practice of early reading* (Vol. 2, pp. 207–227). Hillsdale, NJ: Erlbaum.

Katz, L. G., Evangelou, D., & Hartman, J. (1990). *The case for mixed–age grouping in early education*. Washington, DC: National Association for the Education of Young Children.

Kirk, S. A., Kliebhan, J. M., & Lerner, J. W. (1978). *Teaching reading to slow and disabled learners*. Boston: Houghton Mifflin.

LaSasso, C. (1987). Survey of reading instruction for hearing impaired students in the United States. *Volta Review, 89*(2), 85–98.

Lewkowics, N. (1980). Phonemic awareness training: What to teach and how to teach it. *Journal of Educational Psychology, 72*, 686–700.

Liberman, I. Y., & Shankweiler, D. (1985). Phonology and the problems of learning to read and write. *Remedial and Special Education, 6*, 8–17.

McCloud, B. K., Mitchell, M. M., & Ragland, G. G. (1976). Content analysis of basal reading texts for normal and retarded children. *Journal of Special Education, 10*, 259–264.

McNeil, J. D. (1984). *Reading comprehension: New directions for classroom practice*. Glenview, IL: Scott Foresman.

Mangieri, J. N., & Madigan, F. (1984). Issues in reading instruction. *Roeper Review, 7*(2), 68–70.

Martin, C. E. (1984). Why some gifted children do not like to read. *Roeper Review, 7*(2), 72–74.

Martin, C. E., & Cramond, B. (1983). Creative reading: Is it being taught to the gifted in the elementary schools? *Journal of Education of the Gifted, 6*(2), 70–79.

Mason, J. (1980). When do children begin to read: An exploration of four-year-old children's letter and word reading competencies. *Reading Research Quarterly, 15*, 203–227.

Mason, J. (1986). Kindergarten reading: A proposal for a problem-solving approach. In B. Spodek (Ed.), *Today's kindergarten: Exploring the knowledge base, expanding the curriculum* (pp. 48–66). New York: Teachers College Press.

Maxwell, M. M. (1986, March). Beginning reading and deaf children. *American Annals of the Deaf*, 14–20.

Milgram, N. A. (1973). Cognition and language in mental retardation: Distinctions and implications. In D. K. Routh (Ed.), *The experimental psychology of mental retardation* (pp. 19–34). Chicago: Aldine.

Morrow, L. M. (1986). Promoting responses to literature: Children's sense of story structure. Paper presented at the National Reading Conference, Austin, TX.

Morrow, L. M. (1993). *Literacy development in the early years: Helping children read and write*. Englewood Cliffs, NJ: Prentice-Hall.

Perfetti, C. A. (1985). *Reading ability*. New York: Oxford University Press.

Raines, S. C. (1990). *The whole language kindergarten*. New York: Teachers College Press.

Ramanauskas, S. (1972). Contextual constraints beyond a sentence on close responses of mentally retarded children. *American Journal of Mental Deficiency, 77*, 338–345.

Raver, S. A., & Dwyer, R. C. (1986). Teaching handicapped preschoolers to sight read using language training procedures. *Reading Teacher, 40*(3), 314–321.

Reid, D. K., & Hresko, W. P. (1981). *A cognitive approach to learning disabilities*. New York: McGraw-Hill.

Ross, E. P., & Wright, J. (1987). Matching teaching strategies to the learning styles of gifted readers. *Reading Horizons, 28*(1), 49–56.

Saracho, O. N. (1983). Cognitive style and Mexican American children's perception of reading. In T. Escobedo (Ed.), *Early childhood education: A bilingual perspective* (pp. 202–221). New York: Teachers College Press.

Saracho, O. N. (1984). Young children's conceptual factors of reading. *Early Child Development and Care, 15*(4), 305–314.

Saracho, O. N. (1985a). The impact of young children's print awareness in learning to read. *Early Child Development and Care, 21*(1), 1–10.

Saracho, O. N. (1985b). The roots of reading and writing. *New directions in reading research and practice.* 1985 Yearbook of the State of Maryland International Association, 81–87.

Saracho, O. N. (1986). The development of the preschool reading attitude scale. *Child Study Journal, 16*(2), 113–124.

Saracho, O. N. (1987). Evaluating reading attitudes. *Day Care and Early Education, 14,* 23–25.

Saracho, O. N. (1988). Preschool Reading Attitude Scale. *Early Child Development and Care, 37,* 93–108.

Schickedanz, J. A. (1978). Please read that story again! *Young Children, 33*(5), 48–55.

Schickedanz, J. A. (1982). The acquisition of written language in young children. In B. Spodek (Ed.), *Handbook of research in early childhood education* (pp. 242–263). New York: The Free Press.

Schuele, R., & Van Kleeck, A. (1984). Assessment and intervention: Does "meta" matter? In G. Wallach & K. Butler (Eds.), *Language learning disabilities in school-age children.* Baltimore: Williams & Wilkins.

Simms, R. B., & Falcon, S. C. (1987). Teaching sight words. *Teaching Exceptional Children, 20*(1), 30–33.

Smith, F. (1978). *Psycholinguistics and reading.* New York: Holt, Rinehart & Winston.

Snider, V. E., & Tarver, S. G. (1987). The effect of early reading on acquisition of knowledge among students with learning disabilities. *Journal of Learning Disabilities, 200*(6), 351–356, 373.

Snow, C. E., & Tabors, P. O. (1993). Language skills related to literacy development. In B. Spodek & O. N. Saracho (Eds.), *Language and literacy in early childhood education: Yearbook in early childhood education* (Vol. 4). New York: Teachers College Press.

Spache, G. D., & Spache, E. B. (1986). *Reading in the elementary school* (4th ed.). Boston: Allyn & Bacon.

Spitz, H. (1973). The channel capacity of educable mental retardates. In D. K. Routh (Ed.), *The experimental psychology of mental retardation.* Chicago: Aldine.

Spodek, B. (1985). *Teaching in the early years* (3rd ed.). Englewood Cliffs, NJ: Prentice-Hall.

Spodek, B., Saracho, O. N., & Lee, R. C. (1984). *Mainstreaming young children.* Belmont, CA: Wadsworth.

Stauffer, R.G. (1975). *Directing the reading–thinking process.* New York: Harper & Row.

Stauffer, R.G. (1980). *The language experience approach to the teaching of reading.* New York: Harper & Row.

Sulzby, E. (1985). Children's emergent reading of favorite storybooks. *Reading Research Quarterly, 20,* 458–481.

Teale, W. (1986). The beginning of reading and writing: Written language development during the preschool and kindergarten years. In M. Sampson (Ed.), *The pursuit of literacy: Early reading and writing.* Dubuque, IA: Kendall/Hunt.

Torvey, D. R., & Kerber, J. E. (Eds.) (1986). *Roles in literacy learning: A new perspective.* Newark, DE: International Reading Association.

Venezky, R.L. (1975). *Prereading skills: Theoretical foundations and practical applications* (Theoretical Paper No. 54). Madison: University of Wisconsin, Wisconsin Research and Development Center for Cognitive Learning.

Williams, J. (1979). The ABD's of reading: A program for the learning disabled. In L. B. Resnick and P. A. Weaver (Eds.), *Theory and practice of early reading,* Vol. 3 (pp. 179–195). Hillsdale, NJ: Erlbaum.

Wilson, R. M., and Ribovich, J. K. (1973). Ability grouping? Stop and reconsider! *Reading World, 13,* 84–91.

Yaden, D. D., Jr. (1986). *Metalinguistic awareness: Conceptualizing what it means to read and write.* Portsmouth, NH: Heinemann.

Zjawin, D., Longnecker, N., Pelow, R., & Chant, S. (1981). Everyday reading. *Instructor, 90,* 44–47.

CHAPTER 13

Teaching Social Studies, Science, and Mathematics

CHAPTER OVERVIEW

This chapter discusses:

1. The elements of an early childhood social studies program: intellectualization, socialization, the development of values, and the development of self awareness.
2. Ways of modifying each area of the social studies programs for diverse young children.
3. The goals of early childhood science programs.
4. Ways of modifying science programs for diverse young children.
5. The goals of early childhood mathematics programs.
6. Ways of modifying mathematics programs for diverse young children.

Social studies, science, and mathematics are generally taught to all pupils in their regular class. As with all aspects of mainstreaming, however, responsibility must be shared by both regular and special teachers. This chapter discusses strategies for modifying instruction in these areas for children with special needs.

INTEGRATING SOCIAL STUDIES EDUCATION

Young children need to be helped to understand themselves, the world around them, and their relationship to it. As children receive feedback from the outside world, they also learn about themselves. They need to develop knowledge and skills that are essential both for their everyday life and for future learning. Young children have direct access to the physical world, learning about physical things by touching them, listening to them, or viewing them. Social phenomena are less directly accessible. Although young children have direct contact with people and can observe their behavior directly, they need to learn to interpret these observable behaviors.

Social studies can assist children with special needs to be contributing members of their communities by including a concern for citizenship and providing information, skills, and values development to considerably contribute to their knowledge of the world (Patton, Polloway, & Cronin, 1967).

The basic justification for social studies instruction for all students is just as valid for students with special needs (Patton, Polloway, & Cronin, 1987). Polloway, Payne, Patton, and Payne (1985) suggested the following rationales:

- Providing firsthand experiences that are particularly useful for becoming familiar with one's surroundings.
- Providing opportunities to apply basic skills in meaningful contexts.
- Developing a rich experiential background to establish "knowledge framework into which students can integrate new ideas, relationships, and details".
- Providing opportunities to analyze personal values.
- Providing opportunities to develop critical thinking, information processing skills, and human relations skills.
- Allowing for the acquisition of information and skills that are necessary for adult living and contribute to lifelong interests.

The social studies program, from preschool through the primary grades, should be composed of four processes: intellectualization, socialization, development of values, and the development of self-awareness (Spodek, 1985).

Intellectual Processes

Piaget (1970) stressed the significance of developing logical reasoning. Children experience the world and abstract information from these experiences through their senses. These are organized into *schema*. New experiences are related to prior experiences and to concepts previously attained. Prior concepts are expanded as new information is *assimilated*, or added to the child's existing schema. When prior concepts no longer fit, they are modified through the process of restructuring called *accommodation*. These two processes, assimilation and accommodation, create continual changes toward a balance (or *equilibrium*) in understanding. This equilibration process takes place in relation to social studies knowledge as it does in other areas of knowledge. Piaget spoke of different forms of knowledge including physical knowledge, social knowledge, and logico-mathematical knowledge. *Physical knowledge* is knowledge of the physical attributes of things. We can provide such knowledge through direct experiences, such as field trips, observations, and interviews. Once children gain a sense of the world, we can substitute indirect sources such as texts, audiovisual material, and simulations for direct experiences in the same vein.

Social knowledge—the knowledge of social conventions, symbols, values, rituals, and myths—relates to right and wrong social behavior and rules. It cannot be discovered easily; thus, it must be taught to children either directly or indirectly. *Logico-mathematical knowledge* consists of intellectual processes that are used to organize and make sense of information; these include classifying and ordering objects and events, quantifying objects and events, observing and identifying relationships, and placing things into the proper time-space context. We represent our ideas and feelings through pictures, maps, play activities, and stories. In an inquiry-oriented social studies program, children gather social data, arrange the data, interpret them, and represent the products of their inquiry.

Modifying Programs for Diverse Children

Gifted children have social, physical, and emotional needs similar to all children. The difference between the average and the gifted is that gifted children develop in the areas of intellectual and creative expression at an advanced rate. They also need greater depth and complexity of subject matter than is usual for their age. This intense desire for knowledge, understanding, and creative expression must be met. However, it is also necessary to nurture social, emotional, and physical skills for these children (Neisworth & Bagnato, 1987).

Because gifted children are different, though in a positive way, they encounter problems and pressures. Most of the problems of gifted children probably arise from two major factors: (1) interpersonal differences—wide discrepancies between gifted and normal age-appropriate behavior; and (2) intrapersonal differences—discrepancies among the various levels of development within a given child.

Gifted young children frequently are sensitive to and can accurately read social situations. They begin to sense the differences between themselves and their peers during their early years. Early guidance in how to cope with being different is important to gifted as to children with disabilities. Making and keeping friends is crucial to all children, and all preschoolers need help in learning to cooperate with, tolerate, and accept people who are different (Neisworth & Bagnato, 1987).

Teachers need to encourage young gifted children to engage in higher-order thinking processes and problem-solving strategies, even within the constraints of a prescribed curriculum (Safford, 1989). It is critical that all children, but especially children who are intellectually gifted, use their intelligence (Clark, 1986). This involves assigning more complex—rather than simple, redundant, or repetitive—tasks; providing challenge and novelty; requiring students to anticipate and plan for future consequences; and presenting real problems for which multiple solutions might be considered.

Teachers need to personalize competition in order that gifted young children, like all young children, compete against their own past performance. Disparity among the accomplishments of children within a group are less obvious, for each child's standard of performance is a personal one. Also, errors that perfectionist gifted children see as failures are more likely to be considered a natural component of the learning process (Safford, 1989).

Teachers need to adapt advanced materials so that young gifted children can manage them and be motivated despite their more mature interests and more advanced cognitive levels. In addition, teachers need to modify the time requirements and to incorporate appropriate activity components matched to the individual gifted child's needs in the areas of motor and social skills. A given activity may be geared to the gifted children's level and to their levels in different areas of functioning, some of which may be expected based on their chronological age, others more or less advanced (Safford, 1989).

The concept of children who are at risk suggests a particularly critical role for early childhood education programs in the area of prevention. There is an opportunity to identify early those indicators of at-risk that might be present and, through early intervention, to increase the probability that the child's development will be optimal (Safford, 1989).

Although some disabilities make it more difficult for children to use their intellectual skills in certain subject areas, they should not be avoided. Some children may have language or reading problems. Others may have trouble remembering content and deriving generalizations. Nevertheless, all should be encouraged to continue to work in all curriculum areas and should be provided with the necessary additional resources. If children learn slowly, the expected pace of learning should be modified and a greater variety of activities and experiences provided to illustrate the same ideas. Learning centers such as those discussed in chapter 7 can be established where individuals or small groups of children can work at their own pace. Dramatic play areas can be designed to reflect different social institutions. Audiovisual media including pictures, charts, films, filmstrips, and records can be used. Braille atlases, textured relief maps molded of plastic, and talking books can be made available. Written materials, when they are used, should be at the children's reading level and should be supplemented by other materials, including tapes of the text, maps, charts, newspapers, and magazines. Thematic units or group projects can allow children to help one another and can provide opportunities for informal peer tutoring.

Children who are developmentally delayed usually take longer than their normal peers to learn concepts and may need more, and more varied, experiences to attain concepts at a simpler level. These children and those with learning disabilities should be provided with information in small, manageable steps; and concrete representations of ideas should be offered to them. The teacher can identify problems that arise and provide for the missing links in the learning chain, retracing each step to determine what help is needed for those who failed to learn a concept. Active involvement in inquiry activities, as opposed to passive sitting, looking, and listening, facilitates concept learning. Once children have learned a concept, they need to practice it.

The motor problems of children with cerebral palsy may restrict their capacity to process information. The effects of the disability will depend on the location of the affected areas and the severity of the disability. Cognitive learning becomes a problem when organic or functional language disabilities restrict children's access to information or their capacity to make experiences coherent. Teachers can provide language experiences to these children in a meaningful context while using prompting, fading, and modeling to help them assimilate language learning. Cuing techniques employing verbal instruction along with gestures or other physical means of prodding can also help children remember responses. Selecting appropriate cues to use with individual children requires teachers to analyze which cues work.

Sociodramatic play helps children process information and generate concepts. Some children with disabilities may need additional prompting, cuing, or modeling to act out a role properly. Children can play at shopping in the grocery store with a large number of grocery items (e.g., empty coffee cans, fruit cans, cereal boxes) displayed on a table. Some children can be shoppers, buying groceries in the store, while others are grocery workers, helping with the selection and tallying the cost of what is bought. Shoppers can place their selections in a large paper sack to take home. The children can unpack their groceries and place them on sections of the table labeled *breakfast, lunch,* and *dinner*. Teachers should observe the play and provide whatever support is necessary. Discussion can follow about the process of shopping, what foods are eaten at which meal, and what constitutes a balanced meal.

Similar activities can be designed with other objects that can be categorized and discussed. For example, toy cars, boats, and airplanes can be grouped as means of land, sea, and air transportation. Dollhouse furniture can be classified into kitchen, bedroom, and living room furniture (Walsh, 1980).

Children need to adapt to, relate to, and interpret their environment. Children who are visually impaired may need a greater variety of experiences with objects than other children do. Although these children develop intellectually in the same way as sighted children, they cannot use vision to gather information. A social studies curriculum that focuses on concrete experiences is probably more important for children who are visually impaired than for children who are fully sighted.

Socialization

In socializing children, the teacher helps them learn their roles in both the school community and the larger community and helps them develop social skills. Children must learn the way society is organized and the shared values, rituals, symbols, and myths of the community. Children learn these through holiday celebrations, stories about historic figures and heroes, and traditional stories and songs. Experiences that permit students to inquire about social phenomena provide the children with an understanding of the organization of society and the expectations of their role.

Children need to learn the rules, expectations, mores, and values of the school. This is especially important during preschool and kindergarten, which may be the children's first experience in school. The rituals of daily life and the teacher's classroom organization, way of establishing and enforcing rules, provisions for independent activity, and selection of experiences are all related to children's socialization and are an important part of social studies.

Children with disabilities need to be socialized as much as do children without disabilities, although there may be problems that affect their rate of social development. Children's disabilities influenced their social interaction patterns in several ways. In some settings a disability is a social disturbance, especially when people react negatively to a observed disability. Society tends to punish children with disabilities, restricting their social contacts and impairing their normal social development. Such children may encounter problems in appropriately expressing anger, hostility, guilt, and frustration. They may be highly introverted and fearful. They may also fail to enjoy their achievements and become increasingly dependent on others. Children who are socially incompetent often are mistreated by their classmates, causing them to withdraw even further from social situations. Withdrawn children need to learn to offer positive social reinforcement to their peers in order to become socially accepted (Charlesworth & Hartup, 1967). Keller and Carlson (1974) suggest symbolic modeling—showing appropriate behavior with pictures or stories—as a way to decrease children's fear of interaction with peers.

Children with behavior disorders need more than learning to restrict their behavior and develop academic competencies. Direct attention must be provided to their interpersonal and social needs. McGinnis and Goldstein (1990) provide a program to maintain and generalize social skills. They outline the following steps:

Enhancing motivation
1. Choose skills related to the children's perceptions of their needs.
2. Select the initial skills to be taught by selecting the ones with which the children are more likely to succeed.
3. Provide instruction early so that children practice the skills throughout the remainder of the day.
4. Reinforce the children when they successfully use the skills.

Identifying situations
1. Allow children to identify unique circumstances in which the skill can be used.
2. Identify other skill-related circumstances through observing the children's classroom behavior and querying the participants.

Presenting the behavioral steps
1. Discuss each step and any relevant information regarding that step.
2. Chart the skills steps through illustrations that are easily seen by all group members.

Modeling
1. Provide at least two examples to teach the skill that is demonstrated.
2. Choose circumstances related to the children's life experiences.
3. Provide a model to demonstrate the right sequence for the skill.
4. Provide displays that demonstrate the each step in sequence for the skill. (Extraneous content should be deleted.)
5. Have a model.
6. Have the model say the steps out loud.
7. Portray only positive results.
8. Reinforce the model when the correct skill is used.

Guiding the role play

1. Select a child to be the main actor who will describe an event in his or her own life in which the skill is used effectively.
2. Allow the main actor to select a coactor to remind him or her of a person with whom he or she has a problem.
3. Present related information encompassing the real situation (such as describing the physical setting and situations preceding the problem).
4. Exercise the use of props as much as possible.
5. Review skill steps and direct the primary actor to refer to the skill chart.
6. Persuade the other participants to look out for specific steps in the skill.
7. Instruct the main actor to think out loud.
8. Allow one leader to help the main actor (e.g., point to each behavioral step during role play); let the other leader sit among the rest of the group to direct their attention to the role play.

Performance feedback

1. Pursue feedback from the coactor, observers, leaders, and main actor.
2. Reinforce as soon as possible after the role plays.
3. Reinforce the coactor for being helpful and cooperative.
4. Phrase specific elements of performance.
5. Reinforce consistently based on the extent of the quality of the role play.

Maintenance

Maintain the learned behaviors by using individual or group purposes to observe and reward the skill that was used. Thus, self-monitoring, group emphasis on target skills, awards, and skill folders are appropriate.

Further explanation of this program can be found in *Skillstreaming in Early Childhood* (McGinnis & Goldstein, 1990).

McGinnis, Sauerbry, and Nichols (1985) suggested the following social steps to help children deal with wanting something that is not theirs:

1. Say to yourself, "I want this, but I can't just take it."
2. Say, "It belongs to _____."
3. Think of your choices.
    a. You could ask the person to loan (or share) it.
    b. You could earn the money to buy it.
    c. You could ask the person to trade.
4. Act out your best choice.

Social development can be enhanced if the negative aspects of a disability and its related coping factors are explained and discussed with those who know and care about children with disabilities, helping them learn self-control. A positive, trusting relationship between a child and the significant adults in that child's life can provide the foundation for developing trust. Children who mistrust adults are continuously testing them to discover the status of their relationship. A positive relationship avoids irritation and frustration and can help children cope with their disabilities.

An accepting relationship is essential in a least restrictive environment. Most children with disabilities will probably never lose their disabilities, and parents and teachers need to accept these children's limitations and maximize their capacities for the best possible social development. These children need to function in as normal a social environment as possible. To this end, teachers need to promote active social involvement. Children with disabilities need to learn manners they can apply in different learning situations and settings. Acceptable social behavior learned in the classroom can be used at home, on the playground, or in community settings. Children's interactions affect their social awareness. Appropriate curriculum content and teaching methods can support the socialization processes in early childhood development.

Values

Values are moral principles or standards that are part of an individual's code of living and are employed daily in regular life patterns. They are an integral part of life (e.g., religion, traditions, sense of responsibility, and sexuality) and define the person's thoughts and feelings about components of the social world. Persons select values after considering possible alternatives and the consequences of each alternative, assessing the values, appreciating the choice that was made, and publicly taking stands to defend them. The basic values of early childhood social studies education relate to the worth of the individual, to concepts of freedom and responsibility, to the importance of democratic decision making, and to a concern for the safety of persons and property. Although these values may be taught in different subject matter areas, the social studies have particular responsibility for them.

Children learn the values reflected in the behavior of significant adults including teachers by imitating their behavior and assimilating their perceived values. The pattern of classroom management, decisions about classroom activities, and rules about permissible behavior also influence children's values, as do the types of questions teachers pose to children, for they can lead to further inquiry or lead to stereotyped responses. If a teacher arbitrarily establishes rules for behavior, children may learn not to value rational decision making.

Teachers must be careful not to stereotype boys and girls. They must be especially aware of the possibility for sex-role stereotyping in all aspects of the early childhood program and the possibility for restricting the development of all young children—those who are gifted and those with disabilities (Safford, 1989). It is important that all programs of early childhood education should not only not reflect stereotyping, but should actively try to erase biases that appear in children. Thus there should be a strong multicultural element in the program. The *Anti-Bias Curriculum* (Derman-Sparks & A.B.C. Task Force, 1989) and *Teaching and Learning in a Diverse World* (Ramsey, 1987) are excellent resources to use. One important area to examine for signs of possible bias is the arrangement of play areas and learning centers. Attention should especially be given to the integration of the housekeeping corner (Callahan, 1986).

Valued behavior can be taught through imitation, role playing, creative dramatics, literature, and art experiences. Young children learn from imitating others. Careful planning for modeling can help young children with and without disabilities acquire acceptable behaviors and the values that underlie such behaviors.

Gifted children often show an interest in and excel in a variety of activities, including areas considered inappropriate for their age or sex. Thus, a gifted young boy might become interested in cooking or sewing ("He's going to be a sissy") or in politics ("He's too young for that"). The social pressure to conform to the group and not be weird can obviously create real anxieties for children.

Open-ended stories provide a useful medium for exploring values with young children. The stories should be realistic so that children can identify with the characters. For example, an appropriate story for second- or third-graders could be about two children, Johnny and Ralph, who take a difficult test. Johnny, the school's bully, cheats, and Ralph sees him. Johnny gets a high score while Ralph and the rest of the class fail. What should Ralph do? If he does not report Johnny, everybody will fail and Johnny will be reinforced. If Ralph does report Johnny, Ralph may be accused of jealousy and Johnny might beat him up. Children can provide alternative endings for such a story based on their own values.

Literature can be effective in changing children's values. Stories that can help children value those children with disabilities include:

Brightman, A. (1976). *Like me.* Boston: Little, Brown & Co.

Caudell, R. (1965). *A certain small shepherd.* New York: Holt, Rinehart & Winston.

Charlie, R., and Miller, M. B. (1974). *Handtalk: An ABC of fingerspelling and sign language.* New York: Parents Magazine Press.

Heide, F. (1970). *Sound of sunshine, sound of rain.* New York: Parents Magazine Press.

Keats, E. J. (1971). *Apartment 3.* New York: Macmillan.

Keats, E. J. (1971). *My sister is deaf.* New York: Macmillan.

Klein, G. (1974). *The blue rose.* Westport, CT: Lawrence Hill.

Ominisky, E. (1977). *John O: A special boy.* Englewood Cliffs, NJ: Prentice-Hall.

Parker, M. (1977). *Horses, airplanes, and frogs.* Elgin, IL: Child's World.

Peterson, J. W. (1977). *I have a sister, my sister is deaf.* New York: Harper & Row.

Pursell, M. (1976). *A look at physical handicaps.* Minneapolis: Lerner Publications.

Rinkoff, B. (1972). *The watchers.* New York: Knopf.

Robinet, H. (1976). *Jay and the marigold.* Chicago: Children's Press.

Sobol, H. L. (1977). *My brother is retarded.* New York: Macmillan.

Stein, S. B. (1974). *About handicaps.* New York: Walker & Co.

Tester, S. R. (1976). *Tell me a tale about the trolls*. Elgin IL: Child's World.

Wolf, B. (1977). *Anna's silent world*. New York: Lippincott.

Wolf, B. (1974). *Don't feel sorry for Paul*. New York: Lippincott.

The reasoning abilities of children who are developmentally delayed evolve at a slow pace. These children take longer to distinguish between right and wrong and to develop internal controls. The teacher may need to remind them more often than other children about class rules and restrictions. Class rules can be posted for joint reference when needed.

Teachers need to be less concerned about teaching moral values directly and more concerned about establishing a classroom atmosphere that permits children to go through stages of moral development. A concern for moral development in the classroom should extend beyond the social studies and be integrated throughout all aspects of the classroom.

Self-Awareness

Early childhood educators have always been concerned with the affective aspects of children's development. Many goals of early childhood education focus specifically on the affective domain. Children are helped to explore and enhance their self-concepts, cope with feelings about themselves and others, and learn appropriate ways to express their feelings and interact appropriately with others. Social studies should include a concern for affective goals. Experiences must be provided to strengthen children's self-concepts—experiences that help individuals develop a unique set of perceptions, ideas, and attitudes of themselves. Personal experiences and interaction with others can develop a positive or a negative self-concept. Individuals with a positive self-concept view themselves as important, and able to perform at a normal or superior level; those with a negative self-concept lack the ability to employ learning experiences. An individual's self-concept is usually constant over a wide range of situations and for a long period of time (Saracho, 1980).

Gifted children's self-concept can be promoted by providing them with encouragement, and nurturing and supporting their talent. This avoids the loneliness, unhappiness, or personality change commonly found among gifted children who have not had the opportunity of special intervention programs.

Young children with disabilities need to develop realistic self-images (how they view themselves) and positive self-concepts (how they value themselves). Children with physical and emotional disabilities, developmental delays, divergent language patterns, and other types of disabilities need special attention. Discussions, role playing, storytelling, and similar experiences can be effective in helping children gain a sense of themselves. Children can draw pictures of their homes and they or the teacher can print their addresses and telephone numbers at the bottom of the paper. The teacher can then take a full-length photograph of each child and attach these near the children's pictures of their homes. These drawings and photographs may then be displayed on the wall or bulletin board to help children relate home to school.

Recording and then listening to children's voices can develop their sense of identity and contribute to their self-images. The teacher can record the children singing a song or telling a story on tape. The recordings can then be played back to the children. These are stored in the listening area for children to listen to independently during the day. A full-length mirror in the classroom allows children to examine themselves from head to toe, contributing to a realistic self-image and promoting the children's self-concept. A valid self-image, however, is not enough to ensure a healthy self-concept. Emotional stability is also essential.

To develop the children's positive self-concepts, the teacher must do more than just help them feel good about themselves. A realistic, positive self-concept needs (1) a strong foundation from which to be able to make decisions about interacting with the world, (2) a feeling of competence or mastery, (3) a belief in being able to perform to the limits of one's potential, (4) a sense of social responsibility and a sense of self-sufficiency or self-direction, and (5) an appreciation and enjoyment of oneself along with an appreciation of and respect for others. Individuals who appreciate themselves have a comfortable sense about all components of the self while simultaneously feeling eager to expand their horizons (Peters & Raupp, 1980).

Research on the self-esteem of four-to-eight-year-old children with cerebral palsy show that they vary in their willingness to discuss their disabilities. All of them know that their arms and legs are different, but all of the younger children and half of the older children rejected their being unable to run. Instruction concerning disabilities have focused on elementary and older students. Evidence provided by Dunn, McCartan, and Fuqua (1988) suggests that preschool children may be ready for a basic level of information. Instruction for younger children must emphasize feeling good about themselves and promoting their self-concept.

Children with disabilities need activities to promote an awareness and understanding of the parts of their bodies and of the body as a unified entity. Teachers can plan group experiences such as songs, action plays, art activities, and other improvisation activities. Action games such as "Simon Says," "Hokey Pokey," or "Put Your Finger in the Air" are valuable. Children can also trace each other's bodies on large strips of brown wrapping paper. The children can then add and color in the rest of their features including their clothes. Children's works can be displayed in the classroom with their names on it, helping them become aware of themselves as individuals and as members of a group. The teacher may need to provide some children with special help with their tracing, showing them, for example, the way the legs and arms can be traced.

Asking children to draw their own faces on newsprint paper can also help develop body awareness. Children can later talk about facial features and about the fact that some children need to use eyeglasses and hearing aids to help them see and hear. Children can become aware of the need for other prosthetic devices such as wheelchairs or braces. This activity offers a good opportunity to observe the children's reactions to disabilities, and how they cope with them. Children must learn to deal with their emotions and develop a heightened awareness of themselves, but teachers should not establish unrealistic expectations.

Another facet of self-awareness is that of self-help skills and independence routines. Skills such as grooming, eating, toileting, and dressing play a critical role in helping children with disabilities function independently. The more proficient children become in self-help skills, the less likely they will be placed in special segregated classes. Moreover, children with disabilities who function independently can have more instructional time available in subject areas.

It is important to remember that there are many ways to develop most self-help skills. For example, a coat can be put on in various ways: (1) one arm at a time from the back, (2) arms placed in the sleeves of a coat laid out on a table in front of the child and lifted over the head, (3) a coat laid behind the child into which the child places both arms and then the coat is lifted onto the child's shoulders. If one approach is not successful, the teacher should work with the child to develop another (Alberto, 1979).

In most preschools, children are expected to spend time working and playing independently. Clearly, independence training is an important developmental task. Some disabilities, such as physical disabilities, can limit a child's opportunities to function independently. Preschool materials may need to be modified so that children with limited independence skills can use them. By adapting materials for corrective feedback (e.g., color coding, sorting materials, accompanying puzzles with pictures of the completed work), the teacher can help these children become less dependent on social feedback.

Although most children use their sight to acquire self-help skills, children who are visually impaired must be taught many of these skills directly, including turning their head toward the speaker, holding eating utensils properly, and not engaging in distracting behaviors when someone is speaking. The teacher also needs to coach these children on their personal appearance, dress, and mannerisms. Physical guidance along with modeling and demonstration is often used in teaching these skills. Wehman and Goodwyn (1978) suggested a basic sequence in teaching a self-help skill:

1. The teacher gets the child's attention.
2. The teacher offers instruction including demonstration, encouragement, or imitation.
3. The teacher helps the child respond correctly by prompting, cuing, modeling, and repeating instructions.
4. The teacher manually guides the child through the response if the child proves unable to perform the desired skills.
5. The teacher rewards appropriate responses immediately.
6. The teacher corrects inappropriate responses immediately.

This sequence can be used to teach a number of self-help skills. Oversized buttons can be used at the beginning and gradually be reduced in size to minimize errors in dressing. Color-coded shoe eyelets can help children lace their shoes (Gold & Scott, 1971). Practice in each specific skill is important.

Children must develop positive relationships with others in their social environment. Children develop basic ideas about themselves and others through these relationships. Teachers should help them develop a basis for personal and social understandings. Thoughts that are formed at an early age persist as the nucleus of a lifelong system of developing social relationships.

The residual effects of disabilities often affect children emotionally. They may become lonely, have a negative self-image, or perceive themselves as being unable to meet their parents' expectations. These self-perceptions can make even 4- and 5-year-old children feel ashamed and guilty and impair their relations with peers. A child's inability to meet unrealistic demands can increase the sense of self-pity and frustration that a disability imposes (Draper, Garner, & Resnick, 1978). The problem can be alleviated if children with disabilities understand how others feel, and vice versa.

As children progress in school, their intellectual achievements are reinforced. Constant praise can engender the suspicion that parents or teachers are constantly evaluating the child, and that if the child ever falls short, love will be withdrawn. The fear that parents love their children only because of their accomplishments can be a real problem for gifted children. Although the nature of the relationship is different, Roedell (1986) made this significant observation: Feelings of inadequacy or of being an imposter can result from overdoses of praise or criticism. The general principles of good early childhood education practice that are applicable to this problem (which is more acute with many gifted children, but potentially present in all children) include respect for the child's intrinsic motivation, awareness of the child's sensitivity to unintended adult messages, and valuing of all children as individuals, not on the basis of how they perform or behave (Safford, 1989).

Pictures can help children understand other people's feelings. A photograph, cartoon, illustration, or other visual presentation can depict an important situation. For example, a magazine picture depicting children climbing a chain-link fence with a sign saying, "Danger. High Voltage. Keep Out," can stimulate a discussion about feelings of danger or fear. A picture illustrating a mother holding a broken vase and looking at her 3- or 4-year-old son who is standing before her can stimulate a discussion on how their behavior affects others. Such pictures allow children to identify with other persons and situations and perceive the world from another person's point of view. They also help children develop critical social skills as they analyze situations, identify problems, and predict outcomes (Walsh, 1980).

Self-concept begins to develop during infancy when children begin to differentiate themselves from their mothers and the rest of their environment. Children who do not have volitional control over parts of their own body—who may not be able to move a limb, or move it only with great difficulty, or must wear a prosthesis—need guidance in developing feelings of autonomy and independence. Children with disabilities must also develop a realistic sense of themselves in relation to their physical environment, even if it is a difficult task for them.

Thus, a social studies program in early childhood education should help young children acquire a better understanding of themselves and their social world. It also must offer children reasonable and verifiable knowledge and understanding of their social and physical world that they can use to help make rational decisions.

INTEGRATING SCIENCE EDUCATION

Science is composed of facts, concepts, and generalizations. Science helps children discover and create order out of their daily experiences. As part of the science program, children need to generate and verify knowledge through observations of phenomena, testing hypotheses, and carefully reporting and describing science experiences.

An early childhood science program can be built around children's everyday experiences when they observe and describe physical objects, differentiate between groups of objects based on observable attributes, and categorize objects based on these attributes. Activities should allow free exploration of scientific materials and their use as well as provide more formal learning opportunities. A flexible classroom arrangement and a supportive social climate are essential to stimulate all children's exploration to meet the goals of the science program.

A science curriculum should integrate rigorous and intensive instruction with ample opportunities for exploration, discussion, experimentation, and independent study. Children who are gifted are usually curious about everything. They want to experiment all of the time. They are persistent in problem solving. They have a large fund of information, often more than the teacher does about things that particularly interest them. They are not easily distracted, and want to remain at a particular task until they have mastered it. Their ability to attend and concentrate is usually greater than that of others (Cook, Tessier, & Armbruster, 1992).

Teachers can introduce children who are gifted to a wide variety of topics, activities, and materials in the regular classroom program. Teaching units, field trips in the community, and a wide variety of other activities can capitalize on the inherent curiosity and intrinsic motivation that all young children, especially capable children, bring to learning (Safford, 1989).

In the past, schools often limited the science curriculum of children with disabilities, sometimes appearing as an extension of some element of the curriculum. Guidelines for children with disabilities rarely exist. Mason (1987) reported the suggestions set out in *Science 5-16: A Statement of Policy:*

1. Schools need to be adequately resourced.
2. Science teachers must have access to suitable in-service training.
3. The role of the science advisor in special education needs to be clarified.
4. Schools need to develop policy for science and to formulate suitable guidelines and teaching approaches, perhaps with the help of the science advisor.
5. Links need to be established among science teachers in special and mainstream schools.

This statement holds equally for children below age 5 and for those ages 5 and beyond.

Children who have visual or motoric disabilities, for example, often were seen as being incapable of handling science materials. Thompson (1979) suggested that these erroneous decisions of the past were based on myths about the ability of children with disabilities to function in the regular science curriculum. These children have as much need for a science program as do other children, and programs can be adapted to their disabilities and presented within the regular classroom.

Scientific knowledge is essential for understanding our existence and coping with modern technological living conditions. It also provides individuals with enjoyment, understanding, improved health, and, often, an occupation. Teachers do not have the right to withhold these opportunities from any children. Children with disabilities may need more instructional and practice time and more varied experiences to master science skills or concepts—children with hearing impairments, for example, may require more time to learn the technical vocabulary of science, and that vocabulary may need to be presented differently.

Science for preschool children focuses mainly on having children experience physical and natural phenomena and develop ways of organizing the information that results from these experiences. In primitive ways, the techniques young children use to make sense of the world are not too much different from those used by mature scientists.

When teachers have children with disabilities in their classes, they must be concerned about whether these children can gain the same sensory experiences as their peers and whether they have the ability to process the information gained through their experiences. If there are sensory deficits, then the teacher needs to accommodate to them in planning the program, providing substitute experiences when appropriate and helping children build upon the sensory capacities they do have. Providing sensory experiences alone, however, is not enough to help children learn to understand their physical world. They have to be helped to make sense of the world. Children do this by ordering their information. Children develop concepts as a result of what they come to know. They categorize information based upon these concepts and fit new information into the category system already developed, expanding and modifying the system as needed. They can order objects by some quantifiable attribute and put their understandings into a framework of time and space. Causality, for example, results from placing incidents into a time frame with incidents occurring earlier seen as causing those that follow in time.

Science opportunities for children with special needs should not be limited. Hands-on and problem-solving experiences should be designed to help teachers who do not have training in science be able to implement science into their curriculum (Tunnicliffe, 1987).

Children with disabilities can be offered a wide range of science experiences in preschool, although they may have to be modified for each child's specific disability. Although children with visual impairments may not have visual sensations available to them, they can experience the world through their other senses. The physical environment may need to be adapted for children with orthopedic impairments. Experiences may have to be simplified for children with learning disabilities, and cues provided to signal the activities in which they will engage. With such modifications, the basic processes of science can be approached by every child.

Preschool children, for example, can be given a wide range of objects to sort and classify. Children can view leaves collected in the fall and can identify their color, shape, texture, and other attributes (and similarities and differences among the leaves). The leaves can then be sorted by attribute. Even if some children may not be able to see color, they will be able to feel shape and texture. The teacher might later label one set of leaves as oak, another as maple, and so forth, possibly showing the children the trees from which they dropped.

A variety of similar experiences requiring observation of physical attributes of phenomena and categorization of objects by attributes can be provided. Different colors and sizes of beads of blocks or other small objects that can be grouped by size, shape, color, weight, or some other observable attribute can be grouped in the same way. Sighted children might be asked to order these materials by color, whereas blind children could be asked to order them by texture or shape.

Young children can also be given objects that differ by size or weight and asked to order them from the heaviest to the lightest or from the largest to the smallest. These activities provide practice in seriation skills.

Children can be helped to perceive that they can cause things to happen. The movement of a wheel toy that is pushed and continues to roll, for example, can be discussed in terms of cause and effect. Conditions can be varied to modify the consequences of children's action—the toy can be pushed down a ramp, along a smooth surface of the floor, or along a carpeted section of the floor—and children can begin to see that the consequences of their actions will change depending upon conditions in the environment.

Children who are hyperactive or have temper tantrums may have to be controlled in such activities. They should not be allowed to destroy property or use materials in ways that may harm themselves or others. If a pet is abused or another child harmed, the experience can become a miseducative one. Teachers may have to establish and adhere to special rules with some children or modify the activity to allow all the children to participate. If children are prone to throw containers around the room, the containers used for sorting activities might be fastened to a table. A simple change in the environment may allow the child to participate more fully in learning activities.

In adapting the science program for children with disabilities in kindergarten and the primary grades, individualized instruction must be provided, along with more demonstrations and discussions, perhaps pairing children with and without disabilities. The teacher's attitude is still the most important attribute of a successful class. The desire to teach all children, regardless of their learning needs or difficulties, will lead to programs appropriate for both groups.

Four basic types of instructional methods in science for children with learning disabilities are reading, doing, using media, and discussion. *Reading* involves using a variety of printed materials, such as textbooks, information books, and children's magazines. *Doing* involves engaging children in hands-on learning activities and experiments (discussed later in this chapter). *Media* include use of a range of audiovisual materials.

Probably the most commonly used instructional method in early childhood education involves *discussion,* or talking with children. Children who have short attention spans, memory problems, or language delays, or who manifest inappropriate behavior, may have difficulty with learning through discussion. Students with short attention spans tend to have difficulty staying in their chairs or listening for more than a short period of time; such students may "tune out." Although discussion helps children reflect on their experiences, it is not a substitute for hands-on, firsthand experience. Along with discussions, the teacher must provide a variety of active learning experiences including conducting experiments, completing prescribed activities with materials or learning activity packages at a learning center, using audiovisual aids, playing games, working with peer tutors or volunteers, and writing or illustrating stories about the concept being studied. Students with short attention spans should be seated close to the teacher during discussion periods. Writing a discussion outline on the board and frequently calling upon these students to answer questions can also help.

Children with memory problems tend to forget important information. Teachers need to provide children with disabilities with a summary of key points to remember and a set of exercises and activities to help them recall the critical elements of a discussion. These children can also be given opportunities to associate new information with previously learned concepts. Students with language delays may have problems understanding the technical language of science and comprehending words the teacher uses to define these technical terms. Teachers may need to introduce such new words carefully in context, first writing the definition on index cards in isolation, then presenting the words in a sentence, along with some form of illustration.

Audiovisual materials, including pictures, charts, films, filmstrips, maps, and graphs, can be used effectively with many children with disabilities. Children with learning disabilities and with low reading levels can especially profit from using audiovisual materials since they make information available without the need to read.

Children with hearing impairments can be helped to hear the audio portion of films, filmstrips, and videotapes by being seated close to the machine. Those with severe hearing impairments, however, may need to be provided with captioned films with print on each frame or in each sequence. Students who can speech-read or read sign language can make use of films in which an interpreter appears on a designated portion of the picture. Many children tend to think in nonverbal terms. Logical thinking requires more than language, although language is a vehicle for abstract thinking. Language usage occurs after children develop logical relationships between concrete experiences and objects and events. These children gradually make the transition from concrete to abstract thinking. Science experiences should assist children with this transition without frustrating them with activities that require difficult language and reading skills. Children can be successful when learning is on their terms, and this success will promote further success.

Developing Learning Activities

A classroom science activity center allows children to work on science projects in small groups. The science center should have adequate equipment and materials for children to examine and explore. An abundant supply of paper towels and water should be available. All materials should be labeled. Pictures can help children who cannot read print; Braille should be used if children with visual impairments are in the class. Children with and without disabilities can work together in small groups. The teacher needs to know which children may need assistance and plan to provide for it as unobtrusively as possible. Peer tutoring and social interaction among the children may be all that are necessary.

Science experiences that cannot be adapted for children with a particular disability should be alternated among different groups in the program. Each group can work independently, later joining together to share their findings to promote interaction within the class. The entire class should be together for science demonstrations and discussions. Lengthy discussions or long, dull reports should be avoided, and demonstrations should accompany reports on observations or experiments.

Experiments

Most science experiments can be adapted for children with different disabilities.

Children with Hearing Impairments.   Science experiments for children with hearing impairments should provide task cards that identify the materials in each experiment. The vocabulary used in these cards should be presented during discussion or demonstration periods and referred to when appropriate. Rebus, which combines words and pictures, can be used. Only a few task cards should be used at one time.

Task cards or charts can be prepared ahead of time using questions and directions such as:

- Observe carefully.
- What do you think will happen?
- What did you see?
- How are they the same?
- How are they different?
- What caused the differences? (Hadary & Cohen, 1978)

Children with Visual Impairments.   Teachers should carefully select words used in experiments when children with visual impairments are involved. Phrases such as *blue water* or *green leaves* have no meaning to them for they lack the visual referents. In conducting science experiments with these children, Hadary and Cohen (1978) recommend the following modifications:

- When real objects cannot be directly observed, models should be employed in their place.
- Equipment should be anchored in place so children can find them without knocking them down.
- The exact location of displayed materials should be identified.
- Objects should be described to the visually impaired so they know what is available.
- Paired grouping—a visually impaired child working alongside a sighted partner—is effective. The sighted partner can help the visually impaired child with what cannot be seen.
- A large quantity of paper towels and sufficient water should be accessible in case of spillage. Children with visual impairments, particularly, seem to dislike a mess.

Children with Behavior Disorders.   Science often can serve as therapy for children with behavior disorders, providing rational, logical explanations and offering control over what is otherwise a confusing world. Science facilitates cause-and-effect observations of behavior, separates facts from feelings, and teaches problem-solving strategies that can be used to resolve conflict. Science can offer these children an understanding of life events and reality principles. Exploring and investigating help such children acquire feelings of autonomy, develop self-confidence, and become more comfortable with themselves and their world. The following adaptations in conducting science experiments with children with behavior disorders have been suggested by Hadary and Cohen (1978):

- Experiments should be intellectually stimulating.
- Experiments should be presented in sequential order.
- Discussions of discoveries should be encouraged.
- Emotionally disturbed children can be paired with visually impaired children.
- Thinking about observed processes before responding actively should be encouraged.

Malone and Lucchi (1979) provided the following examples of life science activities for children with disabilities:

Studying seeds: Students can remove seeds from fruits and vegetables to compare the amounts and sizes of these seeds. They can (1) dry and plant the seeds, (2) investigate the types of seeds that can be used for food, and (3) make collages with different kinds of seeds.

Observing snails: Large snails can be used as classroom animals. They are easy for young children to care for. Students can tape a wire harness to a snail to discover the amount of mass it can pull (they might be surprised). Children with visual impairments can touch the load on the snail gently with one finger to find out whether the snail has moved its load. Students can measure the snail's traveling speed. (For younger children, simply setting up an ecosystem with a snail, plants, and water in a jar or aquarium may be enough.)

Studying crayfish: Young children can learn about the structure, function, behavior, and environment of the crayfish. Crayfish are easy to handle. Students can carefully place rubber tubing on their pincers. An aquarium plant (anacharis) can be measured to find out how much of it one crayfish will eat in a specific period of time. Follow-up activities can include composing stories about crayfish, reading books about crayfish, and preparing reports on crayfish. Students will enjoy becoming experts on crayfish and sharing their knowledge with others.

In addition, *Batteries and Bulbs, Mealworms, Mystery Powders,* and other units of the Elementary Science Study science experiments (developed by the Education Development Center, Newton, Massachusetts) can be adapted for children with learning disabilities. These and other hands-on kits of science materials are available from Delta Education (P.O. Box M, Nashua, NH 03061). These are hands-on activities that are effective with all young children.

Most children with disabilities, with the exception of those with serious hearing impairments, can use a tape recorder effectively for science instruction. Children can also dictate the results of their experiments on tape. The tape recorder is helpful as a memory bank since students are able to move it forward or backward until they find the information they need (Eichenberger, 1974).

Children can gain their own sense of order and beauty from their science discoveries. Hadary and Cohen (1978) described a girl with a visual impairment observing seeds grow through her sense of touch and writing about her experience: "I made a greenhouse, a home for a seed; it wasn't just science, it was science and art. The seeds grew and made lines through space" (p. 10).

Science instruction is an important part of the early childhood curriculum. It requires children to act upon materials and experiences and to think about their experiences with physical and natural phenomena, creating their own conclusions. Teachers should not spend a great deal of time telling children science facts but should provide them with opportunities to seek out answers. If an atmosphere of inquiry pervades the classroom, it will support the increasing autonomy of children. The significance in science learning is not the product of scientific inquiry (the conclusions the children make or the different categories they develop), but the processes by which they arrive at them.

INTEGRATING MATHEMATICS EDUCATION

Mathematics programs in early childhood education vary greatly. Some programs emphasize proficiency in counting, in writing numerals, and in other mathematical skills, whereas others focus on generating meanings. Some provide systematic, isolated lessons, and others use children's everyday experiences as the bases for developing competency. Young children naturally search for meanings in their world and in this search have many varied contacts with a world of quantity, space, number, shapes, time, and distance. Teachers need to help children become aware of and understand the numerical, spatial, and measuring aspects of their world.

Young children already have a repertoire of mathematical concepts when they enter kindergarten. Suydam and Weaver (1975) have summarized these for 5-year-olds:

- They are able to count the number of objects to 10, and some have the ability to count to at least 20.
- They can name the number of 10s in order (such as 10, 20, 30, 40), and some can tell the number names when counting by 2s and 5s.
- They know and understand the meaning of *first* and are able to identify ordinal positions through 50.
- They can identify and write the numerals from 1 to 10.
- They can answer simple problems with addition and subtraction combinations presented verbally and may or may not use manipulative materials.
- They know about coins, time, and other measures; about fractions; and about geometric shapes.

This suggests that a considerable amount of mathematics learning takes place during the preschool period.

Early childhood mathematics programs must (1) provide a rich environment in which children can accumulate sensory data about quantity, (2) use a range of teaching techniques for children to develop mathematical concepts, (3) demonstrate the relationship between mathematical experiences and mathematical language, (4) present problems that require children to understand the meaning of situations and apply their mathematical understandings, and (5) focus on methods that promote both computational skills and problem-solving ability.

Helping Young Children Develop Mathematical Concepts

Almost any instructional material can be adapted to meet the needs of children who are gifted. These children often are capable of creative or divergent thinking. Attribute blocks are an obvious example. Most gifted children quickly learn to sort by color, shape, and size. Advanced children can learn to sort the differences among more than one attribute. Making an alternative chain of one or two differences challenges the mind of most preschoolers (Cook et al., 1992).

Children with disabilities develop quantitative concepts in the same order as do all children, but children who are developmentally delayed will develop them later, and children with sensory disorders may have a diminished understanding of the relationships among objects. The ability to understand mathematical concepts is achieved as a result of a combination of learning and maturation. Even repeated drill in the performance of quantitative tasks will not substitute for maturation in the development of these understandings. This does not mean that learning experiences should be withheld from those who are developing less normally; rather, it means that readiness activities in mathematics have to be consistent with what the child can understand.

At the preschool level, mathematics activities can focus on:

- Experiences with object permanence and conservation of number.
- Seriation, classification, and equivalence experiences.
- Combination and identification of sets of various objects.
- One-to-one correspondence.
- Rational counting.
- Number recognition, matching numbers and numerals, and ordination. (Alberto, 1979)

Teachers can use many naturally occurring classroom incidents to teach these concepts. This requires the teacher to systematically analyze daily activities to identify those elements that can help children develop mathematical meanings. Snack time, for example, could allow children to match one cup of juice or one cracker to each child, a way of developing the concept of one-to-one correspondence. In addition, specially planned experiences using manipulative materials can be used. Insert puzzles that require the child to put one puzzle piece into one space provide an experience to help acquire the same concept.

Other activities that can be used include providing children with written numerals and having them match a number; ordering blocks, beads, or other objects according to size; matching patterns of beads on a string to various models the teacher provides; or pointing out groups of two or three objects that exist in the classroom or surrounding area.

Teachers need to select teaching materials that are appropriate to each child, no matter what the strength or disability. In addition, they can modify classroom materials to serve children better. Wooden domino pieces, for example, can have felt dots pasted over the painted dots, so that children with visual impairments can feel the numbers. Cues for putting together puzzles can be created by marking the back of each piece and matching it with a similarly marked space in the puzzle.

In teaching mathematics, teachers will find that some children may need a great deal of practice in order to learn and apply mathematical principles, whereas others will grasp them easily. Many young students with disabilities have difficulty with mathematics. Characteristics that may cause difficulty in mathematics include:

1. *Poor self-concept.* Some children with disabilities learn to accept failure at an early age. They do not attempt new tasks because they are afraid to fail. Teachers have to provide experiences in which these children can succeed and help them understand that failure is sometimes a step toward learning. Children who perceive themselves as worthy and who approach problems with confidence have a better chance at success (Cruikshank, Fitzgerald, & Jensen, 1980).
2. *Poor self-control.* Some children are unable to control their behavior and may exhibit explosive, hyperactive, or erratic behavior. They are constantly in motion, rarely sit still, and wander aimlessly around the room. Such children need an environment that limits distractions (Cruikshank et al., 1980).
3. *Specific mathematics disability.* Children with minimal brain damage often cannot learn quantitative concepts. Perceptual problems such as inability to define a position in space (e.g., near, far, up, down, left, right), inability to distinguish a figure from its background, and poor eye-hand coordination may affect the learning of spatial concepts. Students may be easily distracted by extraneous stimuli, such as too many problems or pictures on a page, or too many objects or people in a classroom. Children with perceptual problems need simple worksheets and a relatively uncluttered classroom environment (Cruikshank et al., 1980).
4. *Brain dominance.* It has been suggested that some children's brains are dominated by the left hemisphere, whereas other children's are

dominated by the right hemisphere. The left hemisphere affects verbal, numerical, and logical functions; the right affects visual, spatial, perceptual, intuitive, and imaginative functions. Teachers usually focus their lessons on skills related to the left hemisphere when they ask children to read, listen, think, and write. This procedure, although appropriate for children whose thinking is dominated by the left hemisphere, may create difficulties for those whose thinking is dominated by the right hemisphere. Some educators suggest providing learning activities that strengthen both hemispheres of the brain and the bonds between them (Cruikshank et al., 1980).

5. *Language problems.* Many children who have language difficulties also encounter problems in learning mathematics. They may have trouble understanding common mathematical terms such as *up, down, in, two,* or *plus* and may not be able to communicate concepts they understand. For these children, the language of mathematics needs to be kept as simple as possible, and any misunderstanding of terms must be clarified immediately. Concepts may be developed more easily by relating physical objects to language (Cruikshank et al., 1980).

6. *Poor memory.* Some children who have difficulty recalling information perceived or learned a few moments before may need to overlearn to ensure retention of information. Practice, drill, and repetition within context are effective in improving recall. Retarded children may remember and may be able to apply skills if transfer is practiced with understanding. Complex problem solving is probably difficult; however, simple rote learning of factual materials such as basic facts can be learned, memorized, and applied (Cruikshank et al., 1980).

7. *Short attention span.* Children with short attention spans can have difficulty with problems that are too elaborate, too long, or not interesting enough. Many children can work for relatively long periods of time if problems are interesting and challenging. Filtering out extraneous information and focusing on pertinent facts can help to sustain a child's attention (Cruikshank et al., 1980).

8. *Visual and auditory discrimination disabilities.* Children who have difficulty recognizing that two separate auditory or visual stimuli or patterns of stimuli are the same or different have problems in comparing like and unlike elements. Almost all mathematical tasks require these types of discrimination. Such a disability is a threat to success in mathematics (Johnson, 1979).

9. *Visual and auditory association disabilities.* Children who have difficulty relating separately perceived visual or auditorial stimuli or sets of stimuli to each other will have difficulty with mathematics. Visual and auditory association are essential in coping with abstractions and elements of mathematics (Johnson, 1979).

10. *Perceptual–motor difficulties.* Children who have difficulty with eye–motor coordination or who cannot relate visual stimuli to motor responses or motor cues to visual stimuli will have problems in

mathematics. Most of the performance skills in mathematics, from writing numbers to moving decimal points, require development of perceptual–motor skills (Johnson, 1979).

11. *Spatial awareness and orientation disabilities.* Children who cannot recognize or adequately employ temporal or spatial relationships between objects (difficulties related to perceptual-motor problems) will have problems with the mathematics curriculum. Telling time, learning simple geometry, and developing the vocabulary of position will be particularly difficult (Johnson, 1979).

12. *Verbal expression disabilities.* Children who cannot communicate information to others (either through speaking or through writing) are unable to communicate or request mathematics information. These children have trouble selecting the appropriate operations needed to solve mathematical problems (Johnson, 1979).

13. *Closure and generalization (convergence and divergence) disabilities.* Some children encounter difficulty interpolating parts from wholes or wholes from parts, a requirement of mathematics. Closure or generalization problems (sometimes called convergence and divergence) prevent children from moving beyond a direct use of mathematics information and ideas. These children are restricted to the demonstrable present. Abstract information creates difficulty for them, as do the analytical processes of mathematics (Johnson, 1979).

14. *Slow development through intellectual stages.* Children who are slow in mathematics may be at an earlier developmental stage than their age mates. Children at different stages need to learn different concepts and have topics presented in different ways. For instance, a preoperational child who cannot conserve numbers is not ready to learn the numbers from 1 to 10 (Cruikshank et al., 1980).

Adapting Experiences for Children with Various Disabilities

Some disabilities interfere more with learning mathematics than others; instructional adaptations should be added accordingly. Children who learn more slowly than their classmates may need special attention in developing early number awareness. Students who suffer from cognitive impairment, learning disabilities, and visual and hearing impairments need to have the mathematics curriculum adjusted for them. Most students who are low achievers in mathematics probably will never completely catch up with grade-level expectations. Thus, the mathematical concepts and skills that retarded students master in mathematics tend to be less than those of their classmates. Teachers need to identify the parts of the mathematics curriculum most relevant to daily living situations and to focus on them for these children (Schulz, Carpenter, & Turnbull, 1984; Turnbull & Schulz, 1979). Children with physical disabilities, on the other hand, will probably not need any special curriculum adjustment in the content of their mathematics program. Less emphasis may be placed on the use of manipulative material, however.

Performance deficits found in children with learning disabilities may be grouped into categories of intellectual, spatial, and verbal reasoning ability. Many mathematics dysfunctions have underlying language deficits such as lexical dyscalculia, verbal dyscalculia, and ideognostic dyscalculia. *Lexical dyscalculia* is a disability in reading mathematical symbols (e.g., digits, numbers, or operational signs) (Kosc, 1974). *Verbal dyscalculia* is the inability to label mathematical terms verbally (e.g., misnaming numbers of items, numerals, and operational symbols). *Ideognostic dyscalculia* (or semantic aphasia) is a disability in understanding mathematical ideas and relations required for mental calculation. Students cannot calculate even the easiest sums and cannot clearly read or write numerals. This mathematical dysfunction also affects children's ability to develop ideas (Blackwell, 1976).

Students with brain injuries may be unable to solve simple mathematics problems or comprehend logical relationships. Such injuries can also disturb pupils' ability to solve verbal problems, especially those requiring a change from one operation to another or those requiring solution of mathematical equations within a complex structure. Children with such problems need an appropriate remedial program. Children with learning disabilities can work with materials such as Tangrams, Pattern Blocks, Mirror Cards, Attribute Blocks, and Geo-Boards, all of which are manipulative materials designed to develop general skills and teach children about shapes.

Children with behavior disorders who have difficulty in mathematics also benefit from working with manipulative materials that offer immediate feedback. Individual work with manipulative materials also limits competition. Children with physical disorders or visual impairments and those with multiple disabilities should be provided with similar materials.

Children with visual impairments, for example, can work through mathematical problems using a Braille abacus. Teachers who do not have access to a Braille abacus can make a memory-assistance device by stringing beads with holes through the center on thin wire. Three or more columns of 10 beads each can be made in this fashion and placed in a wooden frame or attached to the edges of a cardboard box. The beads help students remember intermediate steps in their mathematical operations. The beads are arranged to represent specific numbers and can be separated into groups by attaching small alligator clips to the wire (Eichenberger, 1974).

Learning Activities for Children with Disabilities

There are a variety of activities teachers can provide to allow children with disabilities to learn difficult mathematical concepts. For example, children who do not understand the *-er* and *-est* comparatives can be allowed to compare actual objects to determine the relationships between them. By comparing two objects, they can determine if one object is heavier, lighter, smoother, smaller, or shorter than the other. Specific language can be taught later and comparisons can be developed into precise measurements (Knight & Hargis, 1977).

Balance beams and seesaws help children use their own bodies to develop concepts of weight, equivalence, and balance. They can pretend to be tightrope walkers and use their extended arms to balance themselves (see Figure 13.1). They can also carefully tread a crack in the sidewalk, a line between tiles in the classroom, or a long strip of masking tape attached to the floor.

FIGURE 13.1

Children on a treasure hunt can collect objects of varying weights and discuss the objects they collect in terms of *heavy* and *light*. When students understand these terms, they can learn to compare *heavier than* with *lighter than*. By lifting heavy and light objects, the children sense the meaning of these comparative terms (see Figure 13.2).

Children can construct simple balance scales using a plunger as a base and a notched dowel stick, two pails, two washers, and a pivot screw. Crimping plasticine on the light side will help balance the scale. Children can build individual balance scales, using a ruler that has three holes drilled in it—one on each end and one in the middle. Again, plasticine can help maintain the balance (see Figure 13.3). Children can understand the movement of the scale. They can simulate the action on the balance by holding two pails of different weight on each hand (see Figure 13.4).

Children can then learn to read the dials on simple and one-arm balance scales and check their readings by weighing the same objects in their two-pan balance scales where they employ their own set of standard weights. Other scales can also be used (see Figure 13.5). These activities help children understand the term *weight* and the meaning of the numbers they see on the scale. A variety of balancing and weighing experiences can help children create the necessary mental picture.

Linear measurement can also be learned through concrete experience. Young children are not aware that linear measurement is continuous and that a unit of measure is repeated. Nonstandard units of measure can introduce young children to linear measurement. Bruni and Silverman (1976) suggested using nonstandard units of measure such as a "baby foot" (4 inches long) and a "giant foot" (three baby feet, or 12 inches long). The teacher draws a line down the middle of each baby foot and each

FIGURE 13.2

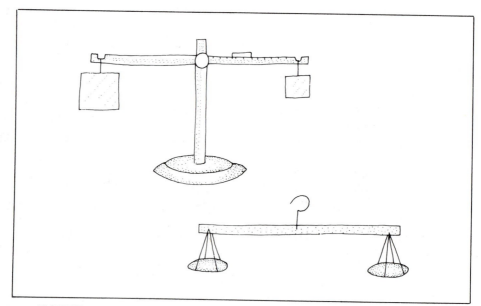

FIGURE 13.3

FIGURE 13.4

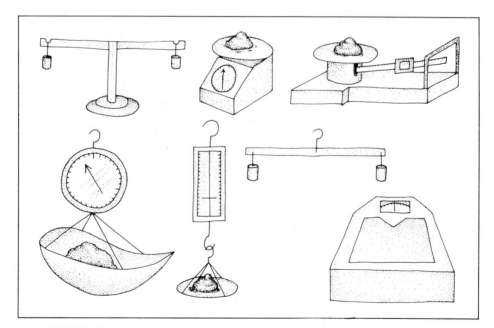

FIGURE 13.5

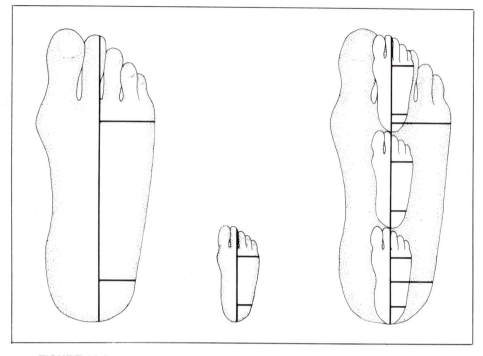

FIGURE 13.6

giant foot to help children focus on a continuous straight line as they employ several units of measure. An arrow indicating direction can be drawn near the toes to enable the children to utilize the baby feet and giant feet the same way each time. If slits are cut on the feet, the children can string the feet along a rope, being careful to avoid overlapping, and use the rope as a measuring instrument (see Figure 13.6).

The ratio of the giant foot's length to the baby foot's length (3 to 1) will allow children to gain a sense of the standard length of foot and yard. This activity can be varied by using the children's own footprints. A child and a partner can trace each other's feet and can use this as a pattern for duplicating more feet. More durable feet can be made from oaktag, felt material, air conditioner filters, or styrofoam.

Before making their measuring ropes, the children should compare lengths of two feet. Feet of different lengths can be stored in cigar boxes. Children can compare two feet, aligning them to find out which one is longer or shorter or if they are the same size. Charts can be made to reinforce these concepts. After a child has compared the lengths of two feet, he or she can tape the feet in the appropriate space.

Children who are able to compare the lengths of two feet can make measuring ropes by stringing baby feet on a string and then begin measuring objects in the room with the rope. They can guess how many baby-feet-long objects are and then measure the objects by laying the measuring rope across them. Children should be sure that their ropes show a continuous line before they count the number of baby feet to the nearest baby foot. Children should be encouraged to use terms such as *about, a little longer than*, and *a little shorter than*.

These experiences can be repeated using giant feet. After the children have measured objects using baby feet and giant feet separately, they can measure the same objects using both nonstandard units. Children take two ropes that are the same length and string baby feet on one rope and string giant feet on the other. Before stringing the baby feet or the giant feet, the children should be encouraged to estimate the number of feet that will be needed.

Following such measurement experiences with nonstandard units, children should be introduced to standard units of measure including English and metric units. Teachers can introduce these units of linear measurement (such as inches, feet, and yards) by providing children with both oaktag strips that are 1 inch wide and 1 foot long and a supply of 1-inch-by-1-inch gummed stickers in two colors. Children can glue the stickers on the oaktag strip, alternating the colors. Before they glue the stickers, have them estimate and then count the number of stickers that will be required. Numbering each sticker in the upper right-hand corner helps children keep track of the count as they glue them down.

Children can then measure the baby feet and the giant feet with their standard foot rules. Before measuring, children should estimate how many gummed stickers long each one is. The words *inch* and *foot* can then be introduced.

Learning to tell time is an important skill for young children; their day is organized around a clock. Initially their general schedule is time for school, dinnertime, and bedtime. Later their schedules become more specific. Although time schedules play an important role in children's lives, often they have difficulty learning to read time from a clock (Krustchinsky & Larner, 1988).

The whole clock method (Lipstreu & Johnson, 1988) of teaching students to tell time has been successfully used with students with a wide range of disabilities. This system helps children generalize about times and understand the continuity of time. Before learning with this system, students should be able to (1) recognize and identify the numbers from 1 to 12 and (2) count around the clock face by 5s as the minute hand moves forward. Then teachers instruct students to tell time around a clock dial in 5-minute intervals from the hour to 55 minutes. Real clocks are used rather than worksheets with clock faces or student-made clocks. Children follow these steps:

1. Children first learn to tell time by the hour (12:00, 2:00, 3:00).
2. Once they have mastered hours, they learn 5 minutes after the hour, then review the hour (12:05, 2:05, 3:05).
3. Then they learn 10 minutes after the hour, reviewing the first two steps.
4. Students then learn the 5-minute interval in a sequences using the face of the real clock (hours first, then :05s, :10s, :15s, :20s, :25s . . . 55s).
5. Times between the hour and the half-hour are learned. (Lipstreu & Johnson, 1988)

Games that repeatedly use the same numerical language help teach mathematics. Play and movement activities that provide children with the opportunity to manipulate objects and build their mathematical language should also be used. It is also important to consistently use the same mathematics vocabulary. For example, in referring to regrouping, renaming, and carrying, which are comparable processes, teachers can reduce student's confusion by consistently using only one of these terms (Lowenbraun & Affleck, 1976).

Visual prompts or demonstrations are often more effective in teaching mathematical language than lengthy verbal explanations. Children need to see what happens to understand a computation. Cawley and Vitello (1972) suggested a comprehensive model of visual prompts or demonstration for mathematics instruction. Their model consists of three cells: "Do," "See," and "Say." The "do" cell includes manipulation of objects and pictures in tasks employing constructing, ordering, arranging, and other similar skills. The "see" cell consists of responding to pictures or to a visual model by pointing or marking; the "say" cell focuses on spoken or written language. This model has been an effective framework in teaching mathematics concepts to children with disabilities. Basically, the sequence of difficulty is from the "do-do" combination (at the easiest level) to "see-see" and then "say-say."

Children make common types of errors, providing clues to their level of understanding. Many computational errors are the result of not knowing basic facts. A basic fact is a combination of one- or two-digit numbers that have a sum (for addition) or subtrahend (for subtraction). For example, the following are basic facts:

$$5 + 6 = 11$$
$$17 - 9 = 8$$

Addition has 100 basic facts, and subtraction has 55. Children who make systematic errors in solving the problems for a particular basic fact are making systematic basic-fact errors. For example, if a child always says that $8 + 5 = 14$, this mistake is a systematic basic-fact error rather than a systematic computational error (Cox, 1975).

Children's mathematical errors can be recorded and analyzed to identify patterns. Recognizing patterns in these errors is the first step toward remediation. Without proper instruction, many children will continue to make the same errors. The appropriateness and effectiveness of various manipulative aids and instructional strategies must be assessed to remediate the errors (Cox, 1975).

Students who have attentional deficits and gross problems with short-term memory can learn subtraction facts by using their visual strengths. Hide-and-seek cards can be very helpful. Five steps that are central to subtraction can be used:

1. Use familiar pictures from addition to represent each double fact. Encourage the student to identify:
   a. The whole that is hidden.
   b. The part that is taken out of hiding.
   c. The part that is still hidden.
2. Teach students how to use the hide-and-seek cards to check answers. Example:
   $10 - 5$ is 5, because $5 + 5 = 10$
3. Provide activities using two partner cards such as $10 - 7$ and $10 - 3$. Students can color the partner facts the same colors or match subtraction fact cards.
4. Emphasize "families" of related addition-subtraction facts very early (such as $9 - 6 = 3; 9 - 3 = 6; 3 + 6 = 9; 6 + 3 = 9$). Introduce students to families of facts to help them understand these relationships and consolidate the learning of known facts.
5. Provide activities to help them practice the work learned in the above four steps. (Thornton & Toohey, 1986)

The five-step sequence to introduce facts of addition and subtraction combined with related activities can help children with disabilities to master basic subtraction facts (Thornton & Toohey, 1985). Modifications in the instruction should include:

- Delaying subtraction until related addition facts are mastered.
- Basing the sequence for studying unknown subtraction facts on retrieval strategies, not on size related to sums.
- Explicitly intervening to teach retrieval strategies.
- Matching the presentation of new facts to the child's idiosyncratic learning style. (Thornton & Toohey, 1986, p. 14)

Hide-and-seek cards can help children with disabilities by focusing their learning on visual strengths and teaching facts using small steps, which their memory can manage.

Though mathematics used to be taught through rote learning, students with learning disabilities have difficulty learning this way. Flexer (1989) believed that:

- Children who learn to add often have just learned to count and are not able to perform either chore effectively or correctly. Even average-ability first- and second-graders who are requested to count 25 counters a number of times will acquire different totals. Also, children assume that the last answer is the correct one and do not bother to check their answers.

- If counting errors lead children to arrive at different answers when they add the same numbers, they are confused concerning which sum should be associated with the specific pair of numbers.

- Place value may be ignored if children learn to add by counting on. They are not aware that 10 ones have been traded for one 10.

Alternative strategies retaining the mathematic conceptual framework must focus on the following goals:

1. Children should understand the concept of addition.
2. They should have access to manipulative materials that concretely model the action of the operation.

3. As models of addition, such manipulatives should extend beyond single-digit numbers.
4. The manipulatives should facilitate the transition to a mental model for constructing addition facts.
5. The model should aid children in remembering addition facts. (Flexer, 1989, p. 22)

General principles of good teaching are important for all children, including those with special needs. Cruikshank, Fitzgerald, and Jensen (1980) developed the following teaching principles for children with disabilities:

1. All children are able to learn if they are taught at their level.
2. Learning should be planned to ensure some success. Immediate feedback is effective.
3. A positive self-concept affects success. Young children must perceive themselves as being important to themselves and to others.
4. Practice is important to develop concrete concepts. Practice provided in practical situations allows for transfer of learning to new situations.
5. A variety of alternative teaching strategies should be planned. If one approach fails, others can be attempted. Sensory approaches can meet each child's individual learning style.
6. Children who have a mathematics disability tend to work slowly and at a concrete level. They may be incapable of performing abstract work and therefore may need to fully develop their concrete levels.
7. Children's errors should be carefully analyzed to understand their thinking processes and to provide clues about ways to clarify their concepts.
8. All children learn differently. An instructional mathematics program should be planned based on careful diagnosis and evaluation.

SUMMARY

When difficulties arise in education, there is a tendency to narrow the curriculum and give greatest priority to the basic skills. There is no denying the importance of the basic academic areas of reading, writing, and arithmetic for all children including those with disabilities. However, if we want children with disabilities to live as normal a life as possible, we need to be careful that the educational experiences we provide them are not too restrictive. Social studies science, and mathematics provide a framework through which children can organize their perception of the physical and social world. These areas allow them to understand their inner world and relate it to the outer world they share with other people.

There is a broad range of activities that teachers can use in providing children with disabilities with experiences in social studies, science, and mathematics. Whenever we deal with individual differences in the classroom, we must modify the basic assumptions we hold about what all children should come to know and how all children learn. When children with disabilities are concerned, we must accept the need for such modification as a matter of course. We should be willing to find ways in which each child can be a competent learner in the classroom and then adapt these learnings to the outside world. Then subject matter areas have a particularly strong contribution to make in normalizing the lives of these children.

REFERENCES

Alberto, P. A. (1979). The young mildly retarded child. In S. G. Garwood (Ed.), *Educating young handicapped children: A developmental approach*. Germantown, MD: Aspen Systems Corporation.

Blackwell, J. H. (1976). When 2 + 2 ain't 4. *Language Arts, 53*, 422–424.

Bruni, J. V., & Silverman, H. (1976). An introduction to weight measurement. *The Arithmetic Teacher, 23*(1), 4–10.

Callahan, C. M. (1986). The special needs of gifted girls. In J. R. Whitmore (Ed.), *Intellectual giftedness in young children: Recognition and development* (pp. 5–15). New York: Haworth Press.

Cawley, J. F., & Vitello, S. J. (1972). Model for arithmetical programming for handicapped children. *Exceptional Children, 39*(2), 101–110.

Charlesworth, R., & Hartup, W. W. (1967). Positive social reinforcement in the nursery school peer group. *Child Development, 38*, 993–1002.

Clark, B. (1986). Early development of cognitive abilities and giftedness. In J. R. Whitmore (Ed.), *Intellectual giftedness in young children: Recognition and development*. New York: Haworth Press.

Cook, R. E., Tessier, A., & Armbruster, V. B. (1992). *Adapting early childhood curricula for children with special needs* (3rd ed.). Columbus, OH: Merrill.

Cox, L. S. (1975). Diagnosing and remediating systematic errors in addition and subtraction computations. *The Arithmetic Teacher, 22*(2), 151–156.

Cruikshank, D. E., Fitzgerald, D. L., & Jensen, J. R. (1980). *Young children learning mathematics*. Boston: Allyn & Bacon.

Derman-Sparks, L., & the A.B.C. Task Force (1989). *Anti-bias curriculum: Tools for empowering young children*. Washington, DC: National Association for the Education of Young Children.

Draper, W., Garner, H. G., & Resnick, R. J. (1978). Emotional and social development. In N. H. Fallen (Ed.), *Young children with special needs* (pp. 245–275). Columbus, OH: Merrill.

Dunn, N. L., McCartan, K. W., & Fuqua, R. W. (1988). Young children with orthopedic handicaps: Self-knowledge about their disability. *Exceptional Children, 55*(3), 249–252.

Eichenberger, R. J. (1974). Teaching science to the blind student. *The Science Teacher, 41*(19), 53–55.

Flexer, R. J. (1989). Conceptualizing addition: Arithmetic instruction for children in special education classes can be more than drill on number facts and computations. *Teaching Exceptional Children, 21*(4), 21–25.

Gold, M. W., & Scott, K. G. (1971). Discrimination learning. In W. B. Stephens (Ed.), *Training the developmentally young*. New York: John Day.

Hadary, D. E., & Cohen, S. H. (1978). *Laboratory science and art for blind, deaf, and emotionally disturbed children: A mainstreaming approach*. Baltimore, MD: University Park Press.

Johnson, S. W. (1979). *Arithmetic and learning disabilities: Guidelines for identification and remediation*. Boston: Allyn & Bacon.

Keller, M. F., & Carlson, P. M. (1974). The use of symbolic modeling to promote social skills in preschool children with low levels of social responsiveness. *Child Development, 45,* 912–919.

Knight, L. N. & Hargis, C. H. (1977). Math language ability: Its relationship to reading in math. *Language Arts, 54*(4), 423–428.

Kosc, L. (1974). Developmental dyscalculia. *Journal of Learning Disabilities, 7*(3), 164–177.

Krustchinsky, R., & Larner, N. (1988). It's about time. *Teaching Exceptional Children, 20*(3), 40–41.

Lipstreu, B. L., & Johnson, M. K. (1988, Spring). Teaching time using the whole clock method. *Teaching Exceptional Children,* 10–12.

Lowenbraun, S., & Affleck, J. Q. (1976). *Teaching mildly handicapped children in regular classes.* Columbus, OH: Merrill.

McGinnis, E., & Goldstein, A. P. (1990). *Skillstreaming in early childhood: Teaching prosocial skills to the preschool and kindergarten child.* Champaign, IL: Research Press.

McGinnis, E., Sauerbry, L., & Nichols, P. (1985, Spring). Skill-streaming: Teaching social skills to children with behavioral disorders. *Teaching Exceptional Children, 17*(3), 160–167.

Malone, L., & Lucchi, L. D. (1979). Life science for visually impaired students. *Science and Children, 16*(5), 20–31.

Mason, H. (1987, January). Science for all? A special case. *Times Educational Supplement,* 19.

Neisworth, J. T., & Bagnato, S. J. (1987). *The young exceptional child: Early development and education.* New York: Macmillan.

Patton, J. R., Polloway, E. A., & Cronin, M. E. (1987). Social studies instruction for handicapped students: A review of current practices. *The Social Studies, 78*(3), 131–135.

Peters, D. L., & Raupp, C. D. (1980). Developing a self-concept of the exceptional child. In T. D. Yawkey (Ed.), *The self-concept of the young child* (pp. 167–176). Provo, UT: Brigham Young University Press.

Piaget, J. (1970). *Science and education and the psychology of the child.* New York: Orion Press.

Polloway, E. A., Payne, J. S., Patton, J. R., & Payne, R. A. (1985). *Strategies for teaching retarded and special needs learners* (3rd ed.). Columbus, OH: Merrill.

Ramsey, P. G. (1987). *Teaching and learning in a diverse world: Multicultural education for young children.* New York: Teachers College Press.

Roedell, W. C. (1986). Socioemotional vulnerabilities of young gifted children. In J. R. Whitmore (Ed.), *Intellectual giftedness in young children: Recognition and development* (pp. 35–54). New York: Haworth Press.

Safford, P. L. (1989). *Integrated teaching in early childhood: Starting the mainstream.* New York: Longman.

Saracho, O. N. (1980). The role of the teacher in enhancing the child's self-concept. In T. D. Yawkey (Ed.), *The self-concept of the young child* (pp. 99–108). Provo, UT: Brigham Young University Press.

Schulz, J. B., Carpenter, C. D., & Turnbull. A. P. (1984). *Mainstreaming exceptional students: A guide for classroom teachers.* Boston: Allyn & Bacon.

Spodek, B. (1985). *Teaching in the early years* (3rd ed.). Englewood Cliffs, NJ: Prentice-Hall.

Suydam, M. N., & Weaver, J. F. (1975). Research on mathematics learning. In J. N. Payne (Ed.), *Mathematics in early childhood,* 37th Yearbook of the National Council of Teachers of Mathematics. Reston, VA: National Council of Teachers of Mathematics.

Teplin, S. W., Howard, J. A., & O'Connor, M. J. (1981). Self concept of young children with cerebral palsy. *Developmental Medicine and Child Neurology, 23,* 730–738.

Thompson, B. (1979). Myth and science for the handicapped. *Science and Children, 7*(3), 16–17.

Thornton, C. A., & Toohey, M. A. (1985). Basic math facts: Guidelines for teaching and learning. *Learning Disabilities Focus, 1*, 44–57.

Thornton, C. A., & Toohey, M. A. (1986). Subtraction facts hide-and-seek cards can help. *Teaching Exceptional Children, 17*, 10–14.

Tunnicliffe, S. D. (1987). Science materials for special needs. *British Journal of Special Education, 14*(2), 73–76.

Turnbull, A. P., & Schulz, J. B. (1979). *Mainstreaming handicapped students.* Boston: Allyn & Bacon.

Walsh, H. M. (1980). *Introducing the young child to the social world.* New York: Macmillan.

Wehman, P., & Goodwyn, R. L. (1978). Self-help skill development. In N. H. Fallen (Ed.), *Young children with special needs* (pp. 159–185). Columbus, OH: Merrill.

CHAPTER 14

Developing Professional Growth

CHAPTER OVERVIEW

This chapter discusses:

1. Ways in which teachers can pursue their own professional development.
2. Types of in-service programs.
3. Important professional associations in general early childhood education and early childhood special education.
4. Professional organizations and publications in early childhood education and early childhood special education.
5. Resources in early childhood education and early childhood special education.

The previous chapters have focused on providing foundation knowledge related to teaching young children of diverse abilities and backgrounds. This knowledge must be integrated with conceptions of curriculum, methods of organizing physical and social resources, and methods of teaching. Ways of evaluating the program and working with parents—also important—have been included.

Preparing to teach at any level is a long-term activity that should extend over a person's entire career. Continued professional development is critical. This chapter discusses ways to enable teachers to extend their professional knowledge.

TEACHERS' PROFESSIONAL GROWTH

Teachers' actions and perceptions of their performance are affected by their own values, attitudes, and perspectives. To change their perceptions, teachers must themselves take responsibility to improve their education (Saracho, 1984; Saracho & Spodek, 1983). Self-knowledge is critical, since teachers' own needs and concerns influence their judgment. Teachers must understand and control their responses toward the children in their classrooms, placing the children's interests above their own personal interests. Self-understanding allows teachers to do this and helps them understand and respond positively toward others. Increased professional knowledge is also required for teachers' growth.

Professional Development

Beginning teachers need to learn more about how to function well in the classroom. Increased knowledge of discipline and classroom management techniques, curriculum ideas, ways to organize learning centers, providing for early literacy training, supporting children's language development, and dealing with transitions are among the topics about which they often express concern.

Some schools provide staff development activities to help teachers increase their knowledge and skills. Schools may

- Help teachers organize their own in-service training programs.
- Help teachers attend conferences and receive publications developed by professional organizations.
- Cooperate with other schools or other school systems to create professional development activities.
- Support teachers who enroll in college or university courses.

Other schools leave teachers to their own resources. Even if schools fail to provide for staff development, teachers have the ultimate responsibility for their own professional growth. They can:

- Participate in the in-service training that is available to them.
- Continue their formal education through university programs.
- Become involved in professional organizations.
- Independently seek the range of educational resources available.

In-Service Programs

In-service meetings, teacher-directed in-service programs, teacher study groups, observing other teachers, mentoring and networking, using technology, and college or university courses are types of in-service programs that support teachers' professional growth.

In-Service Meetings.   In-service meetings should provide information that teachers think they need. Teachers can evaluate their strengths and needs. They also can help each other in providing skills and knowledge. Outside specialists might be used. If teachers in a school feel that the reading program could be improved, a committee could be organized to survey the teachers and come up with topics for workshops and meetings. A reading specialist from a local university might be invited to speak to teachers about new approaches to early reading. Teachers who have outstanding reading programs in their classes could lead workshops on reading instruction or on organizing classrooms for a whole-language approach to teaching reading. Schools could make additional resources, including books and journals, available for teachers to use.

Teacher-Directed In-Service.   Teachers in early childhood schools that do not provide in-service programs can use a team approach to develop a meaningful and systematic in-service program. Teachers can be encouraged to assume responsibility for their own professional development. They can share ideas and coordinate cooperative in-service programs to create an *esprit de corps* in their school and promote teachers' professional development. For example, if a teacher notices that the activity centers seem to bore her children, she might check to see if other teachers have similar concerns. Teachers from neighboring schools might be invited for a series of sessions in which the teachers would share their plans and uses of activity centers. The group also could search through professional books for other ideas to share. Only individuals who have an interest in the topic should participate. Others will develop interest when they hear from teachers who have benefited from such sessions.

Teacher-directed in-service education can support teachers' individual efforts in search of new ideas and new teaching strategies. Teachers learn from each other when they exchange ideas.

Teacher Study Groups.   A teacher study group works on one small, manageable set of problems (such as transitions, flexibility, or short-term planning) at a time. The group identifies an area of study, assesses each participant in the area, develops specific learning plans, and creates a system for getting feedback to improve themselves. For example, if teachers feel that their knowledge of IEPs is inadequate, they might borrow a series of videotapes on IEPs, a videotape player, and a small television set from their school's media center. The teachers could meet weekly during their planning period to view and discuss the tapes.

A teacher study group helps meet the needs of its members by discussing, sharing, and gaining knowledge to meet each person's needs. The group should last as long as the members continue to be satisfied. Dissatisfaction will reduce the members' interest and the group will dissolve.

A study group promotes a more objective view of each individual's own behavior by sharing with others. Teachers learn that others share their concerns and frustrations. It also provides its members with emotional support. As with any in-service program, a teacher study group must continuously be evaluated to assess its worth.

Observing Other Teachers.   Teachers can observe other teachers to improve their teaching. A pair of teachers can observe each other in the same school, or teachers in different schools can collaborate. Visiting other teachers can help a classroom teacher share his or her view of incidents that he or she may not even know exists. In addition, observers can learn new instructional techniques, thus increasing their repertoire of teaching skills. Teachers who become anxious about having observers might be exempted from this activity until they feel secure enough with their colleagues.

Observations also can occur between a teacher and an aide in the same classroom. This may be an unbalanced pair, however, since the aide's qualifications are usually less than the teacher's. They work together as a team, know the classroom situation, and probably share a similar educational philosophy, and they can provide each other with useful feedback. A teacher may schedule occasional observations when one of them is free from other responsibilities, usually for a short period of time (e.g., 10 or 15 minutes). During the observation, the teacher can observe the class more intensely, gaining information about individual children to use in responding to the children's unique developmental levels rather than to some stereotyped characteristics or group norms.

The teacher-aide team may not see everything they do or their effects on their class. The team's expectations of children and their choice of instructional strategies for specific lessons also can affect their view. The observer's perception can eliminate some of the instructor's personal biases.

Mentoring and Networking.   Identifying experienced teachers who can serve as mentors and creating networks of teachers are two important ways to improve teaching. A mentor usually shares accumulated knowledge of practice with a novice teacher, who might feel somewhat unsure of what is happening or why. The mentor can help the novice learn standard procedures, help in the organization of the classroom, and share information about the staff, the children, the parents, and the community.

Mentoring can help a new teacher's transition into the profession and promotes the professional development of both the novice and the experienced teacher. The mentor needs to have a high degree of personal and professional maturity to be effective.

When teachers graduate and enter the teaching profession, they usually lose contact with their fellow graduates. Some groups of graduates create a network of relationships, communicating with each other, sharing ideas, and providing emotional support when necessary. Teachers in a single school or community can develop similar networks. Networking is very helpful in teachers' professional development, including searching for or setting up new networks as they meet new challenges and assume new roles.

Technology.   Technology also promotes teachers' professional development. Video recordings are widely used for in-service training, evaluating teachers, and conducting research. Commercial videotapes are available on a variety of topics in the field. Some universities have developed in-service programs and college courses that are offered through satellite television. Teachers who participate meet in a school or center with a dish antenna that can pull the program down. Often the teachers viewing the course are provided with a telephone link so that they can engage in discussion and ask questions of the instructor or other participants. Project APPLES in Western Illinois University is a good example of a program using such technology.

In addition, videocameras and videocassette recorders allow teachers to view, evaluate, and improve their own teaching. Many teachers reject videotaping, because they feel they lose their spontaneity or they fear their rights might be violated. To protect teachers' rights, their written permission is obtained before they are video-taped or their videotapes are made accessible to others. Teachers must decide who views the tape and when to erase the videotape. Analyzing teachers' classroom instruction through videotapes may be on hold until teachers' rights have been protected.

Professional development requires the effective use of resources that are available in the field. Effective ideas and teaching require that teachers become exposed to emerging practices, products, and research. The professional teacher should have a knowledge of the major literature and information sources, key organizations and agencies, and the dissemination systems in the field.

College or University Courses.   Advanced courses also provide a form of in-service training. Courses can be taken by teachers to allow them to gain an additional certificate or endorsement, or teachers might wish to increase their knowledge in the field in which they are teaching. Some colleges and universities offer courses for teachers in nearby communities. Others schedule classes in late afternoon or evenings, on weekends, and during the summer when teachers are free of professional responsibilities. Often these courses can lead to an advanced degree. Some states require that teachers regularly take advanced courses to maintain a teaching certificate. In addition, some early childhood programs require teachers to regularly complete college courses to ensure that they are up-to-date in the field. Early childhood programs may alter their teachers' work schedule to ease their attendance at a college or university or may pay their tuition. Many programs provide different salary schedules for teachers with advanced education.

Teacher as Researcher.   The traditional view of teachers has seen them as consumers of knowledge that has been generated from research. Their skills were in applying the knowledge that others have created. Recently that view has changed. Increasingly, teachers are seen as producers of knowledge about education as well as consumers of that knowledge. Teachers, alone or in collaboration with others, increasingly are generating research in their own classrooms. Even if this research is not published in the professional journals, it can be shared with others locally as well as more broadly. Often, however, this research is specific to a particular classroom and widespread dissemination is not a concern.

Teachers may engage in *action research,* an approach to systematically address-ing a particular problem. Action research originally developed as a way of dealing with social problems. Both in the 1950s and currently it has also been used to address educational problems, often with teachers collaborating with university professors.

In action research, the teacher will identify a problem in the classroom and will collect information on that problem, often through systematic observation. Once the particulars of the problem are identified, the teacher will generate possible interventions to solve the problem. The most useful intervention is implemented, then information is again collected. If the problem is solved or alleviated, the teacher will move on to other concerns. If the process has not proven effective, then it might begin again, with another intervention tried and information again collected. This systematic identification of problems and testing of interventions, coupled with the careful collection of information about what is happening in the classroom, is a practical form of research that teachers can use. Since things that work in one classroom often can work—possibly with modification—in others, the results of action research are worth disseminating among teachers (Carr & Kemmis, 1986; Oja & Smulyan, 1989).

RESOURCES

Resources include information, services, materials, and other useful products that help teachers become more skillful and effective. Resources include reference books, computerized information research systems, abstracts of professional publications, agencies that provide such materials, and resource people with specific areas of expertise.

Teachers should know what resources are available to them, though this information often is difficult to obtain. Professionals who have access to valuable resources can be more effective. According to Peterson (1987):

> Individuals may not always have the answer to a problem at their fingertips or the information they need tucked away neatly in their heads. But if each of us knows where to find the information we need and how to retrieve it, our ability to perform efficiently and successfully in our jobs is enhanced tenfold. (p. 495)

Professionals need to know how to find such resources as well as how to use or work with each resource to make it meet their needs. A working knowledge of resources in early childhood special education can be an invaluable asset. Following are the broad types of resources in early childhood special education with which teachers should be familiar:

Professional organizations

Professional journals and periodicals

Government documents and reports

Reference materials and bibliographical listings

Information storage and retrieval services

Professional Organizations

Professional organizations provide many valuable ways to promote teachers' professional development. Some of the major professional organizations in early childhood special education include:

Association for Childhood Education International (ACEI), 11501 Georgia Avenue, Suite 315, Wheaton, MD 20902.

ACEI promotes appropriate educational programs and practices for children from birth through the elementary grades. Its goal is to promote teachers' professional growth and disseminate information about school programs. ACEI includes individual members, local affiliate groups, and state and provincial associations. It publishes two journals—*Childhood Education,* which is practice-oriented, and *Journal of Research in Childhood Education,* which is research-oriented—as well as other publications. ACEI holds an annual national study conference as well as international conferences. Its affiliates also hold meetings and workshops locally.

The Council for Exceptional Children (CEC), 1920 Association Drive, Reston, VA 22190.

CEC is the major professional organization concerned with the education of children with disabilities. Although it is a national organization, it includes state affiliates that address more local concerns. The council presents an annual conference and publishes two journals—*Exceptional Children,* more research-oriented, and *Teaching Exceptional Children,* more practice-oriented. The council consists of many divisions, each with its particular concerns. The Division of Early Childhood (DEC), one of several divisions of CEC, is particularly concerned with early childhood special education. It publishes the *Journal of Early Intervention.*

National Association for the Education of Young Children (NAEYC), 1509 16th Street N.W., Washington, DC 20036.

NAEYC is one of the strongest and largest organizations in early childhood education, which it identifies as the education of children from birth through age 8. NAEYC has more than 70,000 members in about 300 affiliated groups who are concerned with the education and well-being of young children. NAEYC offers professional development opportunities to help early childhood educators improve the quality of services they provide for young children. NAEYC publishes two journals, *Young Children* for practitioners and *Early Childhood Research Quarterly* (with Ablex) for researchers. It also offers many separate publications and annually sponsors a national conference. Its affiliates also hold smaller conferences and workshops locally and regionally and publish a range of useful material for practitioners.

World Organization for Early Education, *Organisation Mondial pour l'Education Prescolaire (OMEP)* (French).

This organization promotes the study of the education of young children. It shares information about young children throughout the world on education, development, health and nutrition, playgrounds, and toys. OMEP and UNESCO join their efforts to work on projects of mutual concern. OMEP publishes a journal, *The International Journal of Early*

Childhood Education, and holds a biennial international assembly. An active OMEP committee exists in the United States that holds meetings and publishes a newsletter.

Other Professional Associations. The following are additional organizations related to the education of young children:

American Montessori Society, 150 Fifth Avenue, New York, NY 10010.

Child Welfare League of America, 67 Irving Place, New York, NY 10010.

National Committee on Education of Migrant Children, 1501 Broadway, New York, NY 10016.

Parent Cooperative Preschool International, 9111 Alton Parkway, Silver Spring, MD 20910.

Southern Early Childhood Association, Box 5403 Brady Station, Little Rock, AR 72205.

United States National Committee for Early Childhood Education (a unit of OMEP), 2400 Lahser Road, Southfield, MI 48034.

Professional Journals and Periodicals

There are many professional journals related to the field of early childhood special education. Each journal has its own particular focus. Some journals focus on practical methods to assess and teach children, others are concerned with more theoretical and philosophical issues, and still others report empirical research and reviews of research.

The *Journal of Early Intervention, Topics in Early Childhood Special Education,* and *Infants and Young Children* are three major publications primarily in the early education of young children with disabilities. Other journals related to early childhood-special education include:

- Periodicals in the general areas of special education, child development, and early childhood education.
- Periodicals in specific disability areas of special education.
- Periodicals on related topic areas such as behavior analysis, assessment, mainstreaming, parenting of a child with a disability, and instructional methodology.
- Periodicals relating to services and other professional disciplines directly or indirectly related to individuals with disabilities or young children's growth and development.

The names of various general and more specific journals related to early childhood special education are listed at the end of this chapter. Many organizations and agencies, as well as some private publishers, sponsor publications related to the education and well-being of young children. Among these are:

American Education. Superintendent of Documents, U.S. Government Printing Office, Washington, DC 20402.

Child Care Information Exchange. P.O. Box C-44, Redmond, WA 98052.

Child Care Quarterly. Human Sciences Press, 72 Fifth Avenue, New York, NY 10011.

Child Development, Child Development Abstracts, and *Child Development Monographs.* Society for Research and Child Development, University of Chicago Press, Chicago, IL 60637.

Child Welfare. Child Welfare League of America, Inc., 44 East 23rd Street, New York, NY 10010.

Childhood Education. Association for Childhood Education International, 11141 Georgia Avenue, Suite 200, Wheaton, MD. Bulletins, leaflets, and books are also published.

Children Today. Office of Human Development Services, Department of Health and Human Services, Room 356-G, 200 Independence Avenue, SW, Washington, DC 20201.

Day Care and Early Education. Human Sciences Press, 72 Fifth Avenue, New York, NY 10011.

Dimensions. Southern Early Childhood Association, Box 5403, Brady Station, Little Rock, AR 72215.

Early Years. Allen Raymond, Inc., P.O. Box 1266, Darien, CT 06826.

Instructor. Scholastic, Inc. 730 Broadway, New York, NY 10003.

Journal of Home Economics. American Economics Associations, 2010 Massachusetts Avenue, NW, Washington, DC 20036.

National Parent-Teacher. National Congress of Teachers and Parents, 700 North Rush Street, Chicago, IL 60511. Study guides are also available.

Young Children. National Association for the Education of Young Children, 1509 16th Street, NW, Washington, DC 20036. Bulletins, materials, and books are also published.

Government Documents and Reports

State and national government agencies produce and distribute a range of documents in areas related to areas of early childhood education, including child development, child care, special education, early intervention, child abuse. These publications include technical bulletins, annual reports on programs, population data, investigative series, subject monographs, periodicals, handbooks, regulations on federal programs and services, congressional reports, and copies of federal laws. Government documents are available for purchase from the Superintendent of Documents in Washington, DC. Government bookstores located in regional government office buildings sell these relatively inexpensive publications, which offer a rich source of information. Government publications are also sold by mail. The Government Printing Office produces a *Monthly Catalog of United States Government Publications* (a series of reference volumes containing index listings of available materials with brief abstracts) and a *Subject Bibliography Index.*

The *Monthly Catalog of United States Government Publications* can be found in most university and some public libraries. A series supplement, which lists only periodical publications, also is published. Information on different topics is catalogued by author and subject at the back of each volume, and by the *Series Report Index* (which has the name or number of any published government publication). The indexes show a monthly catalog entry number for each government publication with an abstract describing the publication. The abstract usually includes the original document's call number, the author, the title, the government publishing agency, price, and ordering information. Publications can be ordered directly from the Superintendent of Documents, U.S. Government Printing Office, Washington, DC 20402.

The *Subject Bibliography Index* lists the government's publications on single-subject areas (e.g., child welfare, children, day care, and children with disabilities). Publications are listed in alphabetical order with the federal number and price of the document.

Reference Materials and Bibliographical Listings

Reference materials and bibliographical listings provide comprehensive summaries on a specific topic such as mainstreaming, preschool children with disabilities, or working with parents of young children with disabilities. These resources can be found in books and special publications. The following are examples of these resources:

Carmichael's Manual of Child Psychology (New York, Wiley, 1983). P. H. Mussen edited two large volumes, which include comprehensive summaries of current philosophical and theoretical thoughts and reviews of research in child psychology, such as biological bases of child development, infancy and early experiences, cognitive development, and socialization in young children. The chapters in this manual provide a review of current knowledge in the selected topic areas, with critical analyses of that literature.

Review of Child Development, under the auspices of the Society for Research in Child Development (SRCD), is a series of volumes with integrative reviews of literature about children's development (e.g., history of child development—Vol. 5; development of deaf children—Vol. 5; child abuse—Vol. 5; effectiveness of environment intervention programs—Vol. 3; programs for disadvantaged parents—Vol. 3; psychological testing of children—Vol. 2; genetics and development of intelligence—Vol. 4). The Russell Sage Foundation of New York published Volumes 1 and 2, and the University of Chicago Press published Volumes 3 to 6.

The *Yearbook in Early Childhood Education* (New York, Teachers College Press) is a series of annual publications. Each volume addresses a timely topic of major significance in early childhood education, and each contains chapters that present and interpret current knowledge of aspects of that topic, written by experts in the field. Key issues—including concerns about educational equity, multiculturalism, the needs of diverse populations of children and families, and the ethical dimensions of the field—are woven into the organization of each volume. The first volume deals with *The Preparation of Early Childhood Teachers* (1990). The second volume deals with *Issues in Early Childhood Curriculum* (1991). The third volume deals with *Issues in Child Care* (1992). The fourth volume, issued in 1993, deals with *Language and Literacy in Early Childhood Education*. Future issues will deal with early childhood special education, multilingual/multicultural concerns in early childhood education, and other timely topics.

The *Handbook of Research on the Education of Young Children* (New York, Macmillan, 1993) is a major volume that presents reviews of research on many topics within the field of early childhood education. Each topic is reviewed in a chapter. The topics include various aspects of child development, content areas within the curriculum, policy areas, and methods of doing research. Each chapter reviews a specific aspect of early childhood education and presents implications for the field. Extensive bibliographical references are also provided.

Yearbook of Special Education, published by Marquis Academic Media (Marquis Who's Who, Inc., Chicago) can be found in most university and college libraries and some public libraries. It is published yearly to summarize new developments in special education including different disabilities (e.g., mental retardation) and selected topics such as mainstreaming, rights and litigation, and teacher preparation. It includes bibliographies of educational materials, instruction for parent involvement, evaluation of model special education programs, national and state data on children with disabilities and special education services, and guidelines for assessment of public school services. Information is listed by state in the geographical index.

International Review of Research in Mental Retardation (New York, Academic Press) summarizes research and theory development in the field of mental retardation. For example, chapters include research on mental deficiency during the last decade in France (Vol. 2), measurement of intelligence (Vol. 4), cultural deprivation and cognitive competence (Vol. 6), and physical and motor development of retarded persons (Vol. 7).

Professional information can be obtained by using reference guides that list published materials under alphabetized topic categories. This strategy helps the teacher to know the primary sources for certain information or to obtain a representative sample of literature on a specific topic. There are three types of reference guides:

- *Bibliographical indexes* list periodicals and other published literature under an alphabetized subject listing (author listings may also be provided).

- *Bibliographical abstracts* provide annotated references on publications within defined topic areas in specific professional fields including psychology and child development.

- *Service directories* indicate which agencies can provide information or some type of special service.

The bibliographical indexes and bibliographical abstracts are usually carried by university and college libraries. Community libraries may have smaller collections.

Bibliographical references summarize literature in areas such as special education, general education, child development and early education, psychology, and other related fields. A list of bibliographical references can be found at the end of this chapter. Abstract reference volumes in the areas of young children's early education, and special education are *Psychological Abstracts, Child Development Abstracts,* ERIC abstracts (*Research Relating to Children* and *Current Index to Journals in Education*), and *Education Index.* The content and organization of these materials can be learned by browsing through each of them.

Service directories are published by state or federal agencies, and local community organizations. They usually identify agencies in a specific geographic area that provide specialized services to children, families, or other service agencies. These directories are not widely distributed and may not be available in the library. Usually key state and federal agencies that handle services and funding resources for persons with disabilities (e.g., state departments of education, regional offices of child development, regional offices of developmental disabilities) have these directories. The Educational Resources Information Clearinghouse (ERIC) system may provide a means to retrieve information about existing directories.

The *Directory of National Information Sources on Handicapping Conditions and Related Services* (DHEW Publication No. 80-22007), produced by the U.S. Government Printing Office, is a useful directory of resources. It provides an extended list of other national directories that provide information on services and resources for persons with disabilities.

Other comprehensive directories with an extensive list of agencies and service resources in early childhood-special education are cited at the end of this chapter.

RESOURCES FOR INFORMATION SEARCH AND RETRIEVAL

Professional literature and information on a particular topic can be obtained through search-and-retrieval systems that gather information and make it accessible to potential consumers in the fields of education and psychology. These information retrieval systems identify research literature, government and project reports, teaching materials and aids, and other media for each specified area. An individual specifies several descriptors to retrieve information from the computer bank. This procedure helps to identify the location of specific information and, thus, saves a considerable amount of time.

A number of information search-and-retrieval systems are composed of large data bases of information collected from many different sources (e.g., journal articles, books, government documents, project reports, unpublished reports and products, commercial materials, newsletters, different media). A computer search within those data bases identifies the location of specific information on a topic area.

Educational Resources Information Clearinghouse (ERIC). ERIC, funded by the U.S. Office of Education, has the most widely available print resources to provide materials requested on different educational topics. ERIC is an access system that gathers all kinds of information in printed, microfiche, (small squares of film on which the pages are reproduced), and computer formats. It is composed of a network of 16 specialized clearinghouses in a specific subject area; the information is listed in appropriate reference documents. ERIC clearinghouses are associated with key professional associations, government and private agencies, and training institutions to help them gather materials on new education products and information.

ERIC clearinghouses span the education field for specific subject areas. In the field of early childhood special education, two clearinghouses are of particular importance—the ERIC Clearinghouse on Handicapped and Gifted Children, which is operated by the Council for Exceptional Children in Reston, VA, and the ERIC Clearinghouse on Elementary and Early Childhood Education, which is located at the University of Illinois.

The ERIC system handles information on six interlinking components:

1. A central processing facility receives, enters, and indexes all documents into a computerized collection of the newest documents and journal articles germane to the field.
2. Sixteen specialized clearinghouses throughout the country are responsible for acquiring and handling materials in their specialized area.
3. An ERIC Document Reproduction Service (EDRS) films documents into microfiche form to sell to consumers.
4. The *Current Index to Journals in Education* (CIJE) publishes an extensive monthly annotated bibliography that covers over 700 publications representing the major education periodicals.
5. *Resources in Education* (RIE), published by the U.S. Government Printing Office, summarizes the materials in all 16 specialized ERIC clearinghouses. These materials are available through ERIC in hard copy or microfiche.
6. The central ERIC management team, located within the National Institute of Education, sets ERIC policy and monitors the operation of the ERIC system.

ERIC also has user services such as the following:

- Provides workshops at professional meetings to teach professionals to use its resource system.
- Produces *Computer Search Reprints*, which are documents of current high interest.
- Responds to users' requests by conducting special computerized searches. The *Directory of ERIC Computer Services* identifies the locations where computer searches can be run on special topics. Institutions, universities, and colleges that subscribe to the ERIC computer tapes have their own computer facilities to offer these ERIC resources.

ACCESS ERIC serves as a gateway to the ERIC system. In addition to coordinating the ERIC system, it publishes a journal, *The ERIC Review*. Each issue of this journal, which is published three times a year, addresses a critical and timely topic related to education, such as literacy or parent involvement. The issue contains articles on the topic lists of resource agencies and publications, titles of recent ERIC publications, and a calendar of forthcoming educational events. Subscriptions and additional information are available by calling their toll-free number—1-800-USE-ERIC.

Information can be requested from the appropriate ERIC clearinghouse that taps the appropriate national data base. Current ERIC clearinghouses include:

Adult, Career, and Vocational Education. Center for Vocational Education, Ohio State University, 1960 Kenny Road, Columbus, OH 43210-1090.

Counseling and Personnel Services. 2108 School of Education Building, East University and South University Streets, Ann Arbor, MI 48109-1259.

Early Childhood and Elementary Education (ERIC/EECE). University of Illinois, 804 West Pennsylvania Avenue, Urbana, IL 61801-4897.

Educational Management. University of Oregon, Eugene, OR 97403-5207.

Handicapped and Gifted Children. Council for Exceptional Children, 1920 Association Drive, Reston, VA 22091-1589.

Higher Education. George Washington University, One Dupont Circle, NW, Suite 630, Washington, DC 20036-1183.

Information Resources. School of Education, Syracuse University, 150 Marshall Avenue, Syracuse, NY 13244-2340

Junior Colleges. University of California at Los Angeles, 405 Hilgard Avenue, Los Angeles, CA 90024-1564.

Language and Linguistics. Center for Applied Linguistics, 1118 22nd Street, NW, Washington, DC 20037-0037

Reading and Communication Skills. Indiana University, 2805 East 10th Street, Bloomington, IN 47408-2698.

Rural Education and Small Schools. Appalachia Educational Laboratory, 1031 Quarrier Street, P.O. Box 1348, Charleston, WV 25325-1348.

Science, Mathematics, and Environmental Education. Ohio State University, 1929 Kenny Road, Columbus, OH 43210-1081.

Social Studies/Social Science Education. Indiana University, 2805 East 10th Street, Bloomington, IN 47408-2373

Teacher Education. American Association of Colleges of Teacher Education, One Dupont Circle, NW, Suite 610, Washington, DC 20036-2412.

Tests, Measurement, and Evaluation. American Institute for Research, 3333 K Street, NW, Washington, DC 20007

Urban Education. Teachers College, Columbia University, 525 West 120th Street, Box 40, New York, NY 10027-9998.

Materials from the ERIC system are available on microfiche in many university and public libraries. These can be read on a microfiche reader, which magnifies them and projects them on a screen for the individual to read. They can also be copied on paper.

In order to determine what material is available in the ERIC system, each document is abstracted and identified by key topical words. An individual can make an ERIC search by identifying those documents in the system that are related to the topics he or she wishes to study. These abstracts are stored in a computer data base that is available for on-line searches. They are also stored on CD-ROM (compact disk, read-only memory) disks that are available in many libraries and are upgraded regularly, making a computer search more accessible.

SUMMARY

Teachers can improve themselves professionally in a variety of ways. Staff meetings, invited speakers, films, or workshops can help teachers to upgrade the quality of their teaching. Some schools support staff members' attendance to community workshops, conferences (local, regional, and national), and college or university courses to promote their professional development. They also can share with each other craft activities, songs, or action plays. They can learn through their own experience and from experiences of their fellow teachers.

Professional associations also provide several opportunities. Members of professional organizations are eligible to receive early childhood publications and resource materials, and to attend conferences, workshops, and meetings to keep abreast in the field of early childhood special education. Professional publications are very useful.

Early childhood education is in constant flux. Early childhood and special educators should keep up-to-date to continue their self-education throughout their career.

PERIODICALS IN SPECIAL EDUCATION, CHILD DEVELOPMENT, AND EARLY CHILDHOOD EDUCATION

General Special Education Journals
Exceptional Children

Focus on Exceptional Children

Journal for Special Educators

Journal of Special Education

Remedial and Special Education (formerly *Exceptional Education Quarterly*)

Teacher Education and Special Education

Teaching Exceptional Children

General Child Development and Early Education Journals
Advances in Child Development and Behavior

Developmental Psychology

Early Child Development and Care

Education and Treatment of Children

Infant Behavior and Development

Infants and Young Children

Journal of Experimental Child Psychology

Merrill-Palmer Quarterly

Monographs of the Society for Research in Child Development

Teaching K-8 (formerly *Early Years*)

PERIODICALS IN SPECIFIC AREAS OF DISABILITY

Early Childhood Special Education
Journal of Early Intervention (DEC/CEC)

Topics in Early Childhood Special Education

Mental Retardation
American Journal on Mental Deficiency

Applied Research in Mental Retardation

Education and Training of the Mentally Retarded

Journal of Mental Retardation

Emotional Disturbance or Behavior Disorders
American Journal of Orthopsychiatry

Behavior Therapy

Child Behavior and Development

Child Psychiatry and Human Development

Journal of Autism and Developmental Disorders

Journal of Child Psychology, Psychiatry, and Allied Disciplines

Speech and Hearing Impairments
American Annals of the Deaf

Deaf American

Journal of Child Language

Journal of Speech and Hearing Disorders

Journal of Speech and Hearing Research

Speech Monographs

Volta Review

Blindness and Visual Impairment
Education of the Visually Handicapped

Journal of Visual Impairment and Blindness

New Outlook for Blind (discontinued in 1976)

Orthopedic and Other Health Impairments
Academic Therapy

Learning Disabled

Pediatrics

Learning Disabilities
Journal of Learning Disabilities

Slow Learning Child

Topic in Learning and Learning Disabilities

Gifts and Talents
Gifted Child Quarterly

Journal of Creative Behavior

PERIODICALS ON BEHAVIOR ANALYSIS, ASSESSMENT, MAINSTREAMING, PARENTS, AND METHODOLOGY

Behavior Analysis
Behavior Modification

Journal of Applied Behavior Analysis

Journal of the Experimental Analysis of Behavior

Assessment
Journal of Behavioral Assessment

Legal and Legislative Topics and Children with Disabilities
Exceptional Parent

Volta Review

Mainstreaming/Inclusion
Education Unlimited (discontinued in 1981)

Parents of and Parenting Children with Disabilities
Exceptional Parent

Volta Review

Instructional Methodology and Curriculum
Education and Training of the Mentally Retarded

Learning

Teaching Exceptional Children

Other
Perceptual and Motor Skills

JOURNALS IN PSYCHOLOGY, SOCIAL WORK, AND EDUCATION

Psychology
American Journal of Psychology

American Psychologist

Comparative Psychology

Contemporary Educational Psychology

Contemporary Psychology

Counseling Psychologist

Developmental Psychology

Educational Psychology

Journal of Abnormal and Child Psychology

Journal of Social Psychology

Psychological Bulletin

Psychological Review

Psychology Today

Social Psychology Quarterly

General Education
American Educational Research Journal

Educational Technology

Elementary School Journal

Harvard Educational Review

Journal of Education

Review of Educational Research

Speech Pathology and Audiology
Child Language Teaching and Therapy

Journal of Child Language

Journal of Speech and Hearing Disorders

Journal of Speech and Hearing Research

Topics in Language Disorders

Occupational Therapy
American Journal of Occupational Therapy in Pediatrics

Music Therapy
Journal of Music Therapy

Physical Therapy and Adaptive Physical Education
Journal of American Dietetic Association

Physical Therapy

Medicine and Pediatrics
American Journal of Public Health
Journal of Pediatrics

Interdisciplinary
Analysis and Intervention in Development Disabilities
Learning Disabilities: A Multidisciplinary Journal

BIBLIOGRAPHICAL REFERENCES (INDEX ONLY)

Child Development Abstracts and Bibliography

Current Index to Journal in Education (CIJE)

Dissertation Abstracts International

DSH Abstracts Education (Deafness, speech, hearing)

Education Index

Exceptional Child

Exceptional Child Education Resources (formerly *Exceptional Child Education Abstracts*)

Psychological Abstracts

PsychScan: LD/MR

PsycINFO News

Research in Education (RIE)

Research Relating to Children

DIRECTORIES

Directory for Exceptional Children: A listing of Education and Training Facilities. Porter Sergeant Publishers, Boston, MA 02100.

Directory of National Information Sources on Handicapping Conditions and Related Services. (2nd ed.) Clearinghouse on the Handicapped, Office of Human Development Services, Office for Handicapped Individuals U.S. Government Printing Office, Washington, DC 20402.

Directory of Organizations Interested in the Handicapped. People-to-People Committee for the Handicapped, 1522 K Street, NW, Washington, DC 20005.

Encyclopedia of Associations. Gale Research Co., Book Tower, Detroit, MI 48226.

Guide to Clinical Services in Speech-Language Pathology and Audiology. American Speech-Language-Hearing Association, 10801 Rockville Pike, Rockville, MD 20852.

Handicapped Funding Directory. Box 357, Oceanside, NY 11572.

Information Enterprises. Distributed by Gale Research Co., Book Tower, Detroit, MI 48226.

International Directory of Mental Retardation Resources. President's Committee on Mental Retardation, Washington, DC.

Resource Directory of Research and Training Centers (1980). National Institute of Handicapped Research, Department of Health and Welfare, Washington, DC 20001.

Special Education Programs for Severely Handicapped Students: A Directory of State Education Agency Services. NASDE, 1201–16th Street, NW, Washington, DC 20036.

A Training and Resources Directory for Serving Handicapped Students K through 12. Office of Civil Rights, HEW, Room 5146, 330 Independence Avenue., SW, Washington, DC 20201.

Youth-Serving Organization Directory. Gale Research Co., Book Tower, Detroit, MI 48226.

ORGANIZATIONS RELATED TO PARENTS, DISABILITIES, AND EARLY CHILDHOOD EDUCATION

Parent Organizations
Association for Children with Learning Disabilities

Children's Defense Fund

International Parents' Organization (Deaf)

Parents of Down Syndrome Children

United Cerebral Palsy Foundation

Organizations Relating to Specific Handicapping Conditions
American Association of the Deaf

American Association on Mental Deficiency

American Speech, Language, and Hearing Association

Association for the Education of the Visually Handicapped

National Society for Autistic Children

The Association for Persons with Severe Handicaps (TASH)

Spina Bifida Association of America

Organizations Relating to Early Childhood Education
American Montessori Society

Association for Childhood Education International

Association for the Care of Children's Health

Child Welfare League of America
Day Care and Child Development Council of America
National Association for Education of Young Children

REFERENCES

Carr, W., & Kemmis, S. (1986). *Becoming critical: Education, knowledge and action research.* London: Falmer Press.

Oja, S. N., & Smulyan, L. (1989). *Collaborative action research: A developmental approach.* London: Falmer Press.

Peterson, H. L. (1987). *Early intervention for handicapped and at-risk children.* Denver: Love.

Saracho, O. N. (1984). Perception of the teaching process in early childhood education through role analysis. *Journal of the Association for the Study of Perception, 19*(1), 26–39.

Saracho, O. N., & Spodek, B. (1983). Preparing teachers for multicultural classrooms. In O. N. Saracho & B. Spodek (Eds.), *Understanding the multicultural experience in early childhood education* (pp. 125–146). Washington, DC: National Association for the Education of Young Children.

Index